The Politics of Human Rights

Edited by
Obrad Savić
for the BELGRADE CIRCLE JOURNAL

V

VERSO

London • New York

The editors and Verso gratefully acknowledge the permission of the authors and their publishers to reproduce material in this volume; relevant citations are printed at the end of individual contributions. All contributions without originating-source citations were written specifically for the *Belgrade Circle Journal* and are published here in book form for the first time.

This edition first published by Verso 1999
© in the collection Verso 1999
© in individual contributions the contributors 1999

Verso
UK: 6 Meard Street, London W1V 3HR
US: 180 Varick Street, New York, NY 10014–4606

Verso is the imprint of New Left Books

ISBN 1–85984–727–7

British Library Cataloguing in Publication Data
A catalogue record for this book is available from the British Library

Library of Congress Cataloging-in-Publication Data
A catalog record for this book is available from the Library of Congress

Typeset by M Rules
Printed by Biddles Ltd, Guildford and King's Lynn

Contents

iii

Preface

Terry Eagleton

This book is the outcome of a remarkable encounter between theory and practice, in an age when such fruitful conjunctures are all too rare. The Belgrade Circle is a group of dissident Serbian intellectuals – philosophers, academics, political theorists and the like – who have courageously maintained an opposition to the repressive Yugoslav government, struggling to keep open intellectual channels in danger of being implacably closed. To do so, they have roped in from time to time the contributions of some of the most eminent political philosophers of the West; and it is some of these pieces which are collected together in this volume. What the book represents, then, is an extraordinary exchange between the most ambitiously general questions of political philosophy and the vividly particular destiny of one small, war-torn nation.

It is not only that this sort of liaison is rare these days; it is also that it is not even supposed to be possible. Generality is one thing, while concrete analysis is quite another; and a postmodern era has swung increasingly against the former in favour of the latter. But the concept of human rights insists upon straddling the divide between properly abstract accounts of political society and pressingly particular states of emergency such as we have recently witnessed in Yugoslavia. More to the point, the question of the relationship between universal and specific, theory and practice, global and local, lies at the heart of the issues in question. In this sense, one might claim, this book enacts in its form something of the problems raised by its content.

Traditionally, one of the links between general and particular was the *engagé* intellectual, who sought to bring questions of universal import to bear upon the specific problems of his or her society. It is sometimes argued that this kind of committed intelligentsia passed away with Simone de Beauvoir and Jean-Paul Sartre, and that there is something specious, not to say downright fraudulent, about the intellectual's claim to speak in this totalising way. These days, one can only speak for oneself; and since the whole notion of autonomous selfhood has been called into question, even that is far from certain. The intellectual, in this postmodern conception of the role, must beat a modest retreat from the synoptic standpoint into the shelter of a particular discipline. As such, he or she ends up effectively indistinguishable from the figure in contrast to whom the classical intellectual can be most precisely defined: the academic.

Even so, it is a remarkable fact that history, as so often, perversely insists upon contradicting theory. The intellectual whose patch is political culture as a whole is nowadays often considered either an antediluvian relic or an embarrassing amateur; but how else, after all, can one characterise the work of Raymond Williams, Noam Chomsky, Edward Said, Fredric Jameson, Jürgen Habermas or Pierre Bourdieu? Such work may now be less and less theoretically possible, but it has an irritating habit of existing. It is no longer very fashionable to address oneself to what some may see as the bogus totality of 'society as a whole', but the existence of this book helps one more clearly to see why. For 'society as a whole' is an object which tends to emerge at times of historical crisis; and while this crisis has broken out with a vengeance on the troubled margins of Europe, the Western heartlands can still for the moment indulge the luxury of not seeing themselves from the outside, as a particular, minority form of life, as a specific culture rather than as civilisation itself. It is doubtful that they will be able to afford this luxury for much longer.

So it is, for example, that the distinguished philosopher John Rawls, in his thoughtful essay in this book, can chide those 'outlaw states' which threaten the stability of 'well-ordered peoples' with their 'expansionist' regimes, 'violations of human rights' and determination 'to recognise no geographic limits to the legitimate authority of their established religious or philosophical views' (pp. 34–5). This is not a viewpoint with which the Belgrade Circle are at all likely to disagree. For what after all have they just been witnessing in the form of nightly NATO bombings but the expansionist activities of a rogue superstate which has traditionally been fairly nonchalant about violating human rights, and certainly about setting geographic limits to its ideological ambitions? The United States in particular has always had extreme difficulty in seeing itself from the outside, and something of this self-opacity is revealed in Richard Rorty's richly provocative essay, which finds no difficulty in enlisting in the 'human rights culture' a nation (his own) which has constantly flouted the rights of its own minorities, not to speak of those of cultures far from its shores.

It is timely that we should have this eloquent communication from the edge of Europe, since such communications are in dire danger of being curtailed. Europe, this haven of human rights culture as Rorty would no doubt see it, is now busily slamming down the drawbridge on those uprooted by its own free-market policies, swinging its big guns to face these potential migrants and insurgents rather than the former Soviet lands, and threatening with physical destruction any foreign regime which refuses to be complicit with its own interests. It is this which, in some intellectual circles, passes for the concept of universality. Yet it is from the same Europe, in a rather more heroic, enlightened period of its great bourgeois culture, that the notion of human rights sprang up, and it is still a potent enough lineage to be deployed against much of that Europe's current political practice. At least, as this collection triumphantly demonstrates, ideas can still migrate freely across frontiers, and different cultures still fruitfully interbreed. If the Western liberal intelligentsia is nowadays understandably nervous of appropriating the experience of others by seeking to represent them, there are other intellectual groupings, like the Belgrade Circle, who are part of those whose freedom they espouse. And it is a sign of the urgency of their situation that they call in this volume not necessarily on the politically correct, but on those from whatever ideological camp whose ideas might be of some service to them. As such, the book represents a precious act of solidarity between some of the more privileged intellectuals of the West, who have the time and resources to reflect upon these philosophical matters because there is little need for them to be politically active, and those of their colleagues elsewhere whose situation is often the reverse.

PART I
THE POLITICS OF HUMAN RIGHTS

Introduction

The Global and the Local in Human Rights: The Case of the Federal Republic of Yugoslavia

Obrad Savić

Fifty years ago to this day, the United Nations General Assembly, in its 183rd session, adopted the Universal Declaration of Human Rights. It was a critical turning point in the long quest for freedom and human dignity, comparable in significance to the Magna Carta and the American Declaration of Independence, and declaring a 'common standard for the achievement of all peoples and all nations'. In the final vote, the outline of the Declaration was not adopted unanimously – forty-eight member states voted for it, while eight delegations abstained, including the then Federal People's Republic of Yugoslavia.[1] This lack of consensus was an early indication of future conflicts related to the issue of the limits to a *universal* validity of human rights, which have since become a standard in the evaluation of rights in general.

The modern concept of human rights originated in the context of monstrous abuses during the Second World War: the experience of Nazism (as well as Stalinism) forced the global community to look for international instruments which would defend human life and human rights. However, the United Nations Charter (forerunner to the Universal Declaration), which was adopted on 26 June 1945 before any peace treaty following the war had been signed, was not as far-reaching as some had hoped:

> The human rights provisions which ultimately found their way into the Charter of the United Nations fell far short of the expectations that Roosevelt's vision and the wartime rhetoric had created. (. . .) In retrospect, that was to be expected, for each of the principal victorious powers had troublesome human rights problems of its own. The Soviet Union had its *Gulag*, the United States its *de jure* racial discrimination, France and Great Britain their colonial empires. It was not in their interest to draft a Charter that established an effective international system for the protection of human rights, which is what some nations advocated.[2]

3

What the Charter did do, though, was announce an 'internationalization' of human rights and pave the way for the international conviction that human rights are not something that exist exclusively within the internal jurisdiction of particular countries. 'The Charter remained on the level of a proclamation of human rights and liberties as general values of society, thus providing the broadest basis for the further development and extension of human rights and freedoms of citizens.'[3]

In a formal sense the later Universal Declaration became the first inclusive instrument for a normative regulation of human rights. Since it did not have the status of a regulative legal act, however, there has been a long process, initiated by the Organization of United Nations, during which a general obligation for the protection and improvement of human rights has gradually evolved into concrete provisions. Two international pacts on human rights, two protocols, and many other international conventions and treaties have followed from the Declaration. In addition, several regional organizations, whose work has to be in accord with the aims and principles of the United Nations, have been established within the Council of Europe, the Organisation of the American States, and the Organisation for African Unity. (A regional protection of human rights within the Arab League, or for the Middle East and Asia, has not yet been established.) The main related regional documents are the European Convention for the Protection of Human Rights (1950), the American Human Rights Convention (1950), and the African Charter on Human Rights and the Rights of Peoples (1981).[4]

The European Convention represents the most fully developed and precise of these documents. Its list of human rights contains mostly *civil* and *political* rights, and it provides for more strict mechanisms of implementation and control than the Declaration. In a logical extension, the Convention established the European Human Rights Commission and, somewhat later, the European Court for Human Rights. I will not dwell here on an analysis of the jurisdiction and practical work of these two organizations, but I must note that there is still no mechanism for the implementation or monitoring of *economic* and *social* rights (which are included in the Social Charter). Nor has the Council of Europe shown to date any particular eagerness to act towards improving the so-called right to development.

Other than through the international community and regional organizations, every country is obliged to develop its own mechanisms for the effective establishment, implementation and protection of human rights. In practice, it is only the signatories to the documents mentioned above who have made relevant adjustments to their institutions and legal systems. But the process of the internationalization of human rights has become so powerful that the international obligations of the Declaration cannot be denied, even by those states whose governments refused formally to adopt and ratify them.[5] For example, according to international common law, slavery and genocide are considered crimes against humanity, regardless of whether a state has signed or ratified conventions on slavery or genocide.

The unhindered functioning of human rights and, related to this, the democratic regulation of political and legal life, have become standard criteria for the legitimization of modern states. Only with the presupposition of a respect for human rights is the effective working of a true pluralist-parliamentary democracy possible. Otherwise, what we have is a formal legal simulation which irresponsibly embarks upon the permanent postponing of democracy. The subversive element of natural law which insisted on a delimitation between society and the state ('freedom *from* the state') has nowadays given way to positive law, the operation of human rights within the state's legal order ('*through* constitutional law'). As Habermas suggests, 'the revolutionary moment of turning natural into positive law has been worn out during the long process of the democratic integration of basic rights. This change led to the creation of both political space and a legal framework for citizens' participation in democratic decision-making procedures. The international mechanism for the codification and protection of human rights is binding states with increasing strictness to the creation of decision-making mechanisms which enable all particular interests to be effectively articulated within the 'general will'. Through its conventions, commissions and human rights courts, Europe in particular has already established procedures which for the first time in history make it possible for the *interests of the individual*, of the citizen, to emerge on the international stage, in the field of international law, until now reserved solely for sovereign states. The tendency to 'internalize' human rights indicates the global community's increasing willingness to take into account the sovereignty of the individual, or of minority groups, and not that of states. Respect for human rights is no longer within the domain of a state's internal affairs: care for these rights is progressively being taken over by the international community. This means that the Universal Declaration has in effect initiated a long process of dissolution of state sovereignty. State sovereignty has often been misused, in order to hide violence and lawlessness by the state; the spread of an international consensus on human rights announces the beginning of a new era, 'the age of rights', when human rights will have a real chance to be universalized, to become 'a general law of peoples'.

The end of the Cold War and the disappearance of totalitarian communism, which divided the international community for almost five decades, renewed hopes in a general respect for 'human dignity', as expressed in the Universal Declaration on Human Rights. Things have not moved quickly or dramatically – 'the disappearance of the Soviet empire has not left a world unanimous in its commitment to the idea of human rights or to institutions that give effect to this idea. China – with one fifth of the earth's human population – is at best in slow transition toward constitutionalism, the rule of law, and respect for human rights'[6] – but still a wide international debate has been started:

Following the disappearance of ideological blocs that served to protect the countries which violated human rights, some of these states are now more liable to international pressure to improve human rights conditions. All these factors have enabled the international community to strengthen the normative and institutional framework for dealing with human rights issues in recent years.[7]

A minimal consensus was reached to treat human rights, within a new, modern concept of rights, as a multilateral international right that deals with the protection of individuals and groups against violations of their internationally guaranteed rights by the state. This universalization of human rights uprooted a traditional doctrine of international law, according to which regulation was exclusively at the level of relations between national states: 'To the extent that states had any international legal obligations relating to individuals, they were deemed to be obligations owed to the states whose nationality the individuals possessed.'[8] In a legal sense, a citizen was exclusively within the jurisdiction of his/her own state. Thus, it comes as no surprise to discover that the Pact of the League of Nations, the contract by which the League was founded in 1920, contains absolutely no provision for human rights! Only the Universal Declaration enabled the strengthening of the international mechanisms for the protection of human rights, enabling their jurisdiction to spread to all parts of the world. The moral, political and normative power of the Universal Declaration has enabled the international community to establish extraordinary measures, especially in cases of mass violations of human rights.

Of course, this does not mean that the internationalization of human rights in the second half of the twentieth century can be interpreted only through progress of the humanist 'ideology' that follows a normative concept of social and political justice, that is to say, one that emphasizes ethical solidarity with those who are denied basic human rights. The programme of establishing international humanitarian responsibility has for a number of years been the subject of diplomatic competition and ideological propaganda.

The fact that the normative standards adopted then were looked upon as something redundant or impossible to carry out has undoubtedly enabled the appearance of human rights on a global level. Due to their fear of potential influence of their citizens, liberal democracies were especially eager to adopt norms that would as a matter of fact be redundant. Authoritarian states were ready to accept the normative standards that were extremely at odds with the way they functioned, since it seemed to them that there was no way they could be carried out under the influence of an external factor, nor that they could be reached by an internal pressure. Generally speaking, for liberal democracies, guaranteeing human rights meant advocating values related to ideas about the dignity of the individual. For authoritarian states, who oppressed their citizens, guaranteeing human rights meant acquiring legitimacy with regard to the outside world. Also, human rights to an extent represented moral trump cards in the ideological game that was, in the middle of the Cold War, played for the hearts and souls of people throughout the world.[9]

Both blocs worked equally on minimizing the effective influence of human rights on the processes of government – Western countries which for pragmatic reasons (protection of foreign investment) helped the authoritarian regimes in Eastern Europe, and communist countries which suffocated their own opposition and prevented the appearance of an active civil society. 'Hence, in the course of the first twenty years, foundations for the culture of human rights had been laid, but there were almost no conditions for its realisation, in the sense of improving living conditions for peoples of the world.'[10]

An important step forward came as the result of both a strengthened humanism and the pressure of new relations of political power in various areas of the world. A new geopolitical balance of powers which essentially abolished the barriers between the blocs – accompanied by the anti-colonial movement, a world-wide anti-apartheid campaign, an increased awareness of the right of peoples to self-determination, and widespread civic initiatives – shifted the focus of human rights towards the underdeveloped countries, the Arab world and aboriginal peoples. The Cairo Declaration of Human Rights (1990), for instance, provided for a specifically regional, Islamic acceptance of human rights, and represented an important attempt at codification of the *shari'a* principles in the areas of rights and liberties.[11]

The so-called new world order, heralded by these shifts in global relations, has not made miraculous progress in the area of global human rights, however. For while there is widespread consensual support for the idea of the expansion of civil, political and human rights, the powerful 'neo-liberal' élite have for the most part completely ignored the international economic and social rights of citizens in poor countries. Underdeveloped countries have been coerced into bowing to the mechanisms of the world market, within which, despite all the reforms and privatization, they have no real chance of succeeding. In these circumstances, calls for human rights, and a related insistence on democracy, sound something like post-colonialist interventionism. Moreover, a lack of balance in the distribution of international power and wealth is the very foundation of the prolonged and strong resistance to the generalized moral norms that underpin human rights. 'Globalization from above' produces hegemonic effects which systematically endanger consensual acceptance of the universal status of human rights. As Richard Rorty suggests, 'human rights culture' (the expression was first used by the Argentinian jurist and philosopher Eduardo Rabossi, in his article 'Human Rights Naturalized') can count on universal solidarity only under the condition that it frees itself of pro-Western cultural imperialism. 'We see our task as a matter of making our own culture – the human rights culture – more self-conscious and more powerful, rather than of demonstrating its superiority to other cultures by an appeal to something transcultural.'[12] Human rights, their norms and procedures, discourses and institutions, could be separated from their ambivalent Western origin and latent hegemonism only if they were 'globalized from below', with universalized respect for differences between

countries, regions, cultures and civilizations. Non-violent, consensual internationalization of the universal norms of human rights will in the future
have to be tied to the project of a global civil society, with the programme
of building a cosmopolitan, trans-national democracy.[13] Only under this
condition can the world community become a general guarantor of the universal validity of human rights.

The case of the Federal Republic of Yugoslavia

The development of constitutional rights and civic laws failed to embrace the
young nations which had emancipated themselves from the Ottoman Empire
in the mid nineteenth century. Instead, a process of constituting national
states based on the prevailing private laws and remaining traditional customs developed. That is why the principle of the equality of citizens, which
civic law tries to ensure, 'will be in greatest danger here from the conservative
elements of *kin, not feudal social structure*.'[14] Nineteenth-century Serb constitutional history, for instance, perceived constitutional law as an instrument of
struggle for national independence and the legal means by which to confront
strong absolutism.

> A tendency to limit power that refers only to the narrow circle of individuals
> and a tendency for collective aims are not the best allies of personal rights.
> According to legal historians, rights of the individuals in Serbia at the time
> were most often a chimera, although they were written in constitutions and
> laws. There is even a qualified opinion that up to the First World War, 'no con-
> stitution in Serb constitutional history has been adopted in a legal way.'[15]

Thus, it comes as no surprise to learn that Serbia adopted its first civic law in
1844, under the tutelage of an absolute despot, the illiterate merchant Miloš
Obrenović. According to the research of a sociologist of law,

> A civic law for the Princedom of Serbia was still adopted taking the Austrian
> Civil Law as the model, thus satisfying the demand that the Serb initial civil leg-
> islation should be, in Miloš's own words, 'appropriate to the monarchist
> principle', and that it should not irritate the three patron monarchies, Turkey,
> Russia, and Austria.[16]

In accordance with common law, the first Serbian law founded civil society on the natural-law principle of peasants' cooperatives. After this,
common law increasingly lost importance, and was substituted gradually
with positive legal legislation in the European tradition. However, a legacy of
self-legitimization of political authority (from monarchist absolutism to totalitarian communism) has become a permanent obstacle for the establishment
of a state of law and a rule of law in Yugoslavia, and parliamentary legislation
has never yet functioned according to the ethos of the states under
European jurisdiction.

Belief in 'the rule of law', in the unlimited right of the legislator, led Max Weber to write: 'The most well-known form of legitimacy today is belief in legality.' Unlike constitutional republics based on *the state monopoly on law and legality*, authoritarian systems legitimize themselves through *a political concept of the law*, devoid of any relation to law and justice. Totalitarian states have brought to its final consequence a process of political suspension of law and morals. In the case of Yugoslavia, the reality of legal norms and legislative procedures was absorbed by the political voluntarism of the élite in power. A fleeting remark by Josip Broz Tito – 'We shall not hang on to laws like a drunkard hangs on to a street post' – vividly illustrates the lack of legal order and a collapse of legitimacy through legality.

Twentieth-century societies have, however, developed a legitimizing power of legality. A permanent self-correction in a democratic system is the result of a conviction that 'the source of legitimisation should not be sought one-sidedly, only in the place of either political legislature or judiciary.'[17] In societies of high complexity, as suggested by Habermas, the idea of the state of law and, in connection with it, the autonomizing of the legal system, constantly mesh with morality and politics.

That the remaining idea of *the state of law*, which I have re-formulated, is not euphorical, but that it stems from the ground of the legal reality itself, could, finally, be seen in that the autonomy of a legal system could be measured by that idea only. If the dimension for which legally institutionalised ways of establishing are being opened towards moral argumentation would close, we would no longer know what else the autonomy of law could mean but the autonomy of constitution. The legal system does not acquire autonomy for itself. It is autonomous only inasmuch as institutionalised acts of legislature and judiciary guarantee unbiased creation of courts and will, thus bringing the ethical procedural rationality equally to both law and politics. *There is no autonomy of law without a realized democracy.*[18]

An advancement in the culture of rights can be seen in the acknowledgment that subjective rights are as original as objective ones, and that both constitute the legal order together. The emphasis is on the *inter-subjective sense* of subjective rights, a sense that has long been unrecognized and unacknowledged, because of the individualist understanding and liberalist phrasing.

A right, after all, is neither a gun nor a one-man show. It is a relationship and a social practice, and in both those essential aspects it is an expression of connectedness. Rights are public propositions, involving obligations to others as well as entitlements against them. In appearance, at least, they are a form of social cooperation, no doubt, but still, in the final analysis, cooperation.[19]

The etatistic understanding of objective law, as well as the positivist dogmatics of civil law, is being abandoned:

At a conceptual level, rights do not immediately refer to atomistic and estranged individuals who are possessively set against one another. On the contrary, as elements of the legal order they presuppose collaboration among subjects who recognize one another, in their reciprocally related rights and duties, *as free and equal citizens*. This mutual recognition is constitutive for a legal order.[20]

Progress in the process of legitimacy lay in the first place in the democratic introduction and regulation of rights retroactively referring to the principle of people's sovereignty. From that moment onwards, the idea of human rights and sovereignty became the determining criteria of normative self-understanding of the democratic states of law. A just society could be constituted only where political freedoms were secured through democratic legislature, and where the legitimacy of law was based on universal justice and solidarity. 'The aim of the excursus was to explain why human rights and the principle of popular sovereignty still constitute the sole ideas that can justify modern law.'[21] The task of modern democracies, then, is to resolve a latent tension between the postulated priority of human rights and popular sovereignty, secured through the fact that the legal system creates regular conditions under which 'communicative forms of the Lifeworld' (Habermas) can be institutionalized, since they are indispensable for a politically autonomous legislature. In this regard, 'the substance of human rights then resides in the formal conditions for the legal institutionalization of those discursive processes of opinion- and will-formation in which the sovereignty of the people assumes a binding character.'[22]

In contrast to the long process of democratic consolidation of the state of law in the West, communist Yugoslavia adopted the Bolshevik legal paradigm, which was canonized by the Russian 1918 Constitution and the Soviet 1937 Constitution. This latter openly declared a total abolition of the rights of individuals, a sovereign sphere of his/her personal freedom that stood in the way of unlimited state authority. Laws did not function as legal instruments for the limiting of power, but as political instruments for the unlimited expansion of absolute power. Consequently, the FPRY (Federal People's Republic of Yugoslavia) and the SFRY (Socialist Federal Republic of Yugoslavia) functioned not as legal but as totalitarian states, based on a monopoly of 'legitimate violence'. Traditional means of coercion disabled both the sovereignty and rights of individuals. The lack of legal legitimization created a political space in which the general interest of the majority was suspended by the tyranny of a minority, communist party. 'There is no censorship in Yugoslavia,' philosopher Žarko Puhovski once said, 'but there are many bans, so it turns out that, perversely speaking, there would be progress if a censorship were to be instituted as the sum of rules on bans.'[23] Socialist regimes used the legal infrastructure as a screen behind which the political voluntarism of the one-party state could be hidden. Since the autonomy of civil society was impossible, all citizens, and oppressed and marginal groups in particular, could not participate equally in the shaping of so-called socialist laws. In this respect, the legal order of the SFRY disabled a real balance between the formal and the material interpretation and realization of the adopted Soviet and Russian laws. Such a misbalance between legal norms and legal facts prevented the later FRY from fulfilling the obligations it undertook in a proper, state-like manner.

The question of the legal, political and social status of human rights in the FRY was opened only after the fall of socialism, and intensified under pressure from the international community. The issue gained additional currency against the background of the crumbling of a party and a police state which had failed to evolve into a democratic state ruled by law. Additionally, systematic and wide-scale violation of human rights in the FRY has turned out to be one of the principal obstacles for return to the international community and to possible future integration into the European Union. There are no signs that the FRY authorities are ready to rethink their position on human rights, and even less that they are willing to expose themselves to the risk of international control of their implementation.[24]

When considering the position on human rights as well as the possibilities for their realization in the so-called transition countries, one has to take into account *structural limitations*. First, in the case of the FRY, great changes in society, a crisis of enormous proportions, extraordinary circumstances, war, and, finally, dissolution of the former Yugoslavia, have created *a legal area of excess*, where regulation of public and private life simply does not exist. Second, the emancipation from a totalitarian and authoritarian regime is overlaid by a collectivist heritage insensitive to a liberal culture and individualist tradition. The reform processes came about as a result of demands to establish the freedom not of the individual, but of the nation, of demands for an emancipation of the *ethnos*, not of the citizen. What we have here is a political backlash that is trying to replace a twentieth-century socialist state with a nineteenth-century national state. 'Thus, societies in transition become incapable of resisting national and religious discrimination. Many of them have great troubles with citizenship, which is understood as membership in a dominant, populous, state-making nation, instead of being understood as a simple connection between citizens and state.'[25] Third, normative coordination of national regulations with international legal standards is a necessary, albeit not sufficient, (pre)condition for the full functioning of a state of law, and, related to that, of the consistent rule of law. An inability to establish such a coordination in the FRY has been especially visible in the area of civil and political rights. Some of its fundamental legislation, for example:

> presuppose[s] realisation of human rights based exclusively on the Constitution and laws, without referring to relevant international instruments, which means essentially giving priority to the internal legislature in a sphere which is no longer in the exclusive jurisdiction of the state. [Moreover], realisation and implementation of human rights is brought into the context, or is being implicitly conditioned by the execution of adequate obligations or duties. That is contrary to all the international standards and original

philosophical-juridical and political concepts of human rights.[26]

Fourth, even if a relatively correct legislature was established, and relevant international documents signed, there would be no guarantee, without international control, that political, civil and human rights would be respected. In a state where human rights are treated as an exclusive civil privilege, there can be no effective processual-legal mechanisms for their protection, or international guarantees.

In the context of state suspension of the legal regulation of social and political life, civic initiatives in connection with the implementation of human rights in the FRY acquire special weight and significance. A decisive request to the FRY government to adhere to certain standards of behaviour towards its citizens has come from the inside, from the civil and non-governmental sector in Belgrade, whose 800 or so associations and organizations have become the main internal strongpoint in the struggle for the recognition of political, civic and human rights.[27] Their initiatives contain a potential threat to the legitimacy and sovereignty of a state which is indifferent and cynical to the question of human rights. Under normal circumstances, the improvement of legal norms in the political and legal system would be the task of both state and society. There is still, however, no political or legal culture in the FRY that would conceive of democracy as a double, converging process.

The implications of these points are profound: 'for Democracy to flourish today it has to be reconceived as a double-sided phenomenon: concerned, on the one hand, with the re-form of state power and, on the other hand, with the re-structuring of civil society. The principle of autonomy can only be enacted by recognising the indispensability of a process of double democratisation, the interdependent transformation of both state and civil society.'[28] The process of subversion of state sovereignty is also possible through human rights – although individual citizens of a country are not subjects of international law. Only in the courtroom and in the language of law are rights defended and represented as the achievable rights of individuals, which citizens may legislate for. In this respect, the conditions still do not exist for an individual to win in court proceedings against his/her state in an international court.

This volume is intended to highlight the main directions of the expansion of the idea and culture of human rights. In doing so, it does not succumb to the naïve political euphoria which seems to go hand in hand with the formal legal legitimization of the modern state. The process of an increasingly visible globalization of human rights testifies convincingly to the advantages of the legalist model of legitimation; the 'Western' insistence on the universality of human rights can, however, function virtually as a diplomatic and political alibi for postcolonial interventionism. In all cases, the diffusion of demands for a general recognition of civic, human and political rights must take into account the social and economic, in other words the *structural* limitations of their application. For instance, the emphasis for certain countries that ratify covenants, as Weissbrodt says, would be that 'they must immediately cease torturing their residents, but they are not immediately required to feed, clothe, and house them'.[29] The politics of the globalization of human rights must take into account cultural priorities, regional specificities and local limitations. Otherwise, authoritarian regimes may respond using the geopolitical argument, claiming that the struggle for human rights is nothing but a postcolonial manoeuvre, a conspiracy of the new world order against regional or national interests. Naturally, the global processes of adapting the state to the idea of human rights may also work from below, taking into account all the cultural, regional or national differences. It is the belief of the writers here that modern states follow without hindrance the normative concept of social and political justice, precisely by demonstrating international solidarity with individuals or groups whose basic human rights are jeopardized or completely denied.

Finally, despite a real conflict of global, local and regional interests and needs, one could state the conditions under which a non-violent and general consensus on human rights is possible. The Western discourse of human rights forms an intrinsic value, whose international persuasiveness 'comes from the sense that they are not just features of our legal tradition, that they are not part of what is culturally conditioned, one option among others which human societies can adopt, but fundamental, essential, belonging to human beings as such – in short, inviolable'.[30] That is the minimum around which different groups, states, countries, religious communities, cultures and civilizations could agree. Although they would keep mutually uncoordinated fundamental views on theology, metaphysics and the philosophy of human rights, they could still agree on certain norms and rules that should govern human behaviour. As suggested by Charles Taylor, 'We would agree on the norms, while disagreeing on why they were the right norms. And we would be content to live in this consensus, undisturbed by the differences of profound underlying belief.' When Louis Henkin announced 'The Age of Rights', what he had in mind was a new form of international coexistence, arising under the guise of the broad and non-violent consensus on human rights. Unlike the old compromise, which insisted on fragile coordination, the new, all-encompassing consensus is continually opening up towards individual disagreements around which we could reach some conclusion, so that *a consensus would be renewed*, with mutual respect. I do not see why anyone would willingly abandon *translatio juris* of non-intrusive and wide-reaching consensus about the inviolability of their own human rights. *A singularization of the law*, and not *collectivization of duties* (towards the state, party, nation, race or religion), which, as a rule, undermines a belief that we share similar beliefs and common values, is, in the long term, the only solid basis of a non-violent *universalization* of human rights.

Belgrade, December 1998

Notes

General note: All emphases in quotes are the author's own.

1. The Yugoslav delegation had numerous objections to the proposed outline of the Declaration. First, the Declaration was 'conceptualized individually', seeing citizens as isolated individuals, independent of any given social context. Second, the document favoured individuals as subjects of individual rights, and not the state as a subject of international law. Third, there were no social rights in the proposed list of human rights. Finally, the FPRY delegation particularly insisted upon taking into account the rights of national communities, stating that an individual must be granted certain rights, not just as an isolated individuum, but also as a member of a national community. The political paradox is that a delegation from a communist country insisted on the complete protection of national rights, which, in the period of dissolution of that country, could not be realized without war, violence and violation of human dignity. See 'The Position of the FPRY Delegation', *Arhiv za pravne i društvene nauke*, Belgrade, 1/1949, 126–131.

2. Thomas Buerghental, *International Human Rights in a Nutshell*, West Publishing Co., St Paul, Minn., 1988, p. 18.

3. See Sevima Sali and Zlatan Terzić (eds.), *Međunarodni dokumenti o ljudskim pravima*, Pravni centar BiH, Sarajevo, 1996, p. 32.

4. Miomir Matulović, *Ljudska prava: uvod u teoriju ljudskih prava*, p. 222, Filozofska istraživanja, Zagreb, 1966. For regional rights as a topic of intensive research, see: R. E. Howard, *Human Rights in Commonwealth Africa*, Rowman, New Jersey, 1986; L. J. LeBlanc, *The OAS and the Protection of Human Rights*, Martinus Nijhoff, The Hague, 1977; Karsten Luthke and Bernard Thomasen (eds.), *Der Regional Menschenrechtsshutz in Afrika, Amerika, und Europa*, Fischer Verlag, Frankurt am Main, 1988; A. H. Robertson, *Human Rights in Europe*, Manchester University Press, Manchester, 1986.

5. At the 1993 Vienna World Conference on Human Rights, a Declaration and a Program of Activities were adopted, signed by the representatives of 171 states. At that time, the United Nations had 185 member states. The first article of the Declaration reads: 'Human rights and fundamental liberties are rights of all acquired by birth, their protection and promotion is the first task of the governments. Even if a country did not sign or ratify any convention or agreement on human rights, it is not less *morally* obliged by the Declaration signed in Vienna.' See Kathryn English and Adam Stapleton, *The Human Rights Handbook* (in Croatian), Centar za direktnu zaštitu ljudskih prava, Zagreb, 1998, p. 17.

6. Louis Henkin, *The Age of Rights*, p. xi, Columbia University Press, New York, 1990. For the epistemological foundation of human rights on the idea of dignity, see Ellen Frankel Paul et al. (eds.), *Human Rights*, Basil Blackwell, London, 1986. About the redundant human rights rhetoric, Tom Campbell says: 'The stance that all human beings have certain rights by virtue of their humanity, rights which are not be set aside for any purpose whatsoever, is a *hypnotically arresting ideology*', Tom Campbell et al.(eds.), *Human Rights from Rhetoric to Reality*, Basil Blackwell, Oxford, 1986, p. 1.

7. Thomas Buerghental, *Međunarodna ljudska prava u sažetom obliku*, Beohradski centra za ljudska prava, Belgrade, 1997, pp. 13–14.

8. Buerghental, *International Human Rights in a Nutshell*, p. 2.

9. Richard Folc, 'Traganje za ljudskim pravima u doba globalizacije', in: Konstantin Obradović and Milan Paunović (eds.), *Pravo ljudskih prava*, Beogradski centar za ljudska prava, Belgrade, 1996, pp. 12–13.

10. Ibid., p. 14. A geopolitical critique of the spread of human rights is discussed in Noam Chomsky and Edward Hermann, *The Political Economy of Human Rights*, South End Press, Boston, 1979.

11. Enes Karić, *Ljudska prava u kontekstu islamsko-zapadne debate*, Pravni Centar BiH, Sarajevo, 1996, pp. 275–283.

12. Richard Rorty, 'Human Rights, Rationality, and Sentimentality', in this volume.

13. See David Held, *Democracy and the Global Order*, Stanford University Press, Stanford,

Calif., 1995; David Held and Archibugi Daniele (eds.), *Cosmopolitan Democracy*, Polity Press, Cambridge, Mass., 1994.

14. Aleksandar Molnar, *Društvo i pravo*, vol. 2, Visio Mundi, Novi Sad, 1994, p. 562.

15. Miroslav Prokopijević (ed.), *Ljudska prava*, Institut za evropske studije, Belgrade, 1996, p. 13.

16. Molnar, *Društvo i pravo*, p. 565.

17. Jürgen Habermas, 'Kako je moguća legitimnost putem legalnosti', in Mirjana Kasparović and Nenad Zakošek (eds.), *Legitimnost demokratske vlasti*, Naprijed, Zagreb, 1996, p. 136.

18. Ibid., p. 142.

19. F. Michelman, 'Justification and the Justifiability of Law in a Contradictory World', *Nomos* 18:71, 1986.

20. Jürgen Habermas, *Between Facts and Norms: Contributions to a Discourse Theory of Law and Democracy*, MIT Press, Cambridge, Mass., 1998, p. 88.

21. Ibid., p. 99.

22. Ibid., p. 104.

23. Žarko Puhovski, 'Šta je pravna država?', *Gledišta*, Nos. 10–12: 1989, p. 71.

24. For an account of the disastrous state of human rights in the FRY, see: Elisabeth Rehn, *Question of the Violation of Human Rights and Fundamental Freedoms in any Part of the World – Situation of the Violation of Human Rights in the Territory of the Former Yugoslavia*, Commission resolution, 1996/7 (1. Elizabet Ren, Stanje ljudskih prava na teritoriji bivše Jugoslavije, Beogradski centar za ljudska prava, Beograd, 1996; 2. Elizabet Ren, Izveštaj Specijalnog izvestioca Komisije za ljudska prava Elisabet Ren, Beogradski centar za ljudska prava, Belgrade, 1997); Lidija R. Basta, (ed.), *Constitutional Prerequisites for a Democratic Serbia*, Institut du fédéralisme Fribourg, Switzerland, 1998 (Ustavne pretpostavke za demokratsku Srbiju, Vojin Dimitrijević (ed.), Beogradski centar za ljudska prava, Belgrade, 1997); Vojin Dimitrijević and Goran Svilanović (eds.), *Ljudska prava kao tema u javnosti – Ljudska prava u pravnoj praksi*, Beogradski centar za ljudska prava and Centar za antiratnu akciju, Belgrade, 1997; Aleksandra Jovanović and Slobodanka Nedović, *Economic and Social Rights in the Federal Republic of Yugoslavia*, Belgrade Centre for Human Rights, Belgrade, 1998; Vojin Dimitrijević (ed.), *Human Rights in Yugoslavia 1998*, Belgrade Centre for Human Rights, Belgrade, 1999. An important contribution to the valorization of human rights in the FRY was also given by the following NGOs in Belgrade: Helsinki Committee for Human Rights in Serbia, Fond za humanitarno pravo, Yugoslav Lawyers Committee for Human Rights, Centre for Anti-War Action.

25. Vojin Dimitrijević, 'Tranzicija ka ljudskim pravima', in Vojin Dimitrijević and Milan Paunović (eds.), *Prava i sloboda: međunarodni i jugoslovenski standardi*, p. 213, Beogradski centar za ljudska prava, Belgrade, 1995: 'Our aim is to try to point to the special circumstances of transition, which could bring closer or push away farther the ideal of human rights, and even to make that in the end it could turn out that a transition ends in a state that is the same or even worse when it comes to human rights, compared to the initial situation.' See also Vojin Dimitrijević, *Neizvesnost ljudskih prava*, Izdavačka knjižnica Zoran Stojanović, Sremski Karlovci – Novi Sad, 1993.

26. Nebojša B. Vučinić, 'Jugoslovensko pravo i međunarodni standardi o ljudskim pravima – normativna analiza', in Vojin Dimitrijević and Milan Paunović (eds.), *Prava i sloboda: međunarodni i jugoslovenski standardi*, Beogradski centar za ljudska prava, Belgrade, 1995, pp. 143–170.

27. Branka Petrović and Žarko Paunović, *Directory of Nongovernmental Non-Profit Organizations in the FRY*, CDNPS, Belgrade, 1997.

28. David Held, 'Democracy Today', in his *Models of Democracy*, Stanford University Press, Stanford, Calif., 1987, p. 283.

29. David Weissbrodt, 'Univerzalna Deklaracija o ljudskim pravima', in *Ljudska prava*, nos. 1–2/1998, p. 20.

30. Charles Taylor, 'Conditions of an Unforced Consensus on Human Rights', in this volume.

1

The Law of Peoples

John Rawls

One aim of this essay is to sketch – in a short space, I can do no more than that – how the law of peoples[1] may be developed out of liberal ideas of justice similar to but more general than the idea I called justice as fairness and presented in my book *A Theory of Justice* (1971). By the law of peoples I mean a political conception of right and justice[2] that applies to the principles and norms of international law and practice. In section 58 of the above work I indicated how from justice as fairness the law of peoples might be developed for the limited purpose of addressing several questions of just war. In this essay my sketch of that law covers more ground and includes an account of the role of human rights. Even though the idea of justice I use to do this is more general than justice as fairness, it is still connected with the idea of the social contract: the procedure of construction, and the various steps gone through, is much the same in both cases.

A further aim is to set out the bearing of political liberalism once a liberal political conception of justice is extended to the law of peoples. In particular, we ask: what form does the toleration of non-liberal societies take in this case? Surely tyrannical and dictatorial regimes cannot be accepted as members in good standing of a reasonable society of peoples. But equally not all regimes can reasonably be required to be liberal, otherwise the law of peoples itself would not express liberalism's own principle of toleration for other reasonable ways of ordering society nor further its attempt to find a shared basis of agreement among reasonable peoples. Just as a citizen in a liberal society must respect other persons' comprehensive religious, philosophical and moral doctrines provided they are pursued in accordance with a reasonable political conception of justice, so a liberal society must respect other societies organized by comprehensive doctrines, provided their political and social institutions meet certain conditions that lead the society to adhere to a reasonable law of peoples.

More specifically, we ask: where are the reasonable limits of toleration to be drawn? It turns out that a well-ordered non-liberal society will accept the same law of peoples that well-ordered liberal societies accept. Here I understand a well-ordered society as being peaceful and not expansionist; its legal system satisfies certain requisite conditions of legitimacy in the eyes of its own people; and, as a consequence of this, it honours basic human rights (section IV). One kind of non-liberal society satisfying these conditions is illustrated by what I call, for lack of a better term, a well-ordered hierarchical society. This example makes the point, central for this argument, that although any society must honour basic human rights, it need not be liberal. It also indicates the role of human rights as part of a reasonable law of peoples.

I How a Social Contract Doctrine is Universal in Its Reach

I begin by explaining the way in which a social contract doctrine with its procedure of construction is universal in its reach.

Every society must have a conception of how it is related to other societies and of how it is to conduct itself toward them. It lives with them in the same world and except for the very special case of isolation of a society from all the rest – long in the past now – it must formulate certain ideals and principles for guiding its policies toward other peoples. Like justice as fairness, the more general liberal conception I have in mind – as specified in section III – begins with the case of a hypothetically closed and self-sufficient liberal democratic society and covers only political values and not all of life. The question now arises as to how that conception can be extended in a convincing way to cover a society's relations with other societies to yield a reasonable law of peoples. In the absence of this extension to the law of peoples, a liberal conception of political justice would appear to be historicist and to apply only to societies whose political institutions and culture are liberal. In making the case for justice as fairness, and for similar more general liberal conceptions, it is essential to show that this is not so.

The problem of the law of peoples is only one of several problems of extension for these ideas of justice. There is the additional problem of extending these ideas to future generations, under which falls the problem of just savings. Also, since the ideas of justice regard persons as normal and fully cooperating members of society over a complete life, and having the requisite capacities to do this, there arises the problem of what is owed to those who fail to meet this condition, either temporarily or permanently, which gives rise to several problems of justice in health care. Finally, there is the problem of what is owed to animals and the rest of nature.

We would eventually like an answer to all these questions, but I doubt that we can find one within the scope of these ideas of justice understood as political conceptions. At best they may yield reasonable answers to the first three problems of extension: to other societies, to future generations and to certain cases of health care. With regard to the problems which these liberal ideas of justice fail to address, there are several things we might say. One is that the idea of political justice does not cover everything and we should not expect it to. Or the problem may indeed be one of political justice but none of these ideas is correct for the question at hand, however well they may do for other questions. How deep a fault this shows must wait until the question itself can be examined, but we should not expect these ideas, or I think any account of political justice, to handle all these matters.

Let's return to our problem of extending liberal ideas of justice similar to but more general than justice as fairness to the law of peoples. There is a clear contrast between these and other familiar views in the way they are universal in reach. Take, for example, Leibniz's or Locke's doctrines: these are universal both in their source of authority and in their formulation. By that I mean that their source is God's authority or the divine reason, as the case may be; and they are universal in that their principles are stated so as to apply to all reasonable beings everywhere. Leibniz's doctrine is an ethics of creation. It contains the idea of morals as the *imitatio Dei* and applies straightaway to us as God's creatures endowed with reason. In Locke's doctrine, God having legitimate authority over all creation, the natural law – that part of God's law that can be known by our natural powers of reason – everywhere has authority and binds us and all peoples.

Most familiar philosophical views – such as rational intuitionism, (classical) utilitarianism and perfectionism – are also formulated in a general way to apply to us directly in all cases. Although they are not theologically grounded, let's say their source of authority is (human) reason, or an independent realm of moral values, or some other proposed basis of universal validity. In all these views the universality of the doctrine is the direct consequence of its source of authority and of how it is formulated.

By contrast, a constructivist view such as justice as fairness, and more general liberal ideas, do not begin from universal first principles having authority in all cases.[3] In justice as fairness the principles of justice for the basic structure of society are not suitable as fully general principles: they do not apply to all subjects, not to churches and universities, or to the basic structures of all societies, or to the law of peoples. Rather, they are constructed by way of a reasonable procedure in which rational parties adopt principles of justice for each kind of subject as it arises. Typically, a constructivist doctrine proceeds by taking up a series of subjects, starting, say, with principles of political justice for the basic structure of a closed and self-contained democratic society. That done, it then works forward to principles for the claims of future generations, outward to principles for the law of peoples, and inward to principles for special social questions. Each time the constructivist procedure is modified to fit the subject in question. In due course all the main principles are on hand, including those needed for the various political duties and obligations of individuals and associations.[4] Thus, a constructivist liberal doctrine is universal in its reach once it is extended to give principles for all politically relevant subjects, including a law of peoples for the most comprehensive subject, the political society of peoples. Its authority rests on the principles and conceptions of practical reason, but always on these as suitably adjusted to apply to different subjects as they arise in sequence; and always assuming as well that these principles are endorsed on due reflection by the reasonable agents to whom the corresponding principles apply.

At first sight, a constructivist doctrine of this kind appears hopelessly unsystematic. For how are the principles that apply to different cases tied together? And why do we proceed through the series of cases in one order rather than another? Constructivism assumes, however, that there are other forms of unity than that defined by completely general first principles forming a consistent scheme. Unity may also be given by an appropriate sequence of cases and by supposing that the parties in an original position (as I have called it) are to proceed through the sequence with the understanding that the principles for the subject of each later agreement are to be subordinate to those of subjects of all earlier agreements, or else coordinated with and adjusted to them by certain priority rules. I shall try out a particular sequence and point out its merits as we proceed. There is in advance no guarantee that it is the most appropriate sequence and much trial and error may be needed.

In developing a conception of justice for the basic structure or for the law of peoples, or indeed for any subject, constructivism does not view the variation in numbers of people alone as accounting for the appropriateness of different principles in different cases. That families are smaller than constitutional democracies does not explain why different principles apply to them. Rather, it is the distinct structure of the social framework, and the purpose and role of its various parts and how they fit together, that explain why there are different principles for different kinds of subjects. Thus, it is characteristic of a constructivist idea of justice to regard the distinctive nature and purpose of the elements of society, and of the society of peoples, as requiring persons, within a domain where other principles leave them free, to act from principles designed to fit their peculiar roles. As we shall see as we work out the law of peoples, these principles are identified in each case by rational agents fairly, or reasonably, situated given the case at hand. They are not derived from completely general principles such as the principle of utility or the principle of perfectionism.

II Three Preliminary Questions

Before showing how the extension to the law of peoples can be carried out, I go over three preliminary matters. First, let's distinguish between two parts of justice as fairness, or of any other similar liberal and constructivist conception of justice. One part is worked up to apply to the domestic institutions of democratic societies, their regime and basic structure, and to the duties and obligations of citizens. The other part is worked up to apply to the society of political societies and thus to the political relations between peoples.[5] After the principles of justice have been adopted for domestic justice, the idea of the original position is used again at the next higher level.[6] As before, the parties are representatives, but now they are representatives of peoples whose basic institutions satisfy the principles of justice selected at the first level. We start with the family of societies, each well ordered by some liberal view meeting certain conditions (justice as fairness is an example), and then work out principles to govern their relations with one another. Here I mention only the first stage of working out the law of peoples. As we shall see in section IV we must also develop principles which govern the relations between liberal and what I shall call hierarchical societies. It turns out that liberal and hierarchical societies can agree on the same law of peoples and thus this law does not depend on aspects peculiar to the Western tradition.

It may be objected that to proceed in this way is to accept the state as traditionally conceived, with all its familiar powers of sovereignty. These powers include first, the right to go to war in pursuit of state policies – Clausewitz's pursuit of politics by other means – with the aims of politics given by a state's rational prudential interests.[7] They include second, the state's right to do as it likes with people within its own borders. The objection is misapplied for this reason. In the first use of the original position domestic society is seen as closed, since we abstract from relations with other societies. There is no need for armed forces and the question of the government's right to be prepared militarily does not arise, and would be denied if it did. The principles of domestic justice allow a police force to keep domestic order but that is another matter, and although those domestic principles are consistent with a qualified right of war in a society of peoples, they do not of themselves support that right. That is up to the law of peoples itself, still to be constructed. And, as we shall see, this law will also restrict a state's internal sovereignty, its right to do as it likes to people within its borders.

Thus, it is important to see that in this working out of the law of peoples, a government as the political organization of its people is not, as it were, the author of its own power. The war powers of governments, whatever they should be, are only those acceptable within a reasonable law of peoples. Presuming the existence of a government whereby a people is domestically organized with institutions of background justice does not prejudge these questions. We must reformulate the powers of sovereignty in light of a reasonable law of peoples and get rid of the right to war and the right to internal autonomy, which have been part of (positive) international law for the two and a half centuries following the Thirty Years War, as part of the classical states system.[8]

Moreover, these ideas accord with a dramatic shift in how international law is now understood. Since World War II international law has become far more demanding than in the past. It tends to restrict a state's right to wage way to cases of self-defence (this allows collective security), and it also tends to limit a state's right of internal sovereignty.[9] The role of human rights connects most obviously with the latter change as part of the effort to provide a suitable definition of, and limits on, a government's internal sovereignty, though it is not unconnected with the first. At this point I leave aside the many difficulties of interpreting these rights and limits, and take their general meaning and tendency as clear enough. What is essential is that our elaboration of the law of peoples should fit – as it turns out to do – these two basic changes, and give them a suitable rationale.

The second preliminary matter concerns the question: in working out the law of peoples, why do we start (as I said above) with those societies well ordered by liberal views somewhat more general than justice as fairness? Wouldn't it be better to start with the world as a whole, with a global original position, so to speak, and discuss the question whether, and in what form, there should be states, or peoples, at all? Some writers (I mention them later) have thought that a social contract constructivist view should proceed in this manner, that it gives an appropriate universality from the start.

I think there is no clear initial answer to this question. We should try various alternatives and weigh their pluses and minuses. Since in working out justice as fairness I begin with domestic society, I shall continue from there as if what has been done so far is more or less sound. Thus I build on the steps taken until now, as this seems to provide a suitable starting point for the extension to the law of peoples. A further reason for proceeding thus is that peoples as corporate bodies organized by their governments now exist in some form all over the world. Historically speaking, all principles and standards proposed for the law of peoples must, to be feasible, prove acceptable to the considered and reflective public opinion of peoples and their governments.

Suppose, then, that we are (even though we are not) members of a well-ordered society. Our convictions about justice are roughly the same as those of citizens (if there are any) in the family of societies well ordered by liberal conceptions of justice and whose social and historical conditions are similar to ours. They have the same kinds of reasons for affirming their mode of government as we do for affirming ours. This common understanding of liberal societies provides an apt starting point for the extension to the law of peoples.

Finally, I note the distinction between the law of peoples and the law of nations, or international law. The latter is an existing, or positive, legal order, however incomplete it may be in some ways, lacking, for example, an effective scheme of sanctions such as normally characterizes domestic law. The law of peoples, by contrast, is a family of political concepts with principles of right, justice and the common good, that specify the content of a liberal conception of justice worked up to extend to and to apply to international law. It provides the concepts and principles by which that law is to be judged.

This distinction between the law of peoples and the law of nations should be straightforward. It is no more obscure than the distinction between the principles of justice that apply to the basic structure of domestic society and the existing political, social and legal institutions that actually realize that structure.

III The Extension to Liberal Societies

The three preliminary matters settled, I turn to the extension of liberal ideas of justice to the law of peoples. I understand these ideas of justice to contain three main elements: (i) a list of certain basic rights and liberties and opportunities (familiar from constitutional democratic regimes); (ii) a high priority for these fundamental freedoms, especially with respect to claims of the general good and of perfectionist values; and (iii) measures assuring for all citizens adequate all-purpose means to make effective use of their freedoms. Justice as fairness is typical of these conceptions except that its egalitarian features are stronger. To some degree the more general liberal ideas lack the three egalitarian features of the fair value of the political liberties, of fair equality of opportunity, and of the difference principle. These features are not needed for the construction of a reasonable law of peoples and by not assuming them our account has greater generality.

There are two main stages to the extension to the law of peoples and each stage has two steps. The first stage of the extension I call the ideal, or strict compliance, theory, and unless otherwise stated, we work entirely in this theory. This means that the relevant concepts and principles are strictly complied with by all parties to the agreements made and that the requisite favourable conditions for liberal or hierarchical institutions are on hand. Our first aim is to see what a reasonable law of peoples, fully honoured, would require and establish in this case.

To make the account manageable, we suppose there are only two kinds of well-ordered domestic societies, liberal societies and hierarchical societies. I discuss at the first step the case of well-ordered liberal democratic societies. This leads to the idea of a well-ordered political society of societies of democratic peoples. After this I turn to societies that are well ordered and just, often religious in nature and not characterized by the separation of church and state. Their political institutions specify a just consultation hierarchy, as I shall say, while their basic social institutions satisfy a conception of justice expressing an appropriate conception of the common good. Fundamental for our rendering of the law of peoples is that both liberal and hierarchical societies accept it. Together they are members in good standing of a well-ordered society of the just peoples of the world.

The second stage in working out the law of peoples is that of nonideal theory, and it also includes two steps. The first step is that of noncompliance theory. Here we have the predicament of just societies, both democratic and hierarchical, as they confront states that refuse to comply with a reasonable law of peoples. The second step of this second stage is that of unfavourable conditions. It poses the different problem of how the poorer and less technologically advanced societies of the world can attain historical and social conditions that allow them to establish just and workable institutions, either liberal or hierarchical. In actual affairs, nonideal theory is of first practical importance and deals with problems we face every day. Yet, for reasons of space, I shall say very little about it (sections VI and VII).

Before beginning the extension we need to be sure that the original position with the veil of ignorance is a device of representation for the case of liberal societies. In the first use of the original position, its function as a device of representation means that it models what we regard – you and I, and here and now[10] – as fair conditions for the parties, as representatives of free and equal citizens, to specify the terms of cooperation regulating the

basic structure of their society. Since that position includes the veil of ignorance, it also models what we regard as acceptable restrictions on reasons for
adopting a political conception of justice. Therefore, the conception the
parties would adopt identifies the conception of justice that we regard – you
and I, here and now – as fair and supported by the best reasons.

Three conditions are essential: first, the original position represents the
parties (or citizens) fairly, or reasonably; second, it represents them as rational; and third, it represents them as deciding between available principles for
appropriate reasons. We check that these three conditions are satisfied by
observing that citizens are indeed represented fairly, or reasonably, in virtue
of the symmetry and equality of their representatives' situation in the original position. Next, citizens are represented as rational in virtue of the aim of
their representatives to do the best they can for their essential interests as persons. Finally, they are represented as deciding for appropriate reasons: The
veil of ignorance prevents their representatives from invoking reasons
deemed unsuitable, given the aim of representing citizens as free and equal
persons.

At the next level, when the original position is used to extend a liberal conception to the law of peoples, it is a device of representation because it
models what we would regard – you and I, here and now[11] – as fair conditions
under which the parties, this time as representatives of societies well ordered
by liberal conceptions of justice, are to specify the law of peoples and the fair
terms of their cooperation.

The original position is a device of representation because, as before, free
and equal peoples are represented as both reasonably situated and rational,
and as deciding in accordance with appropriate reasons. The parties as representatives of democratic peoples are symmetrically situated, and so the
peoples they represent are represented reasonably. Moreover, the parties
deliberate among available principles for the law of peoples by reference to
the fundamental interests of democratic societies in accordance with, or as
presupposed by, the liberal principles of domestic justice. And finally, the parties are subject to a veil of ignorance: they do not know, for example, the size
of the territory, or the population, or the relative strength of the people
whose fundamental interests they represent. Although they know that reasonably favourable conditions obtain that make democracy possible, they do
not know the extent of their natural resources, or level of their economic
development, or any such related information. These conditions model what
we, as members of societies well ordered by liberal conceptions of justice,
would accept as fair – here and now – in specifying the basic terms of
cooperation between peoples who, as peoples, regard themselves as free and
equal. We use the original position at the second level as a device of representation as we did at the first.

I assume that working out the law of peoples for liberal democratic societies only will result in the adoption of certain familiar principles of justice,
and will also allow for various forms of cooperative association among
democratic peoples and not for a world state. Here I follow Kant's lead in

Perpetual Peace (1795) in thinking that a world government – by which I mean a unified political regime with the legal powers normally exercised by central governments – would be either a global despotism or else a fragile empire torn by frequent civil strife as various regions and peoples try to gain political autonomy.[12] On the other hand, it may turn out, as I sketch below, that there will be many different kinds of organizations subject to the judgment of the law of democratic peoples, charged with regulating cooperation between them, and having certain recognized duties. Some of these organizations (like the United Nations) may have the authority to condemn domestic institutions that violate human rights, and in certain severe cases to punish them by imposing economic sanctions, or even by military intervention. The scope of these powers is all peoples' and covers their domestic affairs.

If all this is sound, I believe the principles of justice between free and democratic peoples will include certain familiar principles long recognized as belonging to the law of peoples, among them the following:

1. Peoples (as organized by their governments) are free and independent and their freedom and independence are to be respected by other peoples.
2. Peoples are equal and parties to their own agreements.
3. Peoples have the right of self-defence but no right to war.
4. Peoples are to observe a duty of nonintervention.
5. Peoples are to observe treaties and undertakings.
6. Peoples are to observe certain specified restrictions on the conduct of war (assumed to be in self-defence).
7. Peoples are to honour human rights.

This statement of principles is of course incomplete; other principles would need to be added. Further, they require much explanation and interpretation, and some of them are superfluous in a society of well-ordered democratic peoples, for instance, the sixth regarding the conduct of war and the seventh regarding human rights. The main point is that given the idea of a society of free and independent democratic peoples, who are ready to recognize certain basic principles of political justice governing their conduct, principles of this kind constitute the charter of their association.[13] Obviously, a principle such as the fourth – that of nonintervention – will have to be qualified in the general case. Although suitable for a society of well-ordered democratic peoples who respect human rights, it fails in the case of disordered societies in which wars and serious violations of human rights are endemic. Also, the right to independence, and equally the right to self-determination, hold only within certain limits, to be specified by the law of peoples for the general case. Thus, no people has the right to self-determination, or a right to secession, at the expense of the subjugation of another people;[14] nor can a people protest their condemnation by the world society when their domestic institutions violate the human rights of certain minorities living among them. Their right to independence is no shield from that condemnation, or even from coercive intervention by other peoples in grave cases.

There will also be principles for forming and regulating federations (associations) of peoples, and standards of fairness for trade and other cooperative arrangements. There should be certain provisions for mutual assistance between peoples in times of famine and drought, and were it feasible, as it should be, provisions for ensuring that in all reasonably developed liberal societies people's basic needs are met.[15] These provisions will specify duties of assistance in certain situations, and they will vary in stringency depending on the severity of the case.

An important role of a people's government, however arbitrary a society's boundaries may appear from a historical point of view,[16] is to be the representative and effective agent of a people as they take responsibility for their territory and the size of their population, as well as for maintaining its environmental integrity and its capacity to sustain them. The idea here appeals to the point of the institution of property: unless a definite agent is given responsibility for maintaining an asset and bears the loss for not doing so, that asset tends to deteriorate. In this case the asset is the people's territory and its capacity to sustain them in perpetuity; the agent is the people themselves as politically organized. They must recognize that they cannot make up for irresponsibility in caring for their land and conserving their natural resources by conquest in war or by migrating into other people's territory without their consent.[17]

These remarks belong to ideal theory and indicate some of the responsibilities of peoples in a just society of well-ordered liberal societies. Since the boundaries of peoples are often historically the outcome of violence and aggression, and some peoples are wrongly subjected to others, the law of peoples in its nonideal part should, as far as possible, contain principles and standards – or at least some guidelines – for coping with these matters.

To complete this sketch of the law of peoples for well-ordered liberal societies only, let's consider under what conditions we can reasonably accept this part of the law of peoples and regard it as justified.

There are two conditions beyond the three requirements earlier noted in discussing the original position as a device of representation. These requirements were: that the parties (as representatives of free and equal peoples) be represented as reasonably situated, as rational, and as deciding in accordance with appropriate reasons. One of the two further conditions is that the political society of well-ordered democratic peoples should itself be stable in the right way.[18] Given the existence of a political society of such peoples, its members will tend increasingly over time to accept its principles and judgments as they come to understand the ideas of justice expressed in the law among them and appreciate its benefits for all liberal peoples.

To say that the society of democratic peoples is stable in the right way is to say that it is stable with respect to justice, that is, that the institutions and practices among peoples always more or less satisfy the relevant principles of justice, although social conditions are presumably always changing. It is further to say that the law of peoples is honoured not simply because of a fortunate balance of power – it being in no people's interest to upset it – but because, despite the possibly shifting fortunes of different peoples, all are moved to adhere to their common law accepting it as just and beneficial for all. This means that the justice of the society of democratic peoples is stable with respect to the distribution of fortune among them. Here fortune refers not to a society's military success or the lack of it, but to other kinds of success: its achievement of political and social freedom, the fullness and expressiveness of its culture, the economic well-being of all its citizens.

The historical record suggests that, at least so far as the principle against war is concerned, this condition of stability would be satisfied in a society of just democratic peoples. Although democratic societies have been as often involved in war as non-democratic states[19] and have often vigorously defended their institutions, since 1800, as Michael Doyle points out, firmly established liberal societies have not gone to war with one another.[20] And in wars in which a number of major powers were engaged, such as the two World Wars, democratic states have fought as allies on the same side. Indeed, the absence of war between democracies is as close as anything we know to an empirical law in relations between societies.[21] This being so, I shall suppose that a society of democratic peoples, all of whose basic institutions are well ordered by liberal conceptions of justice (though not necessarily by the same conception) will be stable in the right way as above specified. The sketch of the law of such peoples therefore seems to meet the condition of political realism given by that of stability for the right reasons.

Observe that I state what I call Doyle's law as holding between well-established and well-ordered liberal democracies that are significant if not major powers. The reasons for this law's holding (supposing it does) are quite compatible with actual democracies, marked as they are by considerable injustice and oligarchic tendencies, intervening, often covertly, in smaller countries whose democracies are less well established and secure. Witness the United States' overturning the democracies of Allende in Chile, Arbenz in Guatemala, Mossadegh in Iran, and, some would add, the Sandinistas in Nicaragua. Whatever the merits of these regimes, covert operations against them can be carried out by a government bureaucracy at the urging of oligarchic interests without the knowledge or criticism of the public, and presenting it with a fait accompli. All this is made easier by the handy appeal to national security given the situation of superpower rivalry in the Cold War, which allowed those democracies, however implausibly, to be case as a danger. While democratic peoples are not expansionist, they do defend their security interest, and this an oligarchic government can easily manipulate in a time of superpower rivalry to support covert interventions once they are found out.[22]

The last condition for us to accept this sketch of the law of democratic peoples as sound is that we can, as citizens of liberal societies, endorse the principles and judgments of this law on due reflection. We must be able to say that the doctrine of the law of peoples for such societies, more than any other doctrine, ties together our considered political convictions and moral judgments at all levels of generality, from the most general to the more particular, into one coherent view.

IV Extension to Hierarchical Societies

Recall from section III that the extension of liberal ideas of justice to the law of peoples proceeds in two stages, each stage having two steps. The first stage is that of ideal theory and we have just completed the first step of that: the extension of the law of peoples to well-ordered liberal societies only. The second step of ideal theory is more difficult: it requires us to specify a second kind of society – a hierarchical society, as I shall say – and then to state when such a society is well ordered. Our aim is to extend the law of peoples to these well-ordered hierarchical societies and to show that they accept the same law of peoples as liberal societies do. Thus, this shared law of well-ordered peoples, both liberal and hierarchical, specifies the content of ideal theory. It specifies the kind of society of well-ordered peoples all people should want and it sets the regulative end of their foreign policy. Important for us, it has the obvious corollary that non-liberal societies also honour human rights.

To show all this we proceed thus. First, we state three requirements for any well-ordered hierarchical regime. It will be clear that satisfying these requirements does not entail that a regime be liberal. Next, we confirm that, in an original position with a veil of ignorance, the representatives of well-ordered hierarchical regimes are reasonably situated as well as rational, and are moved by appropriate reasons. In this case also, the original position is a device of representation for the adoption of law among hierarchical peoples. Finally, we show that in the original position the representatives of well-ordered hierarchical societies would adopt the same law of peoples that the representatives of liberal societies do. That law thus serves as a common law of a just political society of well-ordered peoples.

The first of the three requirements for a hierarchical society to be well ordered is that it must be peaceful and gain its legitimate aims through diplomacy and trade, and other ways of peace. It follows that its religious doctrine, assumed to be comprehensive and influential in government policy, is not expansionist in the sense that it fully respects the civic order and integrity of other societies. If it seeks wider influence, it does so in ways compatible with the independence of, and the liberties within, other societies. This feature of its religion supports the institutional basis of its peaceful conduct and distinguishes it from leading European states during the religious wars of the sixteenth and seventeenth centuries.

A second fundamental requirement uses an idea of Philip Soper. It has several parts. It requires first, that a hierarchical society's system of law be such as to impose moral duties and obligations on all persons within its territory.[23] It requires further that its system of law be guided by a common good conception of justice, meaning by this a conception that takes impartially into account what it sees not unreasonably as the fundamental interests of all members of society. It is not the case that the interests of some are arbitrarily privileged, while the interests of others go for naught. Finally, there must be sincere and not unreasonable belief on the part of judges and other officials who administer the legal order that the law is indeed guided by a common good conception of justice. This belief must be demonstrated by a willingness to defend publicly the state's injunctions as justified by law. Courts are an efficient way of doing this.[24] These aspects of a legal order are necessary to establish a regime's legitimacy in the eyes of its own people. To sum up the second requirement we say: the system of law is sincerely and not unreasonably believed to be guided by a common good conception of justice. It takes into account people's essential interests and imposes moral duties and obligations on all members of society.

This second requirement can be spelled out further by adding that the political institutions of a well-ordered hierarchical society constitute a reasonable consultation hierarchy. They include a family of representative bodies, or other assemblies, whose task is to look after the important interests of all elements of society. Although in hierarchical societies persons are not regarded as free and equal citizens, as they are in liberal societies, they are seen as responsible members of society who can recognize their moral duties and obligations and play their part in social life.

With a consultation hierarchy there is an opportunity for different voices to be heard, not, to be sure, in a way allowed by democratic institutions, but appropriately in view of the religious and philosophical values of the society in question. Thus, individuals do not have the right of free speech as in a liberal society; but as members of associations and corporate bodies they have the right at some point in the process of consultation to express political dissent and the government has an obligation to take their dissent seriously and to give a conscientious reply. That different voices can be heard is necessary because the sincere belief of judges and other officials has two components: honest belief and respect for the possibility of dissent.[25] Judges and officials must be willing to address objections. They cannot refuse to listen to them on the grounds that they think those expressing them are incompetent and cannot understand. Then we would not have a consultation hierarchy but a purely paternalistic regime.

In view of this account of the institutional basis of a hierarchical society, we can say that its conception of the common good of justice secures for all persons at least certain minimum rights to means of subsistence and security (the right to life),[26] to liberty (freedom from slavery, serfdom and forced occupations) and (personal) property, as well as to formal equality as expressed by the rules of natural justice[27] (for example, that similar cases be treated similarly). This shows that a well-ordered hierarchical society also meets a third requirement: it respects basic human rights.

The argument for this conclusion is that the second requirement rules out violations of these rights. For to satisfy it, a society's legal order must impose moral duties and obligations on all persons in its territory and it must embody a reasonable consultation hierarchy which will protect human rights. A sincere and reasonable belief on the part of judges and other officials that the system of law is guided by a common good conception of justice has the same result. Such a belief is simply unreasonable, if not irrational, when those rights are infringed.

There is a question about religious toleration that calls for explicit mention. Whereas in hierarchical societies a state religion may be on some questions the ultimate authority within society and control government policy on certain important matters, that authority is not (as I have said) extended politically to other societies. Further, their (comprehensive) religious or philosophical doctrines are not unreasonable: they admit a measure of liberty of conscience and freedom of thought, even if these freedoms are not in general equal for all members of society as they are in liberal regimes.[28] A hierarchical society may have an established religion with certain privileges. Still, it is essential to its being well ordered that no religions are persecuted, or denied civic and social conditions that permit their practising in peace and without fear.[29] Also essential, and this because of the inequality of religious freedom, if for no other reason, is that a hierarchical society must allow for the right of emigration.[30] The rights noted here are counted as human rights. In section V we return to the role and status of these rights.

An institutional basis that realizes the three requirements can take many forms. This deserves emphasis, as I have indicated only the religious case. We are not trying to describe all possible forms of social order consistent with membership in good standing of a reasonable society of peoples. Rather, we have specified three necessary conditions for membership of a reasonable society of peoples and then shown by example that these conditions do not require a society to be liberal.

This completes the account of the requirements imposed on the basic institutions of a well-ordered hierarchical society. My aim has been to outline a conception of justice that, although distant from liberal conceptions, still has features that give to societies regulated accordingly the moral status required to be members in good standing in a reasonable society of well-ordered peoples. It is important to see, as I have noted, that an agreement on a law of peoples ensuring human rights is not an agreement only liberal societies can make. We must now confirm this.

Hierarchical societies are well ordered in terms of their own conceptions of justice.[31] This being so, their representatives in an appropriate original position would adopt the same principles as those sketched above, that would be adopted by the representatives of liberal societies. Each hierarchical society's interests are understood by its representatives in accordance with or as presupposed by its conception of justice. This enables us to say in this case also that the original position is a device of representation.

Two considerations confirm this. The first is that, in view of the common good conception of justice held in a hierarchical society, the parties care about the good of the society they represent, and so about its security as assured by the laws against war and aggression. They also care about the benefits of trade and assistance between peoples in time of need. All these help protect human rights. In view of this, we can say that the representatives of hierarchical societies are rational. The second consideration is that they do not try to extend their religious and philosophical doctrines to other peoples by war or aggression, and they respect the civic order and integrity of other societies. Hence, they accept – as you and I would accept[32] – the original position as fair between peoples and would endorse the law of peoples adopted by their representatives as specifying fair terms of political cooperation between them and other societies. Thus, the representatives are reasonably situated and this suffices for the use of the original position as a device of representation in extending the law of peoples to hierarchical societies.[33]

Note that I have supposed that the parties as representatives of peoples are to be situated equally, even though the conception of justice of the hierarchical society they represent allows basic inequalities between its members. For example, some of its members are not granted equal liberty of conscience. There is, however, no inconsistency in this: a people sincerely affirming a non-liberal conception of justice may still think their society should be treated equally in a just law of peoples, even though its members accept basic inequalities among themselves. Though a society lacks basic equality, it is not unreasonable for that society to insist on equality in making claims against other societies.

About this last point, two observations. One is that although the original position at the first level, that of domestic justice, incorporates a political conception of the person rooted in the public culture of a liberal society, the original position at the second level, that of the law of peoples, does not. I emphasize this fact, since it enables a liberal conception of justice to be extended to yield a more general law of peoples without prejudging the case against non-liberal societies.

This leads to a second observation. As mentioned earlier, the law of peoples might have been worked out by starting with an all-inclusive original position with representatives of all the individual persons of the world.[34] In this case the question of whether there are to be separate societies, and of the relations between them, will be settled by the parties behind a veil of ignorance. Off-hand, it is not clear why proceeding this way should lead to different results than, as I have done, proceeding from separate societies outward. All things considered, one might reach the same law of peoples in either case. The difficulty with an all-inclusive, or global, original position is that its use of liberal ideas is much more troublesome, for in this case we are treating all persons, regardless of their society and culture, as individuals who are free and equal, and as reasonable and rational, and so according to liberal conceptions. This makes the basis of the law of peoples too narrow.

Hence I think it best to follow the two-level[35] bottom-up procedure, beginning first with the principles of justice for the basic structure of domestic society and then moving upward and outward to the law of peoples. In so doing our knowledge of how peoples and their governments have acted historically gives us guidance in how to proceed and suggests questions and possibilities we might not otherwise have thought of. But this is simply a point of method and settles no questions of substance. These depend on what can actually be worked out.

One might well be sceptical that a liberal social contract and constructivist[36] idea of justice can be worked out to give a conception of the law of peoples universal in its reach and also applying to non-liberal societies. Our discussion of hierarchical societies should put these doubts to rest. I have noted the conditions under which we could accept the law of liberal peoples we had sketched as sound and justified. In this connection we considered whether that law was stable with respect to justice, and whether, on due reflection, we could accept the judgments that its principles and precepts led us to make. If both these things hold, we said, the law of liberal peoples as laid out could, by the criteria we can now apply, be accepted as justified.

Parallel remarks hold for the wider law of peoples including well-ordered hierarchical societies. Here I simply add, without argument or evidence, but hoping it seems plausible, that these societies will honour a just law of peoples for much the same reasons liberal peoples will do so, and that both we and they will find the judgments to which it leads acceptable to our convictions, all things considered. I believe it is of importance here that well-ordered hierarchical societies are not expansionist and their legal order is guided by a common good conception of justice ensuring that it honours human rights. These societies also affirm a peaceful society of peoples and benefit therefrom as liberal societies do. All have a common interest in changing the way in which politics among peoples – war and threats of war – has hitherto been carried on.

We may therefore view this wider law of peoples as sound and justified. This fundamental point deserves emphasis: there is nothing relevantly different between how, say, justice as fairness is worked out for the domestic case in *A Theory of Justice*, and how the law of peoples is worked out from more general liberal ideas of justice. In both cases we use the same fundamental idea of a reasonable procedure of construction in which rational agents fairly situated (the parties as representatives of citizens in one case and of peoples or societies in the other) select principles of justice for the relevant subject, either their separate domestic institutions or the shared law of peoples. As always, the parties are guided by the appropriate reasons as specified by a veil of ignorance. Thus, obligations and duties are not imposed by one society on another; instead, reasonable societies agree on what the bonds will be. Once we confirm that a domestic society, or a society of peoples, when regulated by the corresponding principles of justice, is stable with respect to justice (as previously defined), and once we have checked that we can endorse those principles on due reflection, then in both domains the ideals, laws and principles of justice are justified in the same way.[37]

V Human Rights

A few of the features of human rights as we have described them are these. First, these rights do not depend on any particular comprehensive moral doctrine or philosophical conception of human nature, such as, for example, that human beings are moral persons and have equal worth, or that they have certain particular moral and intellectual powers that entitle them to these rights. This would require a quite deep philosophical theory that many if not most hierarchical societies might reject as liberal or democratic, or in some way distinctive of the Western political tradition and prejudicial to other cultures.

We therefore take a different tack and say that basic human rights express a minimum standard of well-ordered political institutions for all peoples who belong, as members in good standing, to a just political society of peoples.[38] Any systematic violation of these rights is a serious matter and troubling to the society of peoples as a whole, both liberal and hierarchical. Since they must express a minimum standard, the requirements that yield these rights should be quite weak.

Recall that we postulated that a society's system of law must be such as to impose moral duties and obligations on all its members and be regulated by what judges and other officials reasonably and sincerely believe is a common good conception of justice. For this condition to hold, the law must at least uphold such basic rights as the right to life and security, to personal property, and the elements of the rule of law, as well as the right to a certain liberty of conscience and freedom of association, and the right to emigration. These rights we refer to as human rights.

Next we consider what the imposition of these duties and obligations implies, including (1) a common good conception of justice and (2) good faith on the part of officials to explain and justify the legal order to those bound by it. For these things to hold does not require the liberal idea that persons are first citizens and as such free and equal members of society who hold those basic rights as the rights of citizens. It requires only that persons be responsible and cooperating members of society who can recognize and act in accordance with their moral duties and obligations. It would be hard to reject these requirements (a common good conception of justice and a good faith official justification of the law) as too strong for a minimally decent regime. Human rights, understood as resulting from these requirements, could not be rejected as peculiarly liberal or special to our Western tradition. In that sense, they are politically neutral.[39]

To confirm this last point, I consider an alleged difficulty. Many societies have political traditions that are different from Western individualism in its many forms. In considering persons from a political point of view, these traditions are said to regard persons not as citizens first with the rights of citizens but rather as first being members of groups: communities, associations, or corporations.[40] On this alternative, let's say associationist, view, whatever rights persons have arise from this prior membership and are normally enabling rights, that is, rights that enable persons to perform their duties in the groups to which they belong. To illustrate with respect to political rights: Hegel rejects the idea of one person one vote on the grounds that it expresses the democratic and individualistic idea that each person, as an atomic unit, has the basic right to participate equally in political deliberation.[41] By contrast, in the well-ordered rational state, as Hegel presents it in *The Philosophy of Right*, persons belong first to estates, corporations and associations. Since these social forms represent the rational[42] interests of their members in what Hegel views as a just consultation hierarchy, some persons will take part in politically representing these interests in the consultation process, but they do so as members of estates and corporations and not as individuals, and not all individuals are involved.

The essential point here is that the basic human rights as we have described them can be protected in a well-ordered hierarchical state with its consultation hierarchy; what holds in Hegel's scheme of political rights holds for all rights.[43] Its system of law can fulfil the conditions laid down and ensure the right to life and security, to personal property and the elements of the rule of law, as well as the right to a certain freedom of conscience and freedom of association. Admittedly it ensures these rights to persons as members of estates and corporations and not as citizens. But that does not matter. The rights are guaranteed and the requirement that a system of law must be such as to impose moral rights and duties is met. Human rights understood in the light of that condition cannot be rejected as peculiar to our Western tradition.

Human rights are a special class of rights designed to play a special role in a reasonable law of peoples for the present age. Recall that the accepted ideas about international law changed in two basic ways following World War II, and this change in basic moral beliefs is comparable to other profound historical changes.[44] War is no longer an admissible means of state policy. It is only justified in self-defence and a state's internal sovereignty is now limited. One role of human rights is precisely to specify limits to that sovereignty.

Human rights are thus distinct from, say, constitutional rights, or the rights of democratic citizenship,[45] or from other kinds of rights that belong to certain kinds of political institutions, both individualist and associationist. They are a special class of rights of universal application and hardly controversial in their general intention. They are part of a reasonable law of peoples and specify limits on the domestic institutions required of all peoples by that law. In this sense they specify the outer boundary of admissible domestic law of societies in good standing in a just society of peoples.[46]

Human rights have these three roles:

1. They are a necessary condition of a regime's legitimacy and of the decency of its legal order.
2. By being in place, they are also sufficient to exclude justified and forceful intervention by other peoples, say by economic sanctions, or in grave cases, by military force.
3. They set a limit on pluralism among peoples.[47]

VI Nonideal Theory: Noncompliance

So far we have been concerned solely with ideal theory. By developing a liberal conception of justice we have reviewed the philosophical and moral grounds of an ideal conception of a society of well-ordered peoples and of the principles that apply to its law and practices. That conception is to guide the conduct of peoples toward one another and the design of common institutions for their mutual benefit.

Before our sketch of the law of peoples is complete, however, we must take note of, even though we cannot properly discuss, the questions arising from the highly nonideal conditions of our world with its great injustices and widespread social evils. Nonideal theory asks how the ideal conception of the society of well-ordered peoples might be achieved, or at least worked toward, generally in gradual steps. It looks for policies and courses of action likely to be effective and politically possible as well as morally permissible for that purpose. So conceived, nonideal theory presupposes that ideal theory is already on hand for, until the ideal is identified, at least in outline, nonideal theory lacks an objective by reference to which its questions can be answered. And although the specific conditions of our world at any given time – the status quo – do not determine the ideal conception of the society of well-ordered peoples, those conditions do affect answers to the questions of nonideal theory. They are questions of transition: in any given case, they start from where a society is and seek effective ways permitted by the law of peoples to move the society some distance toward the goal.

We may distinguish two kinds of nonideal theory. One kind deals with conditions of noncompliance, that is, with conditions in which certain regimes refuse to acknowledge a reasonable law of peoples. These we may call outlaw regimes. The other kind of nonideal theory deals with unfavourable conditions, that is, with the conditions of peoples whose historical, social and economic circumstances make their achieving a well-ordered regime, whether liberal or hierarchical, difficult if not impossible.

I begin with noncompliance theory. As we have said, a reasonable law of peoples guides the well-ordered regimes in facing outlaw regimes by specifying the goal they should always have in mind and indicating the means they may use or must avoid in pursuing that goal.

Outlaw regimes are a varied lot. Some are headed by governments that seem to recognize no conception of right and justice at all; often their legal order is at bottom a system of coercion and terror. The Nazi regime is a demonic example of this. A more common case, philosophically more interesting and historically more respectable, is those societies – they would scoff at being referred to as outlaw regimes – whose rulers affirm comprehensive doctrines that recognize no geographic limits to the legitimate authority of their established religious or philosophical views. Spain, France and the Hapsburgs all tried at some time to subject much of Europe and the world to their will.[48] They hoped to spread true religion and culture, sought dominion and glory, not to mention wealth and territory. Such societies are checked only by a balance of power, but as this is changing and unstable, the hegemonic theory of war, so-called, fits nicely.[49]

The law-abiding societies – both liberal and hierarchical – can at best establish a modus vivendi with the outlaw expansionist regimes and defend the integrity of their societies as the law of peoples allows. In this situation the law-abiding societies exist in a state of nature with the outlaw regimes, and they have a duty to their own and to one another's societies and well-being, as well as a duty to the well-being of peoples subjected to outlaw regimes, though not to their rulers and élites. These several duties are not all equally strong, but there is always a duty to consider the more extensive long-run aims and to affirm them as overall guides of foreign policy. Thus, the only legitimate grounds of the right to war against outlaw regimes is defence of the society of well-ordered peoples and, in grave cases, of innocent persons subject to outlaw regimes and the protection of their human rights. This accords with Kant's idea that our first political duty is to leave the state of nature and submit ourselves along with others to the rule of a reasonable and just law.[50]

The defence of well-ordered peoples is only the first and most urgent task. Another long-run aim, as specified by the law of peoples, is to bring all societies eventually to honour that law and to be full and self-standing members of the society of well-ordered peoples, and so secure human rights everywhere. How to do this is a question of foreign policy; these things call for political wisdom, and success depends in part on luck. They are not matters to which political philosophy has much to add. I venture several familiar points.

For well-ordered peoples to achieve this long-run aim they should establish among themselves new institutions and practices to serve as a kind of federative centre and public forum of their common opinion and policy toward the other regimes. This can either be done separately or within institutions such as the United Nations by forming an alliance of well-ordered peoples on certain issues. This federative centre may be used both to formulate and to express the opinion of the well-ordered societies. There they may expose to public view the unjust and cruel institutions of oppressive and expansionist regimes and their violations of human rights.

Even these regimes are not altogether indifferent to this kind of criticism, especially when the basis of it is a reasonable and well-founded law of peoples that cannot be easily dismissed as simply liberal or Western. Gradually over time the well-ordered peoples may pressure the outlaw regimes to change their ways; but by itself this pressure is unlikely to be effective. It must be backed up by the firm denial of all military aid, or economic and other assistance; nor should outlaw regimes be admitted by well-ordered peoples as members in good standing into their mutually beneficial cooperative practices.

VII Nonideal Theory: Unfavourable Conditions

A few words about the second kind of nonideal theory, that of unfavourable conditions. By these I mean the conditions of societies that lack the political and cultural traditions, the human capital and know-how, and the resources, material and technological, that make well-ordered societies possible. In noncompliance theory we saw that the goal of well-ordered societies is somehow to bring the outlaw states into the society of well-ordered peoples. The outlaw societies in the historical cases we mentioned above were not societies burdened by unfavourable resources, material and technological, or lacking in human capital and know-how; on the contrary, they were among the most politically and socially advanced and economically developed societies of their day. The fault in those societies lay in their political traditions and the background institutions of law, property and class structure, with their sustaining beliefs and culture. These things must be changed before a reasonable law of peoples can be accepted and supported.

We must ask the parallel question: what is the goal specified by nonideal theory for the case of unfavourable conditions? The answer is clear. Eventually each society now burdened by unfavourable conditions should be raised to, or assisted toward, conditions that make a well-ordered society possible.

Some writers have proposed that the difference principle, or some other liberal principle of distributive justice, be adopted to deal with this problem and to regulate accordingly the economic inequalities in the society of peoples.[51] Although I think the difference principle is reasonable for domestic justice in a democratic society, it is not feasible as a way to deal with the general problem of unfavourable conditions among societies. For one thing, it belongs to the ideal theory for a democratic society and is not framed for our present case. More serious, there are various kinds of societies in the society of peoples and not all of them can reasonably be expected to accept any particular liberal principle of distributive justice; and even different liberal societies adopt different principles for their domestic institutions. For their part, the hierarchical societies reject all liberal principles of domestic justice. We cannot suppose that they will find such principles acceptable in dealing with other peoples. In our construction of the liberal law of peoples, therefore, liberal principles of domestic distributive justice are not generalized to answer questions about unfavourable conditions.

Confirming this is the fact that in a constructivist conception there is no reason to think that the principles that apply to domestic justice are also appropriate for regulating inequalities in a society of peoples. As we saw at the outset, each kind of subject – whether an institution or an individual, whether a political society or a society of political societies – may be governed by its own characteristic principles. What these principles are must be worked out by a suitable procedure beginning from a correct starting point. We ask how rational representatives suitably motivated, and reasonably situated with respect to one another, would be most strongly moved to select among the feasible ideals and principles to apply to the subject in question. Since the problem and subject are different in each case, the ideals and principles adopted may also be different. As always, the whole procedure and the principles it yields must be acceptable on due reflection.

Although no liberal principle of distributive justice would be adopted for dealing with unfavourable conditions, that certainly does not mean that the well-ordered and wealthier societies have no duties and obligations to societies burdened by such conditions. For the ideal conception of the society of peoples that well-ordered societies affirm directs that in due course all societies must reach, or be assisted to, the conditions that make a well-ordered society possible. This implies that human rights are to be recognized and secured everywhere, and that basic human needs are to be met. Thus, the basis of the duty of assistance is not some liberal principle of distributive justice. Rather, it is the ideal conception of the society of peoples itself as consisting of well-ordered societies, with each people, as I have said, a full and self-standing member of the society of peoples, and capable of taking charge of their political life and maintaining decent political and social institutions as specified by the three requirements earlier surveyed.[52]

I shall not attempt to discuss here how this might be done, as the problem of giving economic and technological aid so that it makes a sustained contribution is highly complicated and varies from country to country. Moreover the problem is often not the lack of natural resources. Many societies with unfavourable conditions don't lack for resources. Well-ordered societies can get on with very little; their wealth lies elsewhere: in their political and cultural traditions, in their human capital and knowledge, and in their capacity for political and economic organization. Rather, the problem is commonly the nature of the public political culture and the religious and philosophical traditions that underlie its institutions. The great social evils in poorer societies are likely to be oppressive government and corrupt élites; the subjection of women abetted by unreasonable religion, with the resulting overpopulation relative to what the economy of the society can decently sustain. Perhaps there is no society anywhere in the world whose people, were they reasonably and rationally governed, and their numbers sensibly adjusted to their economy and resources, could not have a decent and worthwhile life.

These general remarks indicate what is so often the source of the problem: the public political culture and its roots in the background social structure. The obligation of wealthier societies to assist in trying to rectify matters is in no way diminished, only made more difficult. Here, too, in ways I need not describe, an emphasis on human rights may work, when backed by other kinds of assistance, to moderate, albeit slowly, oppressive government, the corruption of élites and the subjection of women.[53]

VIII Concluding Reflections

I have not said much about what might be called the philosophical basis of human rights. That is because, despite their name, human rights are a special class of rights explained by their role in a liberal conception of the law of peoples acceptable to both well-ordered liberal and hierarchical societies. I have therefore sketched how such a law of peoples might be worked out on the basis of a liberal conception of justice.[54] Within this framework I have indicated how respect for human rights is one of the conditions imposed on any political regime to be admissible as a member in good standing into a just political society of peoples. Once we understand this, and once we understand how a reasonable law of peoples is developed out of the liberal conception of justice and how this conception can be universal in its reach, it is perfectly clear why those rights hold across cultural and economic boundaries, as well as the boundaries between nation states, or other political units. With our two other conditions, these rights determine the limits of toleration in a reasonable society of peoples.

About these limits, the following observation: if we start with a well-ordered liberal society that realizes an egalitarian conception of justice such as justice as fairness,[55] the members of that society will nevertheless accept into the society of peoples other liberal societies whose institutions are considerably less egalitarian. This is implicit in our beginning with liberal conceptions more general than justice as fairness as defined in section III. But citizens in a well-ordered egalitarian society will still view the domestic regimes of those societies as less congenial to them than the regime of their own society.

This illustrates what happens whenever the scope of toleration is extended: the criteria of reasonableness are relaxed.[56] In the case we have considered, we seek to include other than liberal societies as members in good standing of a reasonable society of peoples. Hence when we move to these societies, their domestic regimes are less, often much less, congenial to us. This poses the problem of the limits of toleration. Where are these limits to be drawn? Clearly, tyrannical and dictatorial regimes must be outlawed, and also, for basic liberal reasons, expansionist states like those of the Wars of Religion. The three necessary conditions for a well-ordered regime – that it respect the principles of peace and not be expansionist, that its system of law meet the essentials of legitimacy in the eyes of its own people, and that it honour basic human rights – are proposed as an answer as to where those limits lie. These conditions indicate the bedrock beyond which we cannot go.

We have discussed how far many societies of the world have always been, and are today, from meeting these three conditions for being a member in good standing of a reasonable society of peoples. The law of peoples provides the basis for judging the conduct of any existing regime, liberal as well as non-liberal. And since our account of the law of peoples was developed out of a liberal conception of justice, we must address the question whether the liberal law of peoples is ethnocentric and merely Western.

To address this question, recall that in working out the law of peoples we assumed that liberal societies conduct themselves toward other societies from the point of view of their own liberal political conception. Regarding this conception as sound, and as meeting all the criteria they are now able to apply, how else are they to proceed? To the objection that to proceed thus is ethnocentric or merely Western, the reply is: no, not necessarily. Whether it is so turns on the content of the political conception that liberal societies embrace once it is worked up to provide at least an outline of the law of peoples.

Looking at the outline of that law, we should note the difference between it and the law of peoples as it might be understood by religious and expansionist states that reject the liberal conception. The liberal conception asks of other societies only what they can reasonably grant without submitting to a position of inferiority, much less to domination. It is crucial that a liberal conception of the law of peoples not ask well-ordered hierarchical societies to abandon their religious institutions and adopt liberal ones. True, in our sketch we supposed that traditional societies would affirm the law of peoples that would hold among just liberal societies. That law is therefore universal in its reach: it asks of other societies only what they can accept once they are prepared to stand in a relation of equality with all other societies and once their regimes accept the criterion of legitimacy in the eyes of their own people. In what other relations can a society and its regime reasonably expect to stand?

Moreover, the liberal law of peoples does not justify economic sanctions or military pressure on well-ordered hierarchical societies to change their ways, provided they respect the rules of peace and their political institutions satisfy the essential conditions we have reviewed. If, however, these conditions are violated, external pressure of one kind or another may be justified depending on the severity and the circumstances of the case. A concern for human rights should be a fixed part of the foreign policy of liberal and hierarchical societies.

Looking back at our discussion, let's recall that besides sketching how the law of peoples might be developed from liberal conceptions of right and justice, a further aim was to set out the bearing of political liberalism for a wider world society once a liberal political conception of justice is extended to the law of peoples. In particular, we asked: what form does the toleration of non-liberal societies take in this case? Although tyrannical and dictatorial regimes cannot be accepted as members in good standing of a reasonable society of peoples, not all regimes can reasonably be required to be liberal. If so, the law of peoples would not express liberalism's own principle of toleration for other reasonable ways of ordering society. A liberal society must respect other societies organized by comprehensive doctrines, provided their political and social institutions meet certain conditions that lead the society to adhere to a reasonable law of peoples.

I did not try to present an argument to this conclusion. I took it as clear that if other non-liberal societies honoured certain conditions, such as the three requirements discussed in section IV, they would be accepted by liberal societies as members in good standing of a society of peoples. There would be no political case to attack these non-liberal societies militarily, or to bring economic or other sanctions against them to revise their institutions. Critical commentary in liberal societies would be fully consistent with the civic liberties and integrity of those societies.

What conception of toleration of other societies does the law of peoples express? How is it connected with political liberalism? If it should be asked whether liberal societies are, morally speaking, better than hierarchical societies, and therefore whether the world would be a better place if all societies were liberal, those holding a comprehensive liberal view could think it would be. But that opinion would not support a claim to rid the world of non-liberal regimes. It could have no operative force in what, as a matter of right, they could do politically. The situation is parallel to the toleration of other conceptions of the good in the domestic case. Someone holding a comprehensive liberal view can say that their society would be a better place if everyone held such a view. They might be wrong in this judgment even by their own lights, as other doctrines may play a moderating and balancing role given the larger background of belief and conviction, and give society's culture a certain depth and richness. The point is that to affirm the superiority of a particular comprehensive view is fully compatible with affirming a political conception of justice that does not impose it, and thus with political liberalism itself.

Political liberalism holds that comprehensive doctrines have but a restricted place in liberal democratic politics in this sense: fundamental constitutional questions and matters concerning basic rights and liberties are to be settled by a public political conception of justice, exemplified by the liberal political conceptions, and not by those wider doctrines. For given the pluralism of democratic societies – a pluralism best seen as the outcome of the exercise of human reason under free institutions, and which can only be undone by the oppressive use of state power – affirming such a public conception and the basic political institutions that realize it, is the most reasonable basis of social unity available to us.

The law of peoples, as I have sketched it, is simply the extension of these same ideas to the political society of well-ordered peoples. That law, which settles fundamental constitutional questions and matters of basic justice as they arise for the society of peoples, must also be based on a public political conception of justice and not on a comprehensive religious, philosophical, or moral doctrine. I have sketched the content of such a political conception and tried to explain how it could be endorsed by well-ordered societies, both liberal and hierarchical. Except as a basis of a modus vivendi, expansionist societies of whatever kind could not endorse it; but in principle there is no peaceful solution in their case except the domination of one side or the peace of exhaustion.

Notes

1. The term 'law of peoples' derives from the traditional *ius gentium*, and the way I use it is closest to its meaning in the phrase 'ius gentium intra se' (laws of peoples among themselves). In this meaning it refers to what the laws of all peoples had in common. See R. J. Vincent, *Human Rights and International Relations* (Cambridge, England: Cambridge University Press, 1986), 27. Taking these laws to be a core paired with principles of justice applying to the laws of peoples everywhere gives a meaning related to my use of the law of peoples.

2. A political conception of justice has the following three features: (1) it is framed to apply to basic political, economic and social institutions; in the case of domestic society, to its basic structure, in the present case to the law and practices of the society of political peoples; (2) it is presented independently of any particular comprehensive religious, philosophical, or moral doctrine, and though it may be derived from or related to several such doctrines, it is not worked out in that way; (3) its content is expressed in terms of certain fundamental ideas seen as implicit in the public political culture of a liberal society. See my *Political Liberalism* (New York: Columbia University Press, 1993), 11–15.

3. In this and the next two paragraphs I draw on the first section of 'Basic Structure as Subject' (1978), reprinted in *Political Liberalism*.

4. For a detailed example of how this is done in the case of the four-stage sequence of

original position, constitutional convention, the legislature and the courts, see *A Theory of Justice* (Cambridge, Mass.: Harvard University Press, 1971), 195–201. A briefer statement is found in 'Basic Liberties and Their Priority' (1982), reprinted in *Political Liberalism*.

5. By peoples I mean persons and their dependants seen as a corporate body and as organized by their political institutions, which establish the powers of government. In democratic societies persons will be citizens, while in hierarchical and other societies they will be members.

6. See *Theory*, 378ff., where this process is very briefly described.

7. It would be unfair to Clausewitz not to add that for him the state's interests can include regulative moral aims of whatever kind, and thus the aims of war may be to defend democratic societies against tyrannical regimes, somewhat as in World War II. For him the aims of politics are not part of the theory of war, although they are ever present and may properly affect the conduct of war. On this, see the instructive remarks of Peter Paret, 'Clausewitz', in Peter Paret, ed., *The Makers of Modern Strategy* (Princeton, N.J.: Princeton University Press, 1986), 209–13. The view in my text characterizes the *raison d'état* as pursued by Frederick the Great. Or so Gerhard Ritter says in *Frederick the Great*, trans. Peter Paret (Berkeley: California University Press, 1968). See chap. 10, and the statement on p. 197.

8. These powers Charles Beitz characterizes as belonging to what he calls the morality of states in part II of his *Political Theory and International Relations* (Princeton, N.J.: Princeton University Press, 1980). They depend, he argues, on a mistaken analogy between individuals and states.

9. Stanley Hoffman, *Janus and Minerva* (Boulder, Colo. and London: Westview Press, 1987), 374.

10. Note: 'you and I' are 'here and now' citizens of the same liberal democratic society and we are working out the liberal conception of justice in question.

11. In this case 'you and I' are citizens of liberal democratic societies but not of the same one.

12. Kant says at Ak: VIII: 367: 'The idea of international law presupposes the separate existence of independent neighboring states. Although this condition is itself a state of war (unless federative union prevents the outbreak of hostilities), this is rationally preferable to the amalgamation of states under one superior power, as this would end in one universal monarchy, and laws always lose in vigor what government gains in extent; hence a condition of soulless despotism falls into anarchy after stifling seeds of good.' This attitude to universal monarchy was shared by other writers of the eighteenth century. See, for example, Hume's 'Of the Balance of Power' (1752). F. H. Hinsley, *Power and the Pursuit of Peace* (Cambridge, England: Cambridge University Press, 1966), 162ff., also mentions Montesquieu, Voltaire and Gibbon. Hinsley also has an instructive discussion of Kant's ideas in chap. 4. See also Patrick Riley, *Kant's Political Philosophy* (Towanda, Pa.: Rowman and Littlefield, 1983), chaps. 5 and 6. Thomas Nagel, in his *Equality and Partiality* (New York: Oxford University Press, 1991), 169ff., 174, gives strong reasons supporting the same conclusion.

13. See Terry Nardin, *Law, Morality and the Relations of States* (Princeton, N.J.: Princeton University Press, 1983), 269ff., who stresses this point.

14. A clear example regarding secession is whether the South had a right to secede from 1860 to 1861. By this test it had no such right, since it seceded to perpetuate its domestic institution of slavery. This is as severe a violation of human rights as any, and it extended to nearly half the population.

15. By basic needs I mean roughly those that must be met if citizens are to be in a position to take advantage of the rights, liberties and opportunities of their society. They include economic means as well as institutional rights and freedoms.

16. From the fact that boundaries are historically arbitrary it does not follow that their role in the law of peoples cannot be justified. To wit: that the boundaries between the several states of the United States are historically arbitrary does not argue to the elimination of our federal system, one way or the other. To fix on their arbitrariness is to fix on the wrong thing. The right question concerns the political values served by the several states in a federal system. The answer is given by states' function and role: by the political values they serve as subunits, and whether their boundaries can be, or need to be, redrawn, and much else.

17. This remark implies that a people has at least a qualified right to limit immigration. I leave aside here what these qualifications might be.

18. See 'The Domain of the Political and Overlapping Consensus', *New York University Law School Review 64* (1989), 245, sec. VII.

19. See Jack S. Levy, 'Domestic Politics and War', an essay in Robert Rotberg and Theodore Rabb, eds., *The Origin and Prevention of Major Wars* (Cambridge, England: Cambridge University Press, 1989), 87. Levy refers to several historical studies that have confirmed the finding of Small and Singer in the *Jerusalem Journal of International Relations*, vol. 1, 1976, mentioned in note 21 below.

20. See Doyle's two-part article, 'Kant, Liberal Legacies, and Foreign Affairs', *Philosophy and Public Affairs* 12 (1983): 205, 323. A survey of the evidence is in the first part, 106–32. Doyle says: 'These conventions (those based on the international implications of liberal principles and institutions) of mutual respect have formed a cooperative foundation for relations among liberal democracies of a remarkably effective kind. *Even though liberal states have become involved in numerous wars with nonliberal states, constitutionally secure liberal states have yet to engage in war with one another.* [Italicized in the original.] No one should argue that such wars are impossible; but preliminary evidence does appear to indicate . . . a significant predisposition against warfare between liberal states' (213).

21. See Levy, 'Domestic Politics', 88. In these studies most definitions of democracy are comparable to that of Small and Singer as listed by Levy in a footnote: (1) regular elections and the participation of opposition parties, (2) at least ten per cent of the adult population being able to vote for a (3) parliament that either controlled or shared parity with the executive branch (ibid., 88). Our definition of a liberal democratic regime goes well beyond this definition.

22. On this see Alan Gilbert, 'Power-Rivalry Motivated Democracy', *Political Theory 20* (1992), 681, and esp. 684ff.

23. Here I draw upon Philip Soper's *A Theory of Law* (Cambridge, Mass.: Harvard University Press, 1984), esp. 125–47. Soper holds that a system of law, as distinct from a system of mere commands coercively enforced, must be such as to give rise, as I have indicated, to moral duties and obligations on all members of society, and judges and other officials must sincerely and reasonably believe that the law is guided by a common good conception of justice. The content of a common good conception of justice is such as to impose morally binding obligations on all members of society. I mention some of the details of Soper's view here, but I do so rather freely and not with the intent of explaining his thought. As the text shows, my aim is to indicate a conception of justice that, while not a liberal conception, still has features that give to societies regulated accordingly the moral standing required to be members of a political society adhering to a reasonable law of peoples. However, we must be careful in understanding this second requirement. For Soper it is part of the definition of a system of law. It is a requirement which a scheme of rules must satisfy to be a system of law properly thus called. See chap. 4, 91–100. I don't follow Soper in this respect; nor do I reject this idea either, as Soper makes a strong case for it. Rather, it is put aside and the requirement is adopted as a substantive moral principle explicable as part of the law of peoples worked up from a liberal conception of justice. The reason for doing this is to avoid the long debated jurisprudential problem of the definition of law. Also, I don't want to have to argue that the antebellum South, say, didn't have a system of law. I am indebted to Samuel Freeman for valuable discussion of these points.

24. Soper, *A Theory of Law*, 112, 118.

25. Ibid., 141.

26. Henry Shue, *Basic Rights: Substance, Affluence, and U.S. Foreign Policy* (Princeton, N.J.: Princeton University Press, 1980). Shue, p. 23, and Vincent, *Human Rights*, interpret subsistence as including certain minimum economic security, and both hold that subsistence rights are basic. One must agree with this since the reasonable and rational exercise of all liberties, of whatever kind, as well as the intelligent use of property, always implies having certain general all-purpose economic means.

27. On the rules of natural justice, see H. L. A. Hart, *The Concept of Law* (Oxford: Clarendon Press), 156ff.

28. One might raise the question here as to why religious or philosophical doctrines that deny full and equal liberty of conscience are not unreasonable. I did not say, however, that they are reasonable, but rather that they are not unreasonable. One should allow, I think, a space between the reasonable or the fully reasonable, which requires full and equal liberty of conscience, and the unreasonable, which denies it entirely. Traditional doctrines that allow a measure of liberty of conscience but do not allow it fully are views that lie in that space and are not unreasonable. On this see my *Political Liberalism*, lecture II, sec. 3.

29. On the importance of this, see Judith Shklar's *Ordinary Vices* (Cambridge, Mass.: Harvard University Press, 1984), in which she presents what she calls the 'liberalism of fear'. See especially the introduction and chaps. 1 and 6. She once called this kind of liberalism that of 'permanent minorities'. See her *Legalism* (Cambridge, Mass.: Harvard University Press, 1963), 224.

30. Subject to certain qualifications, liberal societies must also allow for this right.

31. These are not political conceptions of justice in my sense; see note 2 above.

32. Here 'you and I' are members of hierarchical societies but again not the same one.

33. Here I am indebted to Lea Brilmayer of New York University for pointing out to me that in my sketch of the law of peoples (October 1990) I failed to state these conditions satisfactorily.

34. Brian Barry, in his splendid *Theories of Justice* (Berkeley: University of California Press, 1989), discusses the merits of doing this. See 183–89ff. Along the way he raises serious objections to what he takes to be my view of the principles of distributive justice for the law of peoples. I do not discuss these important criticisms here, but I do mention questions related to them hereafter.

35. We can go on to third and later stages once we think of groups of societies joining together into regional associations or federations of some kind, such as the European Community, or a commonwealth of the republics in the former Soviet Union. It is natural to envisage future world society as in good part comprised of such federations together with certain institutions, such as the United Nations, capable of speaking for all the societies of the world.

36. Justice as fairness is such an idea. For our purposes other more general liberal ideas of justice fit the same description. Their lacking the three egalitarian elements of justice as fairness noted in the first paragraph of section III does not affect this.

37. There are, however, some differences. The three requirements of legitimacy discussed in this section are to be seen as necessary conditions for a society to be a member in good standing of a reasonable society of peoples; and many religious and philosophical doctrines with their different conceptions of justice may lead to institutions satisfying these conditions. In specifying a reasonable law of peoples, societies with such institutions are viewed as well ordered. However, those requirements do not specify a political conception of justice in my sense (see note 2 above). For one thing, I suppose that a society's common good conception of justice is understood as part of its comprehensive religious or philosophical doctrine. Nor have I suggested that such a conception of justice is constructivist, and I assume it is not. Whether the three requirements for legitimacy can themselves be constructed within a social contract view is another question. I leave it open here. The point, though, is that none of these differences affect the claim in the text that in both domains the ideals and principles of justice are justified in the same way.

38. Here I draw upon T. M. Scanlon's instructive discussion in 'Human Rights as a Neutral Concern', in P. Brown and D. MacLean, eds., *Human Rights and U. S. Foreign Policy* (Lexington, Mass.: Lexington Books, 1979).

39. Scanlon emphasizes this point in 'Human Rights', 83, 89–92. It is relevant when we note later in sections VI and VII that support for human rights should be part of the foreign policy of well-ordered societies.

40. See R. J. Vincent, 'The Idea of Rights in International Ethics', in Terry Nardin, ed. with David Mapel, *Traditions of International Ethics* (Cambridge, England: Cambridge University Press, 1992), 262–65.

41. Hegel, *The Philosophy of Right* (1821), sec. 308.

42. The meaning of *rational* here is closer to *reasonable* than to *rational* as I have used

these terms. The German is *vernünftig*, and this has the full force of reason in the German philosophical tradition. It is far from the economist's meaning of *rational*, given by *zweck-mässig* or *rationell*.

43. There is a complication about Hegel's view in that some rights are indeed rights of individuals. For him the rights to life, security and (personal) property are grounded in personhood; and liberty of conscience follows from being a moral subject with the freedom of subjectivity. I am indebted to Frederick Neuhouser for discussion of these points.

44. See Keith Thomas, *Man and the Natural World* (New York: Pantheon Books, 1983) for an account of the historical change in attitudes toward animals and nature.

45. See Judith Shklar's illuminating discussion of these in her *American Citizenship* (Cambridge, Mass.: Harvard University Press, 1991), with her emphasis on the historical significance of slavery.

46. This fact about human rights can be clarified by distinguishing among the rights that have been listed as human rights in various international declarations. Consider the Universal Declaration of Human Rights of 1948. First, there are human rights proper, illustrated by Article 3: 'Everyone has a right to life, liberty and security of person'; and by Article 5: 'No one shall be subjected to torture or to cruel, degrading treatment or punishment.' Articles 3 to 18 may fall under this heading of human rights proper, pending certain questions of interpretation. Then there are human rights that are obvious implications of these rights. These are the extreme cases described by the special conventions on genocide (1948) and on apartheid (1973). These two classes comprise the human rights.

Of the other declarations, some seem more aptly described as stating liberal aspirations, such as Article 1 of the Universal Declaration of Human Rights of 1948: 'All human beings are born free and equal in dignity and rights. They are endowed with reason and conscience and should act towards one another in a spirit of brotherhood.' Others appear to presuppose specific kinds of institutions, such as the right to social security, in Article 22, and the right to equal pay for equal work, in Article 23.

47. Nardin, *Law, Morality and the Relations of States*, 240, citing Luban's 'The Romance of the Nation-State', 396.

48. On this, see Ludwig Dehio, *The Precarious Balance* (New York: Knopf, 1962).

49. Robert Gilpin, 'The Theory of Hegemonic War', in Rotberg and Rabb, eds., *The Origin and Prevention of Major Wars*.

50. See Kant, *Rechtslehre*, sections 44 and 61.

51. Beitz, *Political Theory and International Relations*; pt. III gives a sustained discussion. This principle is defined in my *A Theory of Justice*, section 13. I do not review the principle here because, as my text says, I believe all liberal distributive principles are unsuitable for the case we are considering.

52. With much of Beitz's view the law of peoples agrees. Thus it seems that he thinks of the difference principle between societies as 'a resource redistribution principle that would give each society a fair chance to develop just political institutions and an economy capable of satisfying its members' basic needs' (141). And 'It [the resource distribution principle] provides assurance to persons in resource-poor societies that their adverse fate will not prevent them from realizing economic conditions sufficient to support just social institutions and to protect human rights' (142). The law of peoples accepts Beitz's goals for just institutions, securing human rights and meeting basic needs. But, as I suggest in the next paragraph, persons' adverse fate is more often to be born into a distorted and corrupt political culture than into a country lacking resources. The only principle that does away with that misfortune is to make the political traditions and culture of all peoples reasonable and able to sustain just political and social institutions that secure human rights. It is this principle that gives rise to the duties and obligations of assistance. We do not need a liberal principle of distributive justice for this purpose.

53. That the insistence on human rights may help here is suggested by Amartya Sen's work on famines. He has shown in *Poverty and Famines* (Oxford: Clarendon Press, 1981), by an empirical study of four well-known historical cases (Bengal, 1943; Ethiopia, 1972–74; Sahel, 1972–73; and Bangladesh, 1974), that food decline need not be the main cause of famine, or even a cause, nor even present. But sometimes it can be an important cause of famine, for

example, in Ireland in the 1840s and in China from 1959 to 1961. In the cases Sen studies, while a drop in food production may have been present, it was not great enough to lead to famine given a decent government that cares for the well-being of all of its people and has in place a reasonable scheme of back-up entitlements provided through public institutions. For Sen 'famines are economic disasters, not just food crises' (162). In the well-known historical cases they revealed faults of the political and social structure and its failure to institute appropriate policies to remedy the effects of shortfalls in food production. After all, there would be massive starvation in any modern Western democracy were there not schemes in place to remedy the losses in income of the unemployed. Since a government's allowing people to starve when this is preventable is a violation of their human rights, and if well-ordered regimes as we have described them will not allow this to happen, then insisting on human rights is exerting pressure in the direction of decent governments and a decent society of peoples. Sen's book with Jean Dreze, *Hunger and Public Action* (Oxford: Clarendon Press, 1989), confirms these points and stresses the success of democratic regimes in coping with these problems. See their summary statement in chap. 13: 257–79. See also the important work of Partha Dasgupta, *An Inquiry into Well-Being and Destitution* (Oxford: Clarendon Press, 1993), chaps. 1–2, 5 and passim.

54. It might be asked why the law of peoples as here constructed is said to be liberal when it is also accepted by well-ordered hierarchical societies. I have called it liberal because the law of peoples is presented as an extension from liberal conceptions of domestic justice. I do not mean to deny, however, that a well-ordered hierarchical society may have conceptions of justice that can be extended to the law of peoples and that its content would be the same as that of liberal conceptions. For the present I leave this question open. I would hope that there are such conceptions in all well-ordered hierarchical societies, as this would widen and strengthen the support for the law of peoples.

55. Three egalitarian elements are the fair value of equal political rights and liberties, fair equality of opportunity, and the difference principle, all to be understood as specified in my *A Theory of Justice*.

56. In the domestic case we are led in parallel fashion to count many comprehensive doctrines reasonable that we would not, in our own case, regard as worthy of serious consideration. See my *Political Liberalism*, lecture II, sec. 3.1 and the footnote.

I am indebted to many people for helping me with this essay. I have indicated specific debts in notes to the text. More general debts I should like to acknowledge are to Ronald Dworkin and Thomas Nagel for discussions about my earlier attempts to consider the law of peoples at their seminars at New York University in the fall of 1990 and 1991; to T. M. Scanlon and Joshua Cohen for valuable criticism and comments; to Michael Doyle and Philip Soper for instructive correspondence; and as always to Burton Dreben. I am especially indebted to Erin Kelly, who has read all the drafts of this essay and proposed many improvements, most of which I have adopted. Her criticisms and suggestions have been essential in my getting right, as I hope, the line of reasoning in section IV.

2

The Rights of Man and Good Will

Emmanuel Lévinas

I

The discovery of those rights that, under the name rights of man, are associated with the very condition of being a man, independently of qualities by which men differ from one another – such as social rank, physical, intellectual and moral strength, virtue and talents – and the elevation of these rights to the rank of fundamental legislative principles and social order certainly mark an essential moment in Western consciousness. Even if the biblical imperatives 'Thou shalt not kill' and 'Thou shalt love the stranger'[1] had been waiting for thousands of years for rights associated with the humanity of man to enter into the primordial legal discourse of our civilization. Man as man would have the right to an exceptional place in being and, by that very fact, one that was exterior to the determinism of phenomena; the right to independence, or to the freedom of each recognized by all. The right to a position protected from the immediate order of necessities inscribed in the natural laws that command inert objects, living things and thinking beings of a Nature, which, in a sense, however, also concerns and envelops humans. An exceptional place, a right to free will, guaranteed and protected by laws henceforth instituted by man. A right revealing itself in the obligation – incumbent, however, on free men themselves – to spare man the dependence of being but a means to a finality and not its end. An obligation to spare man the constraints and humiliations of poverty, vagrancy, and even the sorrow and torture which are still inherent in the sequence of natural – physical and psychological – phenomena, and the violence and cruelty of the evil intentions of living beings.

The formal essence of the rights of man seen in terms of the exceptional place of man in the determinism of the real, opening up the right to a free will, thus receives a concrete characteristic and a content. It is not always easy, in defence of the rights of man (and this is an important, but practical, problem) to establish an order of priority for those concrete rights. It may vary as a function of the actual situation in each country.

Whence in any case considerable and already revolutionary work, with its inevitable upheavals, in favour of the rights of man. Work that makes possible the science of modern times, a science of the nature of things, men and collectivities. Work that is encouraged by access to the technical procedures opened up by science. The further refinement of a human order of freedom by the elimination of many material obstacles of the contingent and social structures that encumber and pervert the application and exercise of the rights of man. Rights that may not be capable of eradicating completely the ultimate harshness of the Inhuman in being, which, by the insuperable firmness of the stitching consolidating its cloth – material, physiological, psychological and social – always thwarts and limits the free will of man.

Man can also stubbornly go on existing while giving up the attempt to acquire and preserve difficult rights. As if the freedom of rights were itself a limit to freedom, as if freedom were itself a necessity of obligation. What is the meaning of the 'should be' of this right?

II

Even if the fact that the possibility of the consolidation and expansion of the rights of man is bound to the scientific progress of modernity seems to me to explain the relatively recent character of its actualization, and the profound origin of the right seems already acquired, as we said, from the earliest time of our Western destiny, the question of the justification of this right, the question of its very 'should be' remains open. The answer cannot be reduced to a necessity apprehended inductively on the basis of the extension of the interest raised by the right of man and the general consent assumed by this extension. Does not the 'normative energy' of the right of man lead us back to the rigour of the reasonable? By virtue of what, and in what way, could the free or autonomous will claimed by the right of man impose itself on another free will without this imposition implying an *effect*, a violence suffered by that will? Or could it be that the decision of a free will conforms to a maxim of action which can be universalized without being contradicted and unless, thus revealing the reason that inheres in a free will, this will makes itself *respected* by all other wills, which are free because of their rationality? A will Kant has called practical reason. And could it be that the 'intellectual feeling' of *respect* here delineates respect as a *modality* of the true meaning of the situation? An 'intellectual feeling' that, precisely as intellectual, would no longer proceed from sensibility, understood as a source of heteronomy by Kant and that attests – rather than to a wound inflicted by one will on the freedom of the other will – to the fullness of peace in reason. The will that obeys the order of a free will would still be a free will, as reason yielding to reason. The categorical imperative would be the ultimate principle of the right of man.

III

Is it certain, however, that free will lends itself entirely to Kant's notion of practical reason, that height of universal thought also called good will? Does it allow itself to be contained therein without resistance? Does respect for formal universality appease the irrepressible part of spontaneity, which cannot immediately and conveniently be reduced to the impulses of passion and feeling? An irrepressible spontaneity that still allows us to distinguish between the rigorous rationalism of intelligence and the risks of a reasonable will. But is that irrepressible spontaneity of the will not goodness itself, which, sensibility par excellence, would also be the original and generous project of the infinite universality of reason which is required by the categorical imperative? A generous impulse rather than, in its holy imprudence, the pathological one denounced by Kant, which disqualifies all freedom![2]

Goodness, a childish virtue; but already charity and mercy and responsibility for the other, and already the possibility of sacrifice in which the humanity of man bursts forth, disrupting the general economy of the real and standing in sharp contrast with the perseverance of entities persisting in their being; for a *condition* in which the other comes before oneself. Dis-inter-estedness of goodness: the other in his demand which is an order, the other as face, the other who 'regards me' even when he doesn't have anything to do with me, the other as fellow man and always stranger – goodness as transcendence; and I, the one who is held to respond, the irreplaceable, and thus, the chosen and thus truly unique. Goodness for the first one who happens to come along, a right of man. A right of the other man above all. Descartes speaks of generosity. He attaches it both to the 'free disposition of [a man's] will' and to the fact that those who are generous 'do not hold anything more important than to do good to other men and to distain their individual interests'.[3]

IV

In religion and theology it is said that the right is conferred by God on man, that the right of man corresponds to the will of God. Expressions that in any case indicate the unconditional or extraordinary nature of that right in relation to all legal forms that already rest on human conventions or on the examination of 'human nature'. Here, without bringing in the famous 'proof of the existence of God', are the rights of man constituting a juncture in which God comes to mind,[4] in which the notion of transcendence ceases to remain purely negative and the abusive 'beyond' of our conversations is thought positively in terms of the face of the other person. What I have called an interruption or rupture of the perseverance of beings in their being, of the *conatus essendi* in the dis-inter-estedness of goodness does not indicate that the right of man gives up its absolute status to revert to the level of decisions made by I know not what compassionate subjectivities. It indicates the absolute of the social, the *for-the-other* which is probably the very delineation of the human. It indicates that 'nothing greater' of which Descartes spoke. No doubt it is important in good philosophy not to think of the rights of man in terms of an unknown God; it is permissible to approach the idea of God setting out from the absolute that manifests itself in the relation to the other.

Translated by Michael B. Smith

Notes

1. Deuteronomy 5:17 and 10:19, respectively. [Trans.]

2. See Kant's *Critique of Practical Reason*, in the *Great Books of the Western World Series*, no. 42 (Chicago: Encyclopaedia Britannica, Inc., 1952), p. 327; *Kritik der praktischen Vernunft*, in *Kants Gesammelte Schriften*, vol. 5, Paul Natorp, ed. (Berlin: Königliche Preußischen Akademie, 1908), pp. 151–4. [Trans.]

3. *The Passions of the Soul*, arts 153, 156, respectively. [I have used the translation in *The Philosophical Works of Descartes*, vol. I, Hildane and Ross, tr. (London & New York: Cambridge University Press, 1968), pp. 401, 403.] In French, cf. *Descartes, Oeuvres et lettres* (Paris: Editions Gallimard, 1953), pp. 769, 770. [Trans.]

4. This expression, which forms the title of Lévinas's book *De Dieu qui vient à l'idée* (Paris: Vrin, 1986), has presented a challenge to translators because it draws both on a colloquial French expression meaning 'to come to mind', or 'to occur to', and on the more literal 'God who comes to the idea'. I have taken a middle path, in the hope that 'God comes to mind' will evoke both God's personal, psychological mode and the conceptual guise in which God appears in philosophy. [Trans.]

Reproduced with permission from Emmanuel Lévinas, *Entre Nous: On Thinking-Of-The Other (European Perspectives)*, trans. Michael B. Smith (New York: Columbia University Press, 1998), pp. 155–8.

3

Private and Public Autonomy, Human Rights and Popular Sovereignty

Jürgen Habermas

In German civil-law jurisprudence, which in Germany has been decisive for the understanding of law in general, the theory of 'subjective right', as it was called, was initially influenced by the idealist philosophy of right. According to Friedrich Carl von Savigny, a legal relation secures 'the power justly pertaining to the individual person: an area in which his will rules, and rules with our consent.'[1] This still emphasizes the connection of individual liberties with an intersubjective recognition by legal consociates. As his analysis proceeds, however, an intrinsic value accrues to private law, independent of its authorization by a democratic legislature. Right 'in the subjective sense' is legitimate per se because, starting with the inviolability of the person, it is supposed to guarantee 'an area of independent rule' (*Herrschaft*) for the free exercise of the individual will.[2] For Georg Friedrich Puchta, too, law was essentially subjective right, that is, private law: 'Law is the recognition of the freedom belonging equally to all human beings as subjects with the power of will.'[3] According to this view, rights are negative rights that protect spheres of action by grounding actionable claims that others refrain from unpermitted interventions in the freedom, life and property of the individual. Private autonomy is secured in these legally protected spheres primarily through contract and property rights.

In the later nineteenth century, though, awareness grew that private law could be legitimated from its own resources only as long as it could be assumed that the legal subject's private autonomy had a foundation in the moral autonomy of the person. Once law in general lost its idealist grounding – in particular, the support it had from Kant's moral theory – the husk of the 'individual power to rule' was robbed of the normative core of a freedom of will that is both legitimate and worthy of protection from the start. The only bond that possessed legitimating force was the one that Kant, with the help of his 'principle of right' (*Rechtsprinzips*), had tied between freedom of choice and the person's autonomous will. After this bond was severed, law, according to the positivist view, could only assert itself as a particular form that furnished specific decisions and powers with the force of *de facto* bindingness. After Bernhard Windscheid, individual rights were considered reflexes of an established legal order that transferred to individuals the power of will objectively incorporated in law: 'Right is a power or rule of will conferred by the legal order.'[4]

Rudolf von Ihering's utilitarian interpretation, according to which utility and not will makes up the substance of right,[5] was later included in this definition: 'From a conceptual standpoint, individual rights are powers of law conferred on the individual by the legal order; from the standpoint of its purpose, they are means for the satisfaction of human interests.'[6] The reference to gratification and interest allowed private rights to be extended beyond the class of negative liberties. In certain instances an individual right yields not only a right on the part of person A to something protected from the interference of third parties, but also a right, be it absolute or relative, to a share in organized services. Finally, Hans Kelsen characterized individual rights in general as interests objectively protected by law and as freedoms of choice (or '*Wollendürfen*' in Windscheid's sense) objectively guaranteed by law. At the same time, he divested the legal order of the connotations of John Austin's command theory, which had been influential up to that point in the German version of August Thon. According to Kelsen, individual entitlements are not just authorized by the will of someone with the power to command, but possess normative validity: legal norms establish prescriptions and permissions having the character of an 'ought'. This illocutionary 'ought', however, is understood not in a deontological but in an empirical sense, as the actual validity that political lawgivers confer on their decisions by coupling enacted law with penal norms. The coercive power of state sanctions qualifies the lawgivers' will to become the 'will of the state'.

In Kelsen's analysis the moral content of individual rights expressly lost its reference, namely, the free will (or 'power to rule') of a person who, from the moral point of view, *deserves* to be protected in her private autonomy. To this extent, his view marks the counterpart of that private-law jurisprudence stemming from Savigny. Kelsen detached the legal concept of a person not only from the moral person but even from the natural person, because a fully self-referential legal system must get by with its self-produced fictions. As Luhmann will put it after taking a further naturalistic turn, it pushes natural persons out into its environment. With individual rights, the legal order itself creates the logical space for the legal subject as bearer of these rights: 'If the legal subject . . . is allowed to remain as a point of reference, then this occurs in order to keep the judgment that "a legal subject or person 'has' subjective rights" from becoming the empty tautology "there are subjective rights" . . . For to entitle or to obligate the person would then be to entitle rights, to obligate duties, in short, to "norm" norms.'[7] Once the moral and natural person has been uncoupled from the legal system, there is nothing to stop jurisprudence from conceiving rights along purely functionalist lines. The doctrine of rights hands on the baton to a systems theory that rids itself by methodological fiats of all normative considerations.[8]

The transformation of private law under National Socialism[9] certainly provoked moral reactions in postwar Germany, which decried the so-called 'legal dethronement' (*objektiv-rechtliche Entthronung*) and concomitant hollowing out of the moral substance of rights. But the natural-law-based restoration of the connection between private and moral autonomy soon lost its power to convince. '*Ordo*'-liberalism[10] only rehabilitated the individualistically truncated understanding of rights – the very conception that invited a functionalist interpretation of private law as the framework for capitalist economic relations:

> The idea of 'subjective right' carries on the view that private law and the legal protection grounded in it ultimately serve to maintain the individual's freedom in society, [in other words, the view] that individual freedom is one of the foundational ideas for the sake of which private law exists. For the idea of 'subjective right' expresses the fact that private law is the law of mutually independent legal consociates who act according to their own separate decisions.[11]

In opposition to the threat posed by a functionalist reinterpretation of this conception, Ludwig Raiser has drawn on social law in an attempt to correct the individualistic approach and thus restore to private law its moral content. Rather than going back to Savigny's conceptual framework, Raiser is led by the welfare-state materialization of private law to *restrict* a concept of 'subjective right', which he preserves without alteration, to the classical liberties. In continuity with previous views, these rights are meant to secure 'the self-preservation and individual responsibility of each person within society'. But they must be supplemented with social rights: 'From an ethical and political standpoint, more is required than a recognition of this [private] legal standing. Rather, it is just as important that one also integrate the individual by law into the ordered network of relationships that surround him and bind him with others. In other words, one must develop and protect the legal institutions in which the individual assumes the *status of member*.'[12] 'Primary' rights are too weak to guarantee protection to persons in those areas where they 'are integrated into larger, transindividual orders'.[13] However, Raiser's rescue attempt does not start at a sufficiently abstract level. It is true that private law has undergone a reinterpretation through the paradigm shift from bourgeois formal law to the materialized law of the welfare state.[14] But this reinterpretation must not be confused with a revision of the basic concepts and principles themselves, which have remained the same and have merely been *interpreted* differently in shifting paradigms.

Raiser does remind us of the intersubjective character of rights, though, something the individualistic reading had rendered unrecognizable. After all, such rights are based on the reciprocal recognition of cooperating legal persons. Taken by themselves, rights do not necessarily imply the atomism – the isolation of legal subjects from one another – that Raiser wants to correct. The citizens who mutually grant one another equal rights are one and the same individuals as the private persons who use rights strategically and encounter one another as potential opponents, but the two roles are not identical:

A right, after all, is neither a gun nor a one-man show. It is a relationship and a social practice, and in both those essential aspects it is seemingly an expression of connectedness. Rights are public propositions, involving obligations to others as well as entitlements against them. In appearance, at least, they are a form of social cooperation – not spontaneous but highly organized cooperation, no doubt, but still, in the final analysis, cooperation.[15]

At a conceptual level, rights do not immediately refer to atomistic and estranged individuals who are possessively set against one another. On the contrary, as elements of the legal order they presuppose collaboration among subjects who recognize one another, in their reciprocally related rights and duties, as free and equal citizens. This mutual recognition is constitutive for a legal order from which actionable rights are derived. In this sense 'subjective' rights emerge co-originally with 'objective' law, to use the terminology of German jurisprudence. However, a statist understanding of objective law is misleading, for the latter first issues from the rights that subjects mutually acknowledge. In order to make clear the intersubjective structure of relations of recognition that underlies the legal order as such, it is not enough to append social rights additively. Both the idealist beginnings and the positivist offshoots of German civil-law jurisprudence from Savigny to Kelsen misjudge this structure.

As we have seen, private-law theory (as the doctrine of 'subjective right') got started with the idea of morally laden individual rights, which claim normative independence from, and a higher legitimacy than, the political process of legislation. The freedom-securing character of rights was supposed to invest private law with a moral authority both independent of democratic lawmaking and not in need of justification within legal theory itself. This sparked a development that ended in the abstract subordination of 'subjective' rights to 'objective' law, where the latter's legitimacy finally exhausted itself in the legalism of a political domination construed in positivist terms. The course of this discussion, however, concealed the real problem connected with the key position of private rights: the source from whence enacted law may draw its legitimacy is not successfully explained. To be sure, the source of all legitimacy lies in the democratic lawmaking process, and this in turn calls on the principle of popular sovereignty. But the legal positivism, or *Getsetzespositivismus*, propounded in the Weimar period by professors of public law does not introduce this principle in such a way that the intrinsic moral content of the classical liberties – the protection of individual freedom emphasized by Helmut Coing – could be preserved. In one way or another, the intersubjective meaning of legally defined liberties is overlooked, and with it the relation between private and civic autonomy in which both moments receive their full due.

Trusting in an idealist concept of autonomy, Savigny could still assume that private law, as a system of negative and procedural rights that secure freedom, is legitimated on the basis of reason, that is, of itself. But Kant did not give an entirely unequivocal answer to the question of the legitimation of general laws that could supposedly ground a system of well-ordered egoism. Even in his *Rechtslehre (Metaphysical Elements of Justice)*, Kant ultimately fails to clarify the relations among the principles of morality, law (or right) and democracy (if we call what Kant sees as constituting the republican mode of government a principle of democracy). All three principles express each in its own way, the same *idea of self-legislation*. This concept of autonomy was Kant's response to Hobbes's unsuccessful attempt to justify a system of rights on the basis of the participants' enlightened self-interest alone, without the aid of moral reasons.

If one looks back at Hobbes from a Kantian perspective, one can hardly avoid reading him more as a theoretician of a bourgeois rule of law without democracy than as the apologist of unlimited absolutism; according to Hobbes, the sovereign can impart his commands only in the language of modern law. The sovereign guarantees an order in internal affairs that assures private persons of equal liberties according to general laws: 'For supreme commanders can confer no more to their civil happiness, than that being preserved from foreign and civil wars, they may quietly enjoy that wealth which they have purchased by their own industry.'[16]

For Hobbes, who clearly outfits the status of subjects with private rights, the problem of legitimation naturally cannot be managed *within* an already established legal order, and hence through political rights and democratic legislation. This problem must be solved immediately with the constitution of state authority, in a single blow, as it were; that is, it must be conjured out of existence for the future. Certainly Hobbes wants to explain why absolutist society is justified as an instrumental order from the perspective of all participants, if only they keep to a strictly purposive-rational calculation of their own interests. This was supposed to make it unnecessary to design a rule of law, that is, to elaborate regulations for a legitimate *exercise* of political authority. The tension between facticity and validity built into law itself dissolves if legal authority per se can be portrayed as maintaining an ordered system of egoism that is favoured by all the participants anyhow: what appears as morally right and legitimate then issues spontaneously from the self-interested decisions of rational egoists or, Kant will put it, a 'race of devils'. The utilitarian grounding of the bourgeois order of private law – that this type of market society makes as many people as possible well off for as long as possible[17] – bestows material justice on the sovereignty of a ruler who by definition can do nothing unlawful.

However, to carry out his intended demonstration, Hobbes must do more than simply show why such an order equally satisfies the interests of all participants *ex post* facto, that is, from the standpoint of readers who already find themselves in a civil society. He must in addition show why such a system could be *preferred* in the same way by each isolated, purposive-rational actor while still in the state of nature. Because Hobbes ascribes the same success-oriented attitude to the parties in the state of nature as private law ascribes to its addressees, it seems reasonable to construe the original act of association along the lines of an instrument available in private law, the contract – specifically, to construe this act as a civil contract in which all the parties jointly agree to install (but not to bind) a sovereign. There is one circumstance Hobbes does not consider here. Within the horizon of their individual preferences, the subjects make their decisions from the perspective of the first-person singular. But this is not the perspective from which parties in a state of nature are led, on reflection, to trade their natural, that is, mutually conflicting but unlimited, liberties for precisely those civil liberties that general laws at once limit and render compatible. Only under two conditions would one expect subjects in the state of nature to make a rationally motivated transition from their state of permanent conflict to a cooperation under coercive law that demands a partial renunciation of freedom on the part of everyone.

On the one hand, the parties would have to be capable of understanding what a social relationship based on the principle of reciprocity even means. The subjects of private law, who are at first only virtually present in the state of nature, have, prior to all association, not yet learned to 'take the perspective of the other' and self-reflexively perceive themselves from the perspective of a second person. Only then could their own freedom appear to them not simply as a natural freedom that occasionally encounters factual resistance but as a freedom constituted through mutual recognition. In order to understand what a contract is and know how to use it, they must already have at their disposal the sociocognitive framework of perspective-taking between counterparts, a framework they can acquire only in a social condition not yet available in the state of nature. On the other hand, the parties who agree on the terms of the contract they are about to conclude must be capable of distancing themselves in yet another way from their natural freedoms. They must be capable of assuming the social perspective of the first-person plural, a perspective always already tacitly assumed by Hobbes and his readers but withheld from subjects in the state of nature. On Hobbesian premises, these subjects may not assume the very standpoint from which each of them could first judge whether the reciprocity of coercion, which limits the scope of each's free choice according to general laws, lies in the equal interest of all and hence can be willed by all the participants. In fact, we find that Hobbes does acknowledge in passing the kinds of moral grounds that thereby come into play; he does this in those places where he recurs to the Golden Rule – Quod tibi fieri non vis, alteri ne feceris – as a natural law.[18] But morally impregnating the state of nature in this way contradicts the naturalism presupposed by the intended goal of Hobbes's demonstration, namely, to ground the construction of a system of well-ordered egoism on the sole basis of the enlightened self-interest of any individual.[19]

The empiricist question – how a system of rights can be explained by the interlocking of interest positions and utility calculations of accidentally related rational actors – has never failed to hold the attention of astute philosophers and social scientists. But even the modern tools of game theory have yet to provide a satisfactory solution. If for no other reason, Kant's reaction to the *failure* of this attempt continues to deserve consideration.

Kant saw that rights cannot for their part be grounded by recourse to a model taken from private law. He raised the convincing objection that Hobbes failed to notice the structural difference between the social contract, which serves as a model for legitimation, and the private contract, which basically regulates exchange relationships. In fact, one must expect something other than a merely egocentric attitude from the parties concluding a social contract in the state of nature: 'the contract establishing a civil constitution . . . is of so unique a kind that . . . it is in principle essentially different from all others in what it founds.'[20] Whereas parties usually conclude a contract 'to some determinate end', the social contract is 'an end in itself'. It grounds 'the right of men [to live] under public coercive law, through which each can receive his due and can be made secure from the interference of others'.[21] In Kant's view the parties do not agree to appoint a sovereign to whom they cede the power to make laws. Rather, the social contract is unique in not having any specific content at all; it provides instead the model for a kind of sociation ruled by the principle of law. It lays down the performative conditions under which rights acquire legitimate validity, for 'right is the limitation of each person's freedom so that it is compatible with the freedom of everyone, insofar as this is possible in accord with a general law.'[22]

Under this aspect, the social contract serves to *institutionalize* the single 'innate' right to equal liberties. Kant sees this primordial human right as grounded in the autonomous will of individuals who, as moral persons, have at their prior disposal the social perspective of a practical reason that tests laws. On the basis of this reason, they have *moral* – and not just prudential – grounds for their move out of the condition of unprotected freedom. At the same time, Kant sees that the 'single human right' must differentiate itself into a *system of rights* through which both 'the freedom of every member of society as a human being' as well as 'the equality of each member with every other as a subject' assume a positive shape.[23] This happens in the form of 'public laws', which can claim legitimacy only as acts of the public will of autonomous and united citizens: establishing public law 'is possible through no other will than that belonging to the people collectively (because all decide for all, hence each for himself); for only to oneself can one never do injustice'.[24] Because the question concerning the legitimacy of freedom-securing laws must find an answer *within* positive law, the social contract establishes the principle of law by binding the legislator's political will-formation to conditions of a *democratic procedure*: under these conditions the results arrived at in conformity with this procedure express per se the concurring will or rational consensus of all participants. In this way, the morally grounded primordial human right to equal liberties is intertwined in the social contract with the principle of popular sovereignty.

The human rights grounded in the moral autonomy of individuals acquire a positive shape solely through the citizens' political autonomy. The principle of law seems to mediate between the principle of morality and that of democracy. But it is not entirely clear how the latter two principles are related. Kant certainly introduces the concept of autonomy, which supports the whole construction, from the pre-political viewpoint of the morally judging individual, but he explicates this concept along the lines of the universal-law version of the Categorical Imperative, drawing in turn on the model of a public and democratic self-legislation borrowed from Rousseau. From a conceptual standpoint, the moral principle and the democratic principle reciprocally explain each other, but the architectonic of Kant's legal theory conceals this point. If one accepts this reading, then the principle of law cannot be understood as the middle term between the principles of morality and democracy, but simply as the reverse side of the democratic principle itself because the democratic principle cannot be implemented except in the form of law, both principles must be realized *uno actu*. How these three principles are related certainly remains unclear, which stems from the fact that in Kant, as in Rousseau, there is still an unacknowledged *competition* between morally grounded *human rights* and the *principle of popular sovereignty*.

But what significance can such a discussion of the history of political ideas have for a systematic treatment of private and public autonomy? Before going any further, I insert an excursus intended to clarify the impact of modern political theory.

Excursus

The two ideas of human rights and popular sovereignty have determined the normative self-understanding of constitutional democracies up to the present day. We must not look on the idealism anchored in our constitutional principles simply as a closed chapter in the history of political ideas. On the contrary, this history of political theory is a necessary element and reflection of the tension between facticity and validity built into law itself, between the positivity of law and the legitimacy claimed by it. This tension can be neither trivialized nor simply ignored, because the rationalization of the lifeworld makes it increasingly difficult to rely only on tradition and settled ethical conventions to meet the need for legitimating enacted law – a law that rests on the changeable decisions of a political legislator. Here let me briefly recall the rationality potential, at work in both cultural and socialization processes, that has increasingly made itself felt in the law since the first great codifications of private and public law at the end of the eighteenth century.

The classical, primarily Aristotelian, doctrine of natural law, whose influence extended well into the nineteenth century, as well as Thomas Aquinas's remodelled Christian version, still reflected an encompassing societal ethos that extended through all social classes of the population and clamped the different social orders together. In the vertical dimension of the components of the lifeworld, this ethos ensured that cultural value patterns and institutions sufficiently overlapped with the action orientations and motives fixed in personality structures. At the horizontal level of legitimate orders, it allowed the nonnative elements of ethical life, politics and law to intermesh. In the train of developments I interpret as the rationalization of the lifeworld, this clamp sprang open. As the first step, cultural traditions and processes of socialization came under the pressure of reflection, so that actors themselves gradually made them into topics of discussion. To the extent that this occurred, received practices and interpretations of ethical life were reduced to mere conventions and differentiated from conscientious decisions that passed through the filter of reflection and independent judgment. In the process, the use of practical reason reached that point of specialization with which I am concerned in the present context. The modern ideas of *self-realization* and *self-determination* signalled not only different issues but two different kinds of discourse tailored to the logics of *ethical* and *moral* questions. The respective logics peculiar to these two types of questions were in turn manifested in philosophical developments that began in the late eighteenth century.

What was considered 'ethics' since the time of Aristotle now assumed a new, subjectivistic sense. This was true of both individual life histories and of intersubjectively shared traditions and forms of life. In connection with, and in reaction to, a growing autobiographical literature of confessions and self-examinations – running from Rousseau through Kierkegaard to Sartre – a kind of reflection developed that altered attitudes toward one's own life. To put it briefly, in place of exemplary instructions in the virtuous life and recommended models of the good life, one finds an increasingly pronounced, abstract demand for a conscious, self-critical appropriation, the demand that one responsibly take possession of one's own individual, irreplaceable and contingent life history. Radicalized interiority is burdened with the task of achieving a self-understanding in which self-knowledge and existential decision interpenetrate. Heidegger used the formulation 'thrown project' to express the expectation of this probing selection of factually given possibilities that mould one's identity.[25] The intrusion of reflection into the life-historical process generates a new kind of tension between the consciousness of contingency, self-reflection and liability for one's own existence. To the extent that this constellation has an ever broader impact on society through prevailing patterns of socialization, *ethical-existential* or *clinical discourses* become not only possible but in a certain sense unavoidable: the conflicts springing from such a constellation, if they are not resolved consciously and deliberately, make themselves felt in obtrusive symptoms.

Not only the conduct of personal life but also the transmission of culture is increasingly affected by the type of discourse aimed at self-understanding. In connection with, and in reaction to, the rise of the hermeneutical and historical sciences, the appropriation of our own intersubjectively shared traditions became problematic starting with Schleiermacher and continuing through Droysen and Dilthey up to Gadamer. In place of religious or metaphysical self-interpretations, history and its interpretation have now become the medium in which cultures and peoples find their self-reassurance.

Although philosophical hermeneutics got its start in the methodology of the humanities, it responds more broadly to an insecurity provoked by historicism – to a reflexive refraction affecting the public appropriation of tradition in the first-person plural.[26] During the nineteenth century a post-traditional identity first took on a definite shape under a close affiliation between historicism and nationalism. But this was still fuelled by a dogmatism of national histories that has since been in the process of disintegration. A pluralism in the ways of reading fundamentally ambivalent traditions has sparked a growing number of debates over the collective identities of nations, states, cultures and other groups. Such discussions make it clear that the disputing parts are expected to consciously choose the continuities they want to live out of, which traditions they want to break off or continue. To the extent that collective identities can develop only in the fragile, dynamic and fuzzy shape of a decentred, even fragmented public consciousness, *ethical-political discourses* that reach into the depths have become both possible and unavoidable.

The intrusion of reflection into life histories and cultural traditions has fostered individualism in personal life projects and a pluralism of collective forms of life. Simultaneously, however, norms of interaction have also become reflexive; in this way universalist value orientations gain ascendancy. Once again, an altered normative consciousness is reflected in the relevant philosophical theories since the end of the eighteenth century. One no longer legitimates maxims, practices and rules of action simply by calling attention to the contexts in which they were handed down. The distinction between autonomous and heteronomous actions has in fact revolutionized our normative consciousness. At the same time, there has been a growing need for justification, which, under the conditions of postmetaphysical thinking, can be met only by *moral discourses*. The latter aim at the impartial evaluation of action conflicts. In contrast to ethical deliberations, which are oriented to the telos of my/our own good (or not misspent) life, moral deliberations require a perspective freed of all egocentrism or ethnocentrism. Under the moral viewpoint of equal respect for each person and equal consideration for the interests of all, the henceforth sharply focused normative claims of legitimately regulated interpersonal relationships are sucked into a whirlpool of problematization. At the post-traditional level of justification, individuals develop a principled moral consciousness and orient their action by the idea of self-determination. What self-legislation or moral autonomy signifies in the sphere of personal life corresponds to the rational natural-law interpretations of political freedom, that is, interpretations of democratic self-legislation in the constitution of a just society.

To the extent that the transmission of culture and processes of socialization become reflexive, there is a growing awareness of the logic of ethical and moral questions. Without the backing of religious or metaphysical worldviews that are immune to criticism, practical orientations can in the final analysis be gained only from rational discourse, that is, from the reflexive forms of communicative action itself. The rationalization of a lifeworld is measured by the extent to which the rationality potentials built into

communicative action and released in discourse penetrate lifeworld structures and set them aflow. Processes of individual formation and cultural
knowledge-systems offer less resistance to this whirlpool of problematization
than does the institutional framework. It is here, at the level of personality
and knowledge, that the logic of ethical and moral questions first asserted
itself, such that alternatives to the normative ideas dominating modernity
could no longer be justified in the long run. The conscious life conduct of
the individual person finds its standards in the expressivist ideal of self-
realization, the deontological idea of freedom, and the utilitarian maxim of
expanding one's life opportunities. The ethical substance of collective forms
of life takes its standards, on the one hand, from utopias of non-alienated, sol-
idary social life within the horizon of traditions that have been
self-consciously appropriated and critically passed on. On the other hand, it
looks to models of a just society whose institutions are so constituted as to regulate expectations and conflicts in the equal interest of all; the social-welfare
ideas of the progressive increase and just distribution of social wealth are just
further variants of this.

One consequence of the foregoing considerations is of particular interest
in the present context: to the extent that 'culture' and 'personality structures' are charged with ideals of the above sort, a law robbed of its sacred
foundation also comes under duress; as we have seen, the third component
of the lifeworld, 'society' as the totality of legitimate orders, is more intensely
concentrated in the legal system the more the latter must bear the burden
of fulfilling integrative functions for society as a whole. The changes just
sketched in the two other components can explain why modern legal orders
must find their legitimation, to an increasing degree, only in sources that do
not bring the law into conflict with those post-traditional ideals of life and
ideas of justice that first made their impact on persons and culture. Reasons
that are convenient for the legitimation of law must, on pain of cognitive dis-
sonances, harmonize with the moral principles of universal justice and
solidarity. They must also harmonize with the ethical principles of a consciously 'projected' life conduct for which the subjects themselves, at both
the individual and collective levels, take responsibility. However, these ideas
of self-determination and self-realization cannot be put together without
tension. Not surprisingly, social-contract theories have responded to the
modern ideals of justice and the good life with answers that bear different
accents.

The aim of the excursus was to explain why human rights and the principle
of popular sovereignty still constitute the sole ideas that can justify modern
law. These two ideas represent the precipitate left behind, so to speak, once
the normative substance of an ethos embedded in religious and metaphysical traditions has been forced through the filter of post-traditional
justification. To the extent that moral and ethical questions have been
differentiated from one another, the discursively filtered substance of
norms finds expression in the two dimensions of self-determination and

self-realization. Certainly one cannot simply align these two dimensions in direct correspondence with human rights and popular sovereignty. Still, there exist affinities between these two pairs of concepts, affinities that can be emphasized to a greater or lesser degree. If I may borrow a terminological shorthand from contemporary discussions in the United States, 'liberal' traditions conceive human rights as the expression of moral self-determination, whereas 'civic republicanism' tends to interpret popular sovereignty as the expression of ethical self-realization. From both perspectives, human rights and popular sovereignty do not so much mutually complement as compete with each other.

Frank Michelman, for example, sees in the American constitutional tradition a tension between the impersonal rule of law founded on innate human rights and the spontaneous self-organization of a community that makes its law through the sovereign will of the people.[27] This tension, however, can be resolved from one side or the other. Liberals invoke the danger of a 'tyranny of the majority' and postulate the priority of human rights that guarantee the pre-political liberties of the individual and set limits on the sovereign will of the political legislator. The proponents of a civic republicanism, on the contrary, emphasize the intrinsic, noninstrumentalizable value of civic self-organization, so that human rights have a binding character for a political community only as elements of their own consciously appropriated tradition. Whereas in the liberal view human rights all but impose themselves on our moral insight as something given, anchored in a fictive state of nature, according to republicans the ethical-political will of a self-actualizing collectivity is forbidden to recognize anything that does not correspond to its own authentic life project. In the one case, the moral-cognitive moment predominates, in the other, the ethical-volitional. By way of contrast, Rousseau and Kant pursued the goal of conceiving the notion of autonomy as unifying practical reason and sovereign will in such a way that the idea of human rights and the principle of popular sovereignty would *mutually* interpret one another. Nevertheless, these two authors also did not succeed in integrating the two concepts in an evenly balanced manner. On the whole, Kant suggests more of a liberal reading of political autonomy, Rousseau a republican reading.

Kant obtains the 'universal principle of law' by applying the moral principle to 'external' relations. He begins his *Elements of Justice* with the one right owed to each human being 'by virtue of his humanity', that is, the right to equal individual liberties backed by authorized coercion. This primordial right regulates 'internal property'; applying this to 'external property' yields the private rights of the individual (which then become the starting point for Savigny and the German civil-law jurisprudence subsequent to Kant).[28] This system of natural rights, which 'one cannot give up even if one wanted to',[29] belongs 'inalienably' to each human being. It is legitimated, prior to its differentiation in the shape of positive law, on the basis of moral principles, and hence independently of that political autonomy of citizens first constituted only with the social contract. To this extent the principles of private law enjoy the validity of moral rights already in the state of nature; hence 'natural rights', which protect the human being's private autonomy, precede the will of the sovereign lawgiver. At least in this regard, the sovereignty of the 'concurring and united will' of the citizens is constrained by morally grounded human rights. To be sure, Kant did not interpret the binding of popular sovereignty by human rights as a constraint, because he assumed that no one exercising her autonomy as a citizen *could* agree to laws infringing on her private autonomy as warranted by natural law. But this means that political autonomy must be explained on the basis of an *internal* connection between popular sovereignty and human rights. The construct of the social contract is meant to accomplish just this. However, in following a path of justification that *progresses* from morality to law, the construction of Kant's *Rechtslehre* denies to the social contract the central position it actually assumes in Rousseau.

Rousseau starts with the constitution of civic autonomy and produces a fortiori an internal relation between popular sovereignty and human rights. Because the sovereign will of the people can express itself only in the language of general and abstract laws, it has directly *inscribed* in it the right of each person to equal liberties, which Kant took as a morally grounded human right and thus *put ahead of* political will-formation. In Rousseau, then, the exercise of political autonomy no longer stands under the proviso of innate rights. Rather, the normative content of human rights enters into the very mode of carrying out popular sovereignty. The united will of the citizens is bound, through the medium of general and abstract laws, to a legislative procedure that excludes per se all nongeneralizable interests and only admits regulations that guarantee equal liberties for all. According to this idea, the procedurally correct exercise of popular sovereignty simultaneously secures the substance of Kant's original human right.

However, Rousseau does not consistently carry through with this plausible idea, because he owes a greater debt to the republican tradition than does Kant. He gives the idea of self-legislation more of an ethical than a moral interpretation, conceiving autonomy as the realization of the consciously apprehended form of life of a particular people. As is well known, Rousseau imagines the constitution of popular sovereignty through the social contract as a kind of existential act of sociation through which isolated and success-oriented individuals *transform* themselves into citizens oriented to the common good of an ethical community. As members of a collective body, they fuse together into the macrosubject of a legislative practice that has broken with the particular interests of private persons subjected to laws. Rousseau takes the excessive ethical demands on the citizen, which are built into the republican concept of community in any case, to an extreme. He counts on political virtues that are anchored in the ethos of a small and perspicuous, more or less homogeneous community integrated through shared cultural traditions. The single alternative would be state coercion: 'Now the less the individual wills relate to the general will, that is to say customary conduct to the laws, the more repressive force has to be increased. The

Government, then, in order to be good, should be relatively stronger as the people becomes more numerous.'[30]

However, if the practice of self-legislation must feed off the ethical substance of a people who already *agree in advance* on their value orientations, then Rousseau cannot explain how the postulated orientation of the citizens toward the common good can be mediated with the differentiated interest positions of private persons. He thus cannot explain how the normatively construed common will can, without repression, be mediated with the free choice of individuals. This would require a genuinely moral standpoint that would allow individuals to look beyond what is good *for them* and examine what lies equally in the interest of each. In the final analysis, the ethical version of the concept of popular sovereignty must lose sight of the universalistic meaning of Kant's principle of law.

Apparently the normative content of the original human right cannot be fully captured by the grammar of general and abstract laws alone, as Rousseau assumed. The substantive legal equality[31] that Rousseau took as central to the legitimacy claim of modern law cannot be satisfactorily explained by the *semantic* properties of general laws. The form of universal normative propositions says nothing about their validity. Rather, the claim that a norm lies equally in the interest of everyone has the sense of rational acceptability: all those possibly affected should be able to accept the norm on the basis of good reasons. But this can become clear only under the *pragmatic* conditions of rational discourses in which the only thing that counts is the compelling force of the better argument based on the relevant information. Rousseau thinks that the normative content of the principle of law lies simply in the semantic properties of *what* is willed; but this content could be found only in those pragmatic conditions that establish *how* the political will is formed. So the sought-for internal connection between popular sovereignty and human rights lies in the normative content of the very *mode of exercising political autonomy*, a mode that is not secured simply through the grammatical form of general laws but only through the communicative form of discursive processes of opinion- and will-formation.

This connection remains hidden from Kant and Rousseau alike. Although the premises of the philosophy of the subject allow one to bring reason and will together in a concept of autonomy, one can do so only by ascribing this capacity for self-determination to a subject, be it the transcendental ego of the *Critique of Practical Reason* or the people of the *Social Contract*. If the rational will can take shape only in the individual subject, then the individual's moral autonomy must reach through the political autonomy of the united will of all in order to secure the private autonomy of each in advance via natural law. If the rational will can take shape only in the macrosubject of a people or nation, then political autonomy must be understood as the self-conscious realization of the ethical substance of a concrete community; and private autonomy is protected from the overpowering force of political autonomy only by the non-discriminatory form of general laws. Both conceptions miss the legitimating force of a discursive process of opinion- and will-formation, in which the illocutionary binding forces of a use of language oriented to mutual understanding serve to bring reason and will together – and lead to convincing positions to which all individuals can agree without coercion.

However, if discourses (and, as we will see, bargaining processes as well, whose procedures are discursively grounded) are the site where a rational will can take shape, then the legitimacy of law ultimately depends on a communicative arrangement: as participants in rational discourses, consociates under law must be able to examine whether a contested norm meets with, or could meet with, the agreement of all those possibly affected. Consequently, the sought-for internal relation between popular sovereignty and human rights consists in the fact that the system of rights states precisely the conditions under which the forms of communication necessary for the genesis of legitimate law can be legally institutionalized. The system of rights can be reduced neither to a moral reading of human rights nor to an ethical reading of popular sovereignty, because the private autonomy of citizens must neither be set above, nor made subordinate to, their political autonomy. The normative intuitions associated conjointly with human rights and popular sovereignty achieve their *full* effect in the system of rights only if we assume that the universal right to equal liberties may neither be imposed as a moral right that merely sets an external constraint on the sovereign legislator, nor be instrumentalized as a functional prerequisite for the legislator's aims. The co-originality of private and public autonomy first reveals itself when we decipher, in discourse-theoretic terms, the motif of self-legisation according to which the addressees of law are simultaneously the authors of their rights. The substance of human rights then resides in the formal conditions for the legal institutionalization of those discursive processes of opinion- and will-formation in which the sovereignty of the people assumes a binding character.

Translated by William Rehg

Notes

1. F. C. von Savigny, *System des heutigen Römischen Rechts*, vol. 1 (Berlin, 1840), sec. 4. For an English translation of this book, see Savigny, *System of the Modern Roman Law*, vol. 1, trans. W. Holloway (Madras, 1876). [Trans.]

2. Savigny, *System*, sec. 53.

3. G. F. Puchta, *Cursus der Institutionen* (Leipzig, 1865), sec. 4.

4. B. Windscheid, *Lehrbuch des Pandektenrechts* (Frankfurt am Main, 1906), vol. 2, sec. 37. Here one might also note the affirmative reference to Ferdinand Regelsberger's definition: 'We have to do with a subjective right if the legal order cedes the realization of a recognized purpose, i.e., the satisfaction of a recognized interest, to the participant and grants him legal power for this end.'

5. R. von Ihering, *Geist des Römischen Rechts* (Leipzig, 1888), pt. 3, p. 338.

6. L. Enneccerus, *Allgemeiner Teil des Bürgerlichen Rechts*, fifteenth ed. (Tübingen, 1959), sec. 72.

7. H. Kelsen, *Allgemeine Staatslehre* (Bad Homburg, 1968), p. 64.

8. J. Schmidt, 'Zur Funktion der subjektiven Rechte', *Archiv für Rechts- und Sozialphilosophie* 57 (1971), pp. 383–96.

9. B. Rüthers, *Die unbegrenzte Auslegung* (Frankfurt am Main, 1973).

10. Associated with the so-called 'Ordo Circle', this German version of liberal economic and legal thought got started before World War II and considerably influenced postwar policies in Germany. [Trans.]

11. H. Coing, 'Zur Geschichte des Begriffs "subjektives Recht"', in Coing et al., *Das subjektive Recht und der Rechtsschutz der Persönlichkeit* (Frankfurt am Main, 1959), pp. 7–23.

12. L. Raiser, 'Der Stand der Lehre vom subjektiven Recht im Deutschen Zivilrecht (1961)', in Raiser, *Die Aufgabe des Privatrechts* (Frankfurt am Main, 1977), pp. 98ff.

13. Raiser, 'Stand der Lehre', p. 113.

14. See chapter 9 ('Paradigms of Law') in J. Habermas, *Between Facts and Norms* (Cambridge, Mass., 1986), sec. 9.1.2.

15. F. Michelman, 'Justification (and Justifiability) of Law in a Contemporary World', in J. R. Pennock and J. W. Chapman, eds., *Justification, Nomos*, vol. 18 (New York, 1986), pp. 71–99.

16. T. Hobbes, *De Cive*, chap. 13, par. 6 (trans. attributed to Hobbes, in *Man and Citizen*, ed. B. Gert [Indianapolis, 1991]); cf. J. Habermas, 'The Classical Doctrine of Politics in Relation to Social Philosophy', in Habermas, *Theory and Practice*, trans. J. Viertel (Boston, 1973), pp. 41–81.

17. Hobbes, *De Cive*, chap. 13, para. 3.

18. 'Whatsoever you require that others should do to you, that do ye to them.' Hobbes, *Leviathan*, ed. R. Tuck (Cambridge, 1991), p. 92; cf. also pp. 117, 188.

19. Otfried Höffe likewise pursues mutatis mutandis this Hobbesian goal of demonstration. For him justice consists in limitations of freedom that are universally distributed and hence equally advantageous for all sides: 'Because it is advantageous for all, natural justice has no need of moral conscience, nor of personal justice, for its implementation. It can be satisfied with self-interest as a motivating principle.' O. Höffe, *Politische Gerechtigkeit* (Frankfurt am Main, 1987), p. 407. This approach is even more clearly elaborated in Höffe's *Kategorische Rechtsprinzipien* (Frankfurt am Main, 1990) and Höffe, *Gerechtigkeit als Tausch?* (Baden-Baden, 1991). For a critique, see K. Günther, 'Kann ein Volk von Teufeln Recht und Staat moralisch legitimieren?' *Rechtshistorisches Journal* 10 (1991), pp. 233–67.

20. I. Kant, 'On the Proverb: That May Be True in Theory, But Is of No Practical Use', in Kant, *Perpetual Peace and Other Essays*, trans. T. Humphrey (Indianapolis, 1983), p. 71.

21. Ibid, p. 72 (translation slightly altered). [Trans.]

22. Ibid, p. 72.

23. Ibid, p. 72.

24. Ibid, pp. 75–76 (translation slightly altered). [Trans.]

25. Ernst Tugendhat has reconstructed this, using linguistic analysis; see his *Self-Consciousness and Self-Determination*, trans. P. Stern (Cambridge, Mass., 1986).

26. J. Habermas, 'Historical Consciousness and Post-Traditional Identity: The Federal Republic's Orientation to the West', in Habermas, *The New Conservatism*, ed. and trans. S. W. Nicholsen (Cambridge, Mass., 1989), pp. 249–67.

27. F. Michelman, 'Law's Republic', *Yale Law Journal* 97 (1998), pp. 1499ff.: 'I take American constitutionalism – as manifest in academic constitutional theory, in the professional practice of lawyers and judges, and in the ordinary political self-understanding of Americans at large – to rest on two premises regarding political freedom: first, that the American people are politically free insomuch as they are governed by themselves collectively, and, second, that the American people are politically free insomuch as they are governed by laws and not by men. I take it that no earnest, non-disruptive participant in American constitutional debate is quite free to reject either of those two professions of belief. I take them to be premises whose problematic relation to each other, and therefore whose meanings, are subject to an endless contestation.'

28. See I. Kant, *The Metaphysical Elements of Justice*, trans. J. Ladd (New York, 1965), pp. 35, 44–45.

29. Kant, 'On the Proverb', p. 82 (translation slightly altered). [Trans.]

30. J.–J. Rousseau, *Of the Social Contract or Principles of Political Right*, trans. C. M. Sherover (New York, 1984), p. 55 (bk. 3, pt. 1, par. 159).

31. According to Habermas, 'substantive legal equality', or *Rechtsinhaltsgleichheit*, has two components: (a) legal statutes are applied so as to treat like cases alike and different cases differently; and (b) legal statutes regulate matters in a way that is in the equal interest of each person. [Trans.]

4

Human Rights, Rationality and Sentimentality

Richard Rorty

In a report from Bosnia some time ago,[1] David Rieff said: 'To the Serbs, the Muslims are no longer human . . . Muslim prisoners, lying on the ground in rows, awaiting interrogation, were driven over by a Serb guard in a small delivery van.' This theme of dehumanization recurs when Rieff says:

> A Muslim man in Bosanski Petrovac . . . [was] forced to bite off the penis of a fellow-Muslim . . . If you say that a man is not human, but the man looks like you and the only way to identify this devil is to make him drop his trousers – Muslim men are circumcised and Serb men are not – it is probably only a short step, psychologically, to cutting off his prick . . . There has never been a campaign of ethnic cleansing from which sexual sadism has gone missing.

The moral to be drawn from Rieff's stories is that Serbian murderers and rapists do not think of themselves as violating human rights. For they are not doing these things to fellow human beings, but to *Muslims*. They are not being inhuman, but rather are discriminating between the true humans and the pseudohumans. They are making the same sort of distinction as the Crusaders made between humans and infidel dogs, and the Black Muslims make between humans and blue-eyed devils. The founder of my university was able both to own slaves and to think it self-evident that all men were endowed by their creator with certain inalienable rights. He had convinced himself that the consciousness of Blacks, like that of animals, 'participate(s) more of sensation than reflection'.[2] Like the Serbs, Mr Jefferson did not think of himself as violating *human* rights.

The Serbs take themselves to be acting in the interests of true humanity by purifying the world of pseudohumanity. In this respect, their self-image resembles that of moral philosophers who hope to cleanse the world of prejudice and superstition. This cleansing will permit us to rise above our animality by becoming, for the first time, wholly rational and thus wholly human. The Serbs, the moralists, Jefferson and the Black Muslims all use the term 'men' to mean 'people like us'. They think the line between humans and animals is not simply the line between featherless bipeds and all others. They think the line divides some featherless bipeds from others: there are animals walking about in humanoid form. We and those like us are paradigm cases of humanity, but those too different from us in behaviour or custom are, at best, borderline cases. As Clifford Geertz puts it, 'Men's most importunate claims to humanity are cast in the accents of group pride.'[3]

We in the safe, rich democracies feel about the Serbian torturers and rapists as they feel about their Muslim victims: they are more like animals than like us. But we are not doing anything to help the Muslim women who are being gang raped or the Muslim men who are being castrated, any more than we did anything in the thirties when the Nazis were amusing themselves by torturing Jews. Here in the safe countries we find ourselves saying things like 'That's how things have always been in the Balkans', suggesting that, unlike us, those people are used to being raped and castrated. The contempt we always feel for losers – Jews in the thirties, Muslims now – combines with our disgust at the winners' behaviour to produce the semi-conscious attitude: 'a plague on both your houses'. We think of the Serbs or the Nazis as animals, because ravenous breasts of prey are animals. We think of the Muslims or the Jews being herded into concentration camps as animals, because cattle are animals. Neither sort of animal is very much like us, and there seems no point in human beings getting involved in quarrels between animals.

The human-animal distinction, however, is only one of the three main ways in which we paradigmatic humans distinguish ourselves from borderline cases. A second is by invoking the distinction between adults and children. Ignorant and superstitious people, we say, are like children; they will attain true humanity only if raised up by proper education. If they seem incapable of absorbing such education, that shows they are not really the same kind of being as we educable people are. Blacks, the whites in the United States and in South Africa used to say, are like children. That is why it is appropriate to address Black males, of whatever age, as 'boy'. Women, men used to say, are permanently childlike; it is therefore appropriate to spend no money on their education, and to refuse them access to power.

When it comes to women, however, there are simpler ways of excluding them from true humanity: for example, using 'man' as a synonym of 'human being'. As feminists have pointed out, such usages reinforce the average male's thankfulness that he was not born a woman, as well as his fear of the ultimate degradation: feminization. The extent of the latter fear is evidenced by the particular sort of sexual sadism Rieff describes. His point that such sadism is never absent from attempts to purify the species or cleanse the territory confirms Catharine MacKinnon's claim that, for most men, being a woman does not count as a way of being human. Being a nonmale is the third main way of being nonhuman. There are several ways of being nonmale. One is to be born without a penis; another is to have one's penis cut or bitten off; a third is to have been penetrated by a penis. Many men who have been raped are convinced that their manhood, and thus their humanity, has been taken away. Like racists who discover they have Jewish or Black ancestry, they may commit suicide out of sheer shame, shame at no longer being the kind of featherless biped that counts as human.

Philosophers have tried to clear this mess up by spelling out what all and only the featherless bipeds have in common, thereby explaining what is essential to being human. Plato argued that there is a big difference between us and the animals, a difference worthy of respect and cultivation. He thought that human beings have a special added ingredient which puts them in a different ontological category than the brutes. Respect for this ingredient provides a reason for people to be nice to each other. Anti-Platonists like Nietzsche reply that attempts to get people to stop murdering, raping and castrating each other are, in the long run, doomed to fail – for the real truth about human nature is that we are a uniquely nasty and dangerous kind of animal. When contemporary admirers of Plato claim that all featherless bipeds – even the stupid and childlike, even the women, even the sodomized – have the same inalienable rights, admirers of Nietzsche reply that the very idea of 'inalienable human rights' is, like the idea of a special added ingredient, a laughably feeble attempt by the weaker members of the species to fend off the stronger.

As I see it, one important intellectual advance made in our century is the steady decline in interest in the quarrel between Plato and Nietzsche. There is a growing willingness to neglect the question 'What is our nature?' and to substitute the question 'What can we make of ourselves?'. We are much less inclined than our ancestors were to take 'theories of human nature' seriously, much less inclined to take ontology or history as a guide to life. We have come to see that the only lesson of either history or anthropology is our extraordinary malleability. We are coming to think of ourselves as the flexible, protean, self-shaping animal rather than as the rational animal or the cruel animal.

One of the shapes we have recently assumed is that of a human rights culture. I borrow the term 'human rights culture' from the Argentinian jurist and philosopher Eduardo Rabossi. In an article called 'Human Rights Naturalized', Rabossi argues that philosophers should think of this culture as a new, welcome fact of the post-Holocaust world. They should stop trying to get behind or beneath this fact, stop trying to detect and defend its so-called 'philosophical presuppositions'. In Rabossi's view, philosophers like Alan Gewirth are wrong to argue that human rights cannot depend on historical facts. 'My basic point', Rabossi says, is that 'the world has changed, that the human rights phenomenon renders human rights foundationalism outmoded and irrelevant.'[4]

Rabossi's claim that human rights foundationalism is *outmoded* seems to me both true and important; it will be my principal topic in this essay. I shall be enlarging on, and defending, Rabossi's claim that the question whether human beings really have the rights enumerated in the Helsinki Declaration is not worth raising. In particular, I shall be defending the claim that nothing relevant to moral choice separates human beings from animals except historically contingent facts of the world, cultural facts.

This claim is sometimes called 'cultural relativism' by those who indignantly reject it. One reason they reject it is that such relativism seems to them incompatible with the fact that our human rights culture, the culture with which we in this democracy identify ourselves, is morally superior to other cultures. I quite agree that ours is morally superior, but I do not think this superiority counts in favour of the existence of a universal human nature. It would only do so if we assumed that a moral claim is ill-founded if not backed up by knowledge of a distinctively human attribute. But it is not clear why 'respect for human dignity' – our sense that the differences between Serb and Muslim, Christian and infidel, gay and straight, male and female should not matter – must presuppose the existence of any such attribute.

Traditionally, the name of the shared human attribute which supposedly 'grounds' morality is 'rationality'. Cultural relativism is associated with irrationalism because it denies the existence of morally relevant transcultural facts. To agree with Rabossi one must, indeed, be irrationalist in the sense of ceasing to make one's web of belief as coherent, and as perspicuously structured, as possible. Philosophers like myself, who think of rationality as simply the attempt at such coherence, agree with Rabossi that foundationalist projects are outmoded. We see our task as a matter of making our own culture – the human rights culture – more self-conscious and more powerful, rather than of demonstrating its superiority to other cultures by an appeal to something transcultural.

We think that the most philosophy can hope to do is summarize our culturally influenced intuitions about the right thing to do in various situations. The summary is effected by formulating a generalization from which these intuitions can be deduced, with the help of non-controversial lemmas. That generalization is not supposed to ground our intuitions, but rather to summarize them. John Rawls's 'Difference Principle' and the US Supreme Court's construction, in recent decades, of a constitutional 'right to privacy' are examples of this kind of summary. We see the formulation of such summarizing generalizations as increasing the predictability, and thus the power and efficiency, of our institutions, thereby heightening the sense of shared moral identity which brings us together in a moral community.

Foundationalist philosophers, such as Plato, Aquinas and Kant, have hoped to provide independent support for such summarizing generalizations. They would like to infer these generalizations from further premises, premises capable of being known to be true independently of the truth of the moral intuitions which have been summarized. Such premises are supposed to justify our intuitions, by providing premises from which the content of those intuitions can be deduced. I shall lump all such premises together under the label 'claims to knowledge about the nature of human beings'. In this broad sense, claims to know that our moral intuitions are recollections of the Form of the Good, or that we are the disobedient children of a loving

God, or that human beings differ from other kinds of animals by having dignity rather than mere value, are all claims about human nature. So are such counterclaims as that human beings are merely vehicles for selfish genes, or merely eruptions of the will to power.

To claim such knowledge is to claim to know something which, though not itself a moral intuition, can *correct* moral intuitions. It is essential to this idea of moral knowledge that a whole community might come to know that most of their most salient intuitions about the right thing to do were wrong. But now suppose we ask: Is there this sort of knowledge? What kind of question is that? On the traditional view, it is a philosophical question, belonging to a branch of epistemology known as 'metaethics'. But on the pragmatist view which I favour, it is a question of efficiency, of how best to grab hold of history – how best to bring about the utopia sketched by the Enlightenment. If the activities of those who attempt to achieve this sort of knowledge seem of little use in actualizing this utopia, that is a reason to think there is no such knowledge. If it seems that most of the work of changing moral intuitions is being done by manipulating our feelings rather than increasing our knowledge, that will be a reason to think that there is no knowledge of the sort which philosophers like Plato, Aquinas and Kant hoped to acquire.

This pragmatist argument against the Platonist has the same form as an argument for cutting off payment to the priests who are performing purportedly war-winning sacrifices – an argument which says that all the real work of winning the war seems to be getting done by the generals and admirals, not to mention the foot soldiers. The argument does not say, since there seem to be no gods, there is probably no need to support the priests. It says instead: since there is apparently no need to support the priests, there probably are no gods. We pragmatists argue from the fact that the emergence of the human rights culture seems to owe nothing to increased moral knowledge, and everything to hearing sad and sentimental stories, to the conclusion that there is probably no knowledge of the sort Plato envisaged. We go on to argue: since no useful work seems to be done by insisting on a purportedly ahistorical human nature, there probably is no such nature, or at least nothing in that nature that is relevant to our moral choices.

In short, my doubts about the effectiveness of appeals to moral knowledge are doubts about causal efficacy, not about epistemic status. My doubts have nothing to do with any of the theoretical questions discussed under the heading of 'metaethics', questions about the relation between facts and values, or between reason and passion, or between the cognitive and the noncognitive, or between descriptive statements and action-guiding statements. Nor do they have anything to do with questions about realism and anti-realism. The difference between the moral realist and the moral anti-realist seems to pragmatists to be a difference which makes no practical difference. Further, such metaethical questions presuppose the Platonic distinction between inquiry which aims at efficient problem-solving and inquiry which aims at a goal called 'truth for its own sake'. That distinction collapses if one follows Dewey in thinking of all inquiry – in physics as well as in ethics – as practical problem-solving, or if one follows Peirce in seeing every belief as action-guiding.[5]

Even after the priests have been pensioned off, however, the memories of certain priests may still be cherished by the community – especially the memories of their prophecies. We remain profoundly grateful to philosophers like Plato and Kant, not because they discovered truths but because they prophesied cosmopolitan utopias – utopias most of whose details they may have got wrong, but utopias we might never have struggled to reach had we not heard their prophecies. As long as our ability to know, and in particular to discuss the question 'What is man?' seemed the most important thing about us human beings, people like Plato and Kant accompanied utopian prophecies with claims to know something deep and important – something about the parts of the soul, or the transcendental status of the common moral consciousness. But this ability, and those questions, have, in the course of the last two hundred years, come to seem much less important. Rabossi summarizes this cultural sea change in his claim that human rights foundationalism is outmoded. In the remainder of this essay, I shall take up the questions: *why* has knowledge become much less important to our self-image than it was two hundred years ago? Why does the attempt to found culture on nature, and moral obligation on knowledge of transcultural universals, seem so much less important to us than it seemed in the Enlightenment? Why is there so little resonance, and so little point, in asking whether human beings in fact have the rights listed in the Helsinki Declaration? Why, in short, has moral philosophy become such an inconspicuous part of our culture?

A simple answer is that between Kant's time and ours Darwin argued most of the intellectuals out of the view that human beings contain a special added ingredient. He convinced most of us that we were exceptionally talented animals, animals clever enough to take charge of our own future evolution. I think this answer is right as far as it goes, but it leads to a further question: why did Darwin succeed, relatively speaking, so very easily? Why did he not cause the creative philosophical ferment caused by Galileo and Newton?

The revival by the New Science of the seventeenth century of a Democritean-Lucretian corpuscularian picture of nature scared Kant into inventing transcendental philosophy, inventing a brand-new kind of knowledge, which could demote the corpuscularian world picture to the status of 'appearance'. Kant's example encouraged the idea that the philosopher, as an expert on the nature and limits of knowledge, can serve as supreme cultural arbiter.[6] By the time of Darwin, however, this idea was already beginning to seem quaint. The historicism which dominated the intellectual world of the early nineteenth century had created an anti-essentialist mood. So when Darwin came alone, he fitted into the evolutionary niche which Herder and Hegel had begun to colonize. Intellectuals who populate this niche look to the future rather than to eternity. They prefer new ideas about how change can be effected to stable criteria for determining the desirability of change. They are the ones who think both Plato and Nietzsche outmoded.

The best explanation of both Darwin's relatively easy triumph, and our own increasing willingness to substitute hope for knowledge, is that the nineteenth and twentieth centuries saw, among the Europeans and Americans, an extraordinary increase in wealth, literacy and leisure. This increase made possible an unprecedented acceleration in the rate of moral progress. Such events as the French Revolution and the ending of the trans-Atlantic slave trade prompted nineteenth-century intellectuals in the rich democracies to say: it is enough for us to know that we live in an age in which human beings can make things much better for ourselves.[7] We do not need to dig behind this historical fact to non-historical facts about what we really are.

In the two centuries since the French Revolution, we have learned that human beings are far more malleable than Plato or Kant had dreamed. The more we are impressed by this malleability, the less interested we become in questions about our ahistorical nature. The more we see a chance to recreate ourselves, the more we read Darwin not as offering one more theory about what we really are but as providing reasons why we need not ask what we really are. Nowadays, to say that we are clever animals is not to say something philosophical and pessimistic but something political and hopeful, namely: if we can work together, we can make ourselves into whatever we are clever and courageous enough to imagine ourselves becoming. This sets aside Kant's question 'What is Man?' and substitutes the question 'What sort of world can we prepare for our great-grandchildren?'

The question 'What is Man?' in the sense of 'What is the deep ahistorical nature of human beings?' owed its popularity to the standard answer to that question: we are the *rational* animal, the one which can know as well as merely feel. The residual popularity of this answer accounts for the residual popularity of Kant's astonishing claim that sentimentality has nothing to do with morality, that there is something distinctively and transculturally human called 'the sense of moral obligation' which has nothing to do with love, friendship, trust, or social solidarity. As long as we believe *that*, people like Rabossi are going to have a tough time convincing us that human rights foundationalism is an outmoded project.

To overcome this idea of a *sui generis* sense of moral obligation, it would help to stop answering the question 'What makes us different from the other animals?' by saying 'We can know, and they can merely feel.' We should substitute 'We can feel *for each other* to a much greater extent than they can.' This substitution would let us disentangle Christ's suggestion that love matters more than knowledge from the neo-Platonic suggestion that knowledge of the truth will make us free. For as long as we think that there is an ahistorical power which makes for righteousness – a power called truth, or rationality – we shall not be able to put foundationalism behind us.

The best, and probably the only, argument for putting foundationalism behind us is the one I have already suggested: it would be more efficient to do so, because it would let us concentrate our energies on manipulating sentiments, on sentimental education. That sort of education sufficiently acquaints people of different kinds with one another so that they are less tempted to think of those different from themselves as only quasi-human.

The goal of this manipulation of sentiment is to expand the reference of the terms 'our kind of people' and 'people like us'.

All I can do to supplement this argument from increased efficiency is to offer a suggestion about how Plato managed to convince us that knowledge of universal truths mattered as much as he thought it did. Plato thought that the philosopher's task was to answer questions like 'Why should I be moral? Why is it rational to be moral? Why is it in my interest to be moral? Why is it in the interest of human beings as such to be moral?'. He thought this because he believed the best way to deal with people like Thrasymachus and Callicles was to demonstrate to them that they had an interest of which they were unaware, an interest in being rational, in acquiring self-knowledge. Plato thereby saddled us with a distinction between the true and the false self. That distinction was, by the time of Kant, transmuted into a distinction between categorical, rigid, moral obligation and flexible, empirically deter- minable, self-interest. Contemporary moral philosophy is still lumbered with this opposition between self-interest and morality, an opposition which makes it hard to realize the my pride in being a part of the human rights culture is no more external to my self than my desire for financial success.

It would have been better if Plato had decided, as Aristotle was to decide, that there was nothing much to be done with people like Thrasymachus and Callicles, and that the problem was how to avoid having children who would be like Thrasymachus and Callicles. By insisting that he could reeducate people who had matured without acquiring appropriate moral sentiments by invoking a higher power than sentiment, the power of reason, Plato got moral philosophy off on the wrong foot. He led moral philosophers to con- centrate on the rather rare figure of the psychopath, the person who has no concern for any human being other than himself. Moral philosophy has sys- tematically neglected the much more common case: the person whose treatment of a rather narrow range of featherless bipeds is morally impecca- ble, but who remains indifferent to the suffering of those outside this range, the ones he or she thinks of as pseudohumans.[8]

Plato set things up so that moral philosophers think they have failed unless they convince the rational egotist that he should not be an egotist – convince him by telling him about his true, unfortunately neglected, self. But the rational egotist is not the problem. The problem is the gallant and hon- ourable Serb who sees Muslims as circumcised dogs. It is the brave soldier and good comrade who loves and is loved by his mates, but who thinks of women as dangerous, malevolent whores and bitches.

Plato thought that the way to get people to be nicer to each other was to point out what they all had in common – rationality. But it does little good to point out, to the people I have just described, that many Muslims and women are good at mathematics or engineering or jurisprudence. Resentful young Nazi toughs were quite aware that many Jews were clever and learned, but this only added to the pleasure they took in beating them up. Nor does it do much good to get such people to read Kant, and agree that one should not treat rational agents simply as means. For everything turns on who counts as a fellow human being, as a rational agent in the only relevant sense – the sense in which rational agency is synonymous with membership in *our* moral community.

For most white people, until very recently, most Black people did not so count. For most Christians, up until the seventeenth century or so, most heathens did not so count. For the Nazis, Jews did not so count. For most males in countries in which the average annual income is under four thousand dollars, most females still do not so count. Whenever tribal and national rivalries become important, members of rival tribes and nations will not so count. Kant's account of the respect due to rational agents tells you that you should extend the respect you feel for people like yourself to all featherless bipeds. This is an excellent suggestion, a good formula for secularizing the Christian doctrine of the brotherhood of man. But it has never been backed up by an argument based on neutral premises, and it never will be. Outside the circle of post-Enlightenment European culture, the circle of relatively safe and secure people who have been manipulating each others' sentiments for two hundred years, most people are simply unable to understand why membership in a biological species is supposed to suffice for membership in a moral community. This is not because they are insufficiently rational. It is, typically, because they live in a world in which it would be just too risky – indeed, would often be insanely dangerous – to let one's sense of moral community stretch beyond one's family, clan, or tribe.

To get whites to be nicer to Blacks, males to females, Serbs to Muslims, or straights to gays, to help our species link up into what Rabossi calls a 'planetary community' dominated by a culture of human rights, it is of no use whatever to say, with Kant: notice that what you have in common, your humanity, is more important than these trivial differences. For the people we are trying to convince will rejoin that they notice nothing of the sort. Such people are *morally* offended by the suggestion that they should treat someone who is not kin as if he were a brother, or a nigger as if he were white, or a queer as if he were normal, or an infidel as if she were a believer. They are offended by the suggestion that they treat people whom they do not think of as human as if they were human. When utilitarians tell them that all pleasures and pains felt by members of our biological species are equally relevant to moral deliberation, or when Kantians tell them that the ability to engage in such deliberation is sufficient for membership in the moral community, they are incredulous. They rejoin that these philosophers seem oblivious to blatantly obvious moral distinctions, distinctions any decent person will draw.

This rejoinder is not just a rhetorical device, nor is it in any way irrational. It is heartfelt. The identity of these people, the people whom we should like to convince to join our Eurocentric human rights culture, is bound up with their sense of who they are *not*. Most people – especially people relatively untouched by the European Enlightenment – simply do not think of themselves as, first and foremost, human beings. Instead, they think of themselves as being a certain *good* sort of human being – a sort defined by explicit opposition to a particularly bad sort. It is crucial for their sense of who they are that they are *not* an infidel, *not* a queer, *not* a woman, *not* an untouchable. Just in so far as they are impoverished, and as their lives are perpetually at risk, they have little else than pride in not being what they are not to sustain their self-respect. Starting with the days when the term 'human being' was synonomous with 'member of our tribe', we have always thought of human beings in terms of paradigm members of the species. We have contrasted *us*, the *real* humans, with rudimentary, or perverted, or deformed examples of humanity.

We Eurocentric intellectuals like to suggest that we, the paradigm humans, have overcome this primitive parochialism by using that paradigmatic human faculty, reason. So we say that failure to concur with us is due to 'prejudice'. Our use of these terms in this way may make us nod in agreement when Colin McGinn tells us, in the introduction to his recent book,[9] that learning to tell right from wrong is not as hard as learning French. The only obstacles to agreeing with his moral views, McGinn explains, are 'prejudice, vested interest and laziness'.

One can see what McGinn means: if, like many of us, you teach students who have been brought up in the shadow of the Holocaust, brought up believing that prejudice against racial or religious groups is a terrible thing, it is not very hard to convert them to standard liberal views about abortion, gay rights and the like. You may even get them to stop eating animals. All you have to do is convince them that all the arguments on the other side appeal to 'morally irrelevant' considerations. You do this by manipulating their sentiments in such a way that they imagine themselves in the shoes of the despised and oppressed. Such students are already so nice that they are eager to define their identity in non-exclusionary terms. The only people they have trouble being nice to are the ones they consider irrational – the religious fundamentalist, the smirking rapist, or the swaggering skinhead.

Producing generations of nice, tolerant, well-off, secure, other-respecting students of this sort in all parts of the world is just what is needed – indeed *all* that is needed – to achieve an Enlightenment utopia. The more youngsters like this we can raise, the stronger and more global our human rights culture will become. But it is not a good idea to encourage these students to label 'irrational' the intolerant people they have trouble tolerating. For that Platonic-Kantian epithet suggests that, with only a little more effort, the good and rational part of these other people's souls could have triumphed over the bad and irrational part. It suggests that we good people know something these bad people do not know, and that it is probably their own silly fault that they do not know it. All they have to do, after all, is to think a little harder, be a little more self-conscious, a little more rational.

But the bad people's beliefs are not more or less 'irrational' than the belief that race, religion, gender and sexual preference are all morally irrelevant – that these are all trumped by membership in the biological species. As used by moral philosophers like McGinn, the term 'irrational behaviour' means no more than 'behaviour of which we disapprove so strongly that our spade is turned when asked *why* we disapprove of it'. It would be better to teach our students that these bad people are no less rational, no less clearheaded, no more prejudiced, than we good people who respect otherness. The bad people's problem is that they were not so lucky in the circumstances of their upbringing as we were. Instead of treating as irrational all those people out there who are trying to find and kill Salman Rushdie, we should treat them as deprived.

Foundationalists think of these people as deprived of truth, of moral knowledge. But it would be better – more specific, more suggestive of possible remedies – to think of them as deprived of two more concrete things: security and sympathy. By 'security' I mean conditions of life sufficiently risk-free as to make one's difference from others inessential to one's self-respect, one's sense of worth. These conditions have been enjoyed by Americans and Europeans – the people who dreamed up the human rights culture – much more than they have been enjoyed by anyone else. By 'sympathy' I mean the sort of reaction that the Athenians had more of after seeing Aeschylus' *The Persians* than before, the sort that white Americans had more of after reading *Uncle Tom's Cabin* than before, the sort that we have more of after watching TV programmes about the genocide in Bosnia. Security and sympathy go together, for the same reasons that peace and economic productivity go together. The tougher things are, the more you have to be afraid of, the more dangerous your situation, the less you can afford the time or effort to think about what things might be like for people with whom you do not immediately identify. Sentimental education only works on people who can relax long enough to listen.

If Rabossi and I are right in thinking human rights foundationalism outmoded, then Hume is a better advisor than Kant about how we intellectuals can hasten the coming of the Enlightenment utopia for which both men yearned. Among contemporary philosophers, the best advisor seems to me to be Annette Baier. Baier describes Hume as 'the woman's moral philosopher' because Hume held that 'corrected (sometimes rule-corrected) sympathy, not law-discerning reason, is the fundamental moral capacity'.[10] Baier would like us to get rid of both the Platonic idea that we have a true self, and the Kantian idea that it is rational to be moral. In aid of this project, she suggests that we think of 'trust' rather than 'obligation' as the fundamental moral notion. This substitution would mean thinking of the spread of the human rights culture not as a matter of our becoming more aware of the requirements of the moral law, but rather as what Baier calls 'a progress of sentiments'.[11] This progress consists in an increasing ability to see the similarities between ourselves and people very unlike us as outweighing the differences. It is the result of what I have been calling 'sentimental education'. The relevant similarities are not a matter of sharing a deep true self which instantiates true humanity, but are such little, superficial, similarities as cherishing our parents and our children – similarities that do not interestingly distinguish us from many nonhuman animals.

To accept Baier's suggestions, however, we should have to overcome our sense that sentiment is too weak a force, and that something stronger is required. This idea that reason is 'stronger' than sentiment, that only an insistence on the unconditionality of moral obligation has the power to change human beings for the better, is very persistent. I think that this persistence is due mainly to a semiconscious realization that, if we hand our hopes for moral progress over to sentiment, we are in effect handing them over to *condescension*. For we shall be relying on those who have the power to change things – people like the rich New England abolitionists, or rich bleeding hearts like Robert Owen and Friedrich Engels – rather than on something that has power over *them*. We shall have to accept the fact that the fate of the women of Bosnia depends on whether TV journalists manage to do for them what Harriet Beecher Stowe did for black slaves, whether these journalists can make us, the audience back in the safe countries, feel that these women are more like us, more like real human beings, than we had realized.

To rely on the suggestions of sentiment rather than on the commands of reason is to think of powerful people gradually ceasing to oppress others, or ceasing to countenance the oppression of others, out of mere niceness, rather than out of obedience to the moral law. But it is revolting to think that our only hope for a decent society consists in softening the self-satisfied hearts of a leisure class. We want moral progress to burst up from below, rather than waiting patiently upon condescension from the top. The residual popularity of Kantian ideas of 'unconditional moral obligation' – obligation imposed by deep ahistorical non-contingent forces – seems to me almost entirely due to our abhorrence for the idea that the people on top hold the future in their hands, that everything depends on them, that there is nothing more powerful to which we can appeal against them.

Like everyone else, I too should prefer a bottom-up way of achieving utopia, a quick reversal of fortune which will make the last first. But I do not think this is how utopia will in fact come into being. Nor do I think that our preference for this way lends any support to the idea that the Enlightenment project lies in the depths of every human soul. So why does this preference make us resist the thought that sentimentality may be the best weapon we have? I think Nietzsche gave the right answer to this question: we resist out of resentment. We *resent* the idea that we shall have to wait for the strong to turn their piggy little eyes to the suffering of the weak. We desperately hope that there is something stronger and more powerful that will *hurt* the strong if they do *not* – if not a vengeful God, then a vengeful aroused proletariat, or, at least, a vengeful superego, or, at the very least, the offended majesty of Kant's tribunal of pure practical reason. The desperate hope for a non-contingent and powerful ally is, according to Nietzsche, the common core of Platonism, of religious insistence on divine omnipotence, and of Kantian moral philosophy.[12]

Nietzsche was, I think, right on the button when he offered his diagnosis. What Santayana called 'supernaturalism', the confusion of ideals and power, is all that lies behind the Kantian claim that it is not only nicer, but more rational, to include strangers within our moral community than to exclude them from it. If we agree with Nietzsche and Santayana on this point, however, we do not thereby acquire any reason to turn our backs on the Enlightenment project, as Nietzsche did. Nor do we acquire any reason to be sardonically pessimistic about the chances of this project, in the manner of admirers of Nietzsche like Santayana, Ortega, Heidegger, Strauss and Foucault.

For even though Nietzsche was absolutely right to see Kant's insistence on unconditionality as an expression of resentment, he was absolutely wrong to treat Christianity, and the age of the democratic revolutions, as signs of human degeneration. He and Kant, alas, shared something with each other which neither shared with Harriet Beecher Stowe – something which Iris Murdoch has called 'dryness' and which Jacques Derrida has called 'phallogocentrism'. The common element in the thought of both men was a desire for purity. This sort of purity consists in being not only autonomous, in command of oneself, but also in having the kind of self-conscious self-sufficiency which Sartre describes as the perfect synthesis of the in-itself and the for-itself. This synthesis could only be attained, Sartre pointed out, if one could rid oneself of everything sticky, slimy, wet, sentimental and womanish.

Although this desire for virile purity links Plato to Kant, the desire to bring as many different kinds of people as possible into a cosmopolis links Kant to Stowe. Kant is, in the history of moral thinking, a transitional stage between the hopeless attempt to convict Thrasymachus of irrationality and the hopeful attempt to see every new featherless biped who comes along as one of us. Kant's mistake was to think that the only way to have a modest, damped-down, non-fanatical version of Christian brotherhood after letting go of the Christian faith was to revive the themes of pre-Christian philosophical thought. He wanted to make knowledge of a core self do what can be done only by the continual refreshment and re-creation of the self, through interaction with selves as unlike itself as possible.

Kant performed the sort of awkward balancing act required in transitional periods. His project mediated between a dying rationalist tradition and a vision of a new, democratic world, the world of what Rabossi calls 'the human rights phenomenon'. With the advent of this phenomenon, Kant's balancing act has become outmoded and irrelevant. We are now in a good position to put aside the last vestiges of the ideas that human beings are distinguished by the capacity to know rather than by the capacities for friendship and intermarriage, distinguished by rigorous rationality rather than by flexible sentimentality. If we do so, we shall have dropped the idea that assured knowledge of a truth about what we have in common is a prerequisite for moral education, as well as the idea of a specifically moral motivation. If we do all these things, we shall see Kant's *Foundations of the Metaphysics of Morals* as a placeholder for *Uncle Tom's Cabin* – a concession to the expectations of an intellectual epoch in which the quest for quasi-scientific knowledge seemed the only possible response to religious exclusionism.[13]

Unfortunately, many philosophers, especially in the English-speaking world, are still trying to hold on to the Platonic insistence that the principal duty of human beings is to *know*. That insistence was the lifeline to which

Kant and Hegel thought we had to cling.[14] Just as German philosophers in the period between Kant and Hegel saw themselves as saving 'reason' from Hume, many English-speaking philosophers now see themselves saving reason from Derrida. But with the wisdom of hindsight, and with Baier's help, we have learned to read Hume not as a dangerously frivolous iconoclast but as the wettest, most flexible, least phallogocentric thinker of the Enlightenment. Someday, I suspect, our descendants may wish that Derrida's contemporaries had been able to read him not as a frivolous iconoclast, but rather as a sentimental educator, another of 'the women's moral philosophers'.[15]

If one follows Baier's advice one will not see it as the moral educator's task to answer the rational egotist's question 'Why should I be moral?' but rather to answer the much more frequently posed question 'Why should I care about a stranger, a person who is no kin to me, a person whose habits I find disgusting?'. The traditional answer to the latter question is 'Because kinship and custom are morally irrelevant, irrelevant to the obligations imposed by the recognition of membership in the same species'. This has never been very convincing, since it begs the question at issue: whether mere species membership is, in fact, a sufficient surrogate for closer kinship. Furthermore, that answer leaves one wide open to Nietzsche's discomfiting rejoinder: *that* universalistic notion, Nietzsche will sneer, would only have crossed the mind of a slave – or, perhaps, the mind of an intellectual, a priest whose self-esteem and livelihood both depend on getting the rest of us to accept a sacred, unarguable, unchallengeable paradox.

A better sort of answer is the sort of long, sad, sentimental story which begins 'Because this is what it is like to be in her situation – to be far from home, among strangers', or 'Because she might become your daughter-in-law', or 'Because her mother would grieve for her'. Such stories, repeated and varied over the centuries, have induced us, the rich, safe, powerful, people, to tolerate, and even to cherish, powerless people – people whose appearance or habits or beliefs at first seemed an insult to our own moral identity, our sense of the limits of permissible human variation.

To people who, like Plato and Kant, believe in a philosophically ascertainable truth about what it is to be a human being, the good work remains incomplete as long as we have not answered the question 'Yes, but am I under a *moral obligation* to her?'. To people like Hume and Baier, it is a mark of intellectual immaturity to raise that question. But we shall go on asking that question as long as we agree with Plato that it is our ability to know that makes us human.

Plato wrote quite a long time ago, in a time when we intellectuals had to pretend to be successors to the priests, had to pretend to know something rather esoteric. Hume did his best to josh us out of that pretence. Baier, who seems to me both the most original and the most useful of contemporary moral philosophers, is still trying to josh us out of it. I think Baier may eventually succeed, for she has the history of the last two hundred years of moral progress on her side. These two centuries are most easily understood not as a period of deepening understanding of the nature of rationality or of morality, but rather as one in which there occurred an astonishingly rapid progress of sentiments, in which it has become much easier for us to be moved to action by sad and sentimental stories.

This progress has brought us to a moment in human history in which it is plausible for Rabossi to say that the human rights phenomenon is a 'fact of the world'. This phenomenon may be just a blip. But it may mark the beginning of a time in which gang rape brings forth as strong a response when it happens to women as when it happens to men, or when it happens to foreigners as when it happens to people like us.

Notes

1. 'Letter from Bosnia', *New Yorker*, November 23, 1992, 82–95.

2. 'Their griefs are transient. Those numberless afflictions, which render it doubtful whether heaven has given life to us in mercy or in wrath, are less felt, and sooner forgotten with them. In general, their existence appears to participate more of sensation than reflection. To this must be ascribed their disposition to sleep when abstracted from their diversions, and unemployed in labor. An animal whose body is at rest, and who does not reflect must be disposed to sleep of course.' Thomas Jefferson, 'Notes on Virginia', *Writings*, ed. Lipscomb and Bergh (Washington, D.C., 1905), 1, 194.

3. Geertz, 'Thick Description', in his *The Interpretation of Culture* (New York: Basic Books, 1973), 22.

4. Rabossi also says that he does not wish to question 'the idea of a rational foundation of morality'. I am not sure why he does not. Rabossi may perhaps mean that in the past – for example, at the time of Kant – this idea still made a kind of sense, but it makes sense no longer. That, at any rate, is my own view. Kant wrote in a period when the only alternative to religion seemed to be something like science. In such a period, inventing a pseudo-science called 'the system of transcendental philosophy' – setting the stage for the show-stopping climax in which one pulls moral obligation out of a transcendental hat – might plausibly seem the only way of saving morality from the hedonists on one side and the priests on the other.

5. The present state of metaethical discussion is admirably summarized in Stephen Darwall, Allan Gibbard and Peter Railton, 'Toward *Fin de Siècle* Ethics: Some Trends', *The Philosophical Review* 101 (1992), 115–89. This comprehensive and judicious article takes for granted that there is a problem about 'vindicating the objectivity of morality' (127), that there is an interesting question as to whether morals is 'cognitive' or 'non-cognitive', that we need to figure out whether we have a 'cognitive capacity' to detect moral properties (148), and that these matters can be dealt with ahistorically.

When these authors consider historicist writers such as Alasdair MacIntyre and Bernard Williams, they conclude that they are '(meta) *théoriciens malgré eux*' who share the authors' own 'desire to understand morality, its preconditions and its prospects' (183). They make little effort to come to terms with suggestions that there may be no ahistorical entity called 'morality' to be understood. The final paragraph of the paper does suggest that it might be helpful if moral philosophers knew more anthropology, or psychology, or history. But the penultimate paragraph makes clear that, with or without such assists, 'contemporary metaethics moves ahead, and positions gain in complexity and sophistication'. It is instructive, I think, to compare this article with Annette Baier's 'Some Thoughts On How We Moral Philosophers Live Now', *The Monist* 67 (1984), 490. Baier suggests that moral philosophers should 'at least occasionally, like Socrates, consider why the rest of society should not merely tolerate but subsidize our activity'. She goes on to ask, 'Is the large proportional increase of professional philosophers and moral philosophers a good thing, morally speaking? Even if it scarcely amounts to a plague of gadflies, it may amount to a nuisance of owls.'

The kind of metaphilosophical and historical self-consciousness and self-doubt displayed by Baier seems to me badly needed, but it is conspicuously absent in *Philosophy in Review* (the centennial issue of *The Philosophical Review* in which 'Toward *Fin de Siècle* Ethics' appears). The contributors to this issue are convinced that the increasing sophistication of a philosophical subdiscipline is enough to demonstrate its social utility, and are entirely unimpressed by murmurs of 'decadent scholasticism'.

6. Fichte's *Vocation of Man* is a useful reminder of the need that was felt, circa 1800, for a cognitive discipline called philosophy that would rescue utopian hope from natural science. It is hard to think of an analogous book written in reaction to Darwin. Those who couldn't stand what Darwin was saying tended to go straight back past the Enlightenment to traditional religious faith. The unsubtle, unphilosophical opposition, in nineteenth century Britain and France, between science and faith suggests that most intellectuals had become unable to believe that philosophy might produce some sort of superknowledge, knowledge that might trump the results of physical and biological inquiry.

7. Some contemporary intellectuals, especially in France and Germany, take it as obvious that the Holocaust made it clear that the hopes for human freedom which arose in the nineteenth century are obsolete – that at the end of the twentieth century we postmodernists know that the Enlightenment project is doomed. But even these intellectuals, in their less preachy and sententious moments, do their best to further that project. So they should, for nobody has come up with a better one. It does not diminish the memory of the Holocaust to say that our response to it should not be a claim to have gained a new understanding of human nature or of human history, but rather a willingness to pick ourselves up and try again.

8. Nietzsche was right to remind us that 'these same men who, amongst themselves, are so strictly constrained by custom, worship, ritual gratitude and by mutual surveillance and jealousy, who are so resourceful in consideration, tenderness, loyalty, pride and friendship, when once they step outside their circle become little better than uncaged beasts of prey.' *The Genealogy of Morals*, trans. Golffing (Garden City, N.Y.: Doubleday, 1956), 174.

9. Colin McGinn, *Moral Literacy: or, How to Do the Right Thing* (London: Duckworth, 1992), 16.

10. Baier, 'Hume, the Women's Moral Theorist?', in Eva Kittay and Diana Meyers, eds., *Women and Moral Theory* (Totowa, N.J.: Rowman and Littlefield, 1987), 40.

11. Baier's book on Hume is entitled *A Progress of Sentiments: Reflections on Hume's Treatise* (Cambridge, Mass.: Harvard University Press, 1991). Baier's view of the inadequacy of most attempts by contemporary moral philosophers to break with Kant comes out most clearly when she characterizes Allan Gibbard (in his book *Wise Choices, Apt Feelings*) as focusing 'on the feelings that a patriarchal religion has bequeathed to us', and says that 'Hume would judge Gibbard to be, as a moral philosopher, basically a divine disguised as a fellow expressivist' (312).

12. Nietzsche's diagnosis is reinforced by Elizabeth Anscombe's famous argument that atheists are not entitled to the term 'moral obligation'.

13. See Jane Tompkins, *Sensational Designs: The Cultural Work of American Fiction, 1790–1860* (New York: Oxford University Press, 1985), for a treatment of the sentimental novel that chimes with the point I am trying to make here. In her chapter on Stowe, Tompkins says that she is asking the reader 'to set aside some familiar categories for evaluating fiction – stylistic intricacy, psychological subtlety, epistemological complexity – and to see the sentimental novel not as an artifice of eternity answerable to certain formal criteria and to certain psychological and philosophical concerns, but as a political enterprise, halfway between sermon and social theory, that both codifies and attempts to mold the values of its time' (126).

The contrast that Tompkins draws between authors like Stowe and 'male authors such as Thoreau, Whitman and Melville, who are celebrated as models of intellectual daring and honesty' (124), parallels the contrast I tried to draw between public utility and private perfection in my *Contingency, Irony and Solidarity* (Cambridge, England: Cambridge University Press, 1989). I see *Uncle Tom's Cabin* and *Moby Dick* as equally brilliant achievements, achievements that we should not attempt to rank hierarchically, because they serve such different purposes. Arguing about which is the better novel is like arguing about which is the superior philosophical treatise: Mill's *On Liberty* or Kierkegaard's *Philosophical Fragments*.

14. Technically, of course, Kant denied knowledge in order to make room for moral faith. But what is transcendental moral philosophy if not the assurance that the noncognitive imperative delivered via the common moral consciousness shows the existence of a 'fact of reason' – a fact about what it is to be a human being, a rational agent, a being that is something more than a bundle of spatio-temporal determinations? Kant was never able to explain how transcendental knowledge could be knowledge, but he was never able to give up the attempt to claim such knowledge.

On the German project of defending reason against Hume, see Fred Beiser, *The Fate of Reason: German Philosophy from Kant to Fichte* (Cambridge, Mass.: Harvard University Press, 1987).

15. I have discussed the relation between Derrida and feminism in 'Deconstruction, Ideology and Feminism: A Pragmatist View', in *Hypatia*, and also in my reply to Alexander Nehamas in *Lire Rorty* (Paris: Éclat, 1992). Richard Bernstein is, I think, basically right in reading Derrida as a moralist, even though Thomas McCarthy is also right in saying that 'deconstruction' is of no political use.

Reproduced with permission from Richard Rorty, 'Human Rights, Rationality and Sentimentality', in Stephen Shute and Susan Hurley, eds., *On Human Rights* (New York: Basic Books, 1993).

5

Law, Solidarity and the Tasks of Philosophy

Peter Dews

I

Faktizität und Geltung marks a major development in Habermas's thinking in a number of respects, not least – of course – in his conception of the status and social function of law itself. In *The Theory of Communicative Action* Habermas had highlighted a 'paradoxical structure' of the advancing jurid-ification of the social world, whereby the application of legal norms both makes possible the dismantling of inherited, authoritarian power relations, but also produces an effect of 'de-worlding', by disrupting the delicate fabric of lifeworld communication, and the social identities which this sustains.[1] In *Faktizität und Geltung*, however, Habermas reaches the conclusion that this paradox is not inevitable. For he contends that when all citizens, including oppressed and marginalized groups, can participate equally in the shaping of law, bringing forth their *own* interpretations of their needs, they are able to determine for themselves the appropriate point of equilibrium between a formal and a material interpretation of law. They can strike an appropriate balance between the paternalistic restriction of freedom which social-welfare legislation often brings with it, and the limitation of freedom which results from the application of the same legal rule to materially different cases.[2]

It becomes clear on closer inspection, however, that the dilemma which Habermas describes in *Faktizität und Geltung*, one which results from the 'ambivalence of the guaranteeing and withdrawal of freedom',[3] is no longer precisely the same as that explored in *The Theory of Communicative Action*. For in the earlier book the negative side of juridification was not revealed merely by the restrictions on individuals' freedom of choice, through regulations such as those governing the workplace, living conditions, or intrafamilial rela-tions, or even through the imposition of an objectifying form of control on citizens, who are treated as cases to be legally processed. Rather it also involved a 'disintegration' of those life contexts which are intrinsically dependent on social integration, obliging individuals to take up the depersonalizing and instrumentalizing attitude of juridical subjects towards each other.[4] Furthermore, this disruption was not simply the result of the fact that the juridical reshaping of ever more social domains is driven by the aim of opening them up to the imperatives of profit and administrative manipulation. Habermas also stressed that the legal medium was simply 'dysfunctional' for 'domains of life which, from a functional viewpoint, are necessarily dependent on a social integration via values, norms, and processes of reaching understanding'.[5]

Of course, Habermas emphasizes throughout *Faktizität und Geltung* that neither a productive market economy nor an effective public administration are sufficient to hold together a complex modern society: 'The resources which primarily require protective handling are an exhausted natural environment and a social solidarity which is in the process of disintegrating.'[6] However, Habermas will not allow that the continual extension of the legal medium might itself play a role in the aetiology of the second of these problems. It is indeed central to Habermas's perspective on law that the function of law in modern society is to expand, albeit in a controlled and ultimately consensual way, the scope for individual instrumental action. But he maintains that the development of legal regulation must be seen as a *response* to the erosion of traditional *Sittlichkeit*, and not as a causal factor in its decay. It is modern societies, and in particular the autonomous dynamic of their economies, which requires an ever increasing number of 'socio-structurally indispensable strategic interactions',[7] giving rise to the need for a form of regulation of such interactions which can be understood as ultimately grounded in consensus, without depending directly on the solidarity or discursively attained agreement of participants.

However, there is a wide range of evidence which suggests that processes of juridification do indeed weaken a solidaristic sense of responsibility. For example, in an essay on the problems of fostering self-limitation strategies, Claus Offe cites the case of legally backed pollution controls, which may – counterproductively – encourage the view that everything which is not explicitly forbidden is allowed. Indeed, Offe suggests, individuals and organizations may come to assume a 'right to pollute' below the technically established threshold, or even to include the possibility of legal sanctions itself in the calculation of risks and benefits.[8] In *The Theory of Communicative Action* Habermas himself cites a range of evidence suggesting that juridical intervention in areas such as welfare, intrafamilial relations and the school system, leads to counterproductive consequences. He argues, for example, that 'The protection of pupils' and parents' rights against educational measures (such as promotion or non-promotion, examinations and tests, and so forth) or from acts of the school or the department of education that restrict basic rights (disciplinary penalties), is gained at the cost of a judicialization and bureaucratization that penetrates deep into the teaching and learning process. For one thing, responsibility for problems of educational policy and school law overburdens government agencies, just as responsibility for the child's welfare overburdens the wardship courts. For another, the medium of law comes into collision with the form of educational activity. Socialization through the school is fragmented into a mosaic of legally contestable administrative acts.'[9]

One of the reasons why Habermas, just over a decade later, no longer takes this problem so seriously, may perhaps be found in his current conception of the relation between justice and solidarity. In an essay on Lawrence Kohlberg, Habermas has suggested that, because morality is concerned with the vulnerability of individuals, it must also entail a concern for the communities to which they belong, since 'the integrity of individuals cannot be preserved without the integrity of their common lifeworld, which makes possible shared, interpersonal connections and relationships'.[10] From this perspective, justice and solidarity are the two coequal dimensions of a postconventional morality, emerging from the same fundamental form of consciousness. Accordingly, Habermas also suggests that 'every demand for universalization would remain powerless if an awareness of unrenounceable solidarity, the certainty of belonging together in a common life context did not also spring from the consciousness of belonging to an ideal community of communication.'[11]

This account of the relation between justice and solidarity seems far too harmonistic, however. For it could be argued that, far from *springing* from 'consciousness of belonging to an ideal community of communication', solidarity, in the form of relations of trust and concern for the well-being of others with whom we belong in a concrete community, is a precondition for such consciousness to have any effective moral reality. There may be situations where even though, as an individual, I can see what course of action would be in the best interests of everyone, I feel justified in not carrying it out because I have no confidence that others will do the same.

In his impressive study *Autonomie und Anerkennung*, Andreas Wildt has explored this problem in the course of a reconstruction of Hegel's critique of Kant's moral philosophy. The core of Hegel's critique, according to Wildt, is not – as is often supposed – that the validity of moral principles must be relativized in some historicist sense, but rather that there can be situations of 'hopelessly destroyed *Sittlichkeit*' where it is no longer *reasonable* to expect individuals to behave morally. In order to accomodate this possibility, Wildt suggests, we need to distinguish between what is *morally* right and what is *practically* right. We can then acknowledge that there may be circumstances 'in which it is no longer plausible to adopt a moral standpoint, and thus in which the knowledge that one is morally obliged to do something is no longer a sufficient reason so to act'.[12] By contrast, Kant's assumption that moral rightness is unconditional 'categorical' rightness presupposes an over-individualistic concept of autonomy which misleadingly abstracts from the concrete context of motivation.[13]

Interestingly, in *Faktizität und Geltung* this account of the breakdown of moral motivation is part of Habermas's explanation for the emergence and extension of modern law. He stresses that one of the functions of law is to relieve the excessive burden which modernity places on moral consciousness, and which has three important aspects. Firstly, the complexity of the situations to be morally assessed often overstretches the cognitive powers of the individual; secondly, the organizational resources required to fulfil certain duties are beyond the capacities of the individual; and – most importantly for our purposes – the abstraction of postconventional morality from concrete forms of life weakens its motivational force, as does the breakdown of expectations that others will follow the same moral norm. But significantly, Habermas does not seem to consider this breakdown of the ethical mediation of morality as in any sense a socially pathological condition. There are, I would suggest, two contradictory reasons for this. On the one hand, Habermas misleadingly equates acceptance by individuals of the 'non-recoverable' (i.e. morally unenforceable) obligations of trust, benevolence and concern with the subsistence of an intact traditional *Sittlichkeit*.[14] From such a perspective, modern moral consciousness will inevitably suffer from an intrinsic lack of motivational force. As Habermas puts it: 'every post-traditional morality requires a distanciation from the self-evidence of unproblematically habitual life-forms. Moral insights which are disconnected from the concrete *Sittlichkeit* of everyday life no longer automatically have the motivating force which allows judgements to become practically effective.'[15] Yet on the other hand, as we have just seen, Habermas also implies that a commitment to the common good – presumably in a degree sufficient to sustain the moral authority of law as a form of collective self-regulation, even when law supplants *individual* moral consciousness – is built into the idealizing play of intersubjective role-taking which he considers essential to the normative infrastructure of communication in general.

   If one combines these two – apparently incompatible – assumptions, then the transfer of moral responsibilities to the sphere of legal regulation will appear unproblematic. Habermas speaks of an 'interlacing' of law and morality in modern society: 'This comes about through the fact that in constitutional states the means of positive law are employed to distribute burdens of argument and to institutionalize forms of justification which are open for moral argumentation.'[16] Presumably, on this account, the 'solidarity' which is the complement of justice will also be injected into the sphere of law, and indeed, at the beginning of *Faktizität und Geltung*, Habermas writes of solidarity being 'preserved' in 'legal structures'.[17] Yet if the weakness of moral consciousness itself in part derives from a deficiency in forms of collective trust and concern which cannot be legally enforced or required, then the transfer from morality to law will do nothing to address this problem – and indeed, as suggested above, may even aggravate it, perhaps to the extent of triggering a degenerative spiral.

   Habermas does stress, throughout *Faktizität und Geltung*, that the good design of procedures for the making and implementation of law in effect only solves half the problem: 'The rational quality of political legislation depends not only on how elected majorities and protected minorities within parliament operate. It also depends on the level of participation and education, on the level of information and the sharpness of articulation of contested issues, in short on the discursive character of the non-institutionalized formation of opinion in the political public sphere.'[18] In this sense he shares those anxieties that, in the absence of any vivid public commitment to democratic participation, the *Rechtstaat* may become an oppressively hollow shell, which – as Charles Taylor has recently reminded us – are at least as old as De Tocqueville.[19] However, Habermas has little to say, from the standpoint of a philosophically informed social theory, about kinds of solidarity which would encourage such participation. He prefers instead to put his trust in the spontaneous potential of civil society and social movements to respond to the dangers posed by the autonomous dynamic of social systems.[20]

This lack of explicit discussion of the problem of solidarity in *Faktizität und Geltung* becomes more curious when one observes that sensitivity to the 'structural dilemma' which Habermas identified in *The Theory of Communicative Action*, in the context of his discussion of juridification, has not entirely disappeared from his current work. If anything, this dilemma has been identified at a more general level, in the form of an 'ambiguous process of individualization' which Habermas takes to be characteristic of contemporary society. Formerly, as we have seen, Habermas had tended to assume that modern society generated more or less spontaneously the forms of consciousness which could underpin and motivate a universalistic morality.[21] Now, however, influenced by the work of Ulrich Beck, he acknowledges the negative aspect of individualization, namely the process of 'singularization' in which the individual increasingly becomes an isolated rational decision-making unit, understanding him- or herself objectivistically as consumer, taxpayer, voter and so on, engaged in interaction with a range of social systems.[22] In the light of this more pessimistic account of the consequences of modernization, Habermas's concept of the lifeworld has lost some of its originally protective and defensive colouring. For part of the answer to the problem of singularization, Habermas suggests, is that individuals must learn 'to create socially integrated life-forms themselves'.[23] Yet, in his discussions of this issue, Habermas has little to say about the conditions under which such life-forms could be achieved, other than to suggest that individuals must 'recognize each other as autonomous subjects capable of action'.[24] But although this may be a necessary, it is certainly not a sufficient condition for the creation and sustaining of new, non-regressive but solidaristic forms of life, since it omits any consideration of the need for a common ethical orientation which is implied by Habermas's own account of solidarity as grounded in the awareness of sharing a form of life.

II

The theory of recognition developed by Axel Honneth in his recent book *The Struggle for Recognition* can, in one sense, be seen as an attempt to deal with problems of normativity and identity which Habermas's current emphasis on law leaves unaddressed. Recovering and developing a tripartite schema which he finds both in Hegel and in George Herbert Mead, Honneth argues that it is possible to distinguish three qualitatively distinct forms of recognition which must all be in play if the individual is to acquire the 'external and internal freedom, upon which the process of articulating and realizing individual life-goals without coercion depends'.[25] The first form of recognition, which Honneth refers to as 'love', is initially experienced in the balance of separation and fusion which characterizes the relationship between the small child and its primary carer. Honneth contends that the fundamental self-confidence which this 'symbiosis refracted by recognition' provides functions as the basis for the development of more complex social relationships: 'this fundamental level of emotional confidence – not only in experience of needs and feelings, but also in their expression – . . . constitutes the psychological pre-condition for the development of all further attitudes of self-respect.'[26]

By contrast with the affect-laden relation of love, Honneth interprets modern law as involving 'an achievement of purely cognitive understanding' in which individuals are acknowledged as autonomous and morally responsible subjects, a recognition which gives rise to the basic feeling of self-respect.[27] However, perhaps the most innovative aspect of Honneth's study is to be found in his discussion of the third form of recognition, 'solidarity'. For here Honneth emphasizes that the preconditions for the individual's self-understanding as an autonomous and individuated being, and for the capacity to identify with his or her own aims and wishes, include not just the recognition of all social members as of equal dignity in the eyes of the law, but also an appreciation of the specific concrete contribution of individuals to the general well-being of society: 'persons can feel themselves to be "valuable" only when they know themselves to be recognized for the achievements which they precisely do not share in an undifferentiated manner with others.'[28] However, 'esteem' in this sense, as the third form of recognition, can only become a reality if there is 'a social medium . . . able to express the characteristic differences among human subjects in a general – that is, an intersubjectively binding – way. This task of mediation is performed, at the societal level, by a symbolically articulated – yet always open and porous – framework of orientation, in which those ethical values and goals are formulated that, taken together, comprise the cultural self-understanding of a society.'[29]

The difference between Honneth's perspective and that of Habermas emerges clearly if one considers the latter's discussion of contemporary feminist critiques of welfarist legal intervention in *Faktizität und Geltung*.[30] For what is at issue here is not simply whether such intervention restricts the freedom of women, but rather the fact that it treats them as anomalies, and does not reflect an appropriate, non-androcentric valuing of their gender-specific contributions to society. Habermas's solution to this problem is that women, like other groups, should constitute discussion forums within the general space of the public sphere which could articulate their specific feelings, needs and aspirations, and feed them into the formal lawmaking process. From Honneth's perspective, however, this in itself would be insufficient to compensate for a sense of lack of worth, if not accompanied by a transformation in the values which organize the distribution of social esteem. Furthermore, as is well known, in the case of large discrepancies between legal recognition and social value, the effectiveness of law can be seriously undermined.

Such examples seem to confirm Honneth's advocacy of the need for what he terms a 'post-traditional *Sittlichkeit*', which would provide individuals with a sense of worth through acknowledgement of their concrete contributions to the general social welfare. However, Honneth does not believe that a philosophically informed social theory can say anything concrete about the character of such a *Sittlichkeit*, apart from stipulating that it must integrate all three levels of recognition, and be compatible with modern notions of juridical equality.[31] Yet at this point an important asymmetry between the practical function of the philosophical explication of the 'moral point of view', which Habermas's discourse of ethics undertakes, and that of the philosophical definition of the *form* of a functioning 'post-traditional *Sittlichkeit*' comes to light. For although, in demonstrating the possibility of the moral point of view, one can defuse moral scepticism, and to this extent produce a practical effect without advocating any specific moral perspective, it is not possible in the same way to encourage a general social commitment to fostering solidarity, merely by providing a philosophical analysis of *Sittlichkeit*. For no-one wonders whether social solidarity is *possible* – merely what expressions of it, if any, are *desirable*. In concluding *The Struggle for Recognition* Honneth suggests that a future 'post-traditional solidarity' could be organized around a variety of value schemes, from 'political republicanism' or an 'ecologically based asceticism' to a 'collective existentialism'. But, in tune with a certain Marxist tradition of scepticism about moral *desiderata*, he hands over the future predominance of one of these schemes to the outcome of social struggles.[32]

Yet even if Honneth has succeeded in demonstrating that human integrity and well-being presuppose a society and culture which incorporate his three forms of recognition, his agnosticism may well be self-defeating if it requires the philosopher simply to stand back and observe while a variety of socio-ethical conceptions clash with one another intellectually and politically. To be effective, such a demonstration must surely also be accompanied by other forms of philosophical exploration and argument, intended to discover how well – and to what extent – fundamental human concerns and aspirations are articulated by various value schemes, and whether such schemes, or elements of them, can be combined or reconciled with others, which foreground different dimensions of human existence.

This point naturally raises the question of why Honneth strives to restrict his description of *Sittlichkeit* to a 'formal' level. The obvious answer is that he wishes to avoid the imputation that culturally specific values and assumptions have implicitly shaped his general account of the good (social) life, thereby vitiating its universality. But this answer raises two separate sets of difficulties. On the one hand, it seems very unlikely that the material which Honneth uses to substantiate his argument – for example studies of child development drawn from the object-relations tradition in psychoanalysis – has not itself been shaped by culturally specific presuppositions. Honneth tries to avoid this problem by stressing the *empirical* dimension of the enquiries he draws on – indeed, he describes his method, in a somewhat puzzling phrase, as an 'empirically controlled phenomenology'.[33] But this description surely begs the question. For as the history of the social sciences, with its range of competing paradigms, amply demonstrates, the fact that the accounts of recognition on which Honneth relies can find empirical support does nothing to overcome their potential relativity. In his sense, even the supposedly 'formal' concept of *Sittlichkeit* which Honneth wants to provide runs a high risk of resting on material presuppositions, and therefore being *ab initio* non-neutral between competing conceptions of the good (social) life.

On the other hand, even if one accepts, as seems only fair, that Honneth's account of the 'good life' achieves a high level of generality, albeit not pure formality, the range of contents which it can accommodate is still severely restricted by the key concepts around which it is organized. Honneth's three forms of recognition are described as preconditions of autonomy and self-realization, or what Honneth calls the 'unforced articulation and realisation of individual lifegoals'. Yet one can easily imagine other positions, even within the spectrum of contemporary ethics, such as those of Charles Taylor or Emmanuel Lévinas, in which the subordination of individual life-goals to 'the Other who dominates me in his transcendence', in Lévinas's phrase, or the choosing of goals which respond to the claims which an ultimate, divine source of goodness makes upon me, claims which may thwart my personal aspirations, might be considered more important then self-realization understood in terms of individual fulfilment.[34]

Thus, once the deceptive methodological patina is stripped away, it becomes clear that Honneth's work takes a specific ethical perspective on human subjects and their integrity and well-being, and argues this through by drawing both on philosophical reflection and empirical forms of enquiry. This is not to say that the resulting conception is arbitrary, of course – merely that its formality can only be a matter of degree. Accordingly, there seems to be no reason of principle why the claims could not be made even more specific, in the course of an attempt to assess and render compatible insights drawn from a variety of ethical and political traditions and orientations. Naturally, social-scientific, psychoanalytic and other forms of evidence would play a major role in such explorations – there could be no question of a purely philosophical 'deduction' of a picture of the good life. Nevertheless, the question of the ethical texture of the society which we inhabit, and should aspire to inhabit, could then once more become an explicit object of philosophical reflection, in a way which has fallen into disrepute in the Critical Theory tradition ever since Adorno's *Minima Moralia*. The counter-argument that the answer to such a question will always be historically relative does not seem to me to be decisive. For one can fully admit this relativity, while nevertheless insisting that it cannot be total, and that the answer should therefore be informed by an awareness of the constant, fundamental features of human existence.

III

It is interesting to note, in this context, that Habermas does not deprive philosophy of any capacity whatsoever to engage with questions of the structure and integrity of forms of life. On the contrary, his current metaphilosophy distinguishes emphatically between two fundamental functions of philosophy, which he describes as those of 'stand-in' and 'interpreter'. As stand-in, philosophy holds open the space for, and acts as a collaborator with, reconstructive theories in the human sciences, which spell out the implicit knowledge mobilized by certain very general human competencies, and thereby helps to provide the underpinning for universalistic theories of morality and law. In its interpretive function, however, philosophy explores, and may help to correct, the reifications which ensue from the excessive predominance of one rationality complex within the lifeworld, and helps to bring the cognitive and moral resources developed within the institutionally specialized rationality spheres back into its domain – the only place where they can be put democratically to work.[35] According to Habermas, philosophy, in this interpretive role, is a culturally specific activity – it can only help to illuminate a determinate lifeworld, a particular totality of background assumptions, but cannot offer an account of the totality of the world as a whole, the 'object' of traditional metaphysics. As a consequence, philosophy in its role as interpreter is also debarred from producing qualitative rankings of different cultural totalities.

However, a paradox seems to result from this philosophical division of labour between reconstructive and interpretive tasks. On the one hand, Habermas attributes the cognitive progress of modernity to the differentiation of the three value spheres of 'truth', 'rightness' and 'authenticity'. It is only when cognitive claims, for example, can be filtered out from the symbolic and ethical contexts in which they were formerly embedded, and thematized with the aid of specific, institutionalized forms of enquiry, that the epistemic take-off to modern science becomes possible. Similarly, modern moral universalism implies the existence of a sphere within which questions of justice can be treated by legal and other experts who are skilled in isolating normative issues. At the same time, however, Habermas stresses that – within the lifeworld – the three dimensions of validity continue to be intrinsically interwoven. Yet, if this is the case, a question arises concerning which 'ontology' should be taken to be more fundamental. As Martin Seel has expressed the issue: does the lifeworld exhibit an *illusory integration* of rationality dimensions, which is exposed as such by their modern institutional separation, or is it rather the integration of the lifeworld which reveals the *illusory separation* of rationality dimensions characteristic of specialized cultures of expertise?[36] To put this in another way: the problem with Habermas's conception is that natural-scientific knowledge – to take this example – is *universal* in its scope, but can only be produced through a process of cognitive abstraction on the part of subjects who remain existentially embedded in the lifeworld. Such knowledge therefore remains epistemically *derivative* in relation to this context. On the other hand, the life-world, which appears as existentially more *fundamental* in terms of its formal fusion of validity claims, will always appear as particular and *relative* in terms of the content which these validity-claims articulate.

Habermas, in his reply to Seel, appears not to appreciate the force of this objection. He states that each specialized form of argumentation can indeed, under the pressure of problems encountered, be abandoned in favour of another form, and that judgment will play an important role in deciding if and how this takes place. In this way a coherence and interdependence of the forms of argumentation is acknowledged, while at the same time allowing Habermas to claim that 'every discourse stands, so to speak, directly before God'.[37] Habermas goes on to suggest that this is not surprising, since 'communicative action encounters in the different types of argumentation only its own reflected forms'. But this reply omits to consider that the types of argumentation also have *ontological* implications: that discourse within the cognitive-instrumental rationality complex, for example, implies a world of normatively neutral facts, while discourse in the legal-moral sphere, as Habermas conceives it, presupposes the existence of a source of normativity which is logically independent of any specific states of affairs. This splitting of ontological domains is incompatible with the fusion of truth, rightness and aesthetic appeal which characterizes our experience of, and ways of assessing, the everyday human world which we inhabit. So the question arises: which ontology is more fundamental? Are the fusions of fact and value typical of the lifeworld projections which veil an essentially value-neutral reality or not?

In itself, this may appear to be a relatively minor problem for Habermas's position. But it takes on greater importance as soon as one tries to locate philosophy on one side or the other of the divide between the lifeworld and the specialized spheres. In its role of placeholder, philosophy is located unambiguously by Habermas within the institutions of systematic research. But he also stresses that philosophy would betray its age-old inheritance if it were to understand itself merely as one specialized discipline amongst others. In the form of interpretation, philosophy is both closely allied – and radically opposed – to everyday understanding. It moves within – and is related to – the non-objectifiable totality of a lifeworld, in a manner similar to that of common sense, yet at the same time its critical and reflective stance opposes it to everything which is taken for granted.[38] We already know that philosophy, in its function as stand-in, is expected to meet the same fallibilistic criteria of truth as any other specialized science. But now the difficulty arises that these expectations will require philosophy to satisfy a standard which is itself *abstracted* from the lifeworld whose integrity philosophical *interpretation* seeks to explore and sustain.

Habermas himself appears to sense this problem when he remarks that 'this mediating task [of interpretation] is not devoid of a certain paradox, because in the expert cultures knowledge is always treated under individual aspects of validity, whereas in everyday practice *all* functions of language and aspects of validity encroach on each other, constitute a syndrome.'[39]

Although Habermas does not say so directly, the task of mediation appears 'paradoxical' because the philosophical language which translates specialized validity claims back into the terms of the lifeworld must itself fuse the various dimensions of validity, and in this case will not be susceptible to any straightforward assessment of its 'cognitive' truth. According to Habermas's own account, the philosophical task of interpretation embodies 'the interest of the lifeworld in the totality of functions and structures which are bundled and joined together in communicative action. However it sustains this relation to the totality with a degree of reflexivity which is lacking in the background of the lifeworld, which is only intuitively present.'[40] But there is no obvious reason why the introduction of reflexivity as such need disrupt the interfusion of validity dimensions which this account implies – there are, after all, forms of reflexivity other than the cognitive, such as those which we find in works of art.

Yet despite his awareness of this paradox, Habermas, in some of his recent writings, seeks to maintain that philosophy must now satisfy the specialized criteria of cognitive truth. Against the historical background of the institutionalized separation of validity spheres, he argues that: 'Today, philosophy could establish its own distinct criteria of validity – in the name of genealogy, of recollection (*Andenken*), of elucidating *Existenz*, of philosophical faith, of deconstruction, etc. – only at the price of *falling short* of a level of differentiation and justification that has already been reached, i.e. at the price of surrendering its own credibility (*Glaubwürdigkeit*).'[41] Curiously, it does not occur to Habermas to consider the types of philosophical activity which he lists here as primarily concerned not to *evade* a specialized treatment of truth-claims, but rather to perform the *interpretive* task which he immediately goes on to describe as 'an enlightening promotion of lifeworld processes of achieving self-understanding, processes that are related to totality', and which is necessary because 'the lifeworld must be defended against extreme alienation at the hands of the objectivating, the moralizing, *and* the aestheticizing interventions of expert cultures.'[42] This dismissal of the major modalities of contemporary philosophy becomes even more surprising when one recalls that Habermas himself has stressed the necessarily 'multilingual' character of philosophy in its role of interpretive mediator between science, art and the lifeworld.[43] For what can these multiple languages be, if not precisely the genealogical, hermeneutic, phenomenological and deconstructive currents of twentieth-century philosophy? What other discourses are available which weave between validity-dimensions, reflecting upon the textures of the lifeworld as a whole, and thus simultaneously confirming and disrupting them? To suggest that such discourses are not 'credible' (*glaubwürdig*) seems a clumsy accusation at best, since they clearly do not aspire to provide 'knowledge' in the modern, specialized sense. This is not to suggest, of course, that they need be simply taken at face value.[44]

It would seem that the difficulties in which Habermas finds himself here arise from the fact that, on the one hand, he wishes to restrict the *status* of the claims of philosophy to the validity sphere of cognitive truth. Partly in consequence of this, he then restricts the *scope* of the claims of philosophy as interpretation to specific lifeworlds, since it does not appear that the evaluative claims of philosophy could aspire to the strict, transcultural universality typical of successful truth-claims. Indeed, Habermas currently limits the role of philosophy as interpreter primarily to the task of explicating lifeworld intuitions, and defending the force of these intuitions against the invasive movement of technology and science. This already represents a certain defiant reversal of direction in the traffic between the lifeworld and the differentiated spheres of expertise, compared with Habermas's former account of interpretation as the translation of specialized insights into the de-differentiated context of an 'impoverished' lifeworld.[45] Nevertheless, it still remains implausible in its attempt to constrain the universalistic aspirations of philosophical discourse.

IV

I would now like to retrace the argument so far. We have found that, in *Faktizität und Geltung*, Habermas downplays the possibilities for conflict between law and solidarity, arguing rather that law can be understood as a remote but nonetheless still identifiable distillate of solidarity. Habermas does indeed acknowledge that a sense of collective belonging is a necessary though endangered resource in contemporary society, but he proposes no philosophically informed analysis of this situation. By contrast, Axel Honneth's recent work, particularly *The Struggle for Recognition*, develops a theory of solidarity as a third essential dimension of recognition, alongside love and law. But Honneth seeks – not entirely convincingly – to limit himself to a formal account of the good life, and to avoid assessing the relative merits of different structures of value, and of social projects which entail different distributions of social esteem. In this respect Habermas's notion of philosophy as 'interpreter', although underdeveloped, could be seen as filling a lacuna in Honneth's work. Habermas himself, of course, insists that philosophy in its interpretive role is always bound to the horizons of particular traditions, and cannot make claims, even by negation, about the good life in general. Yet, as we have seen, this attempt to restrain the scope of philosophy leads to inconsistencies.

Fundamentally, what is at stake here is the sense in which Habermas's theory can still be regarded as emancipatory – as expressing a viewpoint which is 'anchored extratheoretically in an empirical interest or moral experience', as Axel Honneth puts it,[46] and in this sense as continuing the tradition of Critical Theory. Habermas himself is clear that an emancipatory process involves the conjunction of moral and ethical reflection: 'If in posing "ethical" questions we would like to get clear about who we are and who we would like to be; and if in posing "moral" questions we would like to know what is equally good for all; then an emancipatory transformation of consciousness combines moral insight with a new ethical self-understanding. We recognize who we are because we have also learned to see ourselves differently in relation to others.'[47] Yet while he affirms that philosophy, by reconstructing the normative presuppositions of communication in general, can provide a justification of morality and democracy, Habermas sees no role for philosophy in ethical discourses, the responsibility for which must – he insists – be left to the participants in discussion themselves.

However, this restriction seems to be dictated by Habermas's assumption that the contribution of philosophy to ethical discussion could only consist in the imperious handing down of a priori insights. He affirms, for example: 'I do not at all correspond to the traditional image of the "philosopher", who explains the world from a single point.'[48] Such a perspective fails to recognize that we can be forced into a philosophical investigation of our deep tacit assumptions and presuppositions precisely by ethical tension and conflict. An outstanding recent example of such investigation would be Charles Taylor's critical analysis of the internal contradictions of our modern 'ethics of authenticity'.[49] Habermas might reply, of course, that there is no reason to describe such investigations as 'philosophical' rather than reflectively 'ethical', but such a reply would in turn highlight the difficulties of his attempt to restrain the claims of evaluative discourses *within* the confines of specific traditions.

In his general account of 'evaluative' discourse in *The Theory of Communicative Action*, where he takes aesthetic critique as his main exemplar, Habermas suggests that the claim raised by such discourse is the relative one of the 'appropriateness of standards'.[50] 'Above all', Habermas argues, 'the type of validity-claims with which cultural values appear do not transcend local bounds in the same way as claims to truth or rightness. Cultural values do not count as universal . . . Values can only be made plausible in the context of a specific life-form. For this reason, the critique of value-standards presupposes a common pre-understanding of those who participate in argumentation, which is not at their disposal, but which simultaneously constitutes and limits the domain of the thematized validity-claims.'[51] As an account of 'aesthetic critique', this description must already be considered tendentious, since such critique undoubtedly strives for universality, even while being aware that this is far harder to achieve than in the case of cognitive claims. Furthermore, in cases where the aesthetic standards at the basis of the discussion are themselves problematized by the fact of disagreement, the specifically *philosophical* issue of the appropriateness of these standards, assessed in the light of what is *essential* to a work of art *as such*, cannot help but be raised. Aesthetic critique, and indeed therapeutic critique in many of its modes, and *a fortiori* philosophical interpretation of the ethical sphere, cannot help but address the question of the relation between our culturally embedded standards and values and the ultimate or true nature of the relevant phenomena.

This point could be made in another way by pointing out that Habermas lacks (and indeed *must* lack, given his current assumptions) a 'philosophy of culture'. Despite the centrality of the concept of tradition to his account of interpretation, and indeed to his theory of 'ethical discourse', Habermas gives no account of what culture itself might be, as a fundamental human phenomenon, other than an ultimately contingent constellation of assumptions and values which varies from one society to another. Yet there exists a powerful tradition of thought, prominently represented in Germany, which has plausibly claimed that the varied forms of human culture can be viewed as a repertoire of responses to certain fundamental dilemmas of human existence and self-awareness.[52] This is the perspective of what Merleau-Ponty termed 'vertical history'[53] – as opposed to the horizontal relativity of cultures. Consideration of this dimension might have allowed Habermas to break through the rather shallow linguisticality of his conception of lifeworld, and to accept that no genuine self-exploration of a culture can ultimately avoid confronting the basic questions of human existence as such.

Of course, it is always easy and tempting to be sceptical about the possibility of transcending our cultural and linguistic confines, in the manner currently exemplified by Richard Rorty, who nonchalantly claims that 'we have no prelinguistic consciousness to which language needs to be adequate, no deep sense of how things are which it is the duty of philosophers to spell out in language'.[54] However, such a position overlooks the fact that the linguistically disclosed lifeworld is not simply *a world*, but also *the* world: there is no neutral space in which it could be situated as one self-enclosed world amongst others, since the only neutrality on offer, that of naturalism or physicalism, cannot accommodate lifeworlds conceptually at all. Thus the assumptions and values which structure the lifeworld are not projections onto the screen on an independent reality, but rather perspectival ways of experiencing the world as *such*. Implicitly Habermas recognizes this, since he is highly critical of Rorty's celebration of a supposedly final victory of metaphors of self-creation over metaphors of discovery, insisting that frames of world-disclosure shift in response to the resistance of what they disclose.[55] Yet by describing the task of interpretation as a rendering explicit of the intuitions of a particular lifeworld, Habermas fails to acknowledge that philosophical thought, in its interpretive dimension, cannot help but weave back and forth in the field of tension between a cuturally sedimented interpretation of the world, and the experience of the world *tout court*.[56] Without this depth dimension, Critical Theory would begin to lose its emancipatory point. The vibrant ethical and political culture which Habermas regards as necessary to complement and sustain the formal structures of the *Rechtsstaat* must surely include – albeit as a modest component – philosophical explorations and assessments of our fundamental values and existential orientations. Interpretation without reconstruction may be morally blind; but reconstruction without interpretation is surely empty. Furthermore, interpretation cannot be merely an elucidation of the internal structure of a lifeworld. It must appraise the claims and assumptions made by our culture in the light of a conception of human existence and its place in the world as such, since such claims and assumptions are bound to be multiple and conflictual, and cannot be evaluated simply by appealing to traditions which are themselves susceptible to multiple interpretations.

The reluctance of Critical Theory to take on this task will not result in ethical discourses and struggles for recognition untainted by the uncomfortably absolutist claims of philosophy, as Habermas often seems to imagine. The current influence of a certain philosophical tradition, running from Nietzsche to Foucault and Derrida, in providing the vocabulary for the politics of identity and difference, the pervasiveness of its terminology as the medium of articulation for the self-understanding of oppressed and marginalized groups, suggests that, if Critical Theory abandons the field, then other philosophical resources will inevitably be drawn upon. Such resources often lack the commitment to a thoroughgoing reflexive elucidation of their own genesis in historical experience which is characteristic of the Critical Theory tradition. They can often be insensitive to their own pre-theoretical roots in contemporary social developments, and for this reason may generate categories whose inappropriateness can harbour moral and political confusions – perhaps even dangers. Thus a conjoining of the defence of a democratic understanding of law, as one of the essential frameworks for emancipation, with the articulation of a philosophical self-understanding which could play a role in fostering new forms of social solidarity, and thus help to impede the *overextension* of law, should not be discouraged out of an exaggerated fear of succumbing to metaphysical foundationalism. For different, though related, reasons both Honneth and Habermas consider themselves to have moved unequivocally onto a 'post-metaphysical' terrain. But, as Herbert Schnädelbach has pertinently enquired: 'Does not the post-metaphysical age truly begin when, inundated by the media and other tranquillizers, we simply no longer ask certain questions?'[57]

Notes

1. Cf. Jürgen Habermas, *The Theory of Communicative Action*, vol. 2 (*Lifeworld and System: A Critique of Functionalist Reason*), trans. Thomas McCarthy, Cambridge: Polity Press 1987, pp. 361–73.

2. Jürgen Habermas, *Faktizität und Geltung: Beiträge zur Diskurstheorie des Rechts und des demokratischen Rechtsstaats*, Frankfurt am Main: Suhrkamp 1992, pp. 502–3.

3. *Faktizität und Geltung*, p. 502.

4. *The Theory of Communicative Action*, vol. 2, pp. 362, 369.

5. Ibid., pp. 372–3 (trans. altered).

6. *Faktizität und Geltung*, p. 536.

7. Ibid., p. 44.

8. Claus Offe, 'Bindings, Shackles, Brakes: On Self-Limitation Strategies', in A. Honneth et al., eds, *Cultural-Political Interventions in the Unfinished Discourse of Modernity*, Cambridge MA and London: MIT Press 1992, p. 86. Cf. Gunther Teubner's argument that juridification finds itself confronted with a 'regulatory trilemma': if legal norms do not transgress the boundaries of social domains which have their own internal steering mechanisms, they will remain ineffectual; however, in overstepping these limits they risk triggering consequences which will have 'disintegrative effects' either on the integrity of law itself, or on the integrity of the relevant social domain. (Gunther Tuebner, 'Verrechtlichung – Begriffe, Merkmale, Grenzen, Auswege', in Friedrich Kübler, ed., *Verrechtlichung von Wirtschaft, Arbeit und sozialer Solidarität*, Baden-Baden: Nomos Verlagsgesellschaft, 1984, esp. pp. 313–25.)

9. *The Theory of Communicative Action*, vol. 2. p. 371 (trans. altered).

10. Jürgen Habermas, 'Gerechtigkeit und Solidarität: Zur Diskussion über "Stufe 6"', in *Erläuterungen zur Diskursethik*, Frankfurt am Main: Suhrkamp 1991, p. 69.

11. Ibid., p. 72.

12. Andreas Wildt, *Autonomie und Anerkennung: Hegels Moralitätskritik im Lichte seiner Fichte-Rezeption*, Stuttgart: Klett-Cotta 1982, p. 153.

13. Ibid., p. 176.

14. Axel Honneth has recently pointed out, in a critique of Ulrich Beck, that 'de-traditionalization' should not be automatically equated with processes of the loss of community. Cf. Axel Honneth, *Disintegration: Burchstücke einer soziologischen Zeitdiagnose*, Frankfurt am Main: Fischer 1994, p. 25.

15. *Faktizität und Geltung*, p. 566.

16. Ibid., p. 568.

17. Ibid., p. 12.

18. Ibid., p. 570.

19. Cf. Charles Taylor, *The Ethics of Authenticity*, Cambridge MA: Harvard University Press 1992, pp. 9–10.

20. Habermas claims that: 'One can at least affirm that, to the extent that a rationalized lifeworld encourages the formation of a public sphere with a strong basis in civil society, then the authority of public attitudes in the context of escalating public controversies is strengthened.' (*Faktizität und Geltung*, p. 462.)

21. On this see Claus Offe, 'Bindings, Shackles, Brakes', pp. 63–5.

22. Cf. Jürgen Habermas, 'Edmund Husserl über Lebenswelt, Philosophie und Wissenschaft', in *Texte und Kontexte*, Frankfurt am Main 1981, p. 48, and Ulrich Beck, *Risk Society*, London: Sage 1992.

23. 'Edmund Husserl über Lebenswelt, Philosophie und Wissenschaft', p. 48.

24. Ibid.

25. Axel Honneth, *The Struggle for Recognition: The Moral Grammar of Social Conflicts*, trans. Joel Anderson, Cambridge: Polity Press 1995, p. 174.

26. Ibid., pp. 106–7.

27. Cf. ibid., pp. 107–11.

28. Ibid., p. 125.

29. Ibid., p. 122 (trans. altered).

30. Cf. *Faktizität und Geltung*, pp. 506–15.

31. Cf. *The Struggle for Recognition*, ch. 9.

32. Cf. ibid., p. 179.

33. Ibid., p. 227.

34. Cf. Emmanuel Lévinas, *Totality and Infinity*, trans. Alphonso Lingis, Pittsburgh PA: Duquesne University Press (no date), and Charles Taylor, *Sources of the Self*, Cambridge MA: Harvard University Press 1989. The Lévinas phrase cited is from p. 215.

35. Cf. Jürgen Habermas, 'Philosophy as Stand-In and Interpreter', in Kenneth Baynes, James Bohman and Thomas McCarthy, eds., *After Philosophy: End or Transformation?*, Cambridge MA: MIT Press 1987.

36. Martin Seel, 'Die Zwei Bedeutungen "kommunikativer" Rationalität. Bemerkungen zu Habermas' Kritik der pluralen Vernunft', in Honneth and Joas, eds., *Kommunikatives Handeln*, Frankfurt am Main: Suhrkamp 1986, p. 55.

37. '. . . denn jeder Diskurs ist sozusagen unmittelbar zu Gott'. (Habermas, 'Entgegnung', in *Kommunikatives Handeln*, p. 343.)

38. 'Edmund Husserl über Lebenswelt, Philosophie und Wissenschaft', p. 34.

39. Jürgen Habermas, 'Exkurs: Transzendenz von innen, Transzendenz ins Diesseits', in *Texte und Kontexte*, Frankfurt am Main: Suhrkamp 1991, p. 38.

40. Jürgen Habermas, *Der philosophiche Diskurs der Moderne*, Frankfurt am Main: Suhrkamp 1985, p. 224.

41. Jürgen Habermas, 'Metaphysik nach Kant', in *Nachmetaphysiches Denken*, Frankfurt am Main: Suhrkamp 1988, p. 26.

42. Ibid.

43. 'Edmund Husserl über Lebenswelt, Philosophie und Wissenschaft', p. 41.

44. An important criterion of assessment for such discourses would be the extent to which they merely 'express' a particular constellation of attitudes, or social mood, as

opposed to also taking a reflective distance on the lifeworld context from which they derive.

45. Cf. 'Philosophy as Placeholder and Interpreter', p. 314.

46. Axel Honneth, 'The Social Dynamics of Disrespect: On the Location of Critical Theory Today', in *Constellations*, vol. 1, no. 2, October 1994, p. 255.

47. Jürgen Habermas, *Vergangenheit als Zukunft*, Zurich: Pendo Verlag 1990, p. 136.

48. *Vergangenheit als Zukunft*, pp. 149–50.

49. Cf. *The Ethics of Authenticity*, passim.

50. Jürgen Habermas, *Theorie des kommunikativen Handelns*, vol. 1, Frankfurt am Main: Suhrkamp 1981, p. 66.

51. Ibid., p. 71.

52. Continuing this tradition, which includes such figures as Dilthey, Weber and Scheler, Dieter Henrich has suggested, for example, that 'there is a continuity between the fundamental constitution of conscious life and the cultural process of humanity which is in no sense identical with socialization, and collective self-preservation and need-satisfaction. Of course it is intertwined with these, but in such a way that it co-determines the forms in which this self-preservation is organized.' (Dieter Henrich, *Fluchtlinien*, Frankfurt am Main: Suhrkamp 1982, p. 92.)

53. Cf. Maurice Merleau-Ponty, 'Working Notes', in *The Visible and the Invisible*, Evanston IL: Northwestern University Press, 1968, p. 186.

54. Richard Rorty, *Contingency, Irony and Solidarity*, Cambridge: CUP 1989, p. 21.

55. Cf. 'Philosophy as Placeholder and Interpreter', pp. 296–309.

56. Habermas writes that: 'Instead of *grounding* the lifeworld in the primal founding of an acting subjectivity or in the event of a world-interpretation which prejudices everything, philosophy can concentrate on the task of reconstructing the background knowledge which is connected with our grammatical intuitions. The goal of such an analysis is less the tracking of hidden foundations than the explication of what we always already know and can do.' ('Edmund Husserl über Lebenswelt, Philosophie und Wissenschaft', p. 41.) However, this account overlooks the fact that the recourse to an absolute subject or to the Heideggerian 'sending of Being' (*Seinsgeschick*) must be seen as attempts, albeit unsatisfactory, to account for the relation between the lifeworld and its source in a way which does not leave 'gramatical intuitions' hanging question-beggingly in the air.

57. Herbert Schnädelbach, 'Metaphysik und Religion heute', in *Zur Rehabilitierung des animal rationale, Vorträge und Abhandlungen 2*, Frankfurt am Main: Suhrkamp 1992, p. 138.

6

Conditions of an Unforced Consensus on Human Rights

Charles Taylor

I

What would it mean to come to a genuine, unforced international consensus on human rights? I suppose it would be something like what Rawls describes in his *Political Liberalism* as an 'overlapping consensus'. That is, different groups, countries, religious communities, civilizations, while holding incompatible fundamental views on theology, metaphysics, human nature, etc., would come to an agreement on certain norms that ought to govern human behaviour. Each would have its own way of justifying this from out of its profound background conception. We would agree on the norms, while disagreeing on why they were the right norms. And we would be content to live in this consensus, undisturbed by the differences of profound underlying belief.

The idea was already expressed in 1949 by Jacques Maritain. 'I am quite certain that my way of justifying belief in the rights of man and the ideal of liberty, equality, fraternity is the only way with a firm foundation in truth. This does not prevent me from being in agreement on these practical convictions with people who are certain that their way of justifying them, entirely different from mine or opposed to mine, . . . , is equally the only way founded upon truth.'[1]

Is this kind of consensus possible? Perhaps because of my optimistic nature, I believe that it is. But we have to confess at the outset that it is not entirely clear around what the consensus would form, and we are only beginning to discern the obstacles we would have to overcome on the way there. I want to talk a little about both these issues here.

First, what would the consensus be on? One might have thought this was obvious: on human rights. That's what our original question was about. But there is right away a first obstacle, which has been very often pointed out. Rights talk is something that has roots in Western culture. There are certain features of this talk which have roots in Western history, and there only. This is not to say that something very like the underlying norms expressed in schedules of rights don't turn up elsewhere. But they are not expressed in this language. We can't assume straight off, without further examination, that a future unforced world consensus could be formulated to the satisfaction of everyone in the language of rights. Maybe yes, maybe no. Or maybe: partially yes, partially no, as we come to discriminate some of the things which have been associated together in the Western package.

This is not to say that we already have some adequate term for whatever universals we think we may discern between different cultures. Jack Donnelly speaks of 'human dignity' as a universal value.[2] Yasuaki Onuma criticizes this term, pointing out that 'dignity' has been itself a favourite term in the same Western philosophical stream that has elaborated human rights. He prefers to speak of the 'pursuit of spiritual as well as material well-being' as the universal.[3] Where 'dignity' might be too precise and culture-bound a term, 'well-being' might be too vague and general. Perhaps we are incapable at this stage of formulating the universal values in play here. Perhaps we shall always be incapable of this. This wouldn't matter, because what we need to formulate for an overlapping consensus is certain norms of conduct. The deep underlying values supporting these will, in the nature of the case, belong to the alternative, mutually incompatible justifications.

I have been distinguishing in the above between norms of conduct and their underlying justification. The Western rights tradition in fact exists at both these levels. On the one hand, it is a legal tradition, legitimating certain kinds of legal moves, and empowering certain kinds of people to make them. We could, and people sometimes do, consider this legal culture as the proper candidate for universalization, arguing that its adoption can be justified in more than one way. Then a legal culture entrenching rights would define the norms around which world consensus would supposedly crystallize.

Now some people already have trouble with this; e.g., Lee Kwan Yew, and those in South Asia who sympathize with him. They see something dangerously individualistic, fragmenting, dissolvent of community, in this Western legal culture. (Of course, they have particularly in mind – or in their sights – the United States.) But in their criticism of Western procedures, they also seem to be attacking the underlying philosophy of the West, which allegedly gives primacy to the individual, where supposedly a 'Confucian' outlook would have a larger place for the community, and the complex web of human relations in which each person stands.

For the Western rights tradition also vehicles certain views on human nature, society and the human good. In other words, it also carries some elements of an underlying justification. It might help the discussion to distinguish these two levels, at least analytically, so that we can develop a more fine-grained picture of what our options are here. Perhaps in fact, the legal culture could 'travel' better, if it could be separated from some of its underlying justifications. Or perhaps the reverse is true, that the underlying picture of human life might look less frightening, if it could find expression in a different legal culture. Or maybe, neither of these simple solutions will work (this is my hunch), but modifications need to be made in both; however, distinguishing the levels still helps, because the modifications are different on each level.

In any case, I think a good place to start the discussion would be to give a rapid portrait of the language of rights which has developed in the West, and of the surrounding notions of human agency and the good. We could then proceed to identify certain centres of disagreement across cultures, and we might then see what if anything could be done to bridge these differences.

II

First, let's get at the peculiarities of the language of rights. As has often been pointed out, there is something rather special here. Many societies have held that it is good to ensure certain immunities or liberties to their members – or sometimes even to outsiders (think of the stringent laws of hospitality that hold in many traditional cultures). Everywhere it is wrong to take human life, at least under certain circumstances and for certain categories of persons. Wrong is the opposite of right, and so this is in some sense in play here.

But a quite different sense of the word is invoked when we start to use the definite or indefinite articles, or to put it in the plural, and speak of 'a right' or 'rights': or when we start to attribute these to persons, and speak of your rights or my rights. This is to introduce what has been called 'subjective rights'. Instead of saying that it is wrong to kill me, we begin to say that I have a right to life. The two formulations are not equivalent in all respects. Because in the latter case the immunity or liberty is considered as it were the property of someone. It is no longer just an element of the law that stands over and between all of us equally. That I have a right to life says more than that you shouldn't kill me. It gives me some control over this immunity. A right is something which in principle I can waive.[4] It is also something which I have a role in enforcing.

Some element of subjective right exists perhaps in all legal systems. The peculiarity of the West was, first, that it played a bigger role in European medieval societies than elsewhere in history, and, second, that it was the basis of the rewriting of Natural Law theory which marked the seventeenth century. The older notion that human society stands under a Law of Nature, whose origin was the Creator, and which was thus beyond human will, was now transposed. The fundamental law was reconceived as consisting of natural rights, attributed to individuals prior to society. At the origin of society stands a Contract, which takes people out of a State of Nature, and puts them under political authority, as a result of an act of consent on their part.

So subjective rights are not only crucial to the Western tradition, because they have been an important part of its jurisprudence since the Middle Ages. Even more significant is the fact that they were projected onto Nature, and formed the basis of a philosophical view of humans and their society, one which greatly privileges individuals' freedom and their right to consent to the arrangements under which they live. This view becomes an important strand in Western democratic theory of the last three centuries.

We can see how the notion of (subjective) right both serves to define certain legal powers, and also provides the master image for a philosophy of human nature, of individuals and their societies. It operates both as legal norm, and as underlying justification.

Moreover, these two levels are not unconnected. The force of the underlying philosophy has brought about a steady promotion of the legal norm in our politico-legal systems; so that it now occupies pride of place in a number of contemporary polities. Charters of rights are now entrenched in the constitutions of a number of countries, and also of the European Union. These are the basis of judicial review, whereby the ordinary legislation of different levels of government can be invalidated on the grounds of conflict with these fundamental rights.

That (subjective) rights thus operate today as trumps is the convergence of two different if intertwined lines of promotion. On the one hand, there is the old conception of the fundamental law of our polity, which the decrees or decisions of the authority of the day cannot override. This played a role in pre-modern European societies, even as it did frequently elsewhere. The entrenchment of Charters means that the language of rights has become a privileged idiom for a good part of this fundamental law. This is one line of advance.

At the same time, European thought also had a place for a Law of Nature, a body of norms with even more fundamental status, because they are universal and hold across all societies. Again, analogous concepts can be found elsewhere. The place of rights in our political discourse today shows that it has also become the favoured idiom for this kind of law. We speak of a Universal Declaration of Human Rights. This is the second line of advance.

The rights we now entrench in charters benefit from both these promotions. These rights occupy the niche which already existed in many legal systems, whereby laws were subject to judicial review. While at the same time, their great force in modern opinion comes from the sense that they are not just features of our legal tradition, that they are not part of what is culturally conditioned, one option among others which human societies can adopt, but fundamental, essential, belonging to human beings as such – in short inviolable.

So the Western discourse of rights involves, on the one hand, a set of legal forms, by which immunities and liberties are inscribed as rights, with certain consequences for the possibility of waiver, and for the ways in which they can be secured; whether these immunities and liberties are among those from time to time granted by duly constituted authority, or among those which are entrenched in fundamental law.

And it involves, on the other hand, a philosophy of the person and of society, attributing great importance to the individual, and making significant matters turn on his or her power of consent.

When people protest against the Western rights model, they seem to have this whole package in their sights. Taking it as a whole it is not simply wrong, of course, because the philosophy is plainly part of what has motivated the great promotion enjoyed by this legal form. Nevertheless, it will help to distinguish them, because we can easily imagine situations in which, for all their interconnections, the package could be untied, and either the forms or the philosophy could be adopted alone, without the other. Of course, this might involve some adjustment in what was borrowed, but this inevitably happens whenever ideas and institutions developed in one area are taken up elsewhere.

It might help to understand a little better just what exactly we might want ultimately to converge onto in the world society of the future, as well as to measure our chances of getting there, if we imagine variations separately on the two levels. This is what I want to do in the following pages.

What I propose to do is to look at a number of places in which there seem to be obvious conflicts between the present language of human rights and one or more important cultures in today's world. The goal will be to try to imagine ways in which the conflict might be resolved, and the essential norms involved in the human rights claim preserved, and this through some modification, either of legal forms or of philosophy.

But here I must straightaway make a confession. No merit attaches to this, because I shall be unable in any case to hide what I now avow, as the argument progresses. I am a philosopher, and not a jurist. Consequently, what I have to say about the possible variation of legal forms will be terse to the point of near-silence, and not very interesting. I make the distinction, because I want to say some things about the conflicts which could perhaps be resolved through some greater understanding of alternative philosophical foundations for human rights. But I want to stake out the category of resolution through innovations in legal forms, because I am sure that it will play an important part in arriving at an eventual world consensus.

III

That being said, I would like to look at four kinds of conflict. The first could perhaps be resolved by legal innovation, and I will briefly discuss this possibility. But it can also be tackled on the philosophical level. The other two involve the basic justification of human rights claims. In developing these, I will have to spell out much further the justificatory basis for Western thinking and practice about rights than I have in the rather sparse remarks above about Natural Rights theory. I shall return to this below.

1. Let us take the kind of objection that I mentioned at the outset, that someone like Lee Kwan Yew might raise about Western rights practice, and its alleged unsuitability for other societies, in particular East Asian ones. The basic notion is that this practice supposes that individuals are the possessors of rights, and encourages them to act in consequence, that is, to go out and aggressively seek to make good their rights. But this has a number of bad consequences. First of all, it focuses people on their rights, that is, what they can

claim from society and others, rather than on their responsibilities, what they owe to the whole community, or to its members. It encourages people to be self-regarding, and leads to an atrophy of the sense of belonging. This in turn leads to a higher degree of social conflict, more and more many-sided, tending ultimately to a war of all against all. Social solidarity weakens, and the threat of violence increases.

This scary scenario seems rather overdrawn to some. But to others it seems to have some elements of truth. Including to people within Western societies, which perhaps might make us doubt that we are on to a difference between civilizations here. In fact, there is a long tradition of thinking in the West, warning against pure rights talk outside of a context where the political community has a strong positive value. This 'communitarian' theorizing has taken on a new urgency today, because of the experience of conflict and alienation and the fraying of solidarity in many Western democracies, notably but not only the US. Does this mean that Lee Kwan Yew's formula might offer a solution to present-day America?

The absurdity of this suggestion brings us back to the genuine differences of culture which exist today. But if we follow through on the logic of the 'communitarian' critique in the West we can perhaps find a framework in which to consider these differences.

One of the key points in the critique of a too exclusive focus on rights is that this neglects the crucial importance of political trust. Dictatorships, as Tocqueville pointed out (in *Democracy in America*), try to destroy trust between citizens. But free societies vitally depend on it. The price of freedom is a strong common commitment to the political formula that binds us, because without the commitment the formula would have to be aggressively enforced, and this threatens freedom. But what will very quickly dissolve the commitment for each and every one of us is the sense that the others no longer share it or are willing to act on it. The common allegiance is nourished on trust.

This goes for a political regime centred on the retrieval of rights as much, perhaps more, as for any other. The condition of our being able to go out and seek to enforce our own rights is that the system within which this is carried out retains the respect and allegiance of everybody. Once rights-retrieval begins to eat into this, once it begins to create a sense of embattled grievance pitting group against group, undermining the sense of common allegiance and solidarity, the whole system of free-wheeling rights-enforcement is in danger.

The issue is not 'individualism' as such. There are many forms of this, and some have grown up together with modern, democratic forms of political allegiance. The danger is any form of either individualism or group identity which undercuts or undermines the trust that we share a common allegiance as citizens of this polity.

I don't want to pursue here a search into the conditions of political trust in Western democracies, at least not for its own sake.[5] But I want to use this requirement as a heuristic tool, in search of a point of consensus on human rights. One way of considering a claim, similar to that of Lee Kwan Yew's, that the Western rights focus doesn't fit certain cultural traditions, would be to ask how certain fundamental liberties and immunities could be guaranteed in the society in question, consistent with the maintenance of political trust. This means, of course, that one will not consider satisfactory any solution which doesn't preserve these liberties and immunities, while at the same time being led to accept whatever modifications in legal form one needs, to generate a sense of common acceptance of the guaranteeing process in the society concerned.

This would mean, in the concrete case of Lee Kwan Yew's Singapore, that his claim in its present form is hardly receivable. There is too much evidence of the stifling of dissent, and of the cramping (to say the least) of the democratic political process, in Singapore. But this kind of claim should lead us to reflect further on how immunities of the kind we seek in human rights declarations can best be preserved in 'Confucian' societies.

Turning back to our, Western societies, we note that judges and the judicial process enjoy in general a great deal of prestige and respect.[6] In some countries, this respect is based on a long tradition, in which some notion of fundamental law played an important part, and hence in which its guardians had a special place. Is there a way of connecting rights-retrieval in other societies to offices and institutions which enjoy the highest moral prestige there?

Leaving the example of 'Confucian' societies, and adverting to another tradition, we note how in Thailand, at certain crucial junctions, the immense moral prestige of the monarchy has been used to confer legitimacy and force on moves to end military violence and repression and return to constitutional rule. This was the case following the student demonstrations in October 1973, as well as during the events of May 1992. In both cases, a military junta responded with violence, only to find its position unsustainable and to be forced to give way to a civilian regime and renewed elections. In both these cases, King Bhumibhol played a critical role.[7]

The king was able to play this role because of elements in the traditions which have contributed to the Thai conception of monarchy, some of which go way back, e.g., that of the king as dharmaraja, in the tradition of Asoka,[8] which sees the ruler as charged with establishing dharma in the world.

It was perhaps crucial to the overthrows of 1973 and 1992 that a king with this kind of status played the part he did. The trouble is that, as things are, the power of the royal office can also be used in other direction; as we can see in 1976, when right-wing groups used the slogan 'Nation, King and Religion' as a rallying cry in order to attack democratic and radical leaders. The movement of reaction culminated in the October 1976 coup which relegated the democratic constitution once again to the waste paper basket.[9]

The issue which arises from all this is perhaps the following: can the immense power to create trust and consensus which resides in the Thai monarchy be in some way stabilized, regularized and channelled in support of constitutional rule, and the defence of certain human rights, such as those concerned with the security of the person? In Weberian terms, could the charisma here be 'routinized' enough to import a stable direction to it, without being lost altogether?

I suspect that there is somewhere a positive answer to this question. But I don't have anything concrete to propose here. I just use this as the basis of some hypothetical conjectures. If a way could be found to draw on this royal charisma, together with the legitimacy enjoyed by certain individuals of proven 'merit', who are invested with a lot of moral authority in the Thai tradition, to enhance support for a democratic order respectful of those immunities and liberties we generally describe as human rights, the fact that it might deviate from the standard Western model of judicial review initiated by individuals should be accorded less importance than the fact that it protects human beings from violence and oppression. We would have in fact achieved convergence on the substance of human rights, in spite of differences in form.

IV

2. But suppose we take the 'communitarian' arguments against Western rights discourse emanating from other societies at another level: not questioning so much the legal forms, but expressing disagreement with the underlying philosophical justification?

My example is again drawn from Thailand. This society has seen in the last century a number of attempts to formulate reformed interpretations of the overwhelmingly majority religion of this society: Theravada Buddhism. Some of these have attempted to find a basis in this Buddhism for democracy and human rights.

One main stream of reform consists of movements which (as they see it) attempt to purify Buddhism, to turn it away from a focus on ritual, on gaining merit, and even worldly success through blessings and acts of piety, and to focus more on (what they see as) the original goal of Enlightenment. The late Phutthathat (Buddhadasa) has been a major figure in this regard. This stream tries to return to what (it sees as) the original core of Buddhist teaching, about the unavoidability of suffering, the illusion of the self and the goal of Nibbana. It attacks what it sees as the 'superstition' of those who seek potent amulets, and the blessings of monks, and the like. It wants to separate the search for enlightenment from the seeking of merit through ritual. And it is very critical of the whole metaphysical structure of belief which has developed in mainstream Buddhism, about heavens, hell, gods and demons, which play a large part in popular belief. It has been described by the Sri Lankan anthropologist, Gananath Obeyesekere, as a 'protestant Buddhism'.[10]

It is this stream which seems to be producing new reflections on Buddhism as a basis for democratic society and practice. This is not to say that all of those concerned Buddhists, monks and lay, involved in democratic activism of one kind or another have been of this persuasion. But it is the reform stream which seems to have produced the concern to develop a Buddhist vision of democratic society. One may see something paradoxical in this, in that this rather austere reformism is espoused by a relatively small élite, rather far removed from the religious outlook of the mass of the people. But the dedication of some members of this élite to democracy, equality and human rights commands respect.

Phutthathat's reformism was the very opposite of a disengaged religion, unconcerned with the world. On the contrary, he and those inspired by him have always stressed that the path to enlightenment is inseparable from that of concern for all creatures, from metta (loving kindness) and karuna (compassion). We can't really be concerned with our own liberation without also seeking that of others, just as any acts of injustice towards them redound to our own continued imprisonment in illusion. Saneh Chamarik quotes the Buddha: 'Monks: Taking care of oneself means as well taking care of others. Taking care of others means as well taking care of oneself.'[11] This view leads to an activist concern for social justice and well-being. Phutthathat spoke of a 'dhammic socialism'. It is a spiritual stance which entails heightened standards of personal commitment and responsibility, of probity and dedication to duty, even of self-sacrifice and dedication to the poor and downtrodden. Following Obeyesekere's analogy, one could say that it is reminiscent in this respect of Max Weber's description of early Calvinism, which propagated a 'this-worldly asceticism',[12] that prompted responsible, disciplined social action.

But this concern is not necessarily democratic. It could also find expression in other modes of social reform action, including those which see the agency of reform as a minority with the right intentions. These modes are, after all, well rooted in Theravada Buddhist history, in particular in the paradigm model of the Emperor Asoka as the ideally just ruler and upholder of dharma. This is, indeed, one of the models on which the Thai monarchical state was based. The dharmaraja is undoubtedly understood as an agency for good, for the welfare of the people, but he is not in any normal sense a democratic agency.[13]

Phutthathat himself was not entirely clear on the issue of democratic agency. There has, however, been a democratic strand in this general movement. Panyanantha made a democratic application of Phutthathat's thought, for instance. And something similar could be said for Photirak and his Santi Asok movement. This has acquired additional political relevance recently, in that the charismatic leader of the Palang Dharma party, Chamlong Srimuang, is a follower of Santi Asok.

Beyond these, there are followers of Phutthathat's reformism who are deeply committed to democracy, such as Sulak Sivaraksa and Saneh Chamarik. They and others in their milieu are highly active in the NGO community. They are concerned with alternative models of development, which would be more ecologically sound, concerned to put limits to growth, critical of 'consumerism', and conducive to social equality. The Buddhist commitment lies behind all these goals. As Sulak explains it, the Buddhist commitment to non-violence entails a non-predatory stance towards the environment; and calls also for the limitation of greed, one of the sources of anger and conflict.[14]

We can see here an agenda of universal well-being. But what specifically pushes to democracy, that is, to ensuring that people take charge of their own lives, rather than simply being the beneficiaries of benevolent rule? Two things seem to come together in this outlook to underpin a strong democratic commitment. The first is the notion, central to Buddhism, that ultimately each individual must take responsibility for his or her own Enlightenment. The second is a new application of the doctrine of non-violence, which is now seen to call for a respect for the autonomy of each person, demanding in effect a minimal use of coercion in human affairs. This carries us far from the politics of imposed order, decreed by the wise minority, which has long been the traditional background to various forms and phases of military rule. It is also evident that this underpinning for democracy also offers a strong support for human rights legislation. And that, indeed, is how it is understood by thinkers like Sulak.[15]

There is an outlook here which converges on a policy of defence of human rights and democratic development, but which is rather different from the standard Western justifications of these. It isn't grounded on a doctrine of the dignity of human beings as something commanding respect. The injunction to respect comes rather as a consequence of the fundamental value of non-violence, which also generates a whole host of other consequences (including the requirement for an ecologically responsible development, and the need to set limits to growth). Human rights don't stand out, as they often do in the West, as a claim on their own, independent from the rest of our moral commitments, even sometimes in potential conflict with these.

Interestingly, this Buddhist conception provides an alternative way of linking together the agenda of human rights and that of democratic development. Whereas in the Western framework, these go together because they are both seen as co-requirements of human dignity, and indeed, as two facets of liberty, a connection of a somewhat different kind is visible among Thai Buddhists of this reform persuasion. Their commitment to people-centred and ecologically sensitive development makes them strong allies of those communities of villagers who are resisting encroachment by the state and big business, fighting to defend their lands and forests. This means that they are heavily into what has been recognized as a crucial part of the agenda of democratization in Thailand – decentralization, and in particular the recovery of local community control over natural resources.[16] They form a significant part of the NGO community committed to this agenda. A rather different route has been travelled to a similar goal.

Other differences stand out. Because of its roots in a certain justice agenda, the politics of establishing rights in the West has often been surrounded with anger, indignation, the imperative to punish historic wrong-doing. From this Buddhist perspective comes a caution against the politics of anger, itself the potential source of new forms of violence.

My aim here is not to judge between these approaches, but to point to these differences as the source of a potentially fruitful exchange within a (hopefully) emerging world consensus on the practice of human rights and democracy.

We can in fact see a convergence here on certain norms of action, however they may be entrenched in law. But what is unfamiliar to the Western observer is the entire philosophical basis, and its appropriate reference points, as well as the rhetorical bases of its appeal. In the West, both democracy and human rights have been furthered by the steady advance of a kind of humanism, which stressed how humans stood out from the rest of the cosmos, had a higher status and dignity than anything else. This has its origins in Christianity, and also certain strands of ancient thought, but the distance is greatly exacerbated by what Weber describes as the disenchantment of the world, the rejection of a view of the cosmos as a meaningful order. The human agent stands out even more starkly from a mechanistic universe. For Pascal, the human being is a mere reed, but of incomparably greater significance than what threatens to crush it, because it is a thinking reed. Kant echoes some of the same reflections in his discussion of the sublime in the third critique, and also defines human dignity in terms of the incomparably greater worth of human beings compared to the rest of the contents of the universe.

The human rights doctrine based on this humanism stresses the incomparable importance of the human agent. It centres everything on him/her, makes his/her freedom and self-control a major value, something to be maximized. Consequently, in the Western mind, the defence of human rights seems indissolubly linked with this exaltation of human agency. It is because humans justifiably command all this respect and attention, at least in comparison to anything else, that their rights must be defended. The Buddhist philosophy that I have been describing starts from a quite different place, the demand of ahimsa, and yet seems to ground many of the sane norms. (Of course, there will also be differences in the norms grounded, which raises its own problems, but for the moment I just want to note the substantial overlap.) The gamut of Western philosophical emotions, the exaltation of human dignity, the emphasis on freedom as the highest value, the drama of age-old wrongs righted in valour, all the things which move us in seeing *Fidelio* well performed, seem out of place in this alternative setting. And so do the models of heroism. The heroes of ahimsa are not forceful revolutionaries, not Cola di Rienzi or Garibaldi. And with the philosophy and the models, a whole rhetoric loses its basis.

This perhaps gives us an idea of what an unforced world consensus on human rights might look like. Agreement on norms, yes; but a profound sense of difference, of unfamiliarity, in the ideals, the notions of human excellence, the rhetorical tropes and reference points by which these norms become objects of deep commitment for us. To the extent that we can only acknowledge agreement with people who share the whole package, and are moved by the same heroes, the consensus will either never come or must be forced.

This is the situation at the outset, in any case, where consensus on some aspect of human rights has just been attained. Later a process can follow of mutual learning, moving towards a 'fusion of horizons' in Gadamer's term, where the moral universe of the other becomes less strange. And out of this will come further borrowings, and the creation of new hybrid forms.

After all, something of this has already occurred with another stream of the philosophy of ahimsa, that of Gandhi. Gandhi's practices of non-violent resistance have been borrowed and adapted in the West, in the American Civil Rights Movement, for example, under Martin Luther King. And beyond that, they have become part of a world repertory of political practices, invoked in Manila in 1988, in Prague in 1989, to name just two examples.

Also worthy of remark is one other facet of this case, which may be generalizable as well. An important part of the Western consciousness of human rights lies in the awareness of an historic achievement. They define norms of respect for human beings, more radical and more exigent than have ever existed in the past. They offer in principle greater freedom, greater security from violence, from arbitrary treatment, from discrimination and oppression than humans have enjoyed at least in most major civilizations in history. In a sense they involve taking the rather exceptional treatment accorded to privileged people in the past, and extending it to everyone. That is why so many of the landmarks of the historical development of rights were in their day instruments of élite privilege, starting with Magna Carta.

Now there is a curious convergence in this respect with the strand of reform Buddhism I have been describing. Here too, there is the awareness that very exigent demands are being made, which go way beyond what the majority of ordinary believers recognize as required practice. Reform Buddhism is practised by an élite, as has been the case with most of its analogues in history. But here, too, in developing a doctrine of democracy and human rights, reform Buddhists are proposing to extend what has hitherto been a minority practice, and entrench it in society universally. Here again there is a consciousness of the universalization of the highest of traditional minority practice.

It's as though, in spite of the difference in philosophy, this universalization of an exigent standard, which human rights practice at its best involves, was recognized as a valid move, and re-created within a different cultural, philosophical and religious world. The hope for a world consensus is that this kind of move will be repeatedly made.

V

This example drawn from Thailand provides one model for what the path to world consensus might look like. A convergence on certain norms from out of very different philosophical and spiritual backgrounds. The consensus at first doesn't need to be based on any deep mutual understanding of these respective backgrounds. Each may seem strange to the other, even though both recognize and value the practical agreement attained. Of course, this is not to say that there is no borrowing involved at all. Plainly, democracy and human rights practices originated somewhere, and are now being creatively recaptured (perhaps in a significantly different variant) elsewhere. But a mutual understanding and appreciation of each other's spiritual basis for signing on the common norms may be close to non-existent.

This, however, is not a satisfactory end-point. Some attempt at deeper understanding must follow, or the gains in agreement will remain fragile. And this for at least two closely connected reasons.

The first is that the agreement is never complete. I adverted to this in a parenthesis a couple of pages back, but couldn't go into it there. We already saw how what we can call the ahimsa basis for rights connects to ecological concerns rather differently from the Western humanist basis; how the place of anger, indignation, righteous condemnation and punishment is quite different in the two outlooks. All this must lead to differences of practice, of the detailed schedule of rights, or at least of the priority ordering among them. Now the demands of a world consensus will often include our squaring these differences in practical contexts, our accommodating, or coming to some compromise version that both sides can live with. These negotiations will be inordinately difficult, unless each side can come to some more fine-grained understanding of what moves the other.

The second reason follows on from the first; is in a sense just another facet of it. The continued coexistence in a broad consensus, which continually generates particular disagreements, which have in turn to be negotiated to renewed consensus, all this is impossible without mutual respect. If the sense is strong on each side that the spiritual basis of the other is ridiculous, false, inferior, unworthy, these attitudes cannot but sap the will to agree of those who hold these views, while engendering anger and resentment among those who are thus depreciated. The only cure for contempt here is understanding. This alone can replace the too-facile depreciatory stories about others with which groups often tend to shore up their own sense of rightness and superiority. Consequently the bare consensus must strive to go on towards a fusion of horizons.

Now in the above discussion I have analytically distinguished consensus from mutual understanding, and imagined that they occur sequentially, as successive phases. This is certainly a schematic oversimplification, but perhaps not totally wrong in the Thai case I was examining. There are, however, other situations in which some degree of mutual understanding is an essential condition of getting to consensus. The two can't simply occur successively, because the path to agreement lies through some degree of sympathetic mutual comprehension.

3. I want to look now at another difference which seems to be of this latter type. But in order to lay it out here, I will have to describe more fully another facet of the Western philosophical background of rights, which can hit a wall of incomprehension once one crosses the boundary to other cultures.

This is the Western concern for equality, in the form of non-discrimination. Existing charters of rights in the Western world are no longer concerned only with ensuring certain liberties and immunities to individuals. To an important degree, they also serve to counter various forms of discrimination. This represents a shift in the centre of gravity of rights talk over the last centuries. One could argue that the central importance of non-discrimination enters American judicial review with the 14th Amendment, in the aftermath of the Civil War. Since then non-discrimination provisions have been an important and growing part of schedules of rights both in the United States and elsewhere.

This connection is perhaps not surprising, although it took a long time to come to fruition. In a sense, the notion of equality was closely linked from the beginning to that of Natural Right, in contradistinction to the place of subjective rights in medieval systems of law, which were also those of certain estates or privileged individuals. Once right inheres in nature, then it is hard in the long run to deny it to anyone.

But the connection to equality is the stronger, because of the thrust of modern humanism mentioned above, which defines itself against the view that we are embedded in a meaningful cosmic order. This latter has been a background against which various forms of human differentiation could appear natural, unchallengeable – be they social, racial or sexual. The differences in human society, or gender roles, could be understood to reflect differentiations in the order of things, and to correspond to differences in the cosmos, as with Plato's myth of the metals. This has been a very common form of thinking in almost all human societies.[17]

The destruction of this order has allowed for a process of unmasking of existing social and general differences as merely socially constructed, as without basis in the nature of things, as revocable, and hence ultimately without justification. The process of working this out has been long, and we are not yet at the end; but it has been hard to resist in Western civilization in the last two centuries.

This aspect of Western rights talk is often very hard to export, as it encounters societies in which certain of the social differences are still considered very meaningful, and they are seen in turn as intrinsically linked to certain practices, which in Western societies are now regarded as discriminatory. However hard these sticking points may be for a Westerner to grasp in detail, it is not difficult to understand the general shape of the conflict. Particularly as we in the West are far from having worked out how to combine gender equality with out conflicted ideas of gender difference.

To take this issue of gender equality as our example, we can readily understand how a certain way of framing the difference, however oppressive it may be in practice, also serves as the reference point for deeply felt human identities. So that the rejection of the framework can be felt as the utter denial of the basis of identity, and this not just for the favoured gender, but also for the oppressed one. Throwing off this identity can be an act of liberation, but more than just liberation is involved here; since without an alternative sense of identity, the loss of the traditional one is disorienting and potentially unbearable.

The whole shape of the change that could allow for an unforced consensus on human rights here includes a redefinition of identity, perhaps building on transformed traditional reference points, in such a way as to allow for a recognition of an operative equality between the sexes. This can be a tall order; something we should have no trouble appreciating in the West, because we have yet to complete our own redefinitions in this regard.

Now this identity redefinition will be the easier to effect, the more it can be presented as in continuity with the most important traditions and reference points, properly understood. Correspondingly, it gets maximally difficult when it comes across as a brutal break with the past, involving a condemnation and rejection of it. To some extent, which of these two scenarios gets enacted depends on developments internal to the society. But the relation with the outside world, and particularly the West, can also be determining.

The more the outside portrayal, or attempt at influence, comes across as a blanket condemnation of or contempt for the tradition, the more the dynamic of a 'fundamentalist' resistance to all redefinition tends to get in train; and the harder it will be to find unforced consensus. This is a self-feeding dynamic, in which perceived external condemnation helps to feed extreme reaction, which calls down further condemnation, and hence further reaction, in a vicious spiral. The world is already drearily familiar with this dynamic in the unhealthy relation between the West and the great parts of the Islamic world in our time.

In a sense, therefore, the road to consensus in relation to this difference is the opposite from the one mentioned above. There, the convergence on norms between Western humanism and reform Buddhism might be seen as preceding a phase in which they come better to understand and appreciate and learn from each other. In the field of gender discrimination, it may well be that the order would be better reversed. That is, that the path to consensus passes through greater sympathetic understanding of the situation of each party by the other. In this respect, the West, with its own hugely unresolved issues about equality and difference, is often more of a menace than a help.

VI

4. Before concluding, I want to look at another difference, which resembles in different respects both of the above. That is, it is certainly one in which the dynamic of mutual miscomprehension and condemnation is driving us away from consensus. But it also has potentialities like the Thai case, in that we can see how a quite different spiritual or theological basis might be found for a convergence on norms. I am thinking of the difference between international human rights standards and certain facets of the Shari'a, recently discussed in so illuminating a fashion by Abdullahi Ahmed An-Na'im.[18] Certain punishments prescribed by the Shari'a, such as amputation of the hand for theft, or stoning for adultery, appear excessive and cruel in the light of standards prevalent in other countries.

It is worth while developing here, as I have in the other cases, the facet of

Western philosophical thought and sensibility which has given particular force to this condemnation. This can perhaps best be shown through an example. When we read the opening pages of Michel Foucault's *Surveiller et Punir*,[19] we are struck by its riveting description of the torture, execution and dismemberment of Damien, the attempted assassin of Louis XV in the mid-eighteenth century. We cannot but be aware of the cultural change that we have gone through since the Enlightenment.[20] We are much more concerned about pain and suffering than our forebears; we shrink more from the infliction of gratuitous suffering. It would be hard to imagine people today taking their children to such a spectacle, at least openly and without some sense of unease and shame.

What has changed? Perhaps we can distinguish two factors, one positive and one negative. On the positive side, we see pain and suffering, and gratuitously inflicted death, in a new light because of the immense cultural revolution which has been taking place in modernity, which I called elsewhere[21] 'the affirmation of ordinary life'. What I was trying to gesture at with this term is the momentous cultural and spiritual change of the early modern period, which dethroned the supposedly higher activities of contemplation and the citizen life, and put the centre of gravity of goodness in ordinary living, production and the family. It belongs to this spiritual outlook that our first concern ought to be to increase life, relieve suffering, foster prosperity. Concern above all for the 'good life' smacked of pride, of self-absorption. And beyond that, it was inherently inegalitarian, since the alleged 'higher' activities could only be carried out by an élite minority, whereas leading rightly one's ordinary life was open to everyone. This is a moral temper to which it seems obvious that our major concern must be our dealings with others, in justice and benevolence; and these dealings must be on a level of equality.

This affirmation, which constitutes a major component of our modern ethical outlook, was originally inspired by a mode of Christian piety. It exalted practical agapê, and was polemically directed against the pride, élitism, one might say, self-absorption of those who believed in 'higher' activities or spiritualities.

We can easily see how much this development is interwoven with the rise of the humanism which stands behind the Western discourse of human rights. They converge on the concern for equality, and also for the security of the person against burdens, dangers and suffering imposed from outside.

But this is not the whole story. There is also a negative change. Something has been cast off. It is not as though our ancestors would have just thought the level of pain irrelevant, providing no reason at all to desist from some course of action involving torture and wounds. For us, the relief of suffering has become a supreme value, but it was always an important consideration. It is rather that, in cases like that of Damien, the negative significance of pain was subordinated to other, weightier considerations. If it is necessary that punishment in a sense undo the evil of the crime, restore the balance – what is implicit in the whole notion of the criminal making *amende honourable* – then the very horror of regicide calls for a kind of theatre of the horrible as the medium in which this undoing can take place. In this context, pain takes on a different significance; there has to be lots of it to make the trick. A principle of minimizing pain is trumped.

And so we relate doubly to our forebears of two centuries ago. We have new reasons to minimize suffering; but we also lack a reason to override the minimizing of suffering. We no longer have the whole outlook – linked as it was to the cosmos as meaningful order – which made sense of the necessity of undoing the crime, restoring the breached order of things, in and through the punishment of the criminal.

In general, contemporaries in the West are so little aware of the positive change they have gone through – they tend anachronistically to think that people must always have felt this way – that they generally believe that the negative change is the crucial one that explains our difference from our predecessors. With this in mind, they look at the Shari'a punishments as the simple result of pre-modern illusions, in the same category in which they now place the ancien régime execution scenarios. With this dismissive condemnation, the stage is set for the dynamic I described above, in which contemptuous denunciation leads to 'fundamentalist' reaffirmations, which in turn provoke even more strident denunciations, and so on.

What gets lost in this struggle is what An-Na'im shows so clearly, the possibilities of reinterpretation and reappropriation which the tradition itself contains. And what also becomes invisible is what could be the motor of this change, analogous to the role played by the cultural revolution affirming ordinary life in the West. What this or these could be, it is not easy for an outsider to determine. But the striking Islamic theme of the mercy and compassion of God, reinvoked at the beginning of almost every Sura of the Qur'an, might be the locus of a creative theological development, which might help towards a convergence in this domain. In which case, we might see a consensus out of very different spiritual backgrounds, analogous to the Thai Buddhist views I discussed earlier.

VII

I feel that, if not some conclusion, at least some attempt to draw together the threads of this long and perhaps rambling discussion would now be in order. Perhaps I can bring out the main themes of the preceding pages.

I started from the basic notion that an unforced world consensus on human rights would be something like a Rawlsian 'overlapping consensus', in which convergent norms would be justified in very different underlying spiritual and philosophical outlooks. I then argued that these norms have to be distinguished and analytically separated off not just from the background justifications, but also from the legal forms which give them force. These two could vary, with good reason, from society to society, even though the norms we crucially want to preserve remain constant. We need in other words a three-fold distinction: norms, legal forms and background justifications, which each have to be distinguished from the others.

I then looked at four examples of differences. These by no means exhaust the field, though each is important in the present international exchange on human rights. One of these dealt with the issue of variations in legal forms. In the other three, I tried to discuss issues around the convergence on norms out of different philosophical and spiritual backgrounds.

Two important facets of these convergences emerged. In one way, they involve the meeting of very different minds, worlds apart in their premises, uniting only in the immediate practical conclusions. But from another side, it is clear that consensus requires that this extreme distance be closed, that we come better to understand each other in our differences, that we learn to recognize what is great and admirable in our different spiritual traditions. In some cases, this kind of mutual understanding can come after convergence, but in others it seems almost to be a condition of it.

An obstacle in the path to this mutual understanding comes from the inability of many Westerners to see their culture as one among many. An example of this difficulty was visible in the last difference discussed. To the extent that Westerners see their human rights doctrine as arising simply out of the falling away of previous countervailing ideas – e.g., the punishment scenarios of the ancien régime – which have now been discredited, and leave the field free for the preoccupations with human life, freedom, the avoidance of suffering; to this extent they will tend to think that the path to convergence requires that others too cast off their traditional ideas, that they even reject their religious heritage, and become 'unmarked' moderns like us. It is only if we in the West can recapture a more adequate view of our own history, that we can learn to understand better the spiritual ideas which have been interwoven in our development, and hence can be prepared to understand sympathetically the spiritual path of others towards the converging goal.[22] Contrary to what many people think, world convergence will not come through a loss or denial of traditions all around, but rather by creative re-immersions of different groups, each in their own spiritual heritage, travelling different routes to the same goal.

Notes

1. From the Introduction to *UNESCO, Human Rights: Comments and Interpretations*, London: Allan Wingate 1949, pp. 10–11; cited in Abdullahi A. An-Na'im, 'Towards a Cross-Cultural Approach', pp. 28–9 (see note 18).

2. Jack Donnelly, *Universal Human Rights in Theory and Practice*, Ithaca/London: Cornell University Press, 1989, pp. 28–37.

3. Yasuaki Onuma, 'In Quest of Intercivilizational Human Rights', p. 1, also n. 4.

4. Which is why Locke had to introduce a restrictive adjective to block this option of waiver, when he spoke of 'inalienable rights'. The notion of inalienability had no place in earlier Natural Right discourse, because this had no option of waiver.

5. I have talked about substantially similar issues in somewhat different terms in the last chapter of *The Ethics of Authenticity* (Cambridge, MA: Harvard University Press, 1992), and also in *Philosophical Arguments* (Cambridge, MA: Harvard University Press, 1995), in the chapter 'Liberalism and the Public Sphere'.

6. That is what is so dangerous to public order in cases like the recent O. J. Simpson trial,

which both show up and further entrench a deep lack of respect and trust in the judicial process.

7. There is a Western analogue in the positive part played by Juan Carlos during the coup in Madrid in 1964.

8. See Stanley Tambiah, *World Conqueror and World Renouncer*, Cambridge University Press, 1976.

9. See the discussion in John Girling, *Thailand: Society and Politics*, Cornell University Press, 1981, pp. 154–7. Frank Reynolds in his 'Legitimation and Rebellion: Thailand's Civic Religion and the Student Uprising of October, 1973', in Bardwell L. Smith, ed., *Religion and Legitimation of Power in Thailand, Laos, and Burma*, Chambersburg, PA: Anima Books, 1978, discusses the use by the student demonstrators of the symbols of the 'Nation, Religion, Monarchy'.

10. Richard Gombrich and Gananath Obeyesekere, *Buddhism Transformed: Religious Change in Sri Lanka*, Princeton, NJ: Princeton University Press, 1988, chs. 6 & 7.

11. Saneh Chamarik, *Democracy and Development: A Cultural Perspective*, Bangkok: Local Development Institute, 1993, p. 137.

12. 'Innerweltiche Askese'; see *The Protestant Ethic and the Spirit of Capitalism*, tr. Talcott Parsons, London and NY: Routledge, 1993 (Unwin Counterpoint Paperbacks edition).

13. The reform strand which I am describing generally takes a positive view of the historic dharmaraja tradition of the Thai polity, suitably reinterpreted. But they want to distinguish this quite sharply from the other classical tradition which they reject, that which sees the king as devaraja. This view, of Hindu origin, sees the king as ensuring through his ritual action harmony between polity and cosmos. The emphasis is on ceremony rather than on right rule. Many Buddhist intellectuals today want to distinguish the Sukhotai period as their paradigm from the later Ayutthaya regime, which they claim introduced elements of the Hindu devaraja tradition under alien Cambodian influence. These ancient regimes still have powerful symbolic resonance in today's debates. See Peter Jackson, 'Thai Buddhist Identity Debates on the Thaiphum Phra Ruang', in Craig Reynolds, ed., *National Identity and its Defenders: Thailand 1939–1989*, Clayton, Victoria: Monash Papers on Southeast Asia no. 25, 1991, pp. 191–232.

14. See Sulak Sivaraksa, *Seeds of Peace: A Buddhist Vision for Renewing Society*, Berkeley and Bangkok: Parallax Press, 1992, chapter 9.

15. See Sulak, ibid., especially part 2.

16. See the discussion in Vitit Muntaborn & Charles Taylor, *Roads to Democracy: Human Rights and Democratic Development in Thailand*, Bangkok and Montreal: International Centre for Human Rights and Democratic Development, July 1994, part 3.

17. A good example is Pierre Bourdieu's description of the 'correspondences' between the male-female difference and different colours, cardinal points, and oppositions like wet-dry, up-down, etc. See his *Outline of a Theory of Practice*, Cambridge: Cambridge University Press, 1977.

18. See his 'Towards a Cross-Cultural Approach to Defining International Standards of Human Rights: A Meaning of Cruel, Inhuman, or Degrading Treatment or Punishment', in Abdullahi Ahmed An-Na'im, ed., *Human Rights in Cross-Cultural Perspectives*, Philadelphia: University of Pennsylvania Press, 1992, chapter 1.

19. Paris: Gallimard, 1976.

20. Tocqueville was already aware of the change, when he commented on a passage from Mme de Sévigny in *La Démocratie en Amérique*.

21. See *Sources of the Self*, Cambridge, MA: Harvard University Press, 1989, chapter 13.

22. I have discussed at greater length the two opposed understandings of the rise of modernity which are invoked here, in 'Modernity and the Rise of the Public Sphere', in *The Tanner Lectures on Human Values*.

7

Majority Rule and Individual Rights

Jon Elster

I Introduction

My concern with majority rule[1] and individual rights was spurred by recent developments in Eastern Europe and the former Soviet Union. In this region, majority rule is being adopted across the board. At the same time, individual rights have a precarious existence. To exaggerate somewhat, there has been a shift from the despotism of the Party to the despotism of the majority, both inimical to the protection of minority rights. Although there has been progress of a sort, since the Party did not care for the rights of the majority either, the achievements are decidedly limited. In most countries, constitutional democracy is still in the future.

This story has a precedent, or rather several. In England after 1648, in the United States after 1776 and in France after 1789, the abolition of a despotic regime gave rise to untrammelled majority rule, only to be followed some decades later by a regime subject to constitutional constraints.[2] I shall not discuss the case of England, where the third stage took the form of a constitutional monarchy rather than a democracy, but focus instead on the French and the American experiences. In particular, I have found the debates at the Federal Convention in Philadelphia in 1787 and the Assemblée Constituante in Paris in 1789–91 very useful in illuminating the dangers of majority rule.[3] My strategy in this paper, therefore, is first to use these historical precedents to delineate the range of majoritarian problems and counter-majoritarian solutions, and then to look at some implications for Eastern Europe.

I shall proceed as follows. Section II makes a brief argument for the view that decision by majority vote is the ultimate criterion in any democracy, even in constitutional ones. Section III discusses some of the ways in which majority rule can infringe on individual rights. Section IV introduces four solutions to this conflict: constitutional entrenchment, judicial review, separation of powers, checks and balances. In sections V through VIII, these solutions are considered separately in more detail. Their undesirable side-effects are also canvassed. In these sections I draw extensively, but not exclusively, on materials from the two eighteenth-century debates; I conclude in section IX with a survey of constitutional developments in Eastern Europe.

II Arguments for Majority Rule

At an abstract level, one can offer axiomatic arguments for majority rule.[4] Thus majority voting is the only system of preference aggregation that satisfies the conditions of *anonymity* (the outcome should not depend on the naming of the preference holders), *neutrality* (the outcome should not depend on the naming of the alternatives), *positive responsiveness* (a condition related to that of Pareto optimality) and *universal domain* (the aggregation mechanism should work for all possible combinations of individual preferences). At a deeper level, however, these conditions themselves are in need of justification. Consider in particular the crucial notion of anonymity. In pre-democratic political systems, the idea that everybody's preferences are on a par as inputs to the social decision-making process would be seen as ludicrous.

How, then, can one argue for the condition of anonymity? There has never been a lack of groups claiming a privileged status. The rich, landed property owners, the old, the educated, the intelligent, the nobility, members of the Aryan race or of other ethnic groups, believers of some given religion and the male half of society have all claimed to be inherently superior to their complements. None of these groups will accept the condition of anonymity. A key to majority rule is found, however, in the very multiplicity of these privilege-claiming groups. In the presence of many different groups who compete on the basis of their innate *quality*, only *quantity* can emerge as a peaceful focal-point solution.[5] Marx once observed that the only peaceful way to resolve the conflict between two royal pretenders is to have a republic.[6] In the struggle over which tribe in ex-colonial countries is to impose its language as the official one, the only solution acceptable to all has often been to choose the language of the former colonial power. Majority decision is similar to these formal, second-best solutions. Although people are not equal, they have to be treated as if they were.

What I have just said does not amount to an argument for anonymity or, to use the more familiar word, equality. It yields at best an explanation of why the idea of equality was irresistible or, more precisely, why from a certain time onward the only practical choice was between repression and equality.[7] Among the various positive arguments for majority rule[8] I shall (for reasons made clear in the next paragraph) limit myself to its close link to utilitarianism. If more people prefer x to y, then the choice of x is likely to yield more aggregate welfare than would be realized if y were chosen. Although it is easy to think of counter-examples, because preferences can differ in intensity, the general correlation is not invalidated. Similarly, the effect of the

Condorcet paradox of cyclical majorities is to weaken the correlation, not to eliminate it.

The link between majority rule and utilitarianism is confirmed by the fact that they have the same opponent: the defender of individual rights. There is a large literature on the relation between utility and rights.[9] The relation between majority rule and individual rights – the topic of the present essay – has also been the topic of an extensive legal literature. (These two bodies of writing are, however, rarely related to each other.) In two closely parallel arguments, defenders of individual rights have argued that they trump, respectively, utility maximization and majority rule.[10] To the greatest good for the greatest number and the rule of the many over the few, they oppose respect and concern for the individual. The connection between the two doctrines is undermined, however, if one reason why majority rule has to be constrained by rights is that the majority in the heat of passion may fail to perceive what is in its true interest. In that case, rights are needed to promote aggregate welfare and majority rule becomes the enemy of utilitarianism rather than its natural ally. We shall see, however, that there are other reasons to fear majority rule that do not turn on this argument.

I conclude this section with two remarks that should be kept in mind in what follows. Although one may believe that majority rule needs to be limited and constrained in various ways, these limits and constraints can ultimately have no other normative foundation than a simple majority decision. Consider the ideal case of a constituent assembly operating in a complete historical and social vacuum, for example, a group of settlers writing a constitution for their new country. Although the assembly may decide that a qualified majority shall be required to change the constitution, that decision itself must be taken by a simple majority. If one required a qualified majority at the constitutional convention, two problems arise. First, the assembly might not be able to produce a constitution at all. In constitutional amendments, the existing document serves as the status quo that remains in force when a proposed amendment fails, but in a creation *ex nihilo* there is no status quo that can serve as fallback position. Second, and more important, the decision to use a qualified majority would itself have to be made by a simple majority, to avoid an infinite regress.[11] Although the relevance of this remark is attenuated in actual instances of constitution making, which always take place in a context that imposes or suggests a structure on the process, the fundamental logic of constitution making remains that of a simple majority deciding that a simple majority may not be the best way to decide some issues.

A second, related remark concerns the effects of majoritarian decision making at a constitutional convention when that assembly also serves as an ordinary legislature, as was the case at the Assemblée Constituante. That combination obviously may be undesirable. A main task of a constituent assembly is to strike the proper balance of power between the legislative and the executive branches of government. To assign that task to an assembly that also serves as a legislative body would be to ask it to act as judge in its own cause. A constitution written by a legislative assembly might be expected to give excessive powers to the legislature. In the abstract, this problem could be solved by means similar to the ones used in legislative bodies, by checks and balances. A royal veto over the constitution might, for instance, have kept the legislative tendency to self-aggrandizement in check. However, even those who argued for extensive checks and balances *in* the constitution did not believe in a similar system for deciding *on* the constitution. Mounier, for instance, argued that the strong unicameral assembly necessary to create the constitution would be inappropriate for ordinary lawmaking. Similarly, Mirabeau argued that the king should have a veto in the constitution, but not over the constitution itself. Summarizing both points, Clermont-Tonnerre observed that the 'three-headed hydra' – king, first chamber and second chamber – that the constitution should create could not itself have created a constitution. To get around the problem of self-interested framers, the Assemblée Constituante adopted another solution, voting its members inel- igible to the first ordinary legislature. Robespierre,[12] in his first great speech, won the assembly for this 'self-denying ordinance'.[13] Although sometimes viewed by posterity as a disastrous piece of populist overkill,[14] Robespierre's solution did correspond to a genuine difficulty.

III How Majority Rule May Infringe on Individual Rights

For the purposes of this essay, I need not discuss what rights are, nor which rights individuals have. It is sufficient to consider principles claimed as rights, and how they might be endangered by majority rule. I shall not consider the inappropriately named 'positive rights' that entitle the individual to have part of the social product spent on activities that directly enhance his mate- rial welfare, such as the right to work, to welfare, or to a clean environment. Instead I shall limit myself to the traditional rights, such as civil liberties, polit- ical liberties, property rights and the freedom of contract.

A tripartite division of rights will prove convenient. First, there are the rights that enable real and equal political participation, notably the right to vote and freedom of speech and association. Second, there are rights that promote the rule of law, such as a prohibition of bills of attainder, a ban on retroactive legislation or retroactive taxation, a guarantee of full or fair com- pensation for confiscation of property, a ban on arbitrary search and seizure, and the right to a fair trial. Under this category, I also include the right to be able to count on the laws being reasonably stable.[15] Third, there are rights that protect religious and ethnic groups, by guaranteeing freedom of worship or the right to use and be educated in one's own language. This particular way of classifying rights has no intrinsic merit, except that it is usefully cor- related with ways in which – and motives for which – majority rule might possible infringe on the exercise and the value of rights.

First, a majority government will always be tempted to manipulate political rights to increase its chances of re-election. If it is free to change the timing of the election, it may choose a moment when economic conjunctures are favourable.[16] If electoral district boundaries have to be redrawn because of population changes, the government may try to do so to its advantage. If the majority is free to change the electoral system – for example, proportional representation versus single-member districts – it may exploit this possibility for strategic purposes. If voters have to be registered before they can vote, the government may have an incentive to make registration more difficult to disenfranchise de facto some of those who would have voted for the opposition. In countries with state-owned radio and television, the government may give itself disproportionate time. We may note for later reference that in these cases the attack on rights comes from the majority in parliament, not from the majority in the population. The danger is precisely that the parliamentary majority may have means at its disposal to prevent the popular majority from putting a new government in place.

Second, a majority may set aside the rule of law under the sway of a standing interest or a momentary passion. This was Madison's main worry. 'In all cases where a majority are united by a common interest or passion, the rights of the minority are in danger.'[17] This distinction between interest and passion is crucial.[18] If the poor or relatively propertyless form a majority, their interest might induce them to enact laws that are contrary to the rights of property, by creating paper money, legislating debtor relief and so on. A quite different danger arises if the majority is animated by a sudden passion that makes it deaf to the demands of the rule of law. The impulse may originate either in a majority in parliament or in a popular majority that manages to impose its will on parliament by nonelectoral methods. The risk of such legislation being passed is especially great in wartime and other emergency situations, a famous case being the internment of Japanese–Americans during World War II.

Third, a majority may set aside the rights of an ethnic or religious minority under the sway of what one might call a *standing passion*. In earlier centuries, religious fanaticism has been the mainspring of this form of majoritarian domination. Today, ethnic hatred, sometimes combined with religious differences, is proving a horribly potent source of oppression.

Two distinctions are implicit in what I have said. On the one hand, we have to identify the relevant majority, and notably whether it is parliamentary or popular. On the other hand we have to identify the motives which move the members of the majority to infringe on the rights of the minority. Here I have discussed three cases: standing interests, standing passions and momentary passions. Although all six combinations of actors and motives might be relevant, I shall limit myself to five.

First, there is the case of a parliamentary majority that acts to preserve itself as a majority, by the various procedural stratagems mentioned earlier, or to promote such other interests as it might have. Madison, for instance, noted that 'It had often happened that men who had acquired landed property on credit, got into the Legislatures with a view of promoting an unjust protection against their Creditors.'[19]

Second, there is the case of a parliamentary majority being swayed by the (standing) passion of *amour-propre*, that is, vanity or self-love. Although virtually absent at the Federal Convention, the fear that political agents might act on such motives was often expressed in the Assemblée Constituante. Bergasse argued, for instance, that a suspensive veto of the king would not have the intended effect of making the assembly reconsider its vote, because its *amour-propre* would prevent it from backing down.[20]

Third, there is the case of a popular majority acting (through its representatives) to further its economic interest. A special case is that in which this interest is defined in terms of present value of future income, discounted by some positive factor. If the discount rate is high, members of the majority might find it in their interest to take confiscatory measures against property owners, even if they know that in the long run they or their descendants would be better off respecting property.

Fourth, there is the case of a popular majority acting (through its representatives) under a sudden impulse, a momentary passion. The founders in Philadelphia and the constituents in Paris constantly referred to this danger. In Philadelphia, we find references to 'the turbulence and follies of democracy', 'the fury of democracy', 'the popular passions [which] spread like wild fire, and become irresistable', 'fickleness and passion', 'the turbulency and violence of unruly passion', and to the 'precipitation, changeableness, and excesses of the first branch'. In Paris, Lally-Tollendal referred to the assembly being 'entrainée par l'éloquence, séduite par des sophismes, égarée par des intrigues, enflammée par des passions qu'on lui fait partager, emportée par des mouvements soudains qu'on lui communique, arrêtée par des terreurs qu'on lui inspire'. Others warned against 'les prestiges de l'éloquence, l'effervescence de l'enthousiasme', 'les causes d'erreur, de précipitation ou de séduction oratoire', or 'l'erreur, la précipitation, l'ambition'.[21]

Fifth, there is the case of a popular majority acting (through its representatives) from a standing, permanent passion. A perusal of the quotations in the previous paragraph brings out the predominance of terms such as 'sudden', 'fickle', 'unruly', 'precipitation', 'changeableness' and the like. By contrast, there were few references in the two eighteenth-century assemblies to more permanent passions and prejudices that might fashion the will of the majority. In Philadelphia, for instance, nobody mentioned racism or religious sectarianism as potential threats to individual rights.[22] In the late twentieth century, these problems of ethnicity and religion may prove to be the outstanding danger of majority rule. In addition to the problems in Eastern Europe that I discuss in the concluding section, the spectre of Islamic majoritarianism in Algeria offers a striking example.

I should add a nuance to this somewhat mechanical presentation. Although I believe that the distinction between interest and passion is of fundamental analytical importance, they often go together in practical politics. On the one hand, passion often makes us believe that something is in our interest which really is not. What Tocqueville called 'the democratic sentiment of envy' may dress itself up as a theory that the rich, if not restricted, will use their wealth to subvert the polity. On the other hand, an interest, to be effective in politics, often has to take on the garb of passion. Norms of equality and other social norms can impart a passionate tone to claims that otherwise might be seen as mere expressions of self-interest.[23] In practice, therefore, people will not acknowledge a conflict between interest and passion. But this need not prevent the outside observer from being able to identify one of them as the causally efficacious motive, and the other as its dupe or handmaiden.

IV Countermajoritarian Devices: an Overview

In the following sections I discuss what I believe to be the four main countermajoritarian devices used in modern societies. In this section I offer a broader perspective, by attempting to relate the four devices to each other. First, however, I shall briefly comment on a proposal that, although not immediately relevant for current events, was an important background element for the eighteenth-century assemblies.[24] This is the view that when the polity is too large for direct democracy one can reduce the dangers of representative democracy by a system of bound mandates, perhaps combined with the possibility of recalling delegates at any time if they exceed their briefs. In both Philadelphia and Paris, there was general agreement that this system was undesirable. It would reduce democracy to a mere system of preference aggregation, and leave no room for the transformation of preferences through rational deliberation.[25] For many writers, from Aristotle to the present, majority rule is in fact justified by the opportunity it offers for the exchange of ideas and discussion.[26] In a small polity, this ideal can be realized without creating a legislative body with interests of its own. In a large polity, which requires a representative democracy, the latter danger is an unavoidable concomitant of any attempt to realize the deliberative ideal. Independence inevitably cuts both ways. At the same time, direct democracy is more vulnerable to violent popular passions. Whereas both the town meeting and an assembly of (unbound) representatives allow for discussion, the former is vulnerable to the problem of passionate popular majorities and the latter to the problem of self-interested legislative majorities. A representative system constrained by bound mandates may limit both majoritarian dangers, but at the cost of giving up the benefits of deliberation.[27] If the only purpose of representation was to protect individual rights, this system might be optimal. But an assembly is also created to get things done, to work out compromises and to make good decisions.

The four devices I shall discuss are, to repeat, constitutionalism, judicial review, separation of powers, and checks and balances. In some political systems, these form a tightly knit whole. Judicial review, separation of powers, and checks and balances are all written into the constitution. Judicial review is a mechanism to interpret and enforce the constitution. In doing so, it also serves to prevent usurpation of power by the other organs of state. It can only perform that function, however, if it is reasonably independent of those organs. More generally, checks and balances presupposes some separation of

powers: if A is to act as a check on B, it must have some degree of independence from B.

In other systems, these elements are decoupled from each other to a larger
extent. England, for instance, does not even have a written constitution, and
yet there are limits on majority rule that form part of what has been called the
unwritten constitution.[28] Judicial review may go beyond the constitution and
consider rights not specifically enumerated in that document. Also, the institution of judicial review may not itself be specifically mentioned in the
constitution. This is the case in the United States. Although checks and balances presupposes a separation of powers, the converse is not true. The French
Constitution of 1789, which was 'based on an extreme version of the doctrine
of the separation of powers',[29] had no checks and balances beyond the suspensive veto of the king. In the Constitution of the Fifth French Republic, the
Conseil Constitutionnel was originally created to strengthen the executive
against the legislature. It was only fifteen years later that it was made into (and
made itself into) an institution for independent judicial review.[30]

V Constitutionalism as a Constraint on Majority Rule

Majority rule can be restrained by the constitution, both directly and indirectly. In this section I discuss the direct influence that derives from the
combination of the constitutionalization of certain laws and procedures that
make it difficult to amend the constitution. In later sections I discuss other
restraining devices that may or may not be explicitly mentioned in the constitution but that, if they are, operate in a different manner.

A constitution can affect behaviour by acting on the desire of the majority
to change the law or on its opportunities to do so.[31] The first mechanism
operates by making the process of constitutional amendment very slow and
time-consuming, so that impulsive passions can cool down and reason (or
interest!) reinstate itself. The second operates by requiring qualified majorities for changing the constitution or, at the limit, declaring some clauses
unamendable. Some constitutions (such as the Norwegian one) impose both
qualified majorities and delays; others (such as the Swedish one) require
only delays.[32] Still others (such as the Hungarian one) require only qualified
majorities; New Zealand appears to be unique in that 'only ordinary legislative efforts are required to supplement, modify or repeal the Constitution'.[33]

Delaying devices are designed to counteract sudden impulses and momentary passions among the majority. Qualified majorities are intended to
protect individual rights against the standing interests and passions of the
majority. It is easily seen that these two mechanisms must differ fundamentally in their mode of adoption. If we focus on delays, the following
description is indeed appropriate: 'Constitutions are chains with which men
bind themselves in their sane moments that they may not die by a suicidal
hand in the day of their frenzy.'[34] It is in the straightforward interest of the
majority to prevent itself from making rash decisions under the sway of
passion. However, the use of qualified majorities cannot be explained or

justified by the idea that Peter when sober acts to bind Peter when drunk.[35] If a majority among the founders has a standing interest on some particular issue, that interest will not induce them to set it aside. If they are moved by religious fanaticism, this is a passion they embrace rather than fear. In the eighteenth century the question did not have the importance it assumes today. The founders as a whole, and a fortiori a majority among them, represented a minority élite within the population that could impose its views on the rest. In the United States, for instance, today's majority is bound by a founding minority.

As with the other countermajoritarian devices discussed below, constitutionalism has a potential for creating problems as well as solving them. One should keep in mind a dictum of constitutional lawyers, due to Justice Robert Jackson: the constitution is not a suicide pact. It must be possible to unbind oneself in an emergency. Society must not be confined too tightly.[36] In the debates over the constitutional ban on paper money at the Federal Convention, George Mason said that 'Though he had a mortal hatred to paper money, yet as he could not foresee all emergencies, he was unwilling to tie the hands of the Legislature. He observed that the late war could not have been carried on, had such a prohibition existed.'[37] The ensuing dilemma is very tight. On the one hand, one might wish for the constitution to allow for unforeseen and unforeseeable emergencies. On the other hand, some of the occasions that will be claimed to have emergency status will be the very situations in which the constitution was supposed to act as a protection. An alcoholic will always be able to specify some way in which today is special and exceptional.[38]

VI Judicial Review as a Countermajoritarian Device

The dilemma has been solved by judicial review. Let me first note that having a constitution by itself does not solve anything, unless an apparatus of interpretation and enforcement is in place. Sieyès's claim that the constitution did away with the need for executive veto or similar devices[39] had no force as long as he did not specify a practical mechanism by which violations of the constitution would trigger the necessary corrections. He asserted that in such cases one would have to appeal to an extraordinary constitutional convention, but said nothing about who should have the right to call it. And in any case it is obviously impractical to have to go back to the constituent power to decide charges of unconstitutionality. One needs a less cumbersome way, such as judicial review.

In the two eighteenth-century assemblies, this solution was not a central issue. Other solutions to the problems of majority rule, such as bicameralism and executive veto, had a much more important role.[40] At the Federal Convention, ideas related to judicial review were, nevertheless, considered. On the one hand, the framers distinguished between *ex ante* control and review *ex post*. On the other hand, they drew a distinction between the control of the constitutionality of the laws and scrutiny on broader grounds. These issues were mainly discussed in the context of the proposal of instituting a Council of Revision, which would have the power to veto state and federal laws. In the Virginia proposal, the council was supposed to contain, besides the president, 'a convenient number of the National Judiciary'.

Some speakers argued against any form of *ex ante* involvement of the judges. Gerry, for instance, expressed 'doubts whether the Judiciary ought to form a part of [the Council of Revision], as they will have a sufficient check agst. encroachments on their own department by their exposition of the laws, which involved a power of deciding on their Constitutionality'. King similarly 'was of the opinion that the Judicial ought not to join in the expounding of a Law, because the Judges will have the expounding of those Laws when they come before them; and they will no doubt stop the operation of such as shall appear repugnant to the constitution'.[41]

Others argued that *ex post* judicial review was insufficient because constitutionality was not all that was at stake. 'Laws may be unjust, may be unwise, may be dangerous, may be destructive, and yet not be so unconstitutional as to justify the Judges in refusing to give them effect.' Madison referred to the need for 'an additional check agst. a pursuit of those unwise and unjust measures which constituted so great a portion of our calamities'. Mason observed that although judges 'could declare an unconstitutional law void . . . , with regard to every law, however unjust, oppressive or pernicious, which did not come plainly under this description, they would be under the necessity as Judges to give it a free course'.[42]

In a letter of 1817, Madison pointed to a third possibility. Referring to 'the attempts in the Convention to vest in the Judiciary Dept. a qualified negative on Legislative *bills*,' he commented that 'Such a Controul, *restricted to constitutional points*, besides giving greater stability & system to the rules of expounding the Instrument, would have precluded the question of a Judiciary annulment of Legislative *Acts*.'[43]

Of these various proposals, two correspond to contemporary forms of judicial review. In the United States and Norway, the Supreme Court assesses the constitutionality of laws *ex post*, if seized by a case that turns on this issue. In much of the European continent, constitutional courts may scrutinize the law *ex ante*, before it is promulgated. These continental systems differ among themselves in important ways, notably with respect to the assignment of the right to bring a law before the Court. I conjecture that *ex post* review offers a better protection of individual rights, for two reasons. First, *ex ante* review may create a dangerous complicity between the legislative and the judicial branches of government.[44] Second, a law may have a rights-violating potential that is difficult to anticipate until an actual case has been brought.[45]

Judicial review is basically an answer to the need for an enforcement mechanism. Even when a law is obviously unconstitutional, someone must be assigned the right to assess it as such and to set in motion the machinery that will overturn it. The institution to which this right is assigned can then also address the problem mentioned at the end of the previous section, by providing a method for avoiding the absurd consequences that a literal interpretation of the constitution would sometimes entail. The court can apply an old constitution to new circumstances by supplementing or even violating its letter as long as it remains faithful to the spirit.

It is immediately clear that this solution, too, involves problems of its own. If the courts are allowed to decide what is absurd and what is not, or what violates the spirit of the constitution and what does not, the door is wide open for judicial rule rather than mere judicial review. Instead of being a constraint on majority rule, an unelected court will supplant the majority as the main legislator. In theory, therefore, we are confronted with an impossible choice between textualism and originalism on the one hand, and unconstrained activism on the other. In practice, the existence of a legal culture with shared norms of interpretation keeps courts from behaving in a totally arbitrary and unpredictable fashion. But if that is the case, isn't there a danger that the courts will be agents of the majority rather than a constraint on what it can do? The steady constitutional erosion of property rights, for instance, has probably occurred because changing attitudes towards property in the population at large eventually found their way into the legal culture as well. But isn't that precisely what the constitution was supposed to prevent?

This objection rests on a misunderstanding. Ultimately, as I said, the constitutional protection of rights must be anchored in a simple majority. It makes no difference in principle whether the views of the majority are directly expressed in the constitution or in later reinterpretations of the constitution. What matters is that laws reflect the considered opinion of the majority rather than a passing whim or aberration. In this perspective it is actually more reasonable to put one's trust in a slowly evolving legal culture than in a constituent assembly, the members of which are in no way immune to the influence of passion and interest. It remains true, nevertheless, that legal culture can never be more than a soft constraint on the decision of the courts, and that it will always leave some scope for decisions that reflect neither the views of the founding generation nor the considered views of a current majority. Instead, the court may be swayed by minoritarian ideologies – or even by the majoritarian passions of the moment. An example of the latter is the decision of the US Supreme Court that upheld the internment order of American Japanese, even though it was based on little more than collective suspicion.[46]

VII Separation of Powers

In this section and the following I discuss how the relations among state institutions may be organized so as to reduce the dangers of majority rule. This effect can be obtained in two apparently opposed ways: by making the institutions more independent of each other, or by making them more dependent on each other. The former technique is that of the separation of powers, the latter that of checks and balances.

Let me make a preliminary remark about the relationship between the legislative and the executive powers. In the following section, when I discuss executive veto as a constraint on majority rule, I shall assume something like a monarchical or presidential system. In much of the present section, however, I shall assume a parliamentary system in which the executive springs directly from the legislative majority. In such cases, limits on legislative majority rule take the form of limits on the executive.

For present purposes, the most important part of the separation of powers lies in the independence of the judiciary, both as a guarantee of the rule of law and as a protection of judicial review. One aspect of this independence relates to the mode of appointment, tenure and remuneration[47] of judges. Another aspect concerns the organization of the judicial system, such as the selection of jurors and, especially, the assignment of judges to cases. To prevent the government from selecting 'reliable' judges to preside over 'delicate' cases, many countries have adopted the practice of assigning judges by lot or some other mechanical procedure.

In addition to the traditional trio of executive, legislative and judiciary, the press and more generally the media are sometimes said to constitute a 'fourth power', with the task (among others) of drawing attention to majoritarian abuses. We may understand this idea in a literal way or in a more extended sense. In the literal interpretation we may see public media, such as state-owned radio and television companies, as subject to the principle of the separation of powers. Their independence can be assured partly through the appointment, tenure and remuneration of the director general, partly by some degree of budgetary autonomy. In the extended interpretation, privately owned newspapers and broadcasting companies can also be seen to perform the same functions of control and deterrence. To ensure their independence, freedom of speech must have vigorous legal protection against government interference. In addition, government should not be allowed to hold monopolies on paper, printer's ink and the like.

The independence of a central bank falls in the same conceptual category. If politicians have direct control over monetary policy, the temptation to use this tool for short-term or partisan purposes may become irresistible. To see the connection with the topic of this essay, it is sufficient to note that inflation – a frequent outcome of such manipulations – was traditionally seen as a violation of property rights. Again, appointment, tenure, remuneration and budgetary autonomy are key variables in ensuring independence. As before, this solution to the problem of majority rule may give rise to new problems. Earlier, I referred to George Mason's hesitation with regard to a constitutional prohibition of paper money. Two centuries later, William Nordhaus noted that a similar dilemma arises if one takes the more indirect route of creating an independent central bank. To prevent 'political business cycles' one might, he observes, entrust economic policy to persons that will not be tempted by the sirens of partisan politics. This procedure is typical for monetary policy, which for historical reasons is lodged in the central bank (as in the independent Federal Reserve System in the US or the Bank of England). A similar possibility is to turn fiscal policy over to a Treasury dominated by civil servants. It may be objected, however, that delegating responsibility to an agency that is not politically responsive to legitimate needs is even more dangerous than a few cycles. This danger is frequently alleged regarding central banks which pay more attention to the 'soundness of the dollar' or the latest monetarist craze than to fundamental policy problems.[48]

If for 'soundness of the dollar' we substitute 'respect for the text of the constitution' and instead of 'monetarist craze' we read 'non-interventionist ideology', these remarks also apply to an independent judiciary. But who, then, shall guard these guardians? The generic answer lies in a system of checks and balances, in which the guardians are kept in check by those over whom they keep guard.

VIII Checks and Balances

In a system of checks and balances, the political institutions are limited by each other, not only in the weak sense that each has its circumscribed sphere of power, but in the stronger sense that even within that sphere it is not omnipotent. The legislative power can be overridden by executive veto and by judicial review, whereas an activist court may be controlled by the threat of new appointments or by the threat to limit the reviewing powers of the court. I shall focus on two devices that act as checks on majority rule: bicameralism and executive veto. Very roughly speaking, the two checks correspond to two of the majoritarian dangers identified above. The existence of a second chamber can by a number of mechanisms counteract the (momentary) passions of the majority. The executive veto can block the tendency toward legislative tyranny. But these stark statements need nuances and qualifications. In fact , both devices have been offered as solutions to both problems, as indicated by the following table:

	Problem of passionate majorities	Problem of self-interested legislators
Bicameralism is the solution	Upper house will slow down the process, and also through wealth or wisdom resist a passionate majority	A divided assembly less likely to become an aristocracy
Executive veto is the solution	Veto can serve as an additional check on dangerous impulses	The executive will resist any legislative self-aggrandizement

Bicameralism is the solution to the problem of passionate majorities. This proposition has several aspects. In the first place, bicameralism simply makes for a slower and more cumbersome process, giving hot spirits time to cool down. When Thomas Jefferson asked George Washington why the Convention had established a Senate, Washington replied by asking, 'Why do you pour your coffee into your saucer?' 'To cool it,' Jefferson replied. 'Even so,' Washington said. 'We pour legislation into the Senatorial saucer to cool it.' In France, Mounier observed that the majority might need a cooling-off period to protect itself against the temptation to abdicate from power in favour of a strong man.[49]

This argument does not reply on any special virtues possessed by the senators as compared to the members of the lower house, but appeals merely to the virtues of slowness. It carries over, therefore, to any other delaying or cooling device, such as the need for constitutional changes to be approved by two successive legislatures or the king's suspensive veto. Most bicameral systems, however, have posited some qualitative difference between the senators and the representatives by virtue of which the upper house would be more prudent and conservative and thus act as a brake on the more impetuous lower house. A number of screening mechanisms were envisaged. The lower age limit for senators could be set higher.[50] Senators could be chosen by indirect elections (the original American solution). They could be made subject to longer periods of office, with staggered renewals (also part of the American solution). More controversially, they may be subject to different eligibility requirements with regard to property or income.

In a passage that for me represents the intellectual high point of the Convention, Madison offered a veil-of-ignorance argument for the Senate which serves, he asserted,

> first to protect the people against their rulers: secondly to protect the people agst. the transient impressions into which they themselves might be led. A people deliberating in a temperate moment, and with the experience of other nations before them, on the plan of Govt. most likely to secure their happiness, would first be aware, that those chargd. with the public happiness, might betray their trust. An obvious precaution agst. this danger wd. be to divide the trust between different bodies of men, who might watch & check each other . . . . It would next occur to such a people, that they themselves were liable to temporary errors, thro' want of information as to their true interest, and that men chosen for a short term, & employed but a small portion of that in public affairs, might err from the same cause. This reflection wd. naturally suggest that the Govt. be so constituted, as that one of its branches might have an oppy. of acquiring a competent knowledge of the public interests. Another reflection equally becoming a people on such an occasion, wd. be that they themselves, as well as a numerous body of Representatives, were liable to err also, from fickleness and passion. A necessary fence agst. this danger would be to select a portion of enlightened citizens, whose limited number and firmness might seasonably interpose agst. impetuous counsels. It ought finally to occur to a people deliberating on a Govt. for themselves, that as different interests necessarily result from the liberty meant to be secured, the major interests might under sudden impulses be tempted to commit injustice on the minority.[51]

Bicameralism is the solution to the problem of self-interested legislators. The mechanism behind this argument is a form of 'divide and rule': a homogeneous assembly is more likely to form a united front against the executive than an internally divided one. At the Convention, 'Mr. Dickinson was not apprehensive that the Legislature composed of different branches constructed on such different principles, would improperly unite for the purpose of displacing a judge.' Mason claimed that a single legislature, as proposed in the New Jersey plan, contained the seeds of 'Legislative despotism'. In the Assemblée Constituante, Lally-Tollendal stated the matter quite generally: a single power will devour everything, two will fight each other to death, whereas three will maintain a perfect equilibrium.[52]

In both assemblies there was apprehension that an upper house might turn into an aristocracy. In Philadelphia, Gerry said that as '[the new system] now stands it is as compleat an aristocracy as ever was framed. If great powers should be given to the Senate we shall be governed in reality by a Junto as has been apprehended.' Wilson said that 'he was obliged to consider the whole as having a dangerous tendency to aristocracy; as throwing a dangerous power into the hands of the Senate.' This argument had an even stronger appeal in Paris, where the very idea of an upper house powerfully reminded people of the old system of orders. However, the argument can be turned on its head. It is precisely in order to prevent the formation of the *legislature as aristocracy* that one has to accept an *aristocracy within the legislature.* Although a longer term in office for the Senate may turn their members into an aristocracy, that longer tenure is also needed if it is to be a proper check against the lower branch.[53]

The role of bicameralism in checking legislative tyranny was not uncontroversial. Gouverneur Morris argued that 'The check provided in the 2d. branch was not meant as a check on Legislative usurpation of power, but on the abuse of lawful powers, on the propensity of the 1st. branch to legislate too much to run into projects of paper money & similar expedients. It is no check on Legislative Tyranny. On the contrary it may favor it, and if the 1st. branch can be seduced may find the means of success.'[54] The idea that internal division in the legislature might not reduce – might in fact increase – the tendency to legislative tyranny is not one I have encountered elsewhere in the debates. Nor is it particularly plausible. The idea that internal legislative division might not be a sufficient deterrent to legislative tyranny is more attractive. Executive veto may also be required.

Executive veto is the solution to the problem of passionate majorities. An absolute veto for the executive was not seriously discussed in the American assembly. In the French assembly, it was strongly advocated by some of the 'monarchiens', but in the end overwhelmingly defeated. There are two main ways of retaining a form of executive veto even if an absolute veto is rejected. On the one hand, one can allow the assembly to overrule the veto, but require a qualified majority. This was the solution adopted in Philadelphia. On the other hand, one can allow the assembly to overrule the executive by an ordinary majority, but require that the decision be delayed until a later legislature.[55] This was the solution adopted in Paris, allowing the king to veto a proposal in two successive legislatures before the third one could over-rule him. In both cases, the solution was defended, among other reasons, for its beneficial impact on passionate majorities.

This argument was made several times in the American debates. According to Madison, 'a negative in the Ex: is not only necessary for its own safety, but for the safety of a minority in Danger of oppression from an unjust and interested Majority.' Gouverneur Morris was more specific. On July 19 he argued that the upper house is needed as a check 'on the propensity in the 1st branch to legislate too much to run into projects of paper money and similar expedients'. Two days later he cited the same phe-nomena – 'Emissions of paper money, largesses to the people – a remission of debts and similar measures' – as reasons for a strong executive check. Mason similarly argued that 'Notwithstanding the precautions taken in the Constitution of the Legislature, it would so much resemble that of the indi-vidual States, that it must be expected frequently to pass unjust and pernicious laws.'[56] In other words, the tripartite system provided a *double check on majority rule.*[57]

In the Assemblée Constituante, the argument took different forms.[58] For most deputies, executive veto was simply seen as a delaying and cooling device, a brake on passionate majorities. For the radical members of the assembly, it was rather a device that allowed the nation to act as a check on its representatives. After the first veto, the nation could express its opinion through an election. As LaSalle put it, 'Le veto suspensif est comme une sorte d'appel à la nation, qui la fait intervenir comme juge à la première session, entre le Roi et ses représentants.' The argument came in two versions. Some delegates wanted to leave the decision to the legislature following the final veto. Others wanted primary assemblies to vote directly on the motion that had been opposed by the royal veto.[59]

Executive veto is the solution to the problem of self-interested legislators. The role of the executive veto as a check on the tendency toward legislative tyranny was a permanent theme in the two assemblies. In Paris, Lally-Tollendal, citing England as a precedent, claimed that in 1688 the two chambers of Parliament abdicated some of their powers to the executive in order to prevent legislative tyranny. Many other speakers in the Assemblée Constituante argued for the need for a royal veto to check the tendency toward legislative domination. In doing so, they indulged in considerable amounts of cant, imputing either a perfect harmony of interest between the king and the people that would enable him to check the aristocratic tendencies of the legislature, or a perfect coincidence between the will of the king and the general happiness. In the fall of 1789, nobody said outright that even a weak or depraved king would be a useful check on legislative tyranny. After the king's flight to Varenne, it became more difficult to uphold the illusion of his benevolence and wisdom. In the debates on the king's immunity, Duport and Barnave argued that the king could not serve his constitutional function as check on the legislature unless his person was inviolable. 'Si le monarque était dépendant du Corps législatif, il en résulterait que celui-ci pourrait détruire son propre frein.'[60] I return to this theme below.

The Americans also referred to the British experience: 'Where the Executive really was the palladium of liberty, *King* and *Tyrant*, were naturally associated in the minds of people; not *Legislature and* tyranny. But where the Executive was not formidable, the two last were most properly associated. After the destruction of the King in Britain, a more pure and unmixed tyranny sprang up in parliament than had been exercised by the monarch.'[61] Other historical precedents were cited by Gouverneur Morris. Having first reiterated his motion for an absolute veto, defeated a week previously, he went on to say that

> The most virtuous citizens will often as members of a legislative body concur in measures which afterwards in their private capacity they will be ashamed of. Encroachments of the popular branch of the Government ought to be guarded agst. The Ephori at Sparta became in the end absolute . . . . If the Executive be overturned by the popular branch, as happened in England, the tyranny of one man will ensue – In Rome where the Aristocracy overturned the throne, the consequence was different. He enlarged on the tendency of the legislative Authority to usurp on the Executive and wished the section to be postponed, in order to consider some more effectual check than requiring 2/3 only to overrule the negative of the Executive.[62]

The checks must themselves be kept in check, otherwise there would not be a system of checks *and balances*. In Paris, defenders of an absolute veto for the king argued that the assembly could always overrule him refusing to pay taxes. Several delegates responded that in refusing to vote taxes, the assembly would be cutting off its nose to spite its face: 'faire cesser le payement de l'impôt, c'est se couper la gorge pour guérir une plaie à la jambe.'[63] In Philadelphia, checks on the executive included overruling his veto by a two-thirds majority, impeachment, and the incentives provided by re-eligibility. The question of checks on the Senate did not arise.

Moreover, the checks must be genuinely independent of the institutions on which they are supposed to provide a check. I have already cited Duport's observation in the Assemblée Constituante, that the king cannot serve as a brake on the legislature if the assembly can remove him at will. At the Federal Convention, the question arose with regard to both the executive and the upper house. Regarding the latter, Sherman argued against Randolph's proposal (that 'the first branch of the federal Legislature should have the appointment of the Senators') on the plausible grounds that 'if the Senate was to be appointed by the first Branch and out of that Body . . . it would make them too dependent, and thereby destroy the end for which the Senate ought to be appointed.' Regarding the former, Gouverneur Morris asserted that if the executive is chosen by Congress, 'He will be the mere creature of the Legisl: if appointed & impeachable by that body.' Also arguing against selection of the executive by the legislature, Madison asserted that 'the candidate would intrigue with the legislature, would derive his appointment from the predominant faction, and be apt to render his administration subservient to its views.'[64]

The negative side-effects of a system of checks and balances are obvious: the institutions might balance each other so effectively that nothing can be achieved, leading to paralysis rather than responsible government. Admittedly, devices that merely serve to slow down the legislative process do not present this danger, but neither do they offer a response to all problems of majority rule. To counteract the tendency toward legislative tyranny one might need an absolute veto, which might in turn reduce the ability of the system to respond effectively to urgent problems. The stronger the countermajoritarian remedies, the greater the risk of serious side-effects. At the Federal Convention, the trade-off was discussed in the debate on the Senate majority needed to overrule a presidential veto. Gouverneur Morris, arguing for a three-fourths majority, said that 'The excess rather than the deficiency of laws is to be dreaded.' Gerry, arguing for a two-thirds majority, countered that 'If 3/4 be required, a few Senators having hopes from the nomination of the President to offices, will combine with him and impede proper laws.'[65]

IX Conclusion

I conclude by applying these analytical categories to recent developments in Eastern Europe.[66] After the fall of the communist regimes in 1989, entirely new constitutions have been adopted in Bulgaria, the Czech Republic, Croatia, Romania, Slovakia and Slovenia. The Hungarian Constitution has been totally transformed by piecemeal amendments, whereas the process remains unfinished in Albania and Poland. In the latter country, however, a 'little constitution' that regulates the relation among the main powers of state was adopted on November 17, 1992. Before the break-up of Czechoslovakia, that country, too, saw three years of intense constitutional debates. Although the details vary, two common features can be singled out.

First, most developments took place within the framework of the existing communist constitutions, thus effectively giving them a life after death – in fact *only* after death, since they never mattered before the fall of communism. In Czechoslovakia, for instance, constitutional reform was arguably blocked by the structure of the 1968 Constitution, which gave effective veto power to Slovakian nationalists. Although Czechs outnumber Slovaks two to one, constitutional changes needed three-fifth majorities both in the proportionally elected lower house and in each of the equal-sized Czech and Slovak sections of the upper house. In Poland, the situation is even more ironic. As part of the compromise of the Round Table Talks between Solidarity and the government, an upper house with strong veto powers was introduced into the constitution. Although neither side cared about the Senate itself, or thought that it would become a major political actor, it turned out to be a crucial force (or impediment) in the working out of a new constitution.[67] In

Hungary, the thoroughgoing revision of the constitution that took place in the fall of 1989 was facilitated by the simple amendment procedures.

Second, all the constituent assemblies have at the same time served as ordinary legislatures. As mentioned earlier, one would expect this to result in constitutions that give large powers to the legislature at the expense of the executive and the judiciary. More specifically, one would expect bicameral constituent assemblies to adopt bicameralism in the constitution. The latter prediction has been confirmed in Romania and in Poland, the only countries with bicameral constituent assemblies.[68] By and large, the former, more general prediction has also been confirmed, but the picture is somewhat blurred. We would expect, for instance, legislature-oriented constitution makers to propose indirect elections of the president. Although this is indeed the case in Hungary and in the Czech and Slovak Republics, the Bulgarian and Romanian assemblies chose to have direct elections of the president. Except in Poland the directly elected presidents are not vested with large powers in the constitution, yet the moral legitimacy they derive from the popular vote could give them considerable de facto influence, especially in a crisis.

I shall now briefly survey the role in Eastern Europe of the four counter-majoritarian, rights-protecting devices I discussed earlier: constitutionalism, judicial review, separation of powers, and checks and balances.

Constitutionalism. For our purposes there are two relevant questions. What rights are included in the constitution? How well does the constitution protect them? Concerning the first question, limitations of space prevent me from offering a full answer. Instead, I shall simply point to some anomalies or other salient features, limiting myself to the countries that have completed the constitution-making process.

Although all countries have constitutional provisions guaranteeing the rights of ethnic minorities, the force of this protection differs widely. The Bulgarian Constitution offers by far the weakest protection. For one thing, it contains a ban on political parties formed along 'ethnic, racial or religious lines' (Art. 11.4). For another, the Bulgarian Constitution is special in that it offers to ethnic minorities only the right to study their own language (Art. 36.2), not the right to study (all subjects) in their own language. It has a general ban on reverse discrimination, on grounds of race, nationality, ethnic self-identity, sex, origin, religion, education, opinion, political affiliation, personal or social status, property status (Art. 6.2). The Romanian Constitution contains a limited ban in Article 6.2, requiring the protection of national minorities to 'conform to the principles of equality and non-discrimination in relation to the other Romanian citizens'. Presumably this excludes affirmative action for the purpose, say, of promoting the situation of Gypsies. The Slovakian Constitution contains both a general ban on reverse discrimination and a specific ban on affirmative action in favour of ethnic minorities. It is probably not far-fetched to see these provisions as directly aimed at the Hungarian minority.

In the constitutions of Croatia (Art. 18 of the Constitutional Law of Human Rights and Freedoms), Romania (Art. 59.2) and Slovenia (Art. 64), the political rights of minorities are protected by clauses ensuring their representation in parliament. (One might wonder if this does not contradict Article 6.2 of the Romanian Constitution and indeed the more general principle of political equality.) In Slovenia, Article 80 requiring a two-thirds majority of all elected deputies for changes in the electoral law may also be seen as protecting political rights, making it more difficult for the majority to manipulate the system to its advantage. Article 71.3 of the Hungarian Constitution similarly requires a two-thirds majority of the deputies present for the adoption of electoral laws. With two exceptions, the electoral law itself is not constitutionalized. In Poland, the 'little constitution' lays down the principle of proportional elections. In the Czech Republic, the lower house is to be elected by the proportional system and the Senate by the majority system. These broad guidelines, however, still leave plenty of room for majoritarian manipulation of thresholds and districts.

The difficulty of changing the constitutions varies considerably. In what must be among the least restrictive provisions in the world, Slovakia requires only a three-fifths majority in parliament. In the Czech Republic, amendments require a three-fifths majority in each of the two houses. In Hungary, Poland, Slovenia and Croatia, the basic principle is that two-thirds of all deputies must vote in favour of a proposed amendment, but in each country there are some additional stipulations. In Croatia and Slovenia, constitutional amendments may also be adopted by simple majority vote in a referendum. The Hungarian Constitution specifies that statutory legislation in a number of specific domains, for example electoral laws, also requires a two-thirds majority. The Polish Constitution adds that the constitution may not be changed during a state of emergency. In Romania, there must either be a two-thirds majority in each chamber or a three-quarters majority in a joint session of the two chambers, followed by approval in a referendum. In addition, parliament can amend the constitution by a back door procedure to be discussed below. Here, too, the constitution cannot be changed in a state of emergency.

In Bulgaria, the procedure is more complicated. A 'minor' constitutional change can be adopted by parliament in one of two ways: by three-quarters of the deputies voting for it in three ballots on three different days, or by two-thirds voting in favour on two occasions with an interval of no less than two and no more than five months. Fundamental changes have to be approved by a two-thirds majority of a special constituent assembly, elections to which will take place if two-thirds of the deputies call for them. The most important fundamental changes are those which 'resolve on any changes in the form of state structure or form of government' or which call for a change in Article 57.1 of the constitution asserting that 'The fundamental civil rights shall be irrevocable.'

With the exception of the Bulgarian provisions for major constitutional changes, these systems offer a relatively weak protection against the impulses of passionate majorities. The protection of rights may also be undermined, perhaps more seriously, by the fact that the relevant constitutional clauses are often circumscribed by clauses that render their import somewhat uncertain.

On the one hand, there are many references to further regulation by statute.[69] For instance, Article 30.2 of the Bulgarian Constitution says that 'No one shall be detained or subjected to inspection, search or any other infringement of his personal inviolability, except on the conditions and in a manner established by a law.' Similarly, Article 30.8 of the Romanian Constitution says that 'Indictable offenses of the press shall be established by law.' Although the Hungarian Constitution contains similar clauses, their sting is drawn by Article 8.2 which asserts that statutes 'shall not limit the essential content of fundamental rights', leaving the parliament free to expand the scope of rights but not to shrink them.[70] On the other hand, many rights are limited by public or even private interests. To take a typical example, Article 37.2 of the Bulgarian Constitution says that 'The freedom of conscience and religion shall not be practiced to the detriment of national security, public order, public health and morals.'[71] Whereas many constitutions assert that rights can be limited by the rights of others, the Bulgarian Constitution asserts that they shall not be exercised to the detriment of the 'legitimate interests' of others. To have rights limited by the public interest is no doubt inevitable.[72] If they can also be overriden by private interests, however, the trumplike character of rights disappears entirely.

Judicial review. All countries in the region practise *ex ante* or *ex post* reviews of legislation by constitutional courts.[73] This was also a provision in many of the communist constitutions, with the special feature, however, that decisions by the court could be annulled by parliament. In Poland, this overruling mechanism still obtains, although it is rarely utilized. It is more surprising to see that it is also incorporated in the newly enacted constitution of Romania (Art. 145.1). This is the 'backdoor' technique referred to above, by which the assembly may enact de facto amendments of the constitution without going to a referendum. One can imagine circumstances in which the rights-protecting function of judicial review would be undermined by this procedure. One might also view it, however, as part of a system of checks and balances, that is, as preventing an undemocratic rule by the judiciary.

The Hungarian court has been by far the most active one. In the last few years it has emerged as a major political force, characterized as the most powerful constitutional court in the world.[74] Two sets of decisions that have been especially important concern legal reactions to acts committed under the communist regime. In three cases the court was asked to assess the constitutionality of laws regarding restitution of nationalized land to its pre-communist owners.[75] The court decided that the only reason for discriminating between former landowners and owners of other types of confiscated property or, more crucially, between former owners and 'non-former owners' (meaning those who did not formerly hold any kind of property), would be a forward-looking one. If such discrimination would facilitate the transition to a market economy or otherwise have good social results, it was allowable; if not, not. In particular, the pattern of former property holdings was irrelevant. In a recent decision[76] the court struck down as unconstitutional a law extending the statute of limitations for crimes committed during the old regime that, 'for political reasons', had not been prosecuted. In the first set of decisions, the court let utilitarian considerations take precedence over backward-looking considerations of abstract justice, on the grounds that the latter did not give rise to any subjective rights to restitution. In the more recent decision, the basic premise of the court was the principle of legal certainty, which was violated both by the element of retroactivity inherent in the law and by the vagueness of the phrase 'for political reasons'.

The Bulgarian constitutional court has emerged as a weak defender of minority rights against the illiberal provisions in the constitution. On the basis of Articles 11.4 and 44.2 of the constitution, deputies of the former communist party asked that the Movement for Rights and Freedom – the de facto party for the Turkish and Muslim minorities – be declared unconstitutional. Although six of twelve judges found in favour of the petition and only five were against (one was sick), the petition was rejected on the basis of Article 151.1 which requires 'a majority of more than half of all justices' for a binding decision.[77] The reasoning of the five judges was too tenuous and fragile, however, to provide a very solid guarantee. We may note, moreover, that the party that was created to serve the interests of the Bulgarian Gypsies *was* declared unconstitutional.

Separation of powers. In spite of its extensive powers – or perhaps because of them – the Hungarian constitutional court has actively sought to limit its own jurisdiction. Although the law authorizes the court to emit advisory opinions on drafts of bills, the court has on several occasions refused to do so on the grounds that it would violate the principle of the separation of powers. The task of the court, it has argued, must be the purely negative one of voiding unconstitutional laws, and it must never get involved in positive lawmaking. One might ask, however, whether the latter danger is not almost unavoidable in systems of *ex ante* judicial review such as the Hungarian or German ones. This being said, this threat, if it is one, to the separation of powers does not detract from the protection of rights.

Much more serious than the infringement of the judiciary on the other powers of state is the opposite problem, the dependency of the judiciary on the executive. By all accounts, mental habits created under communism still make judges, especially in lower courts, look to government for advice and guidance. Most of them are, in fact, incapable of independent application of the law because of the abysmally low level of legal education and training under communism. Conversely, governmental habits of steering the outcome are slow in withering away. The former Hungarian Minister of Justice Kálmán Kulcsár has described (in a personal communication to the author) his difficulties in persuading his officials not to interfere with the assignment of judges to cases. The mode of appointment of judges varies widely.[78] Suffice it to say here that it does not seem to pose any obvious threats to the separation of powers. In particular, fixity of tenure is expressly stipulated in most of the constitutions.

An independent central bank has not been a goal for the constitution makers in Eastern Europe, with two exceptions. The main exception is the

Czech Republic, where the Hayekian inspiration behind the constitution shows itself in Article 98.1, which protects the bank from intervention by the executive. In Hungary, Article 32.D of the constitution stipulates that the president of the National Bank is appointed by the president of the Republic for a term of six years. Both the fixity of tenure and the fact that the president rather than the government has the appointment power might seem to indicate an intention to keep the bank out of day-to-day politics. In the ongoing turf battles between president and government in Hungary, however, the appointment powers of the former are now degenerating into a mere formality. The Slovenian Constitution says (Art. 152) that the governor of the central bank shall be appointed by the national assembly, whereas the Bulgarian one (Art. 84.11) says that he shall be elected *and dismissed* by the assembly. Article 40 of the Polish Constitution requires that the president present to the Sejm a motion for the appointment *or recall* of the president of the National Bank; once again, there is not the fixity of tenure which would be a minimal condition for independence.

The need for a provision guaranteeing the independence of state-owned media has been made strikingly clear in several countries, notably Hungary and more recently Slovakia. Nevertheless it is a striking fact that none of the constitutions in the region makes any reference to the mode of governance of state-owned radio or television.

Checks and balances. We can distinguish among a number of versions of the idea of checks and balances. The textbook idea posits three main institutions – the executive, the legislative and the judiciary – which must be so organized as to neutralize any tendency by any one of them to usurp power. In the two eighteenth-century debates, however, the three parties involved in checks and balances were rather the two houses of the legislature and the executive. Today's Eastern Europe differs from the textbook scheme in a different way, not in the division of the legislature into two houses, but in the bifurcation of the executive in president and government. If the president has some nontrivial powers, derived from the text of the constitution or from the legitimacy conferred by direct elections, and if the government has some independence from the parliamentary majority that brought it to power, we obtain a new trinity of checks and balances: parliament, government and president. Such independence can be obtained by the German system of a constructive vote of no confidence, requiring that parliament designate a new prime minister as it simultaneously censures the government in place. An alternative is the French system that allows the government to present bills that are automatically adopted as laws unless parliament brings a vote of no confidence within a specified time limit. Under these systems, government has the same relation to parliament as parliament has to the electorate: it is a trustee, not simply a delegate.

The system with the fewest checks and balances is the Bulgarian one. There is a unicameral assembly, a weak presidential veto (it can be overruled by a simple majority of all elected deputies), and no device that ensures the independence of the government from the parliamentary majority.

Institutionally, the constitutional court is the only counterweight to majoritarian assembly rule. De facto, a popular president may also be able to act as an independent force.

Slovakia is more or less in the same position. Although the president is endowed with substantial powers, he can be dismissed by parliament with a three-fifths majority on political grounds, without any formal impeachment procedure. The assembly is unicameral, and there is no device to ensure the independence of government.

Romania does not fare much better. Here the constitution has adopted a solution that was previously found only in Italy, a bicameral assembly with two essentially identical chambers. It is hard to see how this arrangement can serve in a system of checks and balances, or for any other purposes. Although the adoption in Article 113 of the French system of 'governmental legislation' ensures some independence of government from parliament, this provision has rarely been used so far. The right of the president to call a referendum (Art. 90) offers him some independence from the other powers of state. As noted above, the role of the constitutional court in acting as a brake on parliament is limited by the right of the assembly to overrule the decisions of the court.

Hungary has a unicameral assembly and a largely formal presidency. Although the rule of a constructive vote of no confidence ensures that government has some independence from parliament, the strongest constraint on the legislature is provided by the constitutional court. Slovenia has a somewhat similar system: a second chamber that is essentially consultative, a presidency with few formal powers, the rule of a constructive vote of no confidence, and a potentially powerful constitutional court. Much the same applies to Croatia, except that there is no constructive vote of confidence or any other device to ensure the independence of government.

The Czech Republic has a bicameral system, in which the upper house can force the lower house to adopt a bill by absolute rather than simple majority. In addition, the upper house has to approve changes in the constitution by a three-fifths majority. The president, elected by parliament, has little real power. Nor is there any device to ensure the independence of government from parliament.

Poland is the country with the most extensive system of checks and balances, with an upper house and a president that have the power to force the lower house to adopt laws with, respectively, an absolute and a two-thirds majority. However, the Sejm can set aside the decisions of the constitutional court by a simple majority. This embarrassing survival from the communist era lingers on mainly because the Sejm is in no hurry to abolish a provision that confers great powers on itself.

Broadly speaking, this overview confirms the idea stated at the outset: despotism, when overthrown, gives rise to new forms of despotism. Among the countries I have surveyed, Romania, Slovakia and Bulgaria had the most despotic and totalitarian forms of communist rule. They also seem least included to embrace countermajoritarian devices. At the other extreme, the least despotic country – Hungary – is emerging as the one most strongly wedded to the principles of constitutionalism.

I distinguished earlier between the dangers of majority rule arising from three sources: standing interests, standing passions and momentary passions. I also observed that these dangers can arise in either a parliamentary or a popular majority. In Eastern Europe, the two most acute dangers arise from the standing interest of the parliamentary majority in preserving its power and from the standing passions in the population, notably with regard to ethnic divisions and to backward-looking demands for restitution and retribution. Civil society is not yet sufficiently well organized to give rise to well-defined interest groups that might threaten the rights of minority property owners or creditors. Momentary passions are, almost by definition, unpredictable.

The emerging constitutional courts hold out the promise of being able to restrain standing and temporary passions. By contrast, the system of checks and balances is not, by and large, well designed to counteract self-interested legislators. As noted, this observation applies not only to ordinary legislation, but to the constitution-making process itself. In fact, the deepest flaw in the political processes in Eastern Europe is perhaps the constant intermingling of *la politique politisée* and *la politique politisante*. Almost everywhere, the constitutions emerge as the outcome of bargaining for tactical or partisan purposes. Their clauses are viewed as policy instruments, not as providing a relatively fixed framework for policy. In a period of rapid economic and social transformation, this is not unambiguously a bad thing. But there is a price to be paid for flexibility, and some day the bill will come due.

Notes

1. When used without further qualification, 'majority rule' in this paper always means 'simple majority rule'.

2. A similar story for Norway is told in F. Sejersted, 'Democracy and the Rule of Law', in J. Elster and R. Slagstad, eds., *Constitutionalism and Democracy* (Cambridge, England: Cambridge University Press, 1988), 131–52.

3. References to the American proceedings will be cited from the three volumes of M. Farrand, ed., *Records of the Federal Convention* (New Haven, Conn.: Yale University Press, 1966). References to the French proceedings will be cited from volumes 8 through 30 of the *Archives Parlementaires. Série I: 1789–1799* (Paris: 1875–1888).

4. A good exposition is A. Sen, *Collective Choice and Social Welfare* (San Francisco: Freeman, 1970), chap. 5.

5. Here I draw on B. Barry, 'Is Democracy Special?', reprinted in his *Democracy, Power and Justice* (New York: Oxford University Press, 1989), 24–60. For the idea of focal point, see T. C. Schelling, *The Strategy of Conflict* (Cambridge, Mass.: Harvard University Press, 1960), chap. 2.

6. Karl Marx, *The Eighteenth Brumaire*, in Marx and Engels, *Collected Works* (New York: International Publishers, 1979), vol. 11, 166.

7. Barry, 'Is Democracy Special?', 56. The same idea underlies Tocqueville's *Democracy in America*.

8. For a survey, see E. Spitz, *Majority Rule* (Chatham, N.J.: Chatham House Publishers, 1984), chap. 8 and passim.

9. See, for instance, the essays in R. G. Frey, ed., *Utility and Rights* (Oxford: Blackwell, 1985).

10. For the idea of rights as trumps, see notably R. Dworkin, *Taking Rights Seriously* (London: Duckworth, 1977).

11. One might try to avoid the regress by fixed-point reasoning. Consider the proposal that *x* percent of the votes ($x \geq 50$) is sufficient for a law to be passed. The percentage of members of the assembly who agree with the proposal is some decreasing function $f(x)$. There must then exist some self-sustaining percentage of x^* such that $f(x^*) = x^*$. This is the percentage that should be adopted by the assembly. However, this procedure must itself be voted by simple majority.

12. Mounier, *Archives*, 8: 555; Mirabeau, ibid., 8: 538; Clermont-Tonnerre, ibid., 8: 574; Robespierre, ibid., 26: 124.

13. J. M. Thomson, *Robespierre* (Oxford: Blackwell, 1988), 134ff.

14. F. Furet, *La Révolution 1770–1870* (Paris: Hachette, 1988), 104.

15. L. Fuller, *The Morality of Law* (New Haven, Conn.: Yale University Press, 1969), 79–81.

16. In fact, even when the government cannot choose the date of the election, it can still manipulate the economic conjectures so as to make them more favourable. To overcome this problem, one could time elections randomly, as proposed by A. Lindbeck, 'Stablilization Policy in Open Economies with Endogenous Politicians', *American Economic Review: Papers and Proceedings* 66 (1976): 1–19. I note as a curiosum that in the debates of the Assemblée Constituante the proposal was made (30: 97) to have periodical constitutional conventions called in a quasi-random manner, namely, by linking them to the death of the monarch. However, in these cases, as in many others, the advantages of randomization are easily seen to be offset by its drawbacks. See generally chap. 2 of my *Solomonic Judgements* (Cambridge, England: Cambridge University Press, 1989). An important exception is randomization in the judiciary, as further discussed below.

17. Madison, *Records*, 1: 135.

18. For an analysis of the distinction between interest and passion among the American founders, see M. White, *Philosophy, The Federalist, and the Constitution* (New York: Oxford University Press, 1987), chap. 7. For general discussion, see S. Holmes, 'The Secret History of Self-Interest', in J. Mansbridge, ed., *Beyond Self-Interest* (Chicago: University of Chicago Press, 1990), 267–86, and my *Sadder but Wiser? Studies in Rationality and the Emotions*, forthcoming from Cambridge University Press.

19. Madison, *Records*, 2: 123.

20. Bergasse, *Archives*, 9: 116. Strictly speaking, this example is out of place. It shows how certain solutions to the problem of majority rule might fail to work, rather than instantiating that problem itself.

21. When such short-sighted behaviour is induced by passion rather than representing the permanent subjective interest of the actor, it belongs to the next category. For quotations in this paragraph: Randolph, *Records*, 1: 51; Randolph, ibid., 1: 59; Hamilton, ibid., 1: 289; Madison, ibid., 1:421; Madison, ibid., 1: 430; Morris, ibid., 1: 512; Lally-Tollendal, *Archives*, 8: 516; Grégoire, ibid., 8: 567; Sieyès, ibid., 8: 597; Robespierre, ibid., 9: 81.

22. See, however, Madison's letter to Jefferson of October 24, 1787, for a discussion of religious sects as a threat to the freedom of worship.

23. See also chap. 6 of my *The Cement of Society* (Cambridge, England: Cambridge University Press, 1989).

24. See, for instance, G. Wood, *The Creation of the American Republic* (New York: Norton, 1972), 188–96.

25. See notably Sieyès, *Archives*, 8: 595.

26. Spitz, *Majority Rule*, 149–52.

27. My mother tells me that when she was a girl, she and her friends were obsessed by the following hypothetical choice: given that you could only have two out of the three properties of intelligence, kindness and beauty, which two would you choose? Similarly, the discussion in the text suggests that democracies can only have two out of the following three virtues: enabling deliberation, limiting passionate popular majorities and limiting self-interested legislative majorities.

28. V. Bogdanov, 'Britain: The Political Constitution', in V. Bogdanov, ed., *Constitutions in Democratic Politics* (London: Gower, 1988), 53–72. It has been argued, however, that the

violations of the unwritten British constitution under Mrs Thatcher have created the need for a formal bill of rights (L. Siedentop, 'Thatcherism and the Constitution', *Times Literary Supplement*, January 26, 1990).

29. M. J. C. Vile, *Constitutionalism and the Separation of Powers* (New York: Oxford University Press, 1967), 189.

30. G. Vedel, 'The Development of the Conseil Constitutionnel', in E. Smith, ed., *Constitutional Justice under Old Constitutions* (Deventer: Kluwer Law International, 1995).

31. For applications of the motive-opportunity distinction to political affairs see chaps. 9 and 10 of White, *Philosophy, The Federalist, and the Constitution*, and chap. 4 of my *Political Psychology* (Cambridge, England: Cambridge University Press, 1993).

32. A similar practice obtains in Great Britain: 'Under the Parliament Act of 1911, as amended by the Parliament Act of 1949, a non-money bill can be passed into law over the opposition of the House of Lords if it has been passed by simple majority in two consecutive sessions of the House of Commons and one year has elapsed between the second reading of the Bill in the Commons in the first session and its third reading in the Commons in the second session.' (J. Jaconelli, 'Majority Rule and Special Majorities', *Public Law* [1989], 587–616, at 597.)

33. J. N. Eule, 'Temporal Limits on the Legislative Mandate', *American Bar Foundation Research Journal* (1987), 379–459, at 394. Eule goes on to say, however, that 'even in such a system . . . there remain moral and political restraints on the legislative alteration of constitutional doctrine.'

34. John Potter Stockton in debates over the Ku Klux Klan Act of 1871, as cited in J. E. Finn, *Constitutions in Crisis* (New York: Oxford University Press, 1991), 5. On the general theme of self-binding, see chap. 2 of my *Ulysses and the Sirens*, rev. ed. (Cambridge, England: Cambridge University Press, 1984) and S. Holmes, *The Paradox of Democracy*, forthcoming from University of Chicago Press. On the theme of constitutional self-binding, see my 'Intertemporal Choice and Political Theory', in G. Loewenstein and J. Elster, eds., *Choice over Time* (New York: Russell Sage Foundation, 1992). For a discussion of the putative paradoxes involved in self-binding, see P. Suber, *The Paradox of Self-Amendment* (New York: Peter Lang, 1990).

35. I simplify. The use of qualified majorities can also act as a restraint on momentary passions, because with a larger proportion of people required for the decision, the chances are better that not all of them will be caught up in the collective frenzy. Unamendable clauses, in particular, offer a perfect protection against impulsive rashness.

36. Tocqueville warned against the excessively stringent amendment procedures proposed for the French 1848 Constitution. 'I have long thought that, instead of trying to make our forms of government eternal, we should pay attention to making methodical change an easy matter. All things considered, I find that less dangerous than the opposite alternative. I thought one should treat the French people like those lunatics whom one is careful not to bind lest they become infuriated by the constraint.' See A. de Tocqueville, *Recollections: The French Revolution of 1848* (New Brunswick, N.J.: Transaction Books, 1990), 181. The implication, whether intended or not, is that by making change easier one reduces the desire for change. A similar motive was adduced by the government of East Germany in 1989: by making it clear that everybody could leave for the West, they hoped to ensure that nobody would want to do so. Also, it has been argued that the possibility of divorce makes marriages more stable rather than less: 'We thought we were tying our marriage-knots more tightly by removing all means of undoing them; but the tighter we pulled the knot of constraint the looser and slacker became the knot of our will and affection. In Rome, on the contrary, what made marriages honoured and secure for so long a period was freedom to break them at will.' (Montaigne, *Essays* 2: 15.)

37. Mason, *Records*, 2: 309.

38. See notably G. Ainslie, *Picoeconomics* (Cambridge, England; Cambridge University Press, 1992).

39. Sieyès, *Archives*, 8: 596.

40. See my 'Limits to Majority Rule: Alternatives to Judicial Review in the Revolutionary Epoch', in E. Smith, ed., *Constitutional Justice under Old Constitutions*.

41. Gerry, *Records*, 1: 97; King, ibid., 1: 109.

42. Wilson, *Records*, 2: 73; Madison, ibid., 2: 74; Mason, ibid., 2: 78.

43. Madison, *Records*, 3: 424, italics added.

44. I am indebted to Cass Sunstein for pressing this point on me.

45. I am indebted to Justice Suetens of the Belgian Cour d'Arbitrage for this point.

46. For a review of this case, see G. R. Stone et al., *Constitutional Law*, 2d ed. (Boston: Little, Brown, 1991), 568–81.

47. The Constitution of the United States says only that their compensation 'shall not be diminished during their continuance in office'. At the Convention, however, Madison argued (2: 45) that one should also make it impossible to bribe judges by *increasing* their salary.

48. W. Nordhaus, 'The Political Business Cycle', *Review of Economic Studies* 42 (1975): 169–90, at 188.

49. Mounier, *Archives*, 8: 555.

50. Clermont-Tonnerre, *Archives*, 8: 574; Malouet, ibid., 8: 591.

51. *Records*, 1: 421–22.

52. Dickinson, *Records*, 2: 429; Mason, ibid., 1: 254; Lally-Tollendal, *Archives*, 8: 515.

53. Gerry, *Records*, 2: 286; Wilson, ibid., 2: 522; Madison, ibid., 1: 218–19.

54. Morris, *Records*, 2: 52.

55. Recall here that the same two procedures – qualified majorities and delays – are also used as constraints on constitutional amendments.

56. Madison, *Records*, 1: 108; Morris, ibid., 2: 52, 2: 76; Mason, ibid., 2: 78.

57. Some of the interventions quoted in this paragraph may seem to refer to majoritarian interests rather than passions; see, however, note 21 above.

58. I am indebted to Bernard Manin and Pasquale Pasquino for help in understanding the motivations of the *constituants* on this issue.

59. LaSalle, *Archives*, 8: 529; Lameth, ibid., 8: 551; Grégoire, ibid., 8: 567; LaSalle, ibid., 8: 534; Pétion, ibid., 8: 581.

60. Lally-Tollendal, ibid., 8: 517–18; Mirabeau, ibid., 8: 538; Malouet, ibid., 8: 535–36; Duport, ibid., 28: 263ff.; Barnave, ibid., 28: 326ff.; Duport, ibid., 28: 265.

61. Wilson, *Records*, 2: 301.

62. Morris, ibid., 2: 299–300.

63. D'Antraigues, *Archives*, 8: 544; Mirabeau, ibid., 8: 539; Mounier, ibid., 8: 561; Lanjuinais, ibid, 8: 588.

64. Sherman, *Records*, 1: 60; Morris, ibid., 1: 29; Madison, ibid., 2: 109.

65. Morris, ibid., 2: 585; Gerry, ibid., 2: 586.

66. The following applies to the situation at the time of writing (April 1993). I do not discuss developments in the former Soviet Union, partly because I know less about them and partly because they appear to be less advanced. The total lack of references to Albania is due to the very fluid nature of the constitutional process in that country, together with the difficulty of obtaining accurate information. For obvious reasons I do not consider the new constitution of the rump Yugoslavia (Serbia and Montenegro) that was adopted on April 13, 1992.

67. For details, see W. Osiatynski, 'The Roundtable Negotiations in Poland', working paper from the Center for Study of Constitutionalism in Eastern Europe, University of Chicago Law School.

68. For Poland, see A. Rapaczynski, 'Constitutional Politics in Poland', *University of Chicago Law Review* 58 (1991): 595–632, at 615.

69. For a discussion, see L. Cutler and H. Schwartz, 'Constitutional Reform in Czechoslovakia', *University of Chicago Law Review* 58 (1991): 511–53, at 536.

70. For a discussion, see E. Klingsberg, 'Judicial Review and Hungary's Transition from Communism to Democracy', *Brigham Young University Law Review* 41 (1992): 41–144. Klingsberg concludes that this clause was intended not only to protect rights from being limited by statute, but 'to entrench fundamental rights in the Constitution beyond the reach of the amendment process'.

71. To see the potentially illiberal implications of this clause, the following characterization of communist Bulgarian practices may be useful: 'There are . . . public campaigns

directed at two religious practices which, though phrased in terms of their public health implications, could easily be seen as connecting the campaign against Turkish names with an anti-Islam campaign. The government has directly called for an end to the Ramadan feast and ritual circumcision, calling the former "A Means of Crippling the Individual", while describing the latter as "Criminal Interference with Children's Health."' R. J. McIntyre, *Bulgaria: Politics, Economics and Society* (London: Pinter, 1988), 73.

72. I was told by a judge on the Slovenian constitutional court that the greatest weakness of their constitution, in his opinion, is that rights are limited only by the rights of others, with no room for public-interest limitations.

73. For a survey, see H. Schwartz, 'The New Eastern European Constitutional Courts', *Michigan Journal of International Law* 13 (1992): 741–85.

74. For details, see Klingsberg, 'Judicial Review'.

75. Constitutional Court Decisions No. 21/1990, No. 16/1991 and No. 28/1991. For discussions, see Klingsberg, 'Judicial Review', and P. Paczolay, 'Judicial Review of the Compensation Law in Hungary', *Michigan Journal of International Law* 13 (1992): 806–31.

76. Constitutional Court Decision No. 11/1992.

77. Decision rendered on April 22, 1992.

78. Here is a brief summary. In Slovenia, parliament appoints ordinary judges as well as judges to the constitutional court. In Croatia, ordinary judges are appointed by an independent judicial body, whereas judges to the constitutional court are appointed by parliament. A similar system obtains in Poland. In Romania and Bulgaria, ordinary judges are appointed by independent judicial bodies, whereas the power to appoint judges to the constitutional court is divided among the three powers of state. In Hungary, parliament appoints judges to the constitutional court, whereas the president (de facto the government) appoints ordinary judges.

Reproduced with permission from Jon Elster, 'Majority Rule and Individual Rights', in Stephen Shute and Susan Hurley, eds., *On Human Rights* (New York: Basic Books, 1993).

8

Are Human Rights Truly Universal?

Antonio Cassese

The Problem

Mankind today has a number of great normative texts setting out the fundamental rights and freedoms that ought to be enjoyed by every individual on
earth, and correlatively the self-limitations that states should adopt in order
to guarantee these rights and liberties. It is no coincidence that these texts
were drawn up under the aegis of the organization that brings together
almost all states in the international community: the United Nations. The
texts are known, if not to all, at least to many: the 1948 Universal Declaration
of Human Rights, the 1966 Covenant on Civil and Political Rights, with its
accompanying Optional Protocol (which provides for the right of individuals
to make complaints concerning violations of the Covenant by governments),
and the Covenant on Economic, Social and Cultural Rights, also of 1966.

The first document in this trilogy binds all states in the world; but not with
those relatively heavy bonds deriving from true legal norms. It binds them
through its moral and political weight, and through the authority derived
from the fact that it constitutes a set of natural-law principles to which the
states of the world are invited to adhere. The Covenants have different advantages. Precisely because they are actual treaties, they bind only those
countries that have explicitly accepted them through the formal procedure
of ratification or accession. They are therefore stronger in that they lay down
binding legal imperatives, but at the same time they are also weaker in that
they involve only those states that have agreed to observe them, some 90 out
of 171 states.

The three documents seek to address the whole of mankind with a single
voice. And they do indeed provide the same broad parameters of behaviour
for all states. But it would have been unrealistic for them to set forth rigidly
the same scheme of relationships between governments and individuals for
all countries in the world; they could not, in other words, have projected onto
the world stage the same *model of society* and the same *model of state*. Suffice it

to note that the documents were drawn up by states of vastly diverse kinds: some industrialized, others developing; some with market economies, others with planned economies; pluralist states and one-party states; states with official national religions and others that were secular; military regimes and civilian regimes; monarchies and republics; autocratic governments and parliamentary democracies. It would have been unlikely that any of the 'fathers' of those great treaties would have agreed to the adoption by the world community of a system of government or model of society that was the radical negation of their own domestic regime. It is unrealistic to imagine a state collaborating in the setting up of an international normative framework destined to be used by others to deny the legitimacy of its own domestic political system.

Accordingly, the decalogues set up at the international level in no way 'favour' any of the various political or governmental systems I have just mentioned. They quite rightly do not attempt to make the internal political situation in the various countries fit some absurd Procrustean bed. Each country is left free to adopt the institutional arrangements and political system most congenial to it, those which best reflect its people's needs and its national traditions. All that the texts demand is respect for certain *minimum standards* concerning relations between the citizen and the state: respect for certain essential human rights, certain essential freedoms and the right to self-government. Each country is free to decide how to bring about this self-government (through a multi-party system or a single party; by proportional or first-past-the-post electoral systems, or on the basis of the 'blocked single slate'). Each country also has the right to decide how it will organize the periodic consultations necessary to appoint its ruling bodies, just as each state may decide how it will allow for citizen participation in government. Equally, each state may place restrictions on the fundamental rights and freedoms of its citizens for reasons dictated by requirements of public order or national security, morality or health. Finally, each state has the right to choose its own economic and social system and may place restrictions on the fundamental rights and freedoms of its citizens for reasons dictated by requirements of public order or national security, morality or health. Finally, each state has the right to choose its own economic and social system – whether this be capitalist, socialist or of some other kind – so long as it respects and promotes certain rights enjoyed by individuals in the sphere of economic and social relations.

As can be seen, then, the international decalogues are very flexible. This flexibility is accentuated by the well-recognized limitations inherent in the supervisory mechanisms provided for at the international level. The states bound by the Covenants thus enjoy a large measure of manoeuvre.

Despite all this, the fact remains that the Declaration and the two Covenants set forth rules of universal scope, which are supposed, at least so far as their general thrust is concerned, to be valid for all states in the world, and which have as their beneficiaries the five thousand million inhabitants of the earth. But is this relative universality *real*? Are these rules, these universal precepts, perceived and implemented in the same way throughout the world, or do greater differences and divergences exist than those already allowed by the rules themselves?

One could easily reply that this search for universality is vain or otiose: not even within the most homogeneous group of states – the members of the Council of Europe – can one discern identical views on many crucial problems. Dissimilar views have even been taken by the two international organs responsible for ensuring the proper implementation of the European Convention on Human Rights: the European Commission and Court of Human Rights. By way of illustration, I shall mention the infamous 'five techniques to help interrogation' used by the British Security Forces in Northern Ireland in 1971: while the European Commission held in 1976 that the techniques amounted to torture proper,[1] the European Court found in 1978 that they did not cause a suffering so intense as to constitute torture, and rather amounted to 'inhuman or degrading treatment'.[2] Similarly, the refusal of British authorities to remove from the birth certificate of a male transsexual a reference to his being a female at birth – a reference that produced a good deal of adverse consequences for the social and working life of the person concerned – was unanimously regarded by the European Commission in 1984 as a breach of the 'right to respect for one's private life', whereas the European Court, by a majority vote, took the opposite view in 1986.[3] Plainly, such differences of opinion cannot be eliminated, nor indeed are they to be deprecated: human rights make up such a complex, multifaceted and intricate matter that divergences are inevitable, when it comes to the implementation of those rights.

The questions I have raised do not aim at establishing whether there exists complete uniformity in the interpretation and application of human rights standards. By raising those questions I intended rather to look at the *basic approaches and perceptions* taken by states in the area of human rights, in order to see to what extent they diverge or converge.

Before addressing these questions, I shall briefly dwell on two possible answers that would constitute easy ways out.

First, the questions raised above could be dismissed outright by those who still believe in the famous proposition by Joseph de Maistre: 'I have met in my life French, Italians, Russians, etc.; I even know, thanks to Montesquieu, that one can be Persian; but nowhere have I met in my life the man; if he does exist, this is without my knowing.'[4] It follows logically from this proposition that, as individuals and groups are different – by definition – there cannot exist any similarity of application or even perception of human rights standards in the various nations of the world. And yet, close analysis of the present condition shows, as I shall point out below, that convergences do indeed exist and that many states tend to take the same basic view of human rights.

Another answer to the above questions might be found in the work of the French philosopher Jean Hyppolite. In 1964 Hyppolite wrote of the paradox whereby our epoch is at the same time the one in which the 'existential

sense of universality' is strongest, partly because 'all regions of the earth
have now been discovered and have come into relationship with each other',
and also the one in which there has been the clearest 'decline in universal
foundations and standards'.[5] And yet, this answer, right in itself, is not
enough: there are specific reasons, *peculiar to human rights*, that militate
against this universality.

Divergences in Philosophical Conceptions and Cultural Traditions

Let me say immediately that universality is, at least for the present, a myth.
Not only are human rights observed differently – certainly to differing
degrees – in different countries; but they are also *conceived of* differently. I
shall seek to identify the principal points on which the various countries of
the world still seem far apart: in other words, the points at which the effort at
world unification, pursued in developing the three great documents, has still
not been accomplished.

Firstly, there are profound divergences in the *philosophical conception* of
human rights. The Western countries continue tenaciously to defend their
'natural-law' view of human rights – the one they put forward when the three
great texts were being drafted. For them, human rights are innate in individuals, are an intrinsic factor in the 'quality of the human person', and
hence precede any state structure and must be absolutely respected by governments. A state that violates them in its laws and its actions breaches one of
the very prerequisites of civil coexistence between states and may legitimately
be brought to account.

For the socialist countries, by contrast, human rights exist only in society
and in the state, and only to the extent that they are specifically recognized.
They do not pre-exist the state, but rather are accorded by it. The state may
therefore limit them when circumstances so require.

Another important divergence concerns different *cultural and religious conceptions*. For the West, proclaiming human rights means above all protecting
the sphere of individual freedom against the overweening power of an invasive state. This concept – which, as is well known, goes back to Locke – was
very effectively brought out by Benjamin Constant in his famous essay on
Freedom ancient and modern (1819)[6] – an essay in which many see a moderate
reduction of the lofty principles proclaimed in 1789. 'For the ancients,' wrote
Constant, 'freedom was constituted by active, constant participation in the
commonwealth. Our freedom ought to consist in the peaceful enjoyment of
private independence . . .'[7] Individual autonomy is the foremost modern
need.'[8] For the ancients, freedom 'consisted in the collective, but direct exercise of various parts of the whole sovereignty; in discussing in the public
forum war and peace, in concluding treaties of alliance with foreigners,
voting on laws, in pronouncing judgments, in examining accounts', and so
on; the ancients, though, 'accepted as compatible with this collective freedom the individual's complete subjection to the authority of the whole'.[9] It is
precisely this subjection that man today forcibly rejects. Today, the individual

delegates to others the exercise of political power: what concerns him is 'safety in private enjoyment' ('la sécurité dans les jouissances privées');[10] Constant characterized freedom as 'the guarantees accorded by the institutions for that enjoyment'.[11]

This is, broadly speaking, the Western conception of liberty. There is a markedly different view in the socialist countries and again in the Third World. For the former, the individual's freedom can be realized only in a society in which classes, bound up with the capitalist system of production, have ceased to exist, so that the individual can fully participate without hindrance or inequalities in the life of the community. Taking up concepts that were first put forward by J. J. Rousseau, socialist thinkers and politicians argue that freedom does not necessarily mean putting restraints on an oppressive central power: the central power is an expression of the community and identifies itself with it. Freedom means rather the creation of mechanisms that promote and enhance integration between individual and community. The stress is no longer on the dialectic between liberty and authority, but on the dialectic between individual and community.

A still more radical difference in conception is the one between the Western and the Asian great cultural traditions. In the Buddhist conception, society is patterned on the family: the political leader – the emperor, in the past – is like the father of a family, with all the powers, authority and responsibilities of the *pater familias*. Freedom therefore consists not in guaranteeing a space free from possible invasion or oppression by the authorities, but in harmonizing as far as possible the individual's action with the leader's, in view of the duty of obedience owed to the latter.

Even more inclined to subject individuals to the political leader is the Hindu tradition, which has impregnated the social life, and especially the ideology, of India, right up to its Declaration of Independence, and beyond. In Hindu tradition, division into castes – though legally abolished – still involves an obligation on each member of the caste to accept their social status without rebellion. It is the task of all individuals to strive to act positively within their own caste, in order to pass to a superior caste in the next life, or at least not worsen their social standing after death. There is no question of any struggle against authority or of safeguarding a sphere of freedom against an external power.

Similar considerations hold true for Confucianism, a religion (and also a vision of society and of relations between individuals) that developed first in China and subsequently spread to Japan. In Confucian tradition the fundamental nucleus of society is the family; within this miniature social structure, the primary position goes to the head of the household, who is owed unconditional respect by the other members. This patriarchal vision is extended to the state: the emperor is seen as the head of a family to whom absolute deference is owed. This leaves little room for human rights. The same is also true in the Islamic tradition, or at least in practice in the Islamic countries, which have in some respects steadily moved away from the principles of the Qu'ran. In particular, although there is no radical incompatibility between Islam and the essential principles of human rights, there is a conflict as regards the relationship between man and woman: in Islam these are placed squarely in a relation of subordination, the latter to the former.

In the African tradition, which is to a large extent a tradition of tribal practices and customs, the individual's self-realization is through the community, which is headed by a leader, to whose authority all must bow. There is no reason to fight against the leader, since he does not oppress the members of the community, but rather guides them by acting in such a way as to allow them to integrate fully into the whole: what he does is thus beneficial to the interests of the collectivity.

It will be objected that all these Asian or African traditions have been, as it were, diluted or enfeebled by contact with the modern state: as soon as that characteristic construct of Western Europe has taken root in Africa or Asia, all its characteristic ambiguities and concerns have surfaced, including the dialectic between authority and liberty. This also explains why modern state structures have such difficulty functioning in so many African or Asian countries. It is a plant that puts down roots only slowly, and all too often finds itself there in inhospitable, if not indeed sterile, soil.

Divergences in Treatment of the Problem of International Protection of Human Rights

Looking more closely at the attitude of states, one finds still further divergences and conflicts as regards a number of fundamental issues bound up with human rights.

Firstly, there is a difference between the socialist 'statist' conception of human rights, and the current Western *international*, or rather 'metanational', view. I shall attempt to explain in what this divergence consists.

In the socialist view, it is the task of the international community to agree on a series of broad rules or standards as to the categories or types of human rights to be recognized, that is, as to the restrictions that sovereign states have to accept in order to give sufficient 'space' to individuals within the internal system of each country. Once this step has been taken, it is for each state to lend greater specificity to these broad rules or standards. This is done through domestic legislation laying down the scope of the rights, the powers of the governmental authorities and the procedures open to individuals to seek redress should the rights be breached. At this point, the international community no longer has anything to say on the matter: only sovereign states can decide – though of course within the framework set by the international rules on how human rights are to be observed and implemented. The international community 'passes the baton', as it were, to national systems, particularly as regards checks on observance of the rights in question. This means that so far as the socialist countries are concerned, it is not for other states, or the organized international community, to inquire into the observance of human rights. This would contravene a fundamental principle of international law, namely the prohibition of interference in internal affairs –

a principle that has the essential objective of protecting state sovereignty and keeping every country in the condition of self-sufficient, well-armoured monads. The sole exception to this rule of absolute non-interference in the affairs of other states is where breaches of human rights become so grave and systematic as to constitute a threat to peace. Only in this case is the organized international community entitled to intervene by discussing the situation, making recommendations and, if necessary, going further, even to the point of recommending or, if possible, ordering sanctions (the cases of South Africa, Chile and Israel – the latter for violations in the occupied Arab Territories – being, for the socialist countries, examples of such exceptions to the rule of absolute non-interference).

The position of Western states, particularly Scandinavian countries and some other countries in Western Europe, is radically different. They hold that the modern state ought to become a sort of 'glass house', so that anyone can look in and establish whether what goes on there conforms to international standards. According to the West, this right to outside inspection may be exercised through the creation of international monitoring mechanisms, whose aim is to ascertain whether a state is in fact observing the international obligations it has assumed. In the view of these states it is absurd to make a sharp distinction between accepting obligations concerning human rights at the international level, and implementing those obligations at the national level. There must be a continuum, an uninterrupted chain between international and national actions. Why? For one very simple reason: the state agencies all too often fail to observe international obligations which come from 'outside'; or else national authorities charged with translating international obligations into domestic rules of conduct 'manipulate' these obligations and adapt them to the needs of national sovereignty – all the more so because normally the beneficiaries of the international rules are citizens of the state being called on to apply those rules, that is, the very individuals over whom the government authorities are seeking to maintain their power in other ways. Only the vigilant eye of the international community can ensure the proper observance of international standards, in the interest not of one state or another but of the individuals themselves.

A second difference between East and West closely follows the first: it concerns the main features that international supervisory mechanisms ought to present. After long drawn-out debates, talks and negotiations, the socialist countries have ended up accepting the Western idea that international instruments are needed to ensure, or at least encourage, national respect for international standards on human rights. This conversion to the West's idea was, however, a painful process, which carried with it the dilution of international supervisory procedures and the attachment of so many qualifications as practically to make them a blunt weapon. In the eyes of the West, the most effective form of international scrutiny is for the individual who is denied a right to which he or she is entitled, to 'activate' some form of international guarantee. And yet not even the West shows much enthusiasm for advocating international *judicial* guarantees: that is, international courts

before which individuals could bring actions against states, accusing the
latter of infringing upon human rights. The boldest Western countries (once
again, the Western European states, plus some Scandinavian countries and
Canada) do however assert the need at least to set up international
monitoring agencies. An individual whose rights have been breached could
then seek the moral and political 'condemnation' of the state responsible.
Such a condemnation would not be an actual judgment, but rather a non-
binding verdict. Besides, as is well known, the quasi-judicial procedures
existing within the Council of Europe (procedures hinging on two bodies,
the European Commission and Court of Human Rights) are quite exceptional, for attempts made in Latin America to establish similar mechanisms
have not yet yielded significant results.

For the West the reasons behind this conception of international scrutiny
are obvious. Firstly, only a monitoring system activated by those directly
affected by breaches can prove truly effective, for if it is the case, which it usually is, that breaches have been committed by a state against its own citizens,
no other international subject or agency has an interest in setting in motion
a guarantee mechanism. Secondly, if the supervisory procedures are at least
quasi-judicial, there is an assurance that the findings of fact will be something
approaching the truth. Clearly, only adversarial proceedings, where both
parties (the individual complainant and the accused government) have a
chance to state their cases and an assessment is arrived at by a group of
people truly independent of the parties, can provide the guarantees of equity
and justice required in such a delicate area. The Western states (or at least
many of them) have gradually come to embrace the concept of 'right of
petition to an international body' which France, supported by the Eastern
European countries, had proposed in 1946–8. So the situation is now
reversed with Eastern Europe steadfast against any right of international
petition and the West its staunch supporter. It is too early to say whether the
demise of control by communist parties in Eastern Europe will affect any
change in this area of international relations.

Let us look at the limits within which the socialist countries have come cautiously to approach the Western position on international supervision. For
most states of Eastern Europe, the sole form of acceptable international supervision consisted in *periodic consideration* – by intergovernmental bodies – of
reports on observance of international rules drawn up by the individual states
concerned. For most Eastern European states, this type of monitoring respects
the concept of national sovereignty, while making some cautious concession to
the need for international openness. National sovereignty is fully guaranteed
since the subject of verification is the periodic report drawn up by one individual state itself: accordingly, everything is in full conformity with the notion
that it is for each state to ensure application of the international norms within
its own domestic order in accordance with the modalities it prefers. It is for
the individual state to report to the international bodies on the way in which
it has applied the international rules. The international body may make observations and comments, but never go so far as to make specific criticism, let

alone condemnations. From this point of view too, then, state sovereignty remains intact. It is easy to imagine how this kind of control is implemented in practice: every state tends to depict its own domestic system as a paradise, or something like it, and international bodies must confine themselves to articulating cautious doubts or setting forth considerations of a general nature. State sovereignty emerges victorious; individuals disappear from the international scene, and the violations they have suffered remain unexposed.

Another sharp differentiation, again chiefly between East and West, concerns the conception of the *link between human rights and the maintenance of peace.* For the socialist countries, protection of human rights is one of the ways of promoting the maintenance of peaceful relationships among states. They start from the arguments put forward at the end of the Second World War and 'codified' in the United Nations Charter. The great conflagration that had shaken the world had largely been due to the racist, totalitarian policy of Nazism. Accordingly, if political systems that respected human rights were gradually to be furthered throughout the world, this would help to ward off the threat of another world conflict. This argument, correct in itself, can, however, lead to a fallacious conclusion: peace being the supreme goal, everything else takes *second place*; accordingly, if in some particular circumstance the need to respect human rights is liable to cause friction and conflict, thereby threatening peace, it must be swept under the carpet. Between the two goals, the one that must prevail is that of peace. Understood properly, this view is a logical extension of the idea that everything should turn around the essential pivot of state sovereignty, with its corollary of the prohibition on interference in the domestic affairs of other states. In fact, continually advocating the maintenance of friendly relationships among states as the ultimate goal leads to the perception that requiring some country to respect human rights may be a dangerous source of far-reaching disagreement, and accordingly such action should be rejected, indeed forbidden by the international community. (On this issue see however the qualifications I set out in the last section of this chapter.)

The West's view is radically different. For the Western countries, the need to ensure respect for human dignity is always pre-eminent. It is therefore acceptable for a state or group of states to take initiatives and make *démarches* towards another state to encourage, or even attempt to force it to show, greater respect for human rights, even if this goes against 'good neighbourliness', or friendly relations in general. For the West, the proper balance between the need to respect the domestic affairs of foreign states and the countervailing requirement to do everything possible to promote respect for human rights is as follows. In cases where violations perpetrated in another state become serious, systematic and massive, intervention by other states or by international organs becomes acceptable, even if it necessarily gives rise to disagreements, tensions, or even conflict.

A fourth area, where there is a wide gap between Western countries on the one hand and Third World and socialist states on the other, concerns the role and weight to be given to the 'international context' in the event of breaches of human rights. In the view of developing countries – joined here by Eastern

European states – it is illogical and inappropriate to seek out violations committed in other states and then accuse the governments concerned of trampling on human rights. Breaches of those rights – not only civil and political rights but also, and even more so, economic, social and cultural ones – should instead be considered in the general context of the internal situation of the state being challenged, and also as regards the position of that state vis-à-vis other countries. According to this view, if account is not taken of the overall picture, two risks arise. Firstly, one fails to identify, and come to grips with, the *causes* of the breaches of human rights. These causes normally lie in underdevelopment; in the need to cope adequately with economic and social problems; and in international conditions, in the main economic ones, but also political ones (which are believed to explain why countries are, on occasions, compelled to suspend or restrict certain rights, such as trade union freedom, rights to private property or freedom of movement, in order to meet international economic pressures – for instance, the need to pay debts to foreign banks or cope with a fall in the price of raw materials). The second danger which lies in a 'narrow view' of breaches of human rights is that these breaches can be *instrumentalized* in order to criticize certain countries in which underdevelopment, transitory historical circumstances and so on may make some restriction of freedom necessary. This instrumentalization is, according to those states, most often practised by Western countries, in order to point the finger at developing or socialist countries and condition their actions at home and abroad.

The West's reply to this thesis is that all too often these arguments act merely as a 'rationalization' of domestic failings: facile excuses, to justify serious departures from international standards. These departures very often originate from authoritarian forms of government, particularly from military regimes. For the West there is very little foundation in the two theses mentioned, which amount to nothing more than 'ideology'.

As we can see, in this area too there is a considerable split between two groups, which seem to end up inevitably accusing each other of instrumentalization for propaganda purposes.

A fifth area where the confrontation seems no less bitter concerns the *relationship between two classes of human rights*: civil and political rights on the one hand, and economic, social and cultural ones on the other. According to the developing and many socialist countries, the second group is the one that ought to be favoured in international action. There are two reasons. Firstly, these rights are intrinsically more important. What sense is there in talking of freedom of expression when one is hungry, jobless or homeless? Economic and social rights have absolute priority, for it is only when they are fully realized that it is possible to create the *de facto* equality that makes civil and political rights fully realizable. The second reason is that, especially in developing countries, it is in the economic and social fabric that the most painful shortcomings exist, so that this is where intervention is most needed. In those countries, economic and social backwardness means that not only are roads, hospitals and infrastructures generally lacking, but so are elementary and higher education. This, then, is the area where intervention is needed, to narrow the gap which separates these countries from the industrialized ones. Accordingly, progressive recognition of economic, social and cultural rights must be insisted on, at the international level.

The Western states, by contrast, tend to put the emphasis on civil and political rights. This is firstly because these rights are a 'highlight' in their history, virtually symbolizing the progress of the modern state, having been wrested from despotic power following bitter struggle, rebellion or revolution. A second reason is that for Western countries respect for these rights continues to be of great significance. The major human rights issue in Western industrialized states remains: to what extent is the central apparatus to be limited so as to prevent it excessively invading the individual's sphere? The economic structure of these countries, with a market economy (so that individual initiative and enterprise still have an extremely important role), along with the excessive growth of the state, which tends to penetrate every area of private life, even the most intimate ones, mean that civil and political rights remain crucial. There is nothing more obvious for these states than to *project outwards* their own problems and concerns, and hence, internationally too, to favour this category of rights and freedom. Apart from that, though, there are also less 'ideological' motives. The Western countries stress that full enjoyment of material prosperity is worth little unless one is free to express one's ideas, elect the people one prefers to lead the state, or travel and move freely both at home and abroad. Civil and political rights thus remain indispensable, even if the state's effort has to concentrate primarily on raising the population's standard of living. It follows that it is meaningless to set up a hierarchy among categories of rights; above all, for the states in question, it is meaningless to relegate civil and political freedoms to second place, as if they were a luxury.

As we can see, in this case too the divergences among the various alignments of states are profound, and the diplomatic formulas that have been used to make the twain meet on paper are rather meaningless. One of these formulas speaks about the 'interdependence of civil and political rights with economic, social and cultural ones'. This convenient catchphrase serves to dampen the debate while leaving everything the way it was. The diplomats who thrash out these verbal solutions at international meetings go back home satisfied, each thinking their own interpretation of the (conveniently ambiguous) phrase agreed upon is the right one. In fact, the problems remain, and the political and ideological clashes are postponed, only to emerge even more pointedly at the next opportunity.

Divergences Regarding Particular Human Rights

Turning now to a consideration of specific rights and freedoms, here too we come up against considerable differentiation in the way states see these rights. Clearly, divergences can be noted in the way states apply the 'escape clauses' in order to allow themselves room for manoeuvre. These clauses allow for 'suspension of obligations' for reasons of public order, national security, morals, public health and so on. Admittedly, the various international supervisory bodies have managed to secure acceptance for the principle that these concepts ought not to be interpreted solely and exclusively in the light of corresponding national concepts. This has barred the way to utter fragmentation of those clauses and to total anarchy in the application of the rights that those clauses restrict and constrain. Nevertheless the fact remains that every state, though it cannot simply hide behind its own domestic law, retains considerable discretion, for it is impossible at the international level to furnish a uniform interpretation of the clauses, and the supervisory bodies have no judicial powers that would enable them to lay down binding interpretations. In the last instance, the scope of the escape clauses remains in the hands of the state concerned.

Furthermore, significant differences can be identified in the very conception of some specific human rights. I shall give only a few examples, starting with freedom of movement. For the Western countries, this is one of the most important forms of manifestation of the personality. How can an individual develop and achieve self-realization without being free to move about the national territory, freely choose residence and workplace, in a word, decide the 'area' most in line with individual interests and activities? This freedom also includes the possibility of going abroad, whether for leisure, self-improvement, or just to live in a country where one's qualities are better appreciated or better paid. For the West, freedom of movement is not only part of the concept of freedom of the individual and free enterprise, but also derives from an essential postulate: the human person has potential, and must be free to develop and enrich it. In other words, the basis for that freedom is not only the capitalistic-individualistic conception of the world, but also the conception of man that came to maturity with the Renaissance: the human person is seen as a microcosm containing a number of potential areas for development, all of which deserve an environment which will allow them to grow.

This view is bound to fall on deaf ears in the Third World and in the socialist countries. In the former, the need for economic take-off necessitates drastic limitations on the 'brain-drain'. However much it may be the fault of colonialism, it is a fact that at independence those countries found themselves with very few graduates or other qualified people, and therefore had quickly to train new leaders and managers. It would therefore be illogical from their viewpoint to permit the expatriation of young people attracted abroad by easy gain or by the facilities of modern, well-equipped research centres. Similarly, within those countries there is a need to restrict movement: the rapid formation of a few urban centres, densely populated and with abundant service industries, dangerously impoverishes the countryside – where leaders and managers (technicians, doctors, engineers and so on) are also needed. Somewhat similar considerations have applied so far to many socialist countries; however, there, in addition to economic reasons, there were more strictly political or ideological ones for restricting freedom of movement. All this has made the Third World and socialist concept of freedom of movement diametrically opposite to that prevailing in the West.

Similar differences can be found, as regards the effect of science and technology on the enjoyment of human rights. Debate on this topic was initiated by France at the United Nations in the 1970s. For France and other Western countries, there was a need to identify and restrain the dangerous outcomes that modern technology might have for the privacy of individuals and groups. Not surprisingly, the problem was not seen in the same terms in non-industrial countries where the development of technology was welcomed. Far from seeking restrictions on the possible uses of computers, those countries instead pressed for the introduction of scientific and technological progress to their communities.

A third example concerns the right to development. The Third World, supported by the socialists, latched onto this right as early as the 1970s. For them it was a fundamental right belonging both to individuals and to peoples and states. It was a multivalent right, referring both to improvement in economic conditions, and to social, political and cultural development. The entities on which the obligation to fulfil the right was incumbent were states, above all the industrialized ones. So far as the Western countries were concerned, by contrast, this right was a mere slogan; a subterfuge used to include as a human rights issue a demand that the Third World had long and loudly been proclaiming, namely, a demand for major economic assistance from the industrialized countries. As has been pointed out, utilization of human rights rhetoric for this demand had one clear aim: *to dramatize* it, by transforming it into a 'right' so that its bearers could exact its realization from those who, accordingly, had a 'duty' to respect and realize it. (See, however, the qualifications set out in the next section.)

Are There Points of Convergence?

After what I have written so far, it might be thought the international community was irremediably divided with no meeting point, even on this broad topic of human rights. Every state or group of states, while paying lip-service to a number of commonly accepted precepts, would in fact be serving national needs and interests which are not congruent with those precepts. The 'universality' of human rights standards would be merely a convenient cover, aimed at concealing underlying disputes and differences. That is undoubtedly true. However, there are elements that somewhat moderate and mitigate the ideological and political splits. I shall bring out three essential factors.

Firstly, it is a fact that the Universal Declaration and the various covenants, treaties and declarations that followed ended up involving and, as it were, 'ensnaring' states which were opposed or indifferent to certain aspects of human rights, either due to their historical and cultural traditions or due to different ideologies. Thus, as I have shown elsewhere, the socialist countries, having first shown perplexity over, and indeed hostility towards, the Universal

Declaration, ended up collaborating in drafting it. Admittedly, they began by thinking of using it as a weapon in the Cold War. But they gradually came to believe in the Declaration as a great ethical and political decalogue that should inspire their actions. More or less the same thing happened to many Third World countries, which ended up energetically participating in producing, if not the Declaration (many of them were not yet independent in 1946–8), at least the 1966 Covenants. This involved them in a process of debate and negotiation in which, while they put forward their needs and asserted their demands, they also accepted many Western or socialist conceptions. Thus, gradually, the various parameters included in the three international documents in question finished by offering the prospect of common lines of action. Admittedly, this process of unification remains at the moment mainly at a 'rhetorical' level, that is, a normative and to some extent ideological one. But in a world as divided, and fragmented, as the international community today, the existence of a *set of general standards*, however diversely understood and applied, in itself constitutes an important factor for unification.

I wish to stress a second point: despite the differences I have sought to illustrate, a *restricted core* of values and criteria universally accepted by all the states is gradually emerging.

Firstly, one has the impression that some consensus is coming about as to the *relative order of importance* of the various rights; in other words, an understanding in principle as to their 'hierarchy' (although of course any human right is important and indispensable per se, one may however establish an order of priority, subject to the caveat that this is tentative, historically relative and primarily operates as a sort of working hypothesis). This understanding is to some extent reflected in a speech delivered in 1977 by the then US Secretary of State Cyrus Vance.[12] In his view, the fundamental core of human rights is made up of the right to life and security: the right not to be tortured or killed illegally. There then follow rights relating to the fundamental needs of the human person: the rights to work, to decent housing, to nourishment, to protection of health. Thirdly, still in some sort of order of importance, are some civil and political rights like freedom of expression and of association, the right to choose a government and hold public office, and so on. I feel that this grading departs considerably from traditional Western conceptions and goes some way to meet the aspirations and ideological conceptions of the Third World and the socialist countries. It might therefore be regarded as a point of *rapprochement* between the opposing views (the fact that subsequent US administrations have not consistently upheld Vance's view in no way detracts from its intrinsic importance).

There has also been another convergence. Practically all states in the world seem to share the idea that some of the gravest breaches of human rights are genocide, racial discrimination (in particular, apartheid), the practice of torture, and the refusal to recognize the right of peoples to self-determination. This means that agreement in principle has developed, at least as regards an essential core of human values among almost all states in the world. It is foreseeable that this agreement in principle will gradually come to embrace an increasingly wide range of rights.

Furthermore, some convergence has come about in other important areas. For example, recently Eastern European states seem less unresponsive to the Western view of the *relationship between peace and respect for human rights* (reference to this view was made in the third section of this chapter). They now tend to take a somewhat looser view than before, as is evidenced by their voting in favour of General Assembly Resolution 37/200 of 18 December 1982, where it is stated that the absence of peace can in no way relieve a state from its obligation to ensure respect for the human rights of all those under its jurisdiction. Similarly, most Eastern European countries are in the process of changing their minds as far as *international monitoring* is concerned. They now seem less hostile to outside scrutiny of national implementation of international standards in a number of fields including human rights. Behind this shift in the attitude of Eastern European countries one can discern a change in their approach to the principle of non-interference in domestic affairs. Previously, those countries consistently insisted on the rule that states should neither inquire nor make representations about alleged breaches of human rights in other states, as such action ran counter to the long-standing principle of non-interference. The only permissible exception was where the breaches were so serious, large-scale and systematic as to amount to a threat to international peace. Recently this approach has been relaxed, as is borne out by the final document adopted at Vienna, on 19 January 1989, by the CSCE (Conference on Security and Co-operation in Europe). All but one of the thirty-five states adopted the text on the 'Human Dimension of the CSCE' which is of striking importance (Romania entered a reservation). This text provides that each participating state is entitled to *request* from other states, through diplomatic channels, *information* about cases (including specific cases) which raise questions of human rights. In addition, each state may make *observations* to which responses must be given. Furthermore, each state can bring up those cases in *bilateral* meetings. Once a state has received the requested information or response, it may raise the whole question with other participating states in the CSCE. This shift from a *bilateral* to a *multilateral framework* can take place in two ways: a state can simply pass on the received information or response together with its own comments (if any) to the other participating states; or, it may raise the question at one of the meetings of the CSCE. Although of course the CSCE is primarily a European exercise, to a large extent it reflects emerging trends at the universal level.

Yet another area where *rapprochement* is taking place is the right to development. The cleavage between industrialized Western countries and developing nations, to which I drew attention in the preceding section, is now narrowing. This is borne out by the fact that on 4 December 1986 a number of Western countries (including France, Canada and Italy) voted in favour of a General Assembly Resolution on this matter (Resolution 41/128) (however, the United States cast a negative vote, while other Western states including the United Kingdom, the Federal Republic of Germany, Japan and Sweden abstained). This Resolution to a large extent amalgamated the approach of developing countries and that of the West, by diluting the former and incorporating a great number of Western demands relating to the need for developing countries to respect human rights, if they wish to benefit from economic cooperation with industrialized countries.

The third factor I consider important concerns the value of the Declaration and the two Covenants. Despite differences on their interpretation and application, no state (except perhaps, at the time of writing, South Africa and Iran)[13] today casts doubt on the significance of these documents as 'targets to aim at' (*standards of achievement*, to use the words of the Universal Declaration). That is, states continue to see in these three documents a set of values that one should strive to realize. This implies that the various countries may gradually harmonize their respective conceptions and visions, drawing impetus, ideas and guidance from these three documents, even if retaining at the same time a divergent set of views and conceptions.

This seems to me to be demonstrated by a number of documents recently adopted by groups of states where traditionally human rights issues have been if not alien, at least remote. I am referring in particular to the African Charter on Human and Peoples' Rights, approved in 1981,[14] and the two Islamic Declarations on Human Rights, approved in 1981[15] and 1986.[16] Reading these documents, one is immediately struck by the appearance of new rights, or by changes in the emphasis or character of rights already proclaimed in the three great international normative texts (for instance, the rights of peoples are stressed). This is not to say that these documents in any way contradict the underlying values internationally agreed upon. On the contrary, if anything, the recent documents reaffirm these values. Equally, it may be noted that some rights (for instance, that of equality between men and women, already consecrated in the Universal Declaration and the Covenants but in practice applied restrictively in some Arab countries) are vigorously asserted in the two inter-Arab documents. It is almost as if, despite awareness of the gap between what is and what ought to be, there was a desire to restate faith in an important international value, as being applicable at 'regional' level.

The three factors I have sought to bring out together with the new trends emerging in socialist countries[17] perhaps constitute pointers to an effort at gradual unification which, however slow and difficult, gives one hope that states' positions may come closer together, in the human rights field, as in others.

Notes

1. Report of the Commission of 25 January in *Yearbook of the European Convention of Human Rights*, vol. 19, 1976, pp. 513–949, at pp. 792–4.

2. Judgment of 18 January 1978 *Ireland vs. United Kingdom, Publications European Court of Human Rights*, Series A, vol. 25 (1978) at pp. 66–7.

3. Judgment of 17 October 1986 *Rees Case, Publications European Court of Human Rights*, Series A, vol. 106 (1987). The Commission's Report of 12 December 1984 is annexed to the

judgment at p. 23.

4. J. de Maistre, *Considérations sur la France* (1797), ed. P. Manent (Editions Complexe, Paris, 1988), p. 87.

5. 'Le Phénomène de la Reconnaissance Universelle dans l'Experiénce Humaine' in *Le Fondament des Droits de l'Homme: Actes des Entretiens de l'Aquila 14–19 Septembre 1964* (La Nuova Italia, Florence, 1966), pp. 122–5 at p. 122.

6. 'De la Liberté des Anciens Comparée à celle des Modernes' in *De la Liberté chez les Modernes*, pp. 491–515.

7. Ibid. at p. 501.

8. Ibid. at p. 506.

9. Ibid. at p. 495.

10. Ibid. at p. 502.

11. Ibid. at p. 502.

12. 'Human Rights and Foreign Policy', address at University of Georgia School of Law, 30 April 1977, *Department of State Bulletin*, 23 May 1977, pp. 505ff.

13. It should be stressed that in his speech of 2 February 1990 President de Klerk emphatically stated that South Africa would live up to the general standards on human rights.

14. For the text, see *Human Rights in International Law: Basic Texts* (Council of Europe, Strasbourg, 1985), pp. 207–25.

15. 'Islamic Universal Declaration of Human Rights' declared 19 September 1981 (UNESCO, Paris) by Mr Salem Azzam, Secretary General of the Islamic Council. For the text see *Droits de l'Homme et Droit des Peuples*, Fondation L. Basso pour de Droit et la Libération des Peuples (S. Marino, Ministero della Cultura, 1983), pp. 228–38.

16. The declaration is known as the 'Draft Charter on Human and People's Rights in the Arab World' and is reproduced in *Information Sheet no. 21 H/INF* (87) 1 (Council of Europe, Strasbourg, 1988), Appendix XXXX, pp. 243–61. This draft Charter represents the view of the participants of a conference held in Syracuse, 5–12 December 1986; however, it is based on a draft prepared by the General Administration for Legal Affairs of the Secretariat General of the League of Arab States.

17. It is worth mentioning in this respect the important statement made by President Gorbachev in Rome, on an official visit, on 30 November 1989. He repeatedly stressed the importance of 'eternal moral values, the simple laws of ethics and humanity', which should 'serve as reference points' for the solution of the new tasks which the world is currently facing (p. 4 of the typewritten text of his statement, kindly provided by the Soviet Embassy in Rome; see also ibid., pp. 7, 9, 18). He also stressed that 'the increasing role of the principles common to all of mankind is not obliterating but rather enriching the originality and the role of national and other characteristics' (ibid., p. 5). Another important point made by Gorbachev is that states should strive to attain a 'completely uniform (. . .) understanding and application of international law' (ibid., p. 16).

9

Democracy and Human Rights under Different Conditions of Development

Robert Dahl

I Democracy and Human Rights

It seems to me beyond question that the most comprehensive systems of political rights and liberties exist in democratic countries. That this is so is scarcely surprising. For one thing, extensive political rights and liberties are *integral* to democracy: they are necessary to the functioning of the institutions that distinguish modern democracy from other kinds of political orders. The rights and liberties are therefore an element in what we often *mean* today by democracy or the democratic process, or a democratic country.

The institutions that, taken as a whole, distinguish modern democracy (or polyarchy) from other regimes, contemporary and historical, are a written or unwritten constitutional system that vests control over government decisions about policy in elected officials; the selection of elected officials in frequent and fairly conducted elections; an inclusive right of adults to vote in these elections as well as run for elective office; a broadly defined and effectively protected right to freedom of expression; the existence of alternative and independent sources of information, to which citizens are entitled to gain access; and the right of citizens to form relatively independent organizations, including independent political parties and interest groups.

Each of these institutions is either an effective right to which citizens are entitled, or it implies the existence of effective rights. Therefore in order to classify a country as democratic we are obliged to make a judgment that certain political rights exist in that country in a realistic (not nominal or formal) sense and at a comparatively high level. If the rights do not exist, or do not exist above a certain threshold, then *by definition* the country is not 'democratic'. To avoid misunderstanding, let me say that in distinguishing between democratic and non-democratic countries we of course employ judgments that are mainly qualitative – about the appropriate threshold for 'democracy' and about the condition of the various rights and institutions in specific countries.

The range of rights and liberties available to citizens in democratic countries, however, goes well beyond what is strictly required for the existence of democracy itself, for people in democratic countries tend to value rights and liberties generally. Stable democracies are supported by a broader culture, political and general, that places more than trivial value on such qualities as personal freedom, fairness, legality, due process and the like. While I can conceive of a purely theoretical democratic system in which persons accused of strictly criminal offences had no right to a fair trial, and yet all the political rights and liberties necessary to democracy were perfectly protected, I very much doubt that such a strictly compartmentalized system would ever exist in the real world. Citizens who valued the rights and liberties required for the democratic process would hardly be so morally schizoid as to reject the right to a fair trial for criminal offences.

To say that political rights are more fully protected in democratic than in non-democratic countries should not be misinterpreted as an invitation to complacency about the condition of rights in democratic countries. For one thing, economic and social rights, of which I say nothing in this chapter, are of course also important and vary greatly among both democratic and non-democratic countries. Of more immediate relevance to the argument of this chapter is the fact that rights may be effectively projected above the threshold of 'democracy' or polyarchy, and yet fall well short of the standards to which people in democratic countries tend to aspire. For example, if it were not for recurring invasions of political and civil rights in the United States, the American Civil Liberties Union would soon cease to exist. Whether fundamental rights are protected better or worse in the United States than in other democratic countries I cannot say, but I doubt whether any democratic country fully lives up to its own standards of human rights.

Moreover, even among countries above the democratic threshold, the effectiveness and stability of the rights, liberties, opportunities and institutions integral to democracy vary considerably, and they may also vary over time within a country. In order to discuss these variations, and more importantly those among non-democratic countries, I am going to draw heavily on a recent study by Michael Coppedge and Wolfgang Reinicke.

Coppedge and Reinicke ranked 170 independent countries as of mid-1985 on four criteria: free and fair elections, freedom of political organization, freedom of expression, and availability of alternatives sources of information. Within each criterion Coppedge and Reinicke created three or four categories into which countries could be assigned. For example, on the criterion of free and fair elections, countries were assigned to one of three categories:

1. Elections without significant or routine fraud or coercion.
2. Elections with some fraud or coercion.
3. No meaningful elections: elections without choice of candidates or parties, or no elections at all.

The four criteria and their internal categories resulted in a satisfactory ranking of 163 countries. However, I deliberately made three changes in the original classification. First, because of the rapid changes taking place in the Soviet Union and Eastern Europe, I decided to treat them as special cases. Second, I split the least polyarchal (or most authoritarian) countries into two categories: non-Marxist, and Marxist-dominated countries outside Europe.

Finally, because the forty-one most democratic countries – those above the threshold of democracy (polyarchy) by all four criteria – are far from a homogeneous group, it seemed to me useful to divide them into two categories. The 'old' or 'mature' democracies consist of twenty-one countries – predominantly English-speaking or European – where democratic institutions have existed continuously since 1950 or earlier. The 'new' democracies, then, consist of the remaining twenty countries that had made the transition to democracy since 1950 and where at the time of writing the four democratic institutions were above the threshold of polyarchy (see figure 9.1). Four (Colombia, Venezuela, Spain and Portugal) were large countries that had been redemocratized after repressive periods of military dictatorship. Eleven were mini-states in the Caribbean and Pacific that had only recently gained independence. The total also included the doubtful case of Honduras, where the institutions of polyarchy are recent, fragile, and weak in relation to the independent influence of the military.

Thus even though a country has reached the threshold of democracy, its system of rights and liberties may be precarious; and even a democratic country where rights and liberties are quite sturdy may fall considerably short of its feasible possibilities. While it is true that countries where the institutions of democracy (polyarchy) have been achieved set a relatively high world standard for rights and liberties (both from a historical perspective and in comparison with all non-democratic countries in the world today), the evidence does not permit the complacent conclusion that advocates of human rights living in democratic countries can safely turn their attention exclusively to the plight of people in non-democratic countries.

II Variations in Political Rights in Non-democratic Countries

Nonetheless, given that a preponderant majority of countries are not fully democratic it might seem reasonable to conclude that the best means for advancing basic political rights and liberties in the world would be to bring about democracy in countries now governed by non-democratic regimes. Yet however desirable it would be if all countries were to attain a democratic level of political rights and liberties, for the foreseeable future many countries will continue to be governed by non-democratic regimes.

To help us understand why this is so, I want to make use again of the analysis of Coppedge and Reinicke, as I have revised it in figure 9.1. Ignoring the special cases of the Soviet Union and Eastern Europe, the remaining countries range from the forty-one full polyarchies at one end of the scale to the least polyarchal at the other. In the twenty-two least polyarchal (most authoritarian) countries, both Marxist and non-Marxist, no meaningful elections are held, all organizations are banned or controlled by the government or the official party, all public dissent is suppressed, and no publicly available alternative to official information exists. Between these extremely repressive authoritarian regimes and the democracies at the other end of the scale, however, there is a world of very considerable complexity.

Take the countries classified in figures 9.1–9.4 as nearly polyarchal, for example. Judged by one criterion these ten countries were somewhat below the threshold for full polyarchy; but according to the other three criteria they were above the threshold. Probably many observers, using less stringent standards, would call these countries democracies. But perhaps it is more accurate to call them near-polyarchies. Or consider the next scale type (III). This consists of countries that on two of the four criteria fall somewhat short of the levels attained in the fully democratic countries. Suppose we call them proto-polyarchies. Is it not reasonable to assume that in the foreseeable future near-polyarchies and proto-polyarchies are far more likely to attain democratic levels of political rights than countries near the bottom of the scale?

11.1 Obstacles to democratization

Consequently, I do not see how we can think intelligently about democracy and human rights unless we recognize that in many countries the obstacles to full democratization, and thus to the achievement of a full system of democratic rights and liberties, are enormous. Let me summarize some of the main obstacles.

1. In order for democracy to exist, it is essential that leaders do not employ the major instruments for violent coercion – notably the police and the military – to gain and maintain their power. Yet in a great many countries the government of the state is directly under the control of military leaders; or indirectly under the control of military leaders who govern through civilian agents; or under the control of civilian leaders who make use of violent coercion by police and military forces to maintain their rule; or under the control of civilian leaders who govern within a limited set of options circumscribed by the probable reaction of military leaders to decisions that would violate acceptable limits. Although transitions to democracy are by no means impossible – as in Argentina, Brazil and Uruguay, for example – they are difficult, rare and not necessarily irreversible.

2. As study after study has shown, polyarchy is highly correlated with socioeconomic levels and the nature of the socioeconomic order. Democratic institutions are highly favoured by the existence of a modern, dynamic, organizationally pluralist society with historically high levels of material well-being and rates of economic growth, extensive literacy, widespread access to education, relatively high levels of education, extensive organizational and administrative capacities, plurality of relatively autonomous organizations – economic, social, political – and so on. All the 'mature' democracies exist in countries with such a society.

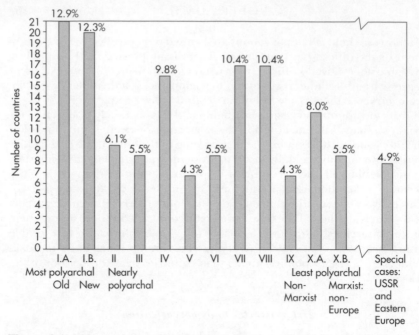

Figure 9.1 163 countries classified by extent to which four institutions of polyarchy existed, mid-1980s

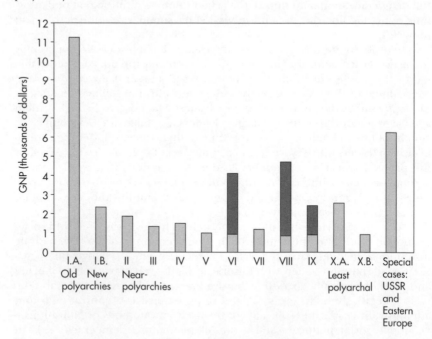

Figure 9.2 Regimes and GNP per capita

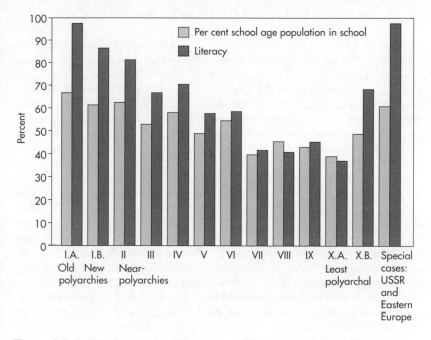

Figure 9.3 Political systems: education and literacy

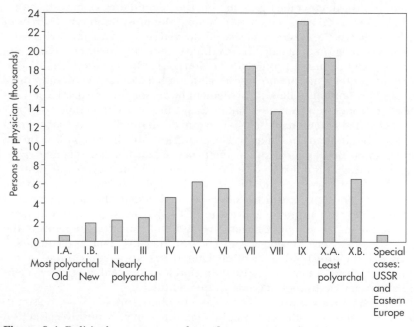

Figure 9.4 Political systems: number of persons per physician

But of course many countries do not possess a society of this kind. Because of the relatively high intercorrelations among the characteristics of these 'advanced' countries, GNP per capita is a convenient if somewhat crude indicator. Figure 9.2 compares GNP per capita among countries that have been democratic (polyarchies) since 1950. As we see from figure 9.2, with a mean GNP per capita of $11,000, the twenty-one older and more stable democratic countries are among the richest in the world. Not surprisingly, they also spent more per capita on health and education than other countries – far more indeed than the poorest countries (see figures 9.3 and 9.4). Because the presence of a few very rich oil sheikdoms among the authoritarian countries enormously raises the average, we might be misled about the relation between poverty and authoritarianism. In figure 9.2, categories VI, VII and IX show the average GNP per capita of these countries with the sheikdoms included; when they are excluded (below the horizontal bar) we see that the remaining countries are among the poorest in the world. Their expenditures on education, health and presumably other social services as well were correspondingly low. To take another example, in the 1980s the GNP per capita of the Soviet Union and most of the other Eastern European countries had reached levels well above those of the European democracies in the 1920s, and probably higher even than that of what was then the wealthiest democratic country, the United States, in 1929.

3. Acute and persistent conflicts that polarize or fragment the people of a country are likely to prevent democratic institutions from fully developing, and to destroy democratic rights and liberties should they be introduced (as in Lebanon, to take an acute case). Among the most important sources of such conflicts is the existence of sharply divided subcultures, formed around the axis of religion, language, race, ethnic group, region and in some cases ideology. Unlike purely economic questions, subcultural differences tend to generate conflicts that are not only too intense but also too deeply 'non-rational' and primordial to allow for settlement by democratic means. To be sure, there are some well-known exceptions, and in a few democratic countries consociational systems have helped to damp down the dangers of subcultural conflict. But in many non-democratic countries subcultural conflicts pose a barrier to the development and maintenance of a system of democratic rights and liberties that is unlikely to be much reduced in the foreseeable future.

4. Nor can we omit the impact of foreign influence and control. Historically, foreign control has often been adverse to the development of self-governing institutions. At least until Gorbachev's glasnost and perestroika, the impact of Soviet hegemony on democratic developments in the countries of Eastern Europe was unrelievedly negative. I am also compelled to say that the direct influence of the United States government has, on the whole, impaired rather than assisted the development of democratic systems in Latin America throughout most of this century.

Surely, however, we would not be gathered here unless we had reason to think that outside influences might sometimes have a positive effect on human rights, and even perhaps on the development of full democracy. No

doubt the most dramatic instance of the positive effects of outside intervention was the pivotal role of the Allied forces of occupation in the postwar
democratization of Germany, Austria and Japan. However, those circumstances were historically unusual, and we can hardly wish for their repetition.
But there is also evidence that outside influences in the form of 'world opinion' and other pressures – requirements concerning rights attached to loans,
grants and other assistance – can sometimes have a positive effect. For example, though the human rights policies of the Carter administration were
sharply criticized by political opponents in the United States and by authoritarian leaders abroad, it is my strong impression that Latin American
advocates of democracy and human rights saw them – and see them in ret-
rospect – as helpful. And it is hardly an accident that democratic rather than
authoritarian regimes have been introduced – and show signs of taking root –
in a number of the Caribbean and Pacific microstates that were until recently
dependencies of Britain, France, Holland or the United States, and on
whom, it may be added, they often continue to depend for financial support.

5. Finally, it would be a profound mistake to neglect the independent effects
of ideas, belief systems, basic attitudes, political culture and similar influences
on the ways people in a country – particularly perhaps the political élites –
think about and orient themselves toward political life and their fellow beings.
While political beliefs, habits and norms of behaviour obviously do not
develop independently of historical experiences and current influences, they
can become deeply rooted and resistant to change. The effects can of course
go either way. A deeply rooted belief system favourable to democracy and
rights is a powerful support to democratic stability, particularly in times of
crisis; but deeply rooted beliefs can also be hostile to democratic institutions
and human rights. In a great many countries a system of democratic rights
finds little support in the beliefs, habits and norms of the people, and more
important, I think, among the political activists and élites.

III Reflections on Limits, Possibilities and Strategies

Because of persistent obstacles to full democratization, a majority of countries
in the world are very likely to be governed by undemocratic regimes in the
foreseeable future – meaning, let us say, for the next fifteen to twenty years.
If this is so, then we ought to consider the limits and possibilities of enhanc-
ing rights in countries governed by *non*-democratic regimes – without
necessarily expecting these countries to become *democratic*.

At this point, if not earlier, one might ask: in saying that 'we ought to consider', just who we 'we' and why 'ought' we to consider these matters? My
assumption is that 'we' may be any persons or any association or organization
concerned about democracy and rights and wishing to act so as to enhance
the prospects for democracy and rights whenever opportunities to do so are
available and our actions might make a difference. The relevant actors,
therefore, might be citizens or subjects of a non-democratic regime who
wish to alter that regime. They might be citizens or officials in a democratic

country who for whatever reason are, or believe themselves to be, in a position to make a difference.

Consequently, I want to cast my thought now in terms somewhat closer to action, to policy – though what I shall say will still be too general and abstract for immediate translation into a feasible policy. By way of advance warning, I want to add that what I am going to propose may seem not only too schematic to do justice to the infinite and subtle variations among countries but unhappily reminiscent at times of the once fashionable and ultimately unrewarding attempt to identify 'stages of development'. I cannot emphasize too strongly how important it is in thinking about prospects for strengthening human rights to avoid mechanistic interpretations, and to pay scrupulous attention to the unique limits and possibilities of a particular country. Yet I also think that a focus on particulars can be enlightened by an awareness of general tendencies.

In considering the limits and possibilities of change in a particular country it seems obvious that we need to ask at least four questions. (1) What is the present state of rights in the country? (2) What is the nature of the underlying conditions (of the kind I just described) that favour or impede the development of democratic rights and liberties? (3) What is the present and, given certain reasonable assumptions, probable future *direction* of change? (4) What is the present and, given certain reasonable assumptions, probable future *rate* of change? It goes without saying that the answers will usually be fraught with uncertainty.

As I have already pointed out, it is absurd to look upon the prospects for democratization and rights in all non-democratic countries as essentially the same. For example, imagine a country that is now only just below the threshold of democracy (let us say a near-polyarchy, or a proto-polyarchy). Suppose further that the underlying conditions I described earlier look on the whole to be favourable to democratization, and the country has been moving more or less steadily, over the long pull at any rate, toward greater democratization. Then obviously the prospects for achieving a full system of democratic rights and liberties are very high. And in so far as actors inside or outside the country are in a position to do anything about it, it would be reasonable for them to try to push the country toward a full system of democratic rights and liberties. But imagine instead that what we have is a country like those in scale type VIII. Suppose further that all five of the conditions mentioned earlier are unfavourable to democracy. Would it not be utterly foolish to clamour for full-scale democracy and immediate elections, on the assumption that all the necessary democratic rights and liberties would somehow come into being? Yet if it is unreasonable in these circumstances for persons deeply committed to democracy to focus on the immediate goal of full democracy, what are they to do?

I want to propose therefore that in attempting to answer the four questions I posed a moment ago, it would be useful to follow a strategy something like the following:

First, because the conditions I mentioned influence but by no means fully determine the characteristics of a regime, we should always (to repeat my earlier warning) pay attention to the unique limits and possibilities of a particular country.

Second, we should look for discrepancies between the conditions of a country and the characteristics of its political system. Perhaps the most important cases are non-democratic countries where the conditions rather strongly favour democratization, i.e., potential democracies; and democratic countries where the conditions provide weak support for democracy, i.e., countries where democratic breakdown is likely. With respect to the potential democracies, we need to search for whatever effective means we have to influence the country to achieve full democratization. Our means may in fact be quite limited. For democratic countries facing potential breakdown we need to identify the major causes. The common tendency to assume economic causes and thus to prescribe economic assistance as a remedy has, I think, often misled us into ignoring other factors, particularly the critical role of the military. Probably American policy has done more harm to democratization in Latin America by assisting military establishments than any gain it has ever achieved through economic aid programmes.

Third, and here I return to the central theme of this article, for non-democratic countries where the conditions are not particularly favourable for democratization, I think it might be useful to adopt a strategy based on the following tentative assumption (or hypothesis if you prefer): *the achievement of certain rights and liberties is likely to precede the achievement of others.* To emphasize the point, let me repeat it in several different ways. Some democratic rights and liberties are unlikely to exist or endure unless they have already been preceded by the attainment of certain other rights and liberties. Or again: full democratization is likely to be achieved only at the end of a process – perhaps often a lengthy process of many vicissitudes – of expanding rights and liberties.

This hypothesis is consistent with the findings of Coppedge and Reinicke, though strictly speaking we cannot infer it from their scale types. Their scale is derived from a cross-section in time, the 1980s. It is a world panoramic snapshot, so to speak. *It is not a set of historical or developmental 'stages' that show* how democratic rights have developed over time. Nonetheless, it is perfectly consistent with the hypothesis that certain democratic rights and liberties are likely to be institutionalized before others. A plausible sequence seems to me as follows:

1. The earliest political right to develop is likely to be the right of access to *alternative sources of information*, independent of government control: samizdat, journals of dissent and opposition, an opposition press and so on.

2. Building on these achievements, *a general freedom of expression* may come to be protected by courts and other institutions. People are able to speak out more or less publicly without fear of reprisal. Governments and oppositions may even become habituated to the notion that so long as people do not actually *organize* into parties or other explicitly political organizations, they may express themselves almost without limit.

3. A dangerous and critical threshold is finally reached with *freedom to*

organize, not only when people may gather together in informal associations but – passing a threshold of extraordinary consequence – like-minded political activists may actually organize themselves freely and openly in political parties that have as their ultimate objective participating in, and possibly winning, elections.

4. Finally, *free and fair elections* may now be achieved. Together with elections the full range of institutions that mark the transition to a democratic polyarchy may now be more or less in place.

In this perspective free and fair elections are the culmination of a process, not its beginning. Indeed, unless and until the other rights and liberties are firmly protected, free and fair elections cannot take place. Except in countries already close to the threshold of democracy, therefore, it is a grave mistake to assume that if only the leaders of a non-democratic country can be persuaded to hold elections, then full democracy will follow. Other than in the near-polyarchies or the proto-polyarchies, elections should be seen as a critical stage following a process of liberalization, probably a lengthy process, in which the prior institutions and appropriate underlying conditions for stable democracy have developed.

What about other, less explicitly political, rights and liberties? It might seem reasonable to conjecture that *political* rights and liberties cannot be assured unless they have been preceded by certain *pre-political* rights. Of these, probably the most important is an effective right to a *fair trial*. For it might be supposed that without fair treatment in the courts, the enforcement of political rights would be virtually impossible.

It is true that historically an effective right to a fair trial did precede democratization in some countries. Yet it seems doubtful to me that this has been or is likely to be the general case. If the sequence of political rights suggested above is roughly correct, the explanation is to be found, I believe, in the relative costs to a non-democratic government of repression and toleration in the different areas. The costs of suppressing all alternative sources of information are so staggering in comparison with the costs of tolerating some sources difficult to control that leaders in a non-democratic regime will often find some degree of toleration preferable to total repression, which may be impossible in any case. Repressing free expression more generally is relatively easier and less costly, though as a society begins to approach a relatively high level of social and economic modernity the costs will rise to a level at which a non-democratic government may well decide that the gains from repression no longer exceed the costs (and the costs of toleration no longer exceed the gains of permitting free expression). Crossing the next two thresholds is not only far more dangerous to non-democratic leaders but easier to prevent. Short of overthrow or collapse, a non-democratic regime can hold out against free and fair elections almost indefinitely. By contrast, the costs of preventing fair trials do not seem to be unusually high, while the costs of accepting or tolerating fair trials, particularly in political cases, may be quite extraordinary. If these assumptions are correct then an effective right to a fair trial need not necessarily come into existence prior to the more strictly political rights necessary to democracy. Evidently then we cannot uncover the relation between democratization and a right to a fair trial without looking at experiences in a large number of countries, and analysis of patterns in a large number of countries.

IV Conclusion

My argument, in summary, is then as follows:

1. The most comprehensive systems of political rights and liberties in the contemporary world exist in democratic countries. Even democratic countries, however, vary in their protection of political (not to mention other) rights.

2. Many countries are not democratic and are unlikely to become so in the foreseeable future because the conditions that tend to favour democracy are weak, or the conditions that tend to favour authoritarian regimes are strong, or both.

3. However, non-democratic countries vary greatly in the extent of political (and pre-political) rights and liberties. They can be arrayed, more or less accurately, on a scale – an ascending series of thresholds – extending from countries in which political rights are virtually non-existent to countries in which political rights are close to the threshold of democracy.

4. Given the wide variety of political systems in the world and the great variation in the conditions that tend to favour democratization or authoritarianism, a feasible strategy for contributing to the development of rights in a non-democratic country would be:

(a) Carefully consider the concrete conditions and characteristics of the country, including the direction and rate of recent changes.
(b) If the underlying conditions are generally favourable for the prospects of democratization, press for full democratization.
(c) If not, adopt an incremental strategy. Identify the next feasible threshold of rights and liberties, and first seek to consolidate rights at this threshold. The immediate aim need not be democracy, but attaining one of the prior rights and liberties necessary for democracy.

Postscript, October 1990

When I wrote the material above for the Oslo meetings in June 1988, I certainly did not foresee the speed with which movements toward democratization would occur in the Soviet Union and Eastern Europe. To what extent does the argument I presented at that time require modification in the light of the extraordinary speed and magnitude of these changes?

The events surely challenge one assumption I then thought reasonable – that 'in the foreseeable future near-polyarchies and proto-polyarchies are far more likely to attain democratic levels of political rights than countries near the bottom of the scale'. The fact is, in the original scale the Soviet

Union and the Eastern European countries were classified by Coppedge and Reinicke, quite properly, at or near the most extreme authoritarian end of the scale. It was only a year later, after the Oslo meetings, that I pulled these countries out and made them special cases, as they are shown in the figures now presented here.

Yet the events do appear to confirm the explanation, in section II.1 above, of the five major obstacles to democratization.

1. When Gorbachev reversed sixty years of policy and practice under which opposition was systematically silenced in the Soviet Union by violent coercion and intimidation, public opposition immediately sprang up and hitherto suppressed demands for political rights and liberties became irresistible. Likewise, when it became evident to people in the countries under Soviet domination that pubic political activity would no longer be coercively suppressed, the democratic oppositions took off like wildfire and helped to bring about the liberalization and democratization of their regimes.

2. As figures 9.2–9.4 illustrate, many of the social and economic characteristics of the USSR and, even more, of countries like Czechoslovakia, Hungary, Poland and East Germany were at variance with the extreme authoritarianism of their regimes. In many respects, in their socioeconomic levels these countries were closer to the mature democratic countries (even though the gaps were great and a major source of discontent) than to the less developed countries with highly authoritarian regimes.

3. When the expansion of political rights and liberties made it possible for hitherto suppressed cleavages to appear, conflicts among sharply divided subcultures rapidly emerged. How, and how successfully, these conflicts will be managed without impairing or reversing the movement toward democratization and liberalization remains highly uncertain, particularly in the Soviet Union. Clearly one part of any solution will be greater autonomy for subgroups conscious of their distinctiveness. Though the problem is too complex to explore here, it is worth stressing that decentralization, increased autonomy, and even separation and independence need not by themselves impair – and may in some circumstances actually enhance – basic rights, liberties and democratic processes. The danger to human rights and democratic institutions arises not from decentralization or autonomy per se but from the intense conflicts and repressive actions that they may stimulate.

4. The events certainly underscore 'the impact of foreign influence and control' on democracy and political liberties. The observation that 'the impact of Soviet hegemony on democratic developments in the countries of Eastern Europe was unrelievedly negative' was abundantly confirmed by the amazing speed of democratization following the withdrawal of the threat of Soviet coercion.

5. Finally, the events seem to me to yield strong support for the independent effects on the prospects for democracy and rights of ideas and beliefs, particularly among political élites. Democratic ideas that were previously suppressed spread with amazing speed among élites and, so far as can be ascertained, among broader publics. Yet influential as they have been, among

many people beliefs in democracy and fundamental political rights have roots so shallow and so weakly embedded in a traditional political culture that they may not survive the economic and political challenges these countries face.

What these five factors neglected, however, was the potentially decisive impact of leadership. No explanation of the transformations in the Soviet Union and Eastern Europe would be complete if it omitted the extraordinary impact of Mikhail Gorbachev in initiating changes that may well have gone beyond anything he originally intended.

Turning now to my 'reflections on limits, possibilities and strategies', several of my suggestions seem to be confirmed by the events, while a few others require qualifications. The events certainly support the view that we should 'pay attention to the unique limits and possibilities of a particular country'. In each of the one-time communist countries the conditions and prospects are different from those of its neighbours; indeed, the republics within the Soviet Union obviously differ too much to allow for generalization.

Certainly, too, 'we should look for discrepancies between the conditions of a country and the characteristics of its political system.' I have already mentioned the tension between the socioeconomic levels of the communist countries and their authoritarian regimes.

I believe also that many of the changes in these countries conform to the 'plausible sequence' I proposed. In fact, the sequence from alternative sources of information, to a wider public expression, then to a plurality of illegal and semi-legal associations and groups seems to me to fit their experiences moderately well.

However, the general tone of my discussion emphasized its slowness:

Other than in the near-polyarchies or the proto-polyarchies, elections should be seen as a critical stage following a process of liberalization, probably a lengthy process, in which the prior institutions and appropriate underlying conditions for stable democracy have developed.

I believe this is correct. Yet I probably underestimated the extent to which the setting of elections can *under some conditions* turn into a driving force that enormously speeds up the whole sequence. What then are the requisite conditions? The answer, a speculative one no doubt, would take a separate essay, and I shall not undertake to provide one here. But surely an answer would include these three factors. First, if any of the five obstacles mentioned above stands massively in the way, elections cannot produce democracy and fundamental rights. The lamentable example of El Salvador, and the less well-known examples of Honduras and Guatemala, demonstrate that elections are not sufficient to transform a regime dominated by a military establishment into a democratic government that respects fundamental rights. Second, the prior elements in the sequence – alternative sources of information, freedom of expression and freedom to organize – must already be in place firmly enough to survive the vicissitudes of the post-election period.

Third, international opinion, information and policy can nowadays exert extraordinary influence on the development of these crucial elements, on the conduct of the elections themselves, and on the post-election transition. It is possible, indeed, that international influences may now help to shorten a process of change that historically was ordinarily quite protracted.

Reproduced with permission from Robert A. Dahl, 'Democracy and Human Rights under Different Conditions of Development', in Asbjorn Eide and Bernt Hagtvet, eds., *Conditions for Civilized Politics, Political Regimes and Compliance with Human Rights* (Oslo: Scandinavian University Press, 1996), pp. 235–51.

The Other's Rights

Jean-François Lyotard

'It seems that a man who is nothing but a man has lost the very qualities which make it possible for others to treat him as a fellow man.'[1] With this sentence, taken from the study on *Imperialism* which forms the second part of *The Origins of Totalitarianism* (1951), Hannah Arendt defines the fundamental condition of human rights: a human being has rights only if he is other than a human being. And if he is to be other than a human being, he must in addition become an *other* human being. Then 'the others' can treat him as their fellow human being. What makes human beings alike is the fact that every human being carries within him the figure of the other. The likeness that they have in common follows from the difference of each from each.

Thou shalt not kill thy fellow human being. To kill a human being is not to kill an animal of the species *Homo sapiens*, but to kill the human community present in him as both capacity and promise. And you also kill it in yourself. To banish the stranger is to banish the community, and you banish yourself from the community thereby.

What is this figure of the other in me, on which, it is said, my right to be treated as a human being rests? It is this question to which I devote the rest of my reflections.

'Nothing but a man', writes Hannah Arendt. That is, nothing other than an individual of the species *Homo sapiens*. A powerful species; in the struggle for life enacted in the theatre of the world, *Homo sapiens* has emerged victorious over all other species. And it continues, successfully, to combat them, using hygiene, sanitary arrangements, the protection of the environment and so on. Each human being is a specimen of this species. He resembles any other member of the species, as a chimpanzee resembles a chimpanzee.

Is the figure of the other (ape) present in every ape? Apes are able to tell each other apart and to distinguish themselves from other species of animal. They can communicate amongst themselves by systems of sensory signals based on the five senses and motility. These systems constitute a sort of language which endows the animals with a sort of community in which affective states (Aristotle's *pathemata*) are exchanged, along with admonitions as to conduct.

This signal-based language is not wholly lacking in the human species, but its role is confined. Animals' capacity to communicate is determined by the genetic stock common to the species, and is of the order of instinct. Human beings have very few instincts. In comparison with their animal brothers, young human beings are slow to realize their capacity in the language of their fellow. And this human language is not common to the species. It functions not by bodily signals, but by signs. These arbitrary signs, combined according to rules which are also arbitrary, but which are fixed by syntactic structures, make it possible to designate any object, real or not, internal or external, as their referent, and to signify something about that object. Finally, and this is what interests us here, this signification is *addressed*.

It is what we today call the 'pragmatic' function of human language which governs the formation of the figure of the other. Explicitly or implicitly, every human sentence is destined to someone or something. Some answer, some response, some link or follow-up is expected. The polarization is marked in our languages by the verbal 'persons' and the personal pronouns. *I* is the one who is speaking now; *you* is the one to whom this communication is currently addressed. *You* are silent when *I* speak, but *you* can speak, has spoken, and will speak.

Animal communication is, we might say, homogeneous. By contrast, the distinguishing characteristic of interlocution is the relation of simultaneous similarity and disparity introduced between the speakers. The instances *I* and *you* cannot merge, since while the one speaks the other speaks no longer or not yet. *I* and *you* are deictics, and as such are correlated with *now*, and *now* designates the present of speech. From it, the temporality of past and future unfold. But relative to the capacity to speak, which by definition is not confined to the present but extends to every possible interlocution, *I* and *you* are alike. Persons capable of speech alternately occupy the instance *I* and the instance *you*. When they say *I*, they are a past or future *you*, and when they are in the position of *you*, they are so because they have spoken or will speak as *I*.

Interlocution thus implies that human beings cannot, as animals can, merge into a community based on signals. They do so only when the impossibility of interlocution reduces them to that meagre resource. In theory, the human *we* does not precede but results from interlocution. In this *we*, the figure of the other remains clearly present to each, to the extent that the other is his possible interlocutor. The one and the other can come to an agreement, after reasoning and debate, and then establish their community by contact. This is the principle of the Greek *politeia* or the modern *republic*. The citizen is the human individual whose right to address others is recognised by those others.

It is important to distinguish the republican principle from the democratic fact. The *demos* is not a contractual but a natural and cultural community. The individual of the *demos* is recognized as such not for his right to speak, but for his birth, language and historical heritage. These individuals form a *nation* (in the medieval sense in which one hears *nature*), whose principal characteristic is the homogeneity of its constituents. Interlocution does not engender this community; between the members of the nation, language and mores function as signals of recognition. Though possessed of interlocutory capacity, the demotic individual, whether a serf or a free man, uses the language to signal emotions and actions to other specimens of the variety of *Homines* to which they collectively belong. This relationship to language excludes the alterity implicit in civic interlocution. The other remains alien, and does not enjoy the rights reserved to nationals. The very Greeks who invented the *politeia* excluded *barbaroi*. The right of interlocution is not granted to every human being. The figure of the other is that of a threat weighing on the national community from without, which cannot help but undermine its integrity.

I oversimplify my description to bring out the essential opposition between the *demotic* and the *civic*. The difference between them is the consideration given to interlocution, which modifies the figure of the other. The people keeps the other out; the city interiorizes the other. In contemporary human communities, for various reasons, these two aspects are for the most part not distinguished: more or less nation, more or less republic. For example, the institution of a European community undoubtedly draws its justification exclusively from the civic principle.

In the republic, there is a principle of universalization which relates to the function, inherent in speech, of *addressing* the other. If a human being can speak, he is a possible interlocutor. The principle is not invalidated merely by the fact of his speaking a language foreign to the national language. *Homo sapiens* has always spoken a multitude of languages. But they are all human languages comprising the structural characteristics I have briefly outlined. These characteristics guarantee that an unknown human language can in principle be translated into a known one. I do not wish to take up here the difficulties and enigmas of translation. The theoretical possibility of translation is quite sufficient to extend interlocution to any human individual whatsoever, regardless of natural or national idiom. Civility may become universal in fact as it promises to do by right.

The form in which civility is in fact extended to national or demotic communities is a serious question. History offers a profusion of different modes, linguistic as well as political and economic. These include: an obligatory single language, an official language alongside which traditional languages are tolerated, compulsory multilingualism, effective multilingualism and so on. The pattern established depends on the balance of military, political, economic and cultural power. These relations determine how interlocution extends, but they cannot curb its extension. There is no limiting the function of destination inherent in the structure of sentences: one may beg a service of a tree or a river, and issue a command to a cat. If the addressee is human, he is immediately vested with the status of interlocutor, capable, in his turn, of addressing the first speaker.

There is no a priori limit to the interlocutory capacity. By its association with the recursiveness and translatability of human language, it cannot help but bind all human speakers in a speech community. From this effective (de facto) power there arises what I shall term an *effect of right (un effet de droit)*. If any human being *can* be an interlocutor for other human beings, he *must be able* to, that is, must be enabled or allowed to. We move from the potential implied by competence to the permission implied by entitlement. We know, however, that capacity does not legitimacy make. But it is tempting to merge the two categories in the case of interlocution, both because the capacity to enter into dialogue with others is possessed equally by everyone, and because interlocution in itself implies reciprocity of speech. Reciprocity respects not only the alterity of interlocution but the parity of the interlocutors. It thus guarantees their respective liberty and their equality before the word. These are the characteristics of justice itself. The slippage here from the fact to the right resembles the contemporary confusion of democracy and republic. But how can we avoid it?

Let us take it that the capacity to speak to others is a human right, and perhaps the most fundamental human right. If the use of this capacity is forbidden, whether de facto, by some injustice of fate, or on principle, for example as a punishment, a harm is inflicted on the speaker thus constrained. He is set apart from the speech community of interlocutors. To no one is he any longer someone other, nor is anyone now his other. There are many ways of imposing silence. Amnesty International knows them better than anyone. Its vocation is modest but decisive. It is *minimal. Amnestos* meant he who is forgotten. Amnesty does not demand that the judgment be revised or that the convicted man be rehabilitated. It simply asks that the institution that has condemned him to silence forget this decree and restore the victim to the community of speakers.

Amnesty's task is in accordance with the provisions of the public law of the republican democracies. I nevertheless maintain that this legality conceals a confusion between a capacity, the aptitude for speech, and a legitimacy, the authority to speak. In other words, there is, strictly speaking, no natural right. It is of the essence of a right that it be merited; no right without duty. The same goes for the capacity to enter into dialogue. It is not true that it realizes itself spontaneously. It requires care and attention, an entire learning process. It requires precisely what is called civilization. The human being as such is no other than a member of the species *Homo*: an animal that can speak. It is true that its language is so constituted that it effectively contains the promise of interlocution. But if he is to bring out and respect the figure of the other that this promise bears in it, he must free himself from that in him which will not recognize the figure of the other, that is, his animal nature. Children do not spontaneously enter into dialogue. There is something in us which resists, something which does perhaps 'speak', but in signals rather than according to the rules of interlocution.

Civilization, understood here as the process of learning how to share dialogue with *you*, requires a moment of silence. Aristotle said: the master speaks and the pupil listens. For that moment, the status of *I* is forbidden to me, I am assigned the position of *you* for the master, at the *tacit* pole of destination. *Tacit* does not imply *passive*. The exaltation of interactivity as a pedagogic principle is pure demagogy. The pupil has the capacity to speak; he has to win the right to speak. To do so, he must be silent. The suspension of inter-locution imposes a silence and that silence is good. It does not undermine the right to speak. It teaches the value of that right. It is the exercise neces-sary for excellence in speech. Like the pupil, writers, artists, scholars and novices must enter into retreat in order to learn what they will have to say to others.

The master, whatever his title, exempts his pupils from the sharing of speech in order to tell them something that they do not know. He may even speak to them in a language that they do not understand. The master is not the figure of the general other, of *you*, but the figure of the *Other* in all its sep arateness. He is the stranger, the foreigner. How can one dialogue with the foreigner? One would have to learn his language. This question is in some measure analogous with that of literature and the arts, testifying to something that is 'present' otherwise than as interlocutory expectation: something opaque, Beckett's the 'Unnamable'.

The silence that the learning process of civilization imposes is the moment of a labour of *estrangement*. It is a matter of speaking otherwise than is my wont and saying something other than what I know how to say. Through the alterity of the master, the strangeness of another logic is, in silence, imposed. He takes me hostage in order to make me hear and say what I do not know. Emmanuel Lévinas has elaborated this theme better than anyone.

From this brief analysis, if follows that the interlocutory capacity changes into a right to speak only if the speech can say something other than the *déjà dit* (what has already been said). The right to speak implies a duty to announce. If our speech announces nothing, it is doomed to repetition and to the conservation of existing meanings. The human community may spread, but it will remain the same, prostrated in the euphoria it feels at being on such very good terms with itself. It is the main function of the media today to reinforce the interlocutory consent of the community. They are boring to the extent that they teach us nothing. Interlocution is not an end in itself. It is legitimate only if, through others, the Other announces to me something which I hear but do not understand.

We should then distinguish three different levels of the 'right to speak'. First, the faculty of interlocution, a principle factually inherent in human lan-guages; second, the legitimation of speech, due to the fact that it announces something other, which it strives to make us understand; and last, the legiti-macy of speech, the positive right to speak, which recognizes in the citizen the right to address the citizen. The latter aspect merges the two former. But this confusion is good. By authorizing every possible speaker to address others, the republic makes it every speaker's duty to announce to those others what they do not know. It encourages announcements; it instructs. And, on the other hand, it forbids that anyone be arbitrarily deprived of speech. It discourages terror. In this way it governs silence in everyone's best interest, authorizing the silence of discipline and outlawing the silence of despotism.

This picture of the republic is idyllic, but the idyll conceals something far from idyllic. The threat of being deprived of speech is not contingent; it weighs constantly on the interlocutory right. This is precisely why the republic is indispensable. The human speaker is always afraid that a 'keep quiet' will debar his words. He complains of the precariousness of his membership in the speech community. Even the good silence of the writer, the monk, or the pupil contains an element of suffering. Any banishment is a harm inflicted on those who undergo it, but this harm necessarily changes to a wrong when the victim is excluded from the speech community. For the wrong is the harm to which the victim cannot testify, since he cannot be heard. And this is precisely the case of those to whom the right to speak to others is refused.

The right to impose silence which the community grants itself as a sanction is always dangerous. The death sentence evidently does an irremediable wrong to the condemned man, even if he is guilty of a heinous crime. But in relation to our present topic, death is not necessarily the wrong done to him. There are, as the Greeks put it, 'beautiful deaths', of which the citizens continue to speak long afterward. It happens that a speaker is more eloquent dead than alive, and does not therefore die for the community. So we must reverse the relation: it is the wrong which is the cause of death, since it implies the exclusion of the speaker from the speech community. The community will not even speak of this exclusion since the victim will be unable to report it and cannot therefore defend himself or appeal.

Those who escaped extermination in the camps are aware of this. Restored to the community, they can describe and narrate what the administration of death was. But how can they communicate the abjection to which they were reduced? It was first and foremost the severing of communication. How can one communicate by means of interlocution the terror of what it means no longer to be destined to anyone or anything? They were not spoken to, they were treated. They were not enemies. The SS or Kapos who called them dogs, pigs, or vermin did not treat them as animals but as refuse. It is the destiny of refuse to be incinerated. The ordeal of being forgotten is unforgettable. It reveals a truth about our relationship to language that is stifled and repressed by the serene belief in dialogue. Abjection is not merely when we are missing from speech, but when we lack language to excess. Our debt to announcement can never be acquitted. The Other in language, the Other that language is, does not say what must be said. It keeps silent. Does it even wait? Excluded from the speech community, the camp victims were rejected into the poverty, the misery of this secret. In that misery resides the true dignity of speech. Clearly, the ordeal of being forgotten cannot be expressed in the sharing of speech, which is, *ex hypothesi*, ignorant of it. Neither *I* nor *you*, the deportee is present in the language of his lords and in that of the deportees themselves only as the third person, who is to be eliminated. He is superfluous as any speaker is superfluous in relation to the Other. But precisely for that reason, absolutely responsible for himself.

The abjection suffered in the camps horribly illustrates the threat of exclusion which weighs on all interlocution. In the school playground, the child to whom the others say 'We're not playing with you' experiences this unspeakable suffering. He suffers a wrong equivalent, on its own scale, to a crime against humanity. Even those who submit themselves to the ascesis of separation in order to exalt the annunciatory power of language run the risk of abjection. True, they forswear the company of others only in order to listen more intently to the foreign master. But this enslavement to the Other is perceived as a suspicious dependence on a power alien to the interlocutory community, as a sort of betrayal. The Latin *sacer* (sacred) expressed the ambivalence of the abject: human refuse excluded from the interests of the speech community, yet a sign, perhaps, in which the Other has left its mark and deserving of respectful fear.

In his analysis of the sublime effect, Edmund Burke termed *horror* the state of mind of a person whose participation in speech is threatened. The power which exceeds the capacity of interlocution resembles night. Though we seek to tame it by dialogue, it does not have the figure of the *you*. It may be well- or ill-disposed. We hear it. We cannot understand it. It may be God, it may be Animal, it may be Satan. In silence we strive to translate its voice in order to announce it to the community of speakers. In this way we seek to make our relation to the Other dialectical. But the strangeness of the other seems to escape any totalization. The effort of translation must be endlessly renewed. It is precisely when we think we have reduced the abject or the sacred to transparent meanings that it becomes most opaque and returns to us from without like an accident. The discontent from which contemporary societies are suffering, the postmodern affliction, is this foreclosure of the Other. It is the reverse of the triumphant identification with the Other which affects modern republics at their birth. Saint-Just enacted law in the name of the Other, and instituted the first totalitarian reign of terror.

Wiser than the dialecticians, the Jacobins and the deciders, Freud acknowledged that abjection was not an episode but a situation constitutive of the human relation to interlocution. As children, we are kept on the margins of interlocution, and condemned to exile. The situation of *infantia* is that of the incomplete human being who *does not yet* speak. The child is spoken to and spoken of, but is not an interlocutor even though he is plunged into the interlocutory community. The statements that concern him have no value for him except as signals or gestures; they are difficult for him to decipher because they are arbitrary, and he has little instinct. He is affected by them, but has no language in which to articulate his own affective states. These reside within him unconsciously, in a forgetfulness which is always present. They do not enter the temporality associated with the instances of destination *I* and *you*. They loom up in the course of the individual life history in apparently unmotivated ways. They block interlocution. With them, the inevitable wrong and abjection of *infantia* erupt into adult relations.

From our native prematurity a mute distress results. It is to this distress that we owe our capacity to question everything around us. But we also owe to it our need to be welcomed, the request that we be authorized to enter the speech community. In interlocution a drama is played out between *me* and *you*; it is the drama of authorization. The question or assertion that we address to others is invariably coupled with an entreaty: deliver me from my abandonment, allow me to belong among you. This entreaty allows of a wide variety of modalities: friendship, hatred, love, and even indifference. But in it resides the foundation of the right to speak. For it is this right that assures me that my request will be heard, and that I will not be rejected into the abjection of *infantia*. Yet at the same time, I have to announce to you the opaque Otherness that I have experienced, and still am experiencing, as a child.

The law says: thou shalt not kill. Which means: you shall not refuse to others the role of interlocutor. But the law that forbids the crime of abjection nonetheless evokes its abiding threat of temptation. Interlocution is authorized only by respect for the Other, in my words and in yours.

Notes

1. H. Arendt, *The Origins of Totalitarianism* (London: Harcourt Brace, 1967), p. 300.

Reproduced with permission from Jean-François Lyotard, 'The Other's Rights', in Stephen Shute and Susan Hurley, eds., *On Human Rights* (New York: Basic Books, 1993), pp. 135–47.

Human Rights in the 'New Europe':
Some Problems

Aaron Rhodes

I

Today the sphere of human rights has become very confused. It is unclear what human rights has come to mean. Many groups holding utterly opposing views on everything from abortion to citizenship, and many groups protecting very narrow, special interests, all claim to base their beliefs and activities on human rights. Recently former US President Jimmy Carter even said, concerning General Cedras of Haiti, 'It's a serious violation of human rights for a citizen to be forced into exile' (*International Herald Tribune*, 21 September 1994, p. 4).

Some of the groups that stood for human rights prior to 1989 have become national, ethnic or political movements and have therefore lost objectivity and credibility as human rights organizations because they stand for particular interests, positions or causes. There is a group promoting equal treatment and respect for obese people, proclaimed by its leader to be a 'human organization'. In some cases human rights have become a professional activity. Some people today live 'off' human rights, as well as (hopefully not 'instead of') 'for' human rights, to use the distinction made by Max Weber in 'Politics as Vocation'. (To an extent I am one of those people who 'live off' human rights, since it is my job to 'manage' a human rights organization.) The professionalization of human rights, which creates financial competition, is one of the fragmenting, centrifugal forces pulling against the centre of human rights.

When we speak of human rights problems we must include the philosophical problems of the human rights movement as such, that is, the loss of the sense of the universality of human rights. In one sense – probably others have said or will say this in this volume – the obligations of intellectuals vis-à-vis human rights are no more or less than anyone else's. Who or what are intellectuals? They are not, properly speaking, a hereditary class or necessarily those upon whom have been conferred special titles, honours, or stigmata. They are the people in any society 'preoccupied with the attainment of an immediate contract with the ultimate principles implicit in their beliefs and actions'. They are more concerned with the 'systematic coherence and the deeper and more general ground of beliefs and standards than other people'. Intellectuals possess an unusual sensitivity to the sacred, an uncommon reflectiveness about the nature of the universe and the rules which govern their society. There is in every society a minority of persons who, more than the ordinary run of their fellow men, are inquiring, and desirous of being in frequent communion with symbols which are more general than the immediate concrete situations of everyday life and remote in their reference both in time and space. There is a need in this minority to externalize this quest in oral and written discourse, in poetic or plastic expression, in historical reminiscence or writing, in ritual performance and acts of worship. This interior need to penetrate beyond the screen of immediate concrete experience marks the existence of intellectuals in every society. (Edward Shils, 'The Intellectuals and the Powers', in *The Intellectuals and the Powers and Other Essays*, Chicago 1972).

Intellectuals are obligated to find the truth. They are supposed to be more capable, by virtue of natural gifts and by virtue of discipline and training, to do so. Furthermore, they are obligated to tell the truth, and to have the courage to do so when and as they find it.

I will speak very briefly about current challenges to the idea of human rights, and a tendency in the scholarly community, which may weaken it intellectually and morally, so that it cannot help threatened societies and peoples – or itself.

II

A huge proportion of human rights abuses now and in the past have been built around various kinds of factual and moral errors that have been exploited by those seeking or possessing political and military power. Such violations of human rights have required the use of disinformation: violations of human rights in the name of ethnic nationalism or race – the abuse of other people because they are not seen as human beings – are an example. Since the nineteenth century the entire idea of race has been destroyed by science, by anthropology. Still, intellectuals have not strongly enough proclaimed the truth, the evidence of history and anthropology, in this matter. The idea of race persists and diminishes the idea of the unity of humankind, which has more scientific validity than the idea of race.

What is more, false ideologies of ethnic nationalism and race intrinsically threaten the idea of intellectual life itself, for they reduce intellectual life to the expression of things outside, beyond the person, and seek to place inappropriate constraints upon intellectual work. Ethnic nationalism is a form of crude determinism denying the idea of intellectual freedom.

If intellectuals care, not only about the gross violations of human rights that follow from ethnic nationalist doctrines but also about the denial of the possibility of true intellectual attainment implicit in those doctrines, they must use the best means available to inform the public of the truths that reveal the futility, the destructiveness and the perversion of such doctrines.

According to Isaiah Berlin's description, nationalist doctrines hold that group identity, defined in terms of common territory, customs, laws, memories, beliefs, language, religious and artistic expression, etc., *completely* shape and inform human beings. The essential unit of human life is not the individual or some form of voluntary association of individuals reflecting the will, but a 'nation', an interdependent collectivity partaking of an organic character.

This unitary organism, the nation, is real in a manner in which individuals are not. The fulfilment of individuals is considered possible only in the context of the nation and is impossible without it. And if the nation does not find its proper destiny, its people cannot hope to redeem themselves as individuals.

According to nationalist doctrines an individual *should* believe something because it is believed by the group, not because of any 'transcendent' values like virtue, justice or liberty.

It follows that the idea of 'civil society' and the idea of the 'rule of law' are basically incompatible with this conception. The ethnic nationalist doctrine means there is really no distinction between the state and society. Law and education are meant to serve the state, as in the doctrines of Carl Shmitt, which provided part of the theoretical foundation for Nazi and communist totalitarianism. No intrinsic legitimacy is thus accorded to institutions created by and for civilians.

There is no acceptance of a 'supra-national' level of reality. There is no commitment to the rights of human beings as such ethnic nationalism by nature denies any 'over-arching criterion or standard by which different national groups can order themselves'. Berlin said that, at its worst, nationalism legitimates and advocates *forcing* others – people outside the 'nation' – to yield. That kind of nationalism is, as William Pfaff termed it, an 'invitation to war'.

III

By obliging conformity to collectively originated views, ethnic nationalism diminishes the grandeur and the nobility of intellectual life and individual excellence. But sadly, many of the so-called 'Western' intellectuals in the intellectual community of NATO countries (without the 'Partnership for Peace) – are busy throwing overboard the philosophical tools that can demonstrate the obligations that obtain from the universality of human rights. There is now a fashion that calls 'outmoded' and 'Eurocentric' the view that the universality of human rights is based on human nature itself and is knowable on the basis of rational ethics.

In a paper named 'Human Rights, Rationality and Sentimentality' (reproduced as chapter 4 in this volume), the American philosopher Richard Rorty articulates a view that is gaining force among intellectuals, the idea that 'there is no big picture'. According to him, the intellectual community is growing less concerned with asking ontological questions like 'What is the nature of man?'. Professor Rorty is pleased with this development. Intellectuals should not cling to the view that human rights are independent of history and historical facts. What he calls 'human rights foundationalism' – the tradition including Plato and Kant and everyone in between – is irrelevant to the practical problems of creating tolerance. The question for him is not 'whether human beings really have the rights enumerated in the Helsinki Declaration'. That question is 'not worth raising', in so far as 'nothing relevant to moral choice separates human beings from animals except historically contingent facts of the world, cultural facts.'

Rationality is no more than an 'attempt' at a coherent 'web of belief'. But still, despite this defeatist admission of epistemological impotence, our task should be making our culture – what Professor Rorty calls 'the human rights culture' – 'more self-conscious and more powerful, rather than . . . demonstrating its superiority to other cultures by an appeal to something transcultural.' 'The most philosophy can hope to do is summarize our culturally influenced intuitions about the right thing to do in various situations.' While Plato, Aquinas and Kant have sought 'independent' support for those summarizing generalizations in claims about human nature, the lack of success of such projects proves no such absolute standards of reference exist. 'If the activities of those who attempt to achieve this sort of knowledge seem of little use in actualizing . . . utopia, that is a reason to think that there is no such knowledge.' Changing moral intuitions is more a matter of 'manipulating feelings' than increasing knowledge, and therefore there is 'reason to think that there is no knowledge of the sort which philosophers like Plato, Aquinas and Kant hoped to acquire.'

As I am not deeply educated in philosophy, perhaps ignorance is what inhibits my understanding of this logic, which seems like saying, 'We have failed, which proves that what we attempted was baseless.' The claim that there is no 'big picture' is like the naively unacknowledged theological quality of atheism. As a classmate of Rorty's during the 1940s recently asked, 'How is the neopragmatic claim that "there's no big picture" *not* a big picture? How is the "no big picture" big picture not the ideology of a comfortable, do-your-own-thing-and-I'll-do-mine culture? And he said that a "social pragmatism" provides no norms to judge the cruel and unjust, and invites either moral paralysis or the raw display of power.' (G. Fackre, letter to the *University of Chicago Magazine*, June 1994.)

Indeed, 'moral paralysis' and the 'raw display of power' are precisely what we have here, now, today. Positions like Professor Rorty's have no answer to ethnic nationalism and even allow it to be justified. We should not pass judgment on it. 'Most people are simply unable to understand why membership in a biological species is supposed to suffice for membership in a moral community.' Professor Rorty writes that since the world is such a dangerous place, people hold those views for good reason. It is useless to employ 'Kantian' arguments about commonality, to apply Kant's secular ethical formula of 'the Christian doctrine of the brotherhood of man'. It is 'Eurocentric' to suggest that others should accept the paradigm of reason, and such arguments are morally offensive to those who do not believe them, whose 'identity . . . is bound up with their sense of who they are *not*'.

The problem with racists, sexists and bigots is not that they lack truth or moral knowledge or a sense of moral obligation. According to Professor Rorty, 'it would be better – more specific, more suggestive of possible remedies – to think of them as deprived of two more concrete things: security and sympathy.' Therefore to address such problems we need to appeal to sentiment and to provide security and sympathy, rather than analyse and diagnose them on the bases of rationality and 'moral law'.

IV

I have not done justice to Professor Rorty's views in this brief gloss of his paper, but would in any event submit that the problems of human rights today demand not more appeals to sentiment but more appeals to the universality of human rights, i.e. *just the opposite from his proposal.* The evidence of the recent past is a strong indication that appeals to sentiment cannot mobilize our societies against injustice and give us courage to identify wrongdoing, to make judgements, to take action. Thanks to television, we are steeped in sentiment. People do feel deeply 'sympathetic' to the victims in the conflicts in the countries of former Yugoslavia, for example. We are steeped in sentiment but we lack knowledge, thus we lack conviction. (In fact, according to Rorty's own logical twist, sentiment has not worked, therefore it is irrelevant.) We are in a sense lost, too easily moved by cheap sentimental appeals, yet disbelieving of everything we see and hear, suspicious, cynical – without a compass, a north star to tell us who or where we are. The 'Western' public seems incapable of identifying moral and political principles by which to interpret very complex conflicts and, through that exercise, to come together on behalf of a course of action.

Indeed, it is romantic to think the 'public' should be responsible for identifying those principles. That is the job of those more concerned with principles than with the here and now, more concerned with things that are true regardless of historical contexts and routine life. In other words, it is the responsibility of intellectuals.

Note: The views expressed above are those of the author, not official positions of the Helsinki Federation. The article is published here with the permission of the author, and is otherwise not for publication without permission.

Prepared for the Croatian Academy of Sciences and Arts, Conference on Peace, Human Rights, and the Responsibility of Intellectuals, September 1994.

12

Hobbes, 'Fearful Discourse', and the Basic Right to Refuse to Bear Arms during Military Service

Aleksandar Molnar

The 1992 Constitution of the Federal Republic of Yugoslavia (FRY) introduced a very important new element in the area of basic human rights. Conscripts in this country (Serbia and Montenegro) are now able, for the first time, and with recourse to the highest law of the land, to legally refuse to bear arms during military service. Article 137 of the Constitution of the FRY reads as follows:

> Military service is general and it is fulfilled in the way specified by federal law.
> A citizen who, due to religious or other reasons, does not want to bear arms shall be able to fulfil military service in the Yugoslav Army without arms, or in the civil service, in accordance with federal law.

The basic right to refuse to bear arms during military service is, therefore, derived from the basic right to conscientious objection. In this regard, the FRY follows the practice which is already established in Europe, although the way of presenting the constitutional material is in this case highly inadequate. In the second part of the constitution, which regulates basic rights, citizens are guaranteed 'freedom of belief, conscience, thought, and the public expression of thought' (Article 35). The concrete realization of this basic right is placed in a rather confused and illogical manner at the very end of the constitution, in the (eighth) part that refers to the Yugoslav Army. Thus, it appears almost as if the writers of the constitution wanted to avoid treating this as a basic human right. However, there is no doubt that the writers of the constitution wanted to follow the standard European and North American models, in which refusal to bear arms during military service is a basic human right, derived from the freedom of conscience.

Based on these legal provisions, the basic right to refuse to bear arms in military service is regulated in greater detail in the Yugoslav Army Law ('Official Bulletin of the FRY' no. 43/1994, Articles 296–300), as well as in the Military Service Regulation Law ('Official Bulletin of the FRY' no.

36/1994, Articles 26–29). In the (provisional) Service Regulation of the Yugoslav Army (which came into effect on 27 December 1993, and is, as far as I know, still valid) there are no provisions with regard to soldiers (i.e. military conscripts serving in the Yugoslav Army) who conscientiously object to the use of arms.

The Law and the Regulation provide that a military conscript who does not want to bear arms should write to the competent military recruiting station within fifteen days of receiving the draft notice. In his written inquiry, the conscript should state the reasons for refusing to bear arms, and state his preference for the institution where he would like to perform civil service (if he does not want to serve in a position within the Yugoslav Army where the use of arms is necessary). The institutions where civil service is possible are military-economic and health institutions, general rescue services, organizations for the rehabilitation of invalids, as well as other organizations that perform activities for the common good. The military recruiting station should decide about the inquiry within sixty days. If the decision is positive, the recruiting station also decides about the institution where the conscript will perform civil service. If it is necessary to select a Yugoslav Army unit for a conscript who refuses to bear arms, the decision will be made by the Army chief of staff. The Regulation and the Law collide when it comes to the duration of military service without bearing arms: while the Regulation stipulates that the recruiting station should decide about the duration, taking into account the specific circumstances of every individual case, the Law uniformly stipulates that this kind of service will last twenty-four months – twice as long as the regular military service. Regarding the decision of the recruiting station, the conscript can object to the District Army Command within fifteen days, and the District Army Command's decision is final.

This is how the basic right to refuse to bear arms during military service is stipulated in constitutional, legal and sub-legal regulations in the FRY. One can immediately say that this does not significantly differ in any regard from the standards accepted in many European countries. Therefore, I will first concentrate on these standards, with particular emphasis on the former Federal Republic of Germany, which has the longest and the richest tradition and can serve as a paradigm for the pluses and minuses of the contemporary understanding of this basic human right. Then I will critically examine the fundamental principles which form the basis for the basic right to refuse to bear arms in military service, and try to derive this basic right from Hobbes's political philosophy, with its special emphasis on fear and cowardice. Then I will, as a contrast, compare the results of this examination with the militaristic ideals of the so-called German '1914 Revolution', which led to the (for the formulation of the basic right to refuse to bear arms in military service, fatal) distinction of heroic vs. cowardly pacifism. Finally, I will draw some conclusions about the possibility of regulating this basic right *de lege ferenda*, which would be based on principles completely different from those now in use.

I The Basic Right to Refuse to Bear Arms during Military Service in the former Federal Republic of Germany

The conscientious objection to arms-bearing appears for the first time in early Christianity. Early Christians considered human life as sacred (a gift of God), and forbade anything that might endanger it ('what God gives, only God can take away'). Origenes formulated this as follows: 'We shall not take up arms against any people, we shall not learn the art of war, for through Jesus we have become the children of peace.' In accordance with this early Christian pacifism, converted soldiers had to throw away their weapons and desert from the Roman army, and many of them became martyrs (Melamed 1909: 105–106). This practice ceased in 314 CE, when the Council criticized soldiers deserting for reasons that had to do with religion, and did its utmost to prevent this in the future. The militarization of Christianity went hand in hand with its promotion to the official state religion, and this led to the birth of the war spirit that in the Middle Ages started wars for the conquest of Jerusalem and, later, religious wars in Europe. However, a number of Christian sects still remained devoted to the original pacifist positions, and forbade their members to take up arms, even if that meant endangering their own lives or bringing them into conflict with secular authorities.

The first serious attempts to legally enable refusal to bear arms in military service occurred in the twentieth century. Before World War I it was still dangerous to promote this idea. Participants in the 12th International Peace Congress in Rouen, in 1903, refused even to discuss the proposition of the Abbé Allégret to form alternative services for the people that refused to bear arms on religious grounds. Four years later, delegates at the 16th International Peace Congress voted for a resolution which explicitly stated that the peace movement was in no way connected with the campaign related to the refusal to bear arms. The situation began to change only after World War I. At the International Miners' Congress in Geneva, in 1920, the first resolution on the refusal to bear arms was voted for. Similar resolutions followed at the International Syndicates Congress in Rome in 1922, the International Congress of Textile Workers in Vienna in 1926, etc. War Resisters International was founded in 1921, in the Dutch town of Bilthoven, its main goal being the 'anti-militaristic revolution' (cf. Runham Brown 1930: 13). Its members called themselves 'war resisters' and 'conscientious objectors', and, following the motto 'War never again', undertook many measures (regardless of legal sanctions) to spread the idea of the necessity of refusing not only to bear arms, but also to participate in the production and distribution of all kinds of weapons, or to participate in any preparation for a concrete military campaign. This International, at the 1925 World Peace Congress in Paris, proposed a resolution on the refusal to bear arms, but it was defeated (195 votes against 145). However, in 1926, delegates to the World Peace Congress in Geneva declared themselves as having the right to refuse to bear arms. Similar decisions were voted for at the national peace congresses in France and Germany. The first anti-militaristic movements of congregationals were formed in England and Switzerland in 1926, with the same basic aim of achieving the right to refuse to bear arms. The international organization of the congregationals was formed in 1928.

At the start of World War I, the UK and the US became the first modern states to accept conscientious objection as a legitimate reason for the refusal to bear arms. After that, Scandinavian countries were the first to provide for the substitution of civil service for armed military service. Denmark introduced an alternative military service in 1917 (which included work in forestry only), and was followed by Sweden (1920 for the congregationals, and in 1925 for all other people stating a conscientious objection) and Norway (in 1922 for the congregationals, and in 1925 for all other people stating a conscientious objection). However, it was still not thought that refusing to bear arms in military service was a basic human right. This changed for the first time in 1949, in Germany. After the horrors of World War II, the idea gained ground that one had to devote much greater attention to the struggle against war. The struggle gained particular importance due to the lack of success of anti-war campaigns between the World Wars, as people realized that it should include all people who were willing to perform military service without bearing arms. Hence, Article 4 of the 1949 Bonn Constitution (of the Federal Republic of Germany) has a formulation later found in the constitutions of almost all European countries: 'No one can be forced to perform military service with arms against his will. The details are regulated by the Federal law.'

The principle adopted by writers of the German Constitution consisted in treating this basic right as a specific evaluation of the basic human right to a free conscience. The formulation of this basic right was considered in the (future) Federal Republic of Germany during the Constitutional Assembly in 1948, not only because of abstract-pacifist motives, but also because of the very concrete attempts of the Germans from the American, British and French occupation zones to avoid being sent to an eventual war to fight against Germans from the Soviet occupation zone. It is very important to bear this in mind, because of the later history of the right to refuse to bear arms in military service: the 'conscientious objection' initially had a quite pragmatic aim of sparing members of an ethnic group the possibility, due to international circumstances, of shooting at each other.

However, the definitive formulation from the Bonn Constitution gave this right a different meaning. The SPD Representative Bergsträsser gave the following explanation for entering this right into the legal material:

> We have included here this additional possibility, since this has to do with the freedom of religion and freedom of conscience. The additional possibility [acknowledges] that people – we had in mind particularly the Mennonites, Jehovah's Witnesses, and members of other sects – do not want to bear arms in military service because of their religious convictions and their conscience. (Krölls 1983: 22–23)

There were four controversies related to the further development of this basic right in Germany. First, there were more and more atheists, who stressed humanistic, ethical, or even political connotations of this basic right (especially after the student movement of 1968), so the idea of religious objection became increasingly lost in a universalistic and religiously neutral concept of 'conscience'. Secondly, an increasing number of people were not refusing to participate in any war against any enemy, but against a specific enemy and in specific circumstances (for example, a nuclear war). Thirdly, there was a question as to whether the reason of conscience should be universally valid for all forms of military service (that is to say, including the civil service), or just for the ones that included arms-bearing. Finally, the possibility of state institutions checking for and determining the existence of an 'authentic' conscience of a person, and then determining whether those individuals should be granted this basic right, was increasingly questioned as well. This led to the proposal that this basic right should be 'untangled' from the right to a free conscience.

Only the third of these controversies has been definitively solved so far. Due to a restrictive and conservative politics of the process of 'acknowldgement' of the existence of the 'conscience' objection (*Anerkennungsverfahren*), a great number of conscripts who wish to invoke their right to refuse to bear arms during military service must hide their political motives, or cloak them in religious or universalistic-ethical concepts (Krölls 1983: 108), while universalizing their own 'situationally conditioned' pacifist views (Böckenförde 1991: 251). In a case when a conscientious objection is recognized for a military conscript, and he is sent to perform some civil service, he loses the right (according to a ruling by the German Constitutional Court) to claim the conscientious objection to refuse to perform this civil service (Löw 1977: 219). Finally, the process of 'recognition' of the conscientious objection was hampered by voluntarism and numerous relics from the system of inquisition (Möhle and Rabe 1972: 53), as well as by the *numerus clausus* approach, which stipulated the exclusion from military service of people up to the number that the state determined informally and arbitrarily (Krölls 1983: 40). However, one has to note that the pressure to use this right is increasing every year, so that the number of military conscripts who performed civil service reached 160,000 in 1995, which is 100 times more than in 1957, when this right was first made possible. That is why one might say that the military needs are still of primary importance, and that the basic right to refuse to bear arms in military service is not used as an authentic unlimited basic human right (as stipulated in the constitution), but as a right that is subject to limitations – as provided in the meantime by the German Constitutional Court (Alexy 1986: 107).

It would be ideal for the state (or for its military) if each year the number of people who refuse to bear arms in military service would be such that: (1) it would not endanger the optimum manpower of the armed forces, (2) it could cover all the 'un-soldierly' people (that is to say, people who would only create problems while in the army, or who would, because of their convictions, just be put into jails), and (3) it would cover only people whose motivation was far removed from the political sphere (because of the reactive influence of the strengthening of pacifism in public opinion). Since this is not the case, the basic right to refuse to bear arms in military service must be defamed and stigmatized. People who refuse to bear arms are subjected to numerous inconveniences, so that the state is not put in the position of refusing this right to a significant number of them – thus making a mockery of the right itself.

A military conscript who wants to refuse to bear arms must first subject himself to a procedure of conscience-examination, which is rightly described as the last remnant of the inquisition in the twentieth century. (The 1984 Law reduces this procedure in normal cases to the examination of a written request.) Even if he manages to convince the state of the strength of his pacifist beliefs, he must spend a much longer time period (compared to the one under his 'normal' military service) performing his civil service, quite often under very difficult conditions (hospitals for the mentally ill, etc.). Even with all this, he is regarded with suspicion, as a member of some minority with which 'there is something wrong', and which is deviant (as compared to the 'healthy military conscripts' who are ready to take up arms in order to bravely defend their motherland). Hence, if the state is to allow the refusal to bear arms, a military conscript is (implicitly) required to be a 'martyr' or a 'hero', who will survive all challenges and bravely resist all temptations thrown at his pacifist conscience. He will 'pay' the state for excluding him from the armed forces with all his troubles and stigmatization, and serve as a negative example for all who do not know whether to follow in his footsteps. In return, the state will have achieved the most stable possible compromise: on the one hand, a (minimal) social stratum that serves as a cover for the state's obligation to protect the basic human right to refuse to bear arms during military service, and, on the other, an exclusion from its armed forces only of 'pacifist heroes' who have proved that their 'soldiering' would bring more harm than usefulness.

It is my intention to present in this paper a critique of this whole construction, as completely incompatible with the logic of constituting a society on the principles of basic human rights. First of all, general military service and a people's army belong (I hope) to the European militant-nationalist past, which started with the Jacobin military revolution of 1793, and which today contradicts European integration processes, based on the principles of democracy and basic human rights. A true contemporary pacifist, democratic and individualistic society should give up on these relics of militant nationalism and accept the professional army as the most appropriate military-organizational principle (as already implemented in Holland, Belgium and Great Britain, and promised for France and – in the near future – Russia). The formation of national professional armies should be as closely coordinated as possible, which could lead to them becoming territorial branches of the 'UN–world police'. Thus, regulation of the basic human right to refuse to bear arms in military service should be understood as a temporary solution for a transitional period. In this period, a system of general military service and a people's army would be completely replaced with one of the military as a profession and a professional army (with a tendency for them to be integrated in the 'UN–world police').

Secondly, it is wrong to assume that armed forces should be the organizational part of a modern state which puts its priorities above the priorities of the other parts of the state apparatus and, even more important, above the ones of citizens themselves. This is a relic of the militaristic consciousness of the supremacy of war ('defence') over politics (diplomacy). This way of reasoning has nothing in common with the logic of basic human rights – quite the contrary, it is a remnant of an authoritarian way of constituting nation-states. Only a state that gives priority to pacifist rights over military obligations, priority to diplomacy over the army, and priority to the Security Council and armed forces of the UN ('UN–world police') over its own armed forces, acts in the spirit of (internationally valid) basic human rights. Hence, the establishment of quotas for people who will use their basic human right to refuse to bear arms during military service is unconstitutional, and it could not be tolerated in a true pacifist legal state (one which is in a process of transition towards a professional-army system).

Thirdly, the aforementioned situation, with the realization of the right to refuse to bear arms, illustrates a society which still regards itself as a 'society of heroes'. From this perspective, 'true' members of society must be 'heroes', whether as patriots or as pacifists, and the refusal to bear arms is not regarded as a right, but as a way for 'the heroes of pacifism' to confirm their true bravery (which they have in common with 'the heroes of patriotism'), and thus secure an adequate social status. I think that this is at the core of the misconceptions about the constitution of a society, as well as in the derivation of the basic human right to refuse to bear arms in military service. Modern societies are not 'societies of heroes', but societies where bravery is an exception. Their members tend to be cowards or, at best, people who fear any (war) situation in which their bravery or cowardice might be demonstrated. If one starts from this axiom in the way a society is constituted, what follows is a conclusion that one needs to define again the content of the basic right to refuse to bear arms in military service. In order to show this, I will use some of the basic postulations of Hobbes's social theory, which, in my opinion, provides for an understanding of military service based on fear and cowardice, in a way which is still very relevant today.

II Hobbes's Understanding of Fear and Cowardice

As far as European history is concerned, fear and cowardice have long been (and to a great extent remain) something shameful and indecent, while bravery has been exalted and considered as an (unattainable) ideal in every man. This is why bravery has been at the same time the basis for the privileges of the rare people who had it, while fear and cowardice have gone hand in hand with the submission and lack of rights of the rank and file (Delimo, 1987: 5 ff.) The theoretical social implications of the value of bravery were addressed long ago by Plato. He considered bravery to be among the four virtues that constituted an (ideal) political community (together with wisdom, moderation and righteousness), and its 'carrier' was the class of warriors. The class-monopolizing of bravery by warriors freed the remaining two classes from an obligation to prove themselves as carriers of this virtue. That is why the question of whether citizens (who do not belong to the warrior class) are brave or not, was irrelevant for the foundation and survival of Plato's 'brave' Republic. It was only important that the warriors were brave, and from that fact one could already draw the conclusion that a class-based republic completely realizes this virtue (Plato, 1976: 114/429b).

An élitist 'hero discourse' is a primary characteristic of medieval class society, where nobles played the dominant role, as virtual protectors of other classes (Duby, 1973: 184). The basic characteristic of this discourse was the non-existence of a firm border between war and politics, that is to say, between an ordinary (state) and extraordinary (martial) law. Up until the seventeenth century, politics and war represented for kings and nobles two sides of the same coin. One moved easily from peace to war, and vice versa. Actually, every peace was half war, and every war half peace. Politics was conducted with the rattling of arms, while wars were conducted alongside diplomatic negotiations. The non-existence of a standing army was a factor that restrained militarism, but, on the other hand, this contributed to the fact that it was much easier to calculate the start of war and the way in which it was going to develop, since the armies of mercenaries employed were a mere means, paid in order to produce certain ends. As for the class of nobles itself, it provided diplomats and generals, without any obstacles in the way of moving from diplomacy into the military, and vice versa. There was no specialization that would strictly separate 'peace experts' from 'war experts'. All together, this influenced the opinion that there was no important difference between peace and war, and thus between politics and the conduct of war (Schmitthenner, 1937: 21–22). Wars did not significantly differ from hunting, and hunting was not that different from other games that filled one's spare time. On the other hand, for the 'mob' (that is to say, the population that was not organized into classes), a military career was as good as any other. For all the people who did not 'suffer' from the problem of ownership and who had personal freedom, labour and war were considered as parts of the same continuum.

In the modern era, things slowly began to change. Bravery and fear were both emancipated from the class framework, and were related instead to rationalist individual ethics. Bravery appears as the highest ideal for every individual, while fear and cowardice were seen as mere pathological forms, as states of lack of bravery. For example, Descartes could not yet see how fear and cowardice would be useful for a man, and treated them as 'passions' that were primarily bad for an individual, and that must be got rid of in any way (Dekart, 1981: 105–106; 174–176). In the early modern era, an 'egalitarization' of the capacities for bravery and heroism placed fear and cowardice in the area of general individual and social pathology. Approximately, from the French Revolution (more precisely, from its Jacobin phase) onwards, this attitude served as a basis for establishing a general military service, and was used to legitimize militaristic components of nationalist doctrines. (I will deal with this in more detail in section III.)

The third attitude, that will completely negate the 'heroic discourse' (whether in a traditional class, or in a new egalitarian sense), shall become possible only when the civil class begins to dominate society, when liberal theory shakes the foundations of the ancien régime, and when a citizen's life and property begin to be important as the main values that a state should protect. This 'fearful discourse' appeared for the first time in seventeenth-century England, during the Civil War, and it was to introduce contemporaries to a new – civil – insight into a relationship between an individual and a state, war and politics, as well as between fear and bravery. One of the best theoretical expressions of this change can be read in the works of Thomas Hobbes.

Hobbes's starting premise is constituted of the dichotomies (freed of all the religious and class connotations) of the natural (warlike) and the state-like (peaceful) state. Thus a State of God becomes completely irrelevant, and the earthly state fits without any problem into a lawful order of the universe, and can survive only if it is founded on the principles of reason. The individuals (supplied with reason) are the ones that should choose between chaos and order, and it is in their power to make peace (if they should choose it) a stable context for state institutions. Hobbes introduces into his theory a duality of the natural law (the principle of freedom) and natural laws (principles of reason), which poses individuals a basic dilemma: to keep their absolute freedom, or to accept a reciprocal (reasonable) limitation, in order to protect the safety of honour, life and property (and thus secure a 'minimum of freedom'). According to Hobbes, a rational man, governed by natural laws, will have to choose the second alternative, and to prefer peace within the state order to all others, especially to all the other violent means of realizing absolute freedom. That is the content of the first natural law which Hobbes mentions in *Leviathan*:

> And therefore, as long as this natural Right of every man to every thing endureth, there can be no security to any man (how strong or wise soever can be), of living out the time, which Nature ordinarily alloweth men to live. And consequently it is a precept, or general rule of Reason, *That every man, ought to endeavour Peace, as farre as he has hope of obtaining it; and when he cannot obtain it, that he may seek, and use, all helps, and advantages of Warre.* (Hobbes, 1966b: 116)

Hence, a state of peace can be achieved only when the individuals prefer a rationally based value of security (of honour, life and property) to the value of unlimited freedom. According to Hobbes, this is in the interest of not only the weakest and the least intelligent, but also the strongest and the wisest, since in that way they reduce the risk of becoming victims to the united weak and unintelligent people. Civilization is the result of the reasonable insights that all people are equal with regard to the possibility of killing each other, that the natural state does not give to anyone a decisive advantage with regard to other people, and that it is necessary to replace the war which governs in that natural state with an order in which there will be a balance of the minimum of freedom and maximum of security.

Mark Gavre has mentioned that Hobbes in his anthropological pessimism followed Calvin, and that his very theory of civil society shows some influences of Calvinism, which was an unquestioned dogma of all the British Protestant sects in the seventeenth century. Gavre's main conclusion is that 'the structure of Hobbes' argument follows that of Calvin, with the change that religious faith has been replaced by reason' (Gavre, 1974: 1551). That thesis is undoubtedly true, but it is not sufficient. Hobbes did not think that one can get from the natural state into the social one with the aid of reason alone. He states quite explicitly in *Leviathan* that the possibility of man getting out of the natural state lies

> partly in the passions, partly in his reason. The passions that incline men to peace, are fear of death; desire of such things as are necessary to commodious living; and a hope by their industry to obtain them. And reason suggesteth convenient articles of peace, upon which men may be drawn to agreement. These articles, are they, which otherwise are called the Laws of Nature (Hobbes, 1966b: 66)

Thus, a civil society is based not only on reason, but also on three 'passions': the fear of death, the wish for things necessary for a comfortable life, and the hope that they can be achieved through normal production. However, all of these passions can be reduced to the one fundamental one of fear. Indeed, Hobbes concludes that for the stability of a civil society, '[t]he passion to be reckoned upon, is fear' (Hobbes, 1966b: 116) – fear of death, the loss of property, and all the things necessary for a comfortable life.

Such a belief in fear as the fundamental 'passionate' basis of a civil society cannot be understood without taking into account the scholastic tradition, where the word 'fear' (*timor*) meant more a rational than an irrational activity of thinking of future evil, and taking some concrete steps in order to stop that evil. Influenced by this, Hobbes made a distinction between fear and a state of being afraid (*being affrighted*) (Laird, 1968: 172–173). In *De cive*, Hobbes gives a clear distinction between these two psychic events:

> It is objected: it is so improbable that man should grow into civil societies out of fear, that if they had been afraid, they would not have endured each other's looks. They presume, I believe, that to fear is nothing else than to be affrighted. I comprehend in this word *fear*, a certain foresight of future evil; neither do I conceive flight the sole property of fear, but to distrust, suspect, take heed, provide so that they may not fear, is also incident to the fearful. They who go to sleep, shut their doors; they who travel, carry their swords with them, because they fear thieves. Kingdoms guard their coasts and frontiers with forts and castles; cities are compact with walls; and all for fear of neighbouring kingdoms and towns. Even the strongest armies, and most accomplished for fight, yet

sometimes parley for peace, as fearing each other's power, and lest they might be overcome. It is through fear that men secure themselves by flight, indeed, and in corners, if they think they cannot escape otherwise; but not for the most part by arms and defensive weapons; whence it happens that daring to come forth they know each other's spirits. But then if they fight, civil society ariseth from victory; if they agree, from their agreement. (Hobbes, 1966a: 6n)

It clearly follows that only a rationally founded fear, as a reflexive principle of self-preservation and security, can be the basis of a civil society, while an instinctively caused psychic state of fear is worthless, and is as dangerous for a civil society as other – non-social – passions. Only individuals moved by the rational fear, who look for the security of a civil society, can seriously undertake the conclusion of a valid social contract. Obligations that follow from that social contract will bind them only in so far as in the social state they do not feel as endangered as they were in the natural state. As noted by Howard Warrender, fear and a wish for security are for Hobbes not just a driving force for man to develop from his natural state; they also guide his reason to recognize when he is endangered in the social state, so that he must resort to the means of war, characteristic of the natural state. 'If Hobbes' theory is, however, as we suggested, that I am obliged by my covenant unless some *subsequent* cause of fear invalidates it, the function of the sovereign is not to make valid a covenant that was previously invalid, but to prevent (by taking away subsequent causes of fear) what is already a valid covenant from being invalidated.' Thus, 'the obligation of the individual is contingent upon "sufficient security", and where this security is lacking, he may attempt to preserve himself by any means which seems justifiable to him in terms of his own circumstances and fears' (Warrender, 1961: 44, 320–321).

When describing in this way members of a civil society, it seems that Hobbes has in mind extremely materialistic-oriented people, who mostly fear loss of life and property, and subsume to these values all others. However, this is not true, since Hobbes puts the value of honour above the value of life. According to him, 'because all signs of hatred and contempt provoke most of all to brawling and fighting, insomuch as most men would rather lose their lives (that is to say, their peace) than suffer slander' (Hobbes, 1966a: 38). Thus, if their honour is sullied, 'most' people would not hesitate to give their lives – primarily in a duel – in order to wash the slander from themselves and their name. However, perhaps Hobbes here went a step further than the basic premises of his theory allow for, since, in order to preserve their honour, it is not necessary for people to risk their lives in duels; in a society that would efficiently protect not just lives and property, but also honour all its members, a regular court procedure of protection would be quite enough to satisfy even the most honour-abiding among them. A more plausible solution is possibly to be found in *Leviathan*, where Hobbes pleads for 'such time as there shall be Honour ordained for them that refuse Duels, and Ignominy for them that make the Challenge' (Hobbes, 1966b: 81).

In any case, honour should not be mixed with glory, which is attained through bravery and heroic deeds, and for which Hobbes does not find a high place in the hierarchy of the generally accepted social values. There is a passage in *Leviathan*, where we find his opinion that 'a glory (. . .) is a generosity too rarely found to be presumed on, especially in the pursuers of wealth, command, or sensual pleasure; which are the greatest part of mankind' (Hobbes, 1996b: 128–129). Thus, a stable civil society must count on the fact that all or at least the majority of its people do not long for glory and that they place the greatest value on their honour, and then life and property, and that they are interested in the survival of the civil society in which they live only as long as it guarantees them these values. Having left a natural state, in which these fundamental values were under pressure, people expect of civil society a state in which they can be free from the fear of their honour, life and property being endangered, and begin to build an order in which they can live and work in peace. That is why they cannot authorize a sovereign to endanger them in a way that existed in the natural state. 'More generally, Hobbes' views would be consistent only if, in the nature of things, certain powers could never be transferred to any ruler, so that absolutism meant simply that all the powers that could be transferred were in fact bestowed upon the ruler' (Laird, 1968: 204). Among 'the powers that could never be transferred to any ruler' are powers to preserve honour, life and property. An individual can never renounce these. Thus, when speaking of the united powers of a sovereign to protect his subjects, Hobbes never includes among them these 'untransferable powers'. Moreover, their existence – in the sense of an inviolable minimum of the natural law obtaining in a civil society – presupposes the *raison d'être* of any social condition, and their strengthening is directed to the reason of building and maintenance of every *suprema potestas*: 'The obligation of subject to the sovereign, is understood to last as long, and no longer, than the power lasteth, by which he is able to protect them' (Hobbes, 1996b: 208).

At the moment when the politics of a sovereign cannot secure the safety of his subjects, they free themselves from obligations towards him, and revert to the state of *bellum omnium contra omnes*. But, in order for a civil society to be really stable and permanent, it is not enough for a sovereign alone to take care of it; the cooperation of all its members is needed. That also means a maximum rationalization of all the actors, in accordance with the provisions of the natural laws. A sovieragn's obligation to enable his people to be 'educated' is derived from this; in other words, an obligation not to keep them rooted in the basic fear of losing life (or property or 'other pleasures'), but allowing them to learn about their rights according to natural laws (which a good sovereign should transform into civil laws). Because, if he does not do this, and if he establishes an order contrary to natural laws, a sovereign will, sooner or later, suffer a rebellion of his subjects united against him, as a natural consequence – a sanction for the breaking of natural laws. Thus, a rebellion by his subjects is something quite normal, it is the effect of a monarch's lack of education which deprives his subjects of protection, driving them into rebellion against him.

As does every man, so a sovereign has an obligation according to the first natural law (that he must posit into a civil law) to seek and keep peace. If he does not do so, he is moving towards the state of war, and provoking his subjects to unite against himself and his army. Hobbes is quite clear in *De cive*: '[A] person who rules without right – or, more precisely, against laws – is "enemy" and may be put to death' (Hobbes, 1966a: 153). In the meantime, based on the experiences of the English Civil War, Hobbes saw that people might rush to war, seduced by the 'war propaganda' of some leaders, which provokes the lowest instincts in them. In the English Civil War the leaders, with their sweet talk, won over ordinary people who were politically indifferent and willing to 'take any side for pay and plunder' (Hobbes, 1966d: 166). Although he excluded King Charles I from his critique of the leaders of the Civil War, Hobbes was conscious of the fact that a sovereign can use 'war propaganda' himself in order to awaken the lowest instincts among his subjects, as well as a blind wish 'for pay and plunder'. That is why in *Behemoth* we find an (albeit implicit) theory of the monarch's power 'by the consent of the people'. The consent of the people

> establishes the sovereign as the final arbiter in disputes because he represents the people or, according to the legal fiction of authorisation, because he *is* the people. Although it is doubtful that Hobbes ever intended this consent to occur as a historical fact, he did expect it to have a real effect in preventing self-appointed wise men and prophets from deceiving the people into surrendering their minds to authority. (Kraynak, 1982: 846, also Orwin, 1975)

Let us now consider how Hobbes's solution for the relationship of a successfully constituted civil society looks so far as war is concerned. From everything said so far, it follows clearly that Hobbes made a distinction between two separate orders: *nature-war-chaos* and *state-peace-order*. The state starts where the war ends, and vice versa. Where civil war is concerned, Hobbes is quite explicit:

> But in those places where there is a civil law at any time, at the same time there are neither laws, nor commonwealth, nor society, but only temporal league, which every discontented soldier may depart from when he pleases, as being entered by each man for his private interest, without any obligation of conscience: there are therefore almost at all times multitudes of lawless men. (Hobbes, 1966c: 184)

Thus, in the state of civil war, there can be only 'temporal league' among warriors, not among states.

However, a problem arises at the international level. We do not find in Hobbes's work any hints about the possibilities of solving the problems of overcoming wars and achieving security in international relations in the same way as with the state – i.e. by creating a *civitas maxima*. Moreover, Hobbes clearly started from the premise that peace can be established only within the borders of a state, while relations between states are, so to speak, in a constant state of war.

> For WAR, consisteth not in battle only, or the act of fighting; but in a tract of time, wherein the will to contend by battle is sufficiently known; and therefore the notion of *time*, is to be considered in the nature of war; (. . .) so the nature of war, consisteth not in actual fighting; but in the known disposition thereto, during all the time there is no assurance to the contrary. All other time is PEACE. (Hobbes, 1966b: 113)

Starting from this definition of war, Hobbes could indeed calmly conclude that 'in all times, kings, and persons of sovereign authority, because of their independency, are in continual jealousies, and in the state and posture of gladiators', that is to say, in the state of war (Hobbes, 1966b: 115). And not only that. Presupposing that people long for security and that in unregulated relations – such as in the natural state – security is protected with weapons, the universal rule is that the most opportunistic thing is to attack first, so that one is not taken by surprise.

> And for this difference of one another, there is no way for any man to secure himself, so reasonable, as an anticipation; that is, by force, or wiles, to master the persons of all men he can, so long, till he see no other power great enough to endanger him; and this is no more than his own conservation requireth, and is generally allowed. (Hobbes, 1966b: 111)

Hence, it is also best for states to initiate wars against their enemies, so that they will not be attacked at inopportune moments.

Two principles of Hobbes's social philosophy are in direct conflict here: on the one hand, according to the first law of nature, a sovereign must always strive for peace, while on the other, general insecurity in international relations obliges every sovereign to lead 'preventive' wars. The antagonism is to an extent present in the very constitution of a state, since only citizens enter into a state of peace, while a sovereign remains in the natural state (with sovereigns in all other states). If one takes into account the plurality of states and sovereigns, this can lead to a conclusion that states are special oases of peace and security, secured by the wars that sovereigns wage among themselves. In such a way, in global relations, the superseding of the natural state has never occurred, it has simply been 'functionalized' to protect these oases of peace and security in states. One should take into account that Hobbes writes at a time when nationalism had not yet succeeded in making a sovereign a national leader, or in making wars 'a question of life or death of the whole nation'. In his time, wars are almost 'private affairs' of monarchs fighting for their own aims and interests, and their subjects are interested in these wars only in as much as they wish to be spared all their unfavourable consequences – most of all, the endangering of honour, life and property. That is why subjects can calmly accept a new sovereign who defeats their old sovereign in a war, if he offers them the same, or even better conditions of security.

> In his [Hobbes's] account, persons who fall into the hands of a foreign conqueror who is willing to protect them may submit to him, just as they are released from any obligation to obey their own sovereign, if it has failed to provide protection. (. . .) Hobbes' theory, indeed, does not provide any reason why an individual person should prefer his own sovereign to a foreign one. (Bull, 1981: 726)

This is certainly the most anachronistic part of Hobbes's theory. It (as we shall see later) implies, but does not clearly meet, a world that will be divided into national states, in which irrational ideologies will transform national leaders into almost living gods, and their subjects into believers ready to give up their honour, life and property for their leader. Hobbes still has the hope that the peace of all the people on earth will be secured in such a way as to allow their sovereigns to fight and kill each other, while each sovereign will offer to all their subjects more or less identical conditions of guaranteeing security (according to the first law of nature). This has enabled Hobbes's approach to an international order to be, as Hedley Bull says, both 'realistic' and deeply pacifist at the same time.

Even though, as we have seen, he accepts the possibility of the coexistence of war and peace on the global (world) scale, Hobbes has excluded war activity from a social order, putting it beyond the reach of citizens. War could not be a part of the state order, or a political aim, but merely a private business which belonged to the domain of a sovereign and his paid army. In that sense, Hobbes anticipated a famous saying of the Prussian King Frederick II, a century later, that a sovereign has to lead a war in such a way that his nation would not realize that it is at war (Haffner, 1979: 77).

That is how we reach the problem of the military service of citizens: does a citizen have an obligation to go to war for his sovereign or not? A negative answer might be expected based on what has been said so far. However, Hobbes' reply is very sophisticated:

> Upon this ground, a man that is commanded as a soldier to fight against the enemy, though his sovereign have the right enough to punish his refusal with death, may nevertheless in many cases refuse, without injustice (. . .). And there is allowance to be made for natural timorousness; not only to women, of whom no such a dangerous duty is expected, but also to men of feminine courage. When armies fight, there is on one side, or both, a running away; yet when they do it not out of treachery, but fear, they are not esteemed to do it unjustly, but dishonourably. For the same reason, to avoid battle, is not injustice, but cowardice. But he that inrolleth himself a soldier or taketh imprest money, taketh away the excuse of a timorous nature; and is obliged, not only to go to the battle, but also not to run from it, without his captain's leave. And when the defence of the commonwealth requireth at once the help of all that

are able to bear arms, every one is obliged; because otherwise the institution of the commonwealth, which they have not the purpose, or courage to preserve, was in vain. (Hobbes, 1966b: 205)

There were different interpretations of such a solution. According to Leo Strauss, by tying military service to a lack of fear Hobbes 'destroyed a moral basis of the national defence', so, if he wanted to express a consequent pacifist solution, it would have been better if he had opted for the model of the world state as the best one to avoid war and the fear of citizens for their own safety (Strauss, 1971: 171–172). The trouble with this criticism is that it does not take into account the fact that Hobbes was at the same time both a 'realist' and a pacifist. Thus, he had to settle in some other way his totally 'realistic' conviction of the eternity of fights between states (which *a priori* prevents the creation of a world state), with a pacifist value attitude, expressed in the first law of nature. Hobbes found a way for this in a theory that, according to Josef Popper-Lynkeus, for the first time demands an essentially voluntarist military service (Popper-Lynkeus, 1921: 188).

This conclusion seems a bit hasty. For, if one takes a better look, Hobbes's argument does not postulate anywhere the free will of a state's citizens to accept military service. What does Hobbes really say in the passage from *Leviathan* quoted above? First of all, he talks about military service *in war*. As there was no general military service in his time, based on the principles of recruiting and garrisons in preparation for (some future, eventual) war, Hobbes simply had in mind the cases when a monarch calls citizens to go directly to a war which either has yet to start, or is taking place already. Hence, when Hobbes speaks of military service, he has in mind these very concrete cases of true *war*. However, at the same time, he distinguishes two sorts of war – a class-knightly one and a national-defensive one – each of which gives a totally different meaning to military service. A class-knightly war was a common war of the time, and Hobbes treats it as a 'normal case'. In this kind of conflict, monarchs and nobles fight for various things, and knightly rules specify both the way of fighting and the sparing of the civilian population. That is why, according to Hobbes, if a sovereign thinks that he can fill his army not only with mercenaries, but also with his citizens, they can refuse his call by pointing to their fearful nature. The argument follows logically from Hobbes's theory that we mentioned earlier. Citizens enter the social state and transfer all of their 'transferable power' to a sovereign, in order to live in peace and security. The exceptions are paid soldiers, who, by the act of accepting paid military service, renounce the right to invoke their 'fearful nature'. The fact that a sovereign will fight on the battlefields with his mercenaries, far away from city life, does not interest citizens as long as it does not endanger their lives and property. In other words, a sovereign can test his power with other sovereigns, far from city life, and if he falls as a victim of the enemy, citizens will simply have a new sovereign. But a new sovereign, just like the previous one, will not be able to impose on them any obligatory military service. The reason is the same: citizens will be able to invoke their fearful nature and to imply that – if sent to war – they will leave the battlefield at the moment when it gets 'tough'. Thus, the anticipated cowardice mentioned by Hobbes is, in the case of a class-knightly war, the basis for a citizen's basic right to refuse to bear arms in military service out of rational fear (i.e. avoiding the state in which their cowardice will be revealed).

The case of a national-defensive war is quite different. Here is presupposed a type of war that has as its aim the plundering, killing and enslaving of a civilian population. Thus, faced with this direct danger to his honour, life and property, a citizen cannot invoke his fearful nature and avoid going to war. Moreover, in a national-defensive war, he does not have the possibility of invoking any reason to refuse military service, since the victory of the enemy means disaster for the whole population. In this case a sovereign and his people are united together in the face of an external danger. Hobbes assumes that in this sort of war all the classes (that comprise the people) can see danger in the enemy that intends to conquer and plunder their 'commonwealth', and that all therefore have an obligation to come under the command of a sovereign and to defend their country. Fear and a wish for security cannot be expressed as a basis for refusing to serve in the military, since they are already negated by the enemy's intent. Thus, in this case, the protection of honour, life and property presupposes accepting the war, which does not mean reverting to the natural state, but rather defending the principles of civil society on its edges, from the outbreak of forces from the surrounding natural state.

Two conclusions can be drawn from Hobbes's premise. First, every civil society is constituted on fear (for one's honour, life and property), and on the wish for security, and that is why a citizen cannot be forced into any military service that would endanger this constitutive basis. Secondly, there is a difference when more than this fear-based constitution is threatened. In a case when a civil society itself is endangered, every citizen must, *out of the rationally founded fear for his honour, life and property*, suppress an instinctive cowardice within himself, and accept the struggle for the defence of the principles of his civil society. The same argument can be applied to a sovereign himself: at the very moment when he starts endangering the life, honour and property of his citizens, they must listen to the rational fear within themselves, suppress cowardice, accept war against him, and 'put him to death' as an enemy.

III 'Fearful Discourse' and 'Heroic Discourse' in Modern Society

Hobbes's understanding of military service as mentioned above can be understood as part of a 'fearful discourse'. In this 'fearful discourse', an individual enters civil society out of fear (for his honour, life and property), retaining the natural right to cowardice as long as the civil society is secure, but at the moment when that security disappears, he has (out of a rationally founded fear) to take decisive – including military – steps against anyone endangering him, regardless of whether it is a foreign enemy, or a sovereign himself. Hobbes has been sharply criticized for these opinions by those who defended a diametrically opposed 'heroic discourse' in the constitution of a society.

The 'heroic discourse' brought to paroxysm a modern-age longing for egalitarization – and it did so in the area of the virtue of bravery. As we saw with Descartes, establishment of the ideal of bravery for all individuals without exception led to declaring fear and cowardice as something patho-logical, both in an individual and in a social sense. Modern nationalist ideologies radicalized the whole matter, declaring whole peoples as 'heroic', and putting them completely at the disposal of their 'glorious' army leaders. To put things in a more concrete perspective, we shall see how this 'heroic discourse' functioned among members of the German '1914 Revolution', so-called (on that 'revolution' in more detail, see Mommsen, 1990, and Lübbe, 1963).

For the German '1914 Revolutionaries', Hobbes was certainly one of the greatest ideological enemies. His greatest 'sins' were his materialistic and atheist convictions that, according to them, led Hobbes into thinking that a man is 'naturally' free, and that he has certain rights that precede state. For example, Houston Stewart Chamberlain assumed that nature does not know of any freedom, but only necessity, while freedom comes to man from God only, and from the (equally deified) national state. Hence, Chamberlain declared Hobbes to be the most ardent materialist and atheist, who despises everything that comes from philosophy and religion and talks of 'nonsense such as "natural laws"' (Chamberlain, 1917: 3). Freedom and right are, according to Chamberlain, totally on the other side – in the wars led by a national state, in order to win in the 'struggle for survival' and achieve world supremacy. Unlike Chamberlain, Werner Sombart did not object to Hobbes's insistence on natural rights (within a materialist and atheist world-view), but to a 'philistine spirit' (Krämergeist) that negated all heroic values. According to him, with Hobbes's teaching on state, that philistine cowardly spirit entered English political theory, and the theories of the social contract and basic human rights thereafter became unquestioned (Sombart, 1915: 22–23). This was equal to a national death, since a private logic took control of the public sphere and prevented the development of a real and authentic 'heroic spirit' (which was characteristic for Germans).

Hobbes did not fare any better in Germany later, with the National Socialists, who continued the '1914 Revolution'. There were some attempts to proclaim him one of the founders of totalitarianism, but these came to little. (The same goes for less ambitious attempts to recognize in Hobbes a theorist who grounded an authoritarian 'state-philosophical model of confidence into an absolute powerholder' – as Martin Kriele claims even today, for exam-ple in Kriele, 1983: 219–220.) It is well known that Carl Schmitt has himself denied the possibility that Hobbes was even a member, let alone a founder, of the theory of the totalitarian or authoritarian state. The reason was clear: Hobbes clearly insisted on the view that citizens acquire the right to a revolution at the very moment when a sovereign deprives them of security and endangers their life or property (Schmitt, 1937: 163). This was totally incompatible with the 'heroic discourse' initiated by the '1914 Revolutionaries' and finished by the '1933 Revolutionaries'.

The '1914 Revolutionaries' were, during World War I and immediately after it, trying to prove that Germany was a 'country of heroes' (contrary to the English, who had become that 'cowardly philistine people'), and that thus it had to win the (First World) war. One of the leaders of this revolution, Werner Sombart, believed in the sharp antagonism between a heroic and a philistine spirit (embodied in the 'principal' antagonism between Germany and England). While a hero thinks about his duties, a merchant is only interested in his rights; a hero wishes to sacrifice his own life, while a merchant wants to get something from his own life; a hero fulfils every task that comes from the 'higher authority', which is totally unthinkable for a merchant, whose interest lies in 'limiting' authority; finally, a hero finds his existence only in his fatherland, especially if he is at war, while a merchant cannot even conceive of a 'fatherland', because he is a hard-core individualist (Sombart, 1915: 63–66). A philistine spirit projects its merchant beliefs onto a state and looks at it as a 'social contract' among individuals, whose basic rights are higher than any state functions. When war occurs, a philistine cannot have any other relation to it than a pacifist one. His ideal is a 'perpetual peace'. If he cannot avoid war, then he conducts it as a defensive war, forming a paid army, which goes to war as it would do any other job – for a profit (Sombart, 1915: 28–29).

Ernst Jünger gave the most articulate form to this critique of pacifism. He was one of the 'conservative revolutionaries' who spent the whole of World War I at the front, only to begin to theoretically develop and propagate his critique (for the future) after defeat. According to him, one must take into account that pacifism itself has two forms: one is cowardly, and inspired by egoism and a fear of war (this mostly corresponds to Hobbes's pacifism), while the other is a matter of an idea and a principle, and 'has to be respected'. For this latter form of pacifism the basic things are ideas and 'consciousness': the idea of humanity is higher than the idea of people, and that is why a 'heroic pacifist' fights for its realization out of conviction, and not out of fear or for material goods (Jünger, 1958: 444). That is the logic which is still valid today, with the addition of some other elements of the pacifist's rhetoric, at the bottom of the basic right to refuse to bear arms during military service, derived from the basic right to a freedom of conscience.

The actual core of the 'heroic discourse' of today, what remains if Jünger's ideas are deprived of their radical militarism, is a belief that only 'heroes' are worthy of being treated seriously by military authorities (and then also freed from an obligation to bear arms in military service). Their most important attribute is 'conscience', which drives them so hard to reject weapons that they are able heroically and martyr-like to suffer all the negative consequences derived from this (and which would 'break' a coward immediately, and force him to look upon all the other 'normal people' and take up his place in the military). There is no mercy towards cowards, they are not worthy of that, and that is why they can be made into, finally, 'cannon fodder'. This 'heroic discourse' has particularly dreadful consequences in times of war. Then every individual is forced to prove his heroism through his own deeds, which can frequently result in complete disaster (as the example of Germany during World War I clearly shows). The essence of this danger was nicely summed up right after World War I by Ivan Aleksandrovič Iljin, and there is nothing that one could add to it or take away from it even today:

> During war, every nation goes through such a spiritual and moral strain, that always exceeds its capabilities: a mass heroism is expected from it, although heroism is a matter of exceptions; it is required to show massive self-sacrifice, although self-sacrifice is a matter of high virtue; it is required to show a strength of character, a victory of spirit over the body, unconditional devotion to spiritual things, and all of it is connected to a deed of mass killing, for a deed of enemy and destruction. (Iljin, 1995: 131–132)

IV Possible Meanings of the Basic Human Right to Refuse to Bear Arms during Military Service

Based on what has been said here, a different understanding – different, that is, from the one that lies behind contemporary legal provisions – of the meaning of the basic human right to refuse to bear arms during military service shall now be suggested. At the same time, it shall be insisted that only a professional army is appropriate for a contemporary pacifist society and that all *de lege ferenda* solutions of the basic right to refuse to bear arms in military service should be provisional only, until a professional army is introduced (tendentially, as a part of the 'UN–World Police'). According to this understanding, Paragraph 2 of Article 137 of the Constitution of the FRY should be deleted, and instead there should be included the following article in the second part of the constitution, the one devoted to basic human rights:

> Every military conscript is guaranteed the right to refuse to bear arms during military service. This right differs from the obligation to refuse to use arms in military conflicts, when every soldier has an obligation to refuse to use arms if by doing so he would commit a crime, according to the provisions of international law.
>
> Every military conscript who does not wish to fulfil military service with arms, out of fear or other reasons, shall be enabled to fulfil his service, according to his own choice, either without arms in the Yugoslav Army, or in the civil service, according to Federal law.
>
> Every military conscript who does not refuse to bear arms during military service shall be enabled to refuse to use arms for reasons of conscience, in special cases, stipulated by Federal law.
>
> Every soldier has the right to desert out of cowardice or other reasons, if the

Yugoslav Army takes actions that endanger sovereignty, territory, and constitutional order of the country.

From this it follows that there is a difference between a right and an obligation to refuse to use arms. The use of arms must always be refused when it would result in crimes against peace, crimes against humanity, and war crimes. According to the Nuremberg principles, an individual cannot be freed from responsibility if he has participated in committing any of these crimes. He can eventually be punished more lightly if:

he acted under the order of the government or the superiors; and
'if the court establishes that justice so requires' (as put in the Nuremberg charter).

However, he is responsible in any case, and his responsibility cannot be nullified by invoking the phrase 'obeying orders'. That is why it is necessary to differentiate the cases of an *obligatory* refusal to use arms from the cases when an individual has only a *right* to refuse. During the Vietnam War, there were cases in the US when military conscripts refused to go to war by invoking their conscience and the possibility of finding themselves in a Catch-22-type situation (that is to say, being convicted either of refusal to obey orders, or of committing a war crime), but the courts did not accept this argument (Whittome, 1989: 30). In a sense, the attitude of the American courts was logically correct: everyone going to war in principle accepts the possibility that he will enter a situation where it is necessary to choose between refusing an order and committing a crime. If any military conscript was given a right to refuse to go to war in order to avoid getting into a Catch-22 situation, then the same would have to be done with all the other military conscripts. His is a paradox that follows from the very legal regulation of war crimes, and it will remain even after people's armies are transformed into professional ones.

Every basic right to refuse to bear arms during military service would include three different items, under three different conditions:

a universal right to refuse to bear arms during military service out of fear (or some other reason),
a refusal to bear arms during military service in individual cases because of reasons of conscience, and
deserting out of cowardice (or some other reason).

In the first – general – case, every military conscript should be enabled a choice in the way service is fulfilled, without invoking *numerus clausus*, and even the simple invoking of fear would be quite enough for avoiding having to bear arms. A conscript would have a right to decide whether he wanted to serve without arms in the Yugoslav Army, or outside of it, in the civil service. In that case, the service could last twice as long as ordinary military service only under the condition that a conscript choosing this option was freed of all the additional military obligations in the reserves, except general mobilization in cases of direct war danger.

In the second – special – case, a military conscript, who is not a universal pacifist, and who accepts the possibility of taking up arms and participating in some future war, would have the right to refuse to use arms, because of a conscientious objection, in a precisely determined war (or, more precisely, in a concrete armed conflict). That would be enabled if his reasons were in accordance with federal law and approved in a special procedure; if, for example, someone refused to shoot at UN soldiers (seeing in them legitimate 'world police'), or at his compatriots, who would under the circumstances be on the enemy side.

Finally, the third case, which is certainly the most delicate one. Every soldier would have the right to desert if the Yugoslav Army broke the conditions for the fulfilling of military service: if it ceased to protect the sovereignty, territory, independence and constitutional order of the country (Article 133 of the constitution), or if it embarked on a war of conquest. In these cases, the army would not guarantee a social contract that a soldier had agreed upon, and thus he would be able to use his natural right, and look for security from whoever seemed the most capable of providing it. In other words, in these cases there would be a regression into – as Hobbes would say – a natural state, where each individual would have to decide whose side to take, and thus save his honour, life and property. Should the army endanger the constitutional order of a country, every soldier would have the right to desert if he disagrees with the change of the constitutional order; if the army embarks on a war of conquest, every soldier on the foreign territory concerned would have the right to desert if he did not want a territorial expansion of his country; finally, if, in a civil war, a regular army ceased to defend the territorial integrity of the country and joined a struggle for its territorial division, every soldier would have the right to desert if he did not wish to remain to live on the territory defended by his army, or if he thought that the enemy army would offer him better protection. Of course, in the case that the army fought in order to protect or re-establish the constitutional order and territorial integrity of the country (as well as its sovereignty and independence), the right to desert could not be fulfilled, since every soldier would still be bound by his earlier joining of the social contract (that would in such a way defend him from the 'forces of the natural state').

Postscript

When this essay was being finished (May 1996), a proposal for a Law on Amnesty entered into the procedure of the Parliament of the Federal Republic of Yugoslavia, which should, for lack of prisoners of war, refer only to deserters from the Yugoslav People's Army during the war in Croatia in 1991. Even though it is obvious that there is a political will to free deserters from that war of any guilt, there still remains the question of how this can be done. From what has been said above, a conclusion follows that it can be done through the acknowledgment of their cowardice, in conditions where the Yugoslav People's Army refused to protect the territorial integrity of their country and took sides in the war for the new division of territories in the former Yugoslavia.

Translated by Aleksander Bošković

Bibliography

Alexy, Robert (1986): *Theorie der Grundrechte*, Frankfurt am Main: Suhrkamp.

Böckenförde, Ernst-Wolfgang (1991): 'Das Grundrecht der Gewissensfreiheit (1970)', in: *Staat, Verfassung, Demokratie, Studien zur Verfassungstheorie und zum Verfassungsrecht*, Frankfurt am Main: Suhrkamp.

Bull, Hedley (1981): 'Hobbes and the International Anarchy', *Social Research* 48 (4): 717–738.

Chamberlain, Houston Stewart (1917): *Demokratie und Freiheit*, Munich: Hugo Bruckmann.

Dekart, Rene (1981): *Strasti duše*, Belgrade: Grafos (original: Descartes: *Les passions de l'ame*).

Delimo, Žan (1987): *Strah na Zapadu (Od XIV do XVIII veka). Opsednuti grad*, vol. 1, Novi Sad: Književna zajednica Novog Sada i Dnevnik (original: Jean Delimeau: *Le Peur en Occident (XIVᵉ – XVIIIᵉ siècles). Une cité assiégé*).

Duby, Georges (1973): *Guerriers et paysans. VIIᵉ – XIIᵉ siécle. Premier essor de l'économie européene*, Paris: Gallimard.

Gavre, Mark (1974): 'Hobbes and His Audience', *The American Political Science Review* 68 (4): 1542–1556.

Haffner, Sebastian (1979): *Preußen ohne Legende*, Hamburg: Wilhelm Goldmann Verlag.

Hobbes, Thomas (1966a): *Philosophical Rudiments Concearning Government and Society*, in: *English Works of Thomas Hobbes of Malmesbury* (ed. by Sir William Molesworth), Aalen: Scientia Verlag (second reprint), vol. 2.

Hobbes, Thomas (1966b): *Leviathan, or the Matter, Form, and Power of a Commonwealth Ecclesiastical and Civil*, in: ibid., vol. 3.

Hobbes, Thomas (1966c): *The Questions Concearning Liberty, Necessity, and Chance, Clearly Stated and Debated between Dr. Bramhall, Bishop of Derry, and Thomas Hobbes of Malmesbury*, in: ibid., vol. 5.

Hobbes, Thomas (1966d): *Behemoth: the History of the Cause of the Civil Wars of England*, in: ibid., vol. 6.

Iljin, Ivan Aleksandrovič (1995): 'O suprotstavljanju zlu silom', in: Obrad Savić (ed.): *Evropski diskurs rata*, Belgrade: Beogradski krug, 1995.

Jünger, Ernst (1958): 'Der Kampf als inneres Eriebnis', in: *Werke*, Stuttgart: Ernst Klett Verlag, vol. 5.

Kraynak, Robert (1982): 'Hobbes's *Behemoth* and the Argument for Absolutism', *The American Political Science Review* 76 (4): 837–847.

Kriele, Martin (1983): 'Staatsphilosophische Lehren aus dem Nationalsozialismus', in:

Hubert Rottleuthner (ed.): *Recht, Rechtsphilosophie und Nationalsozialismus. Voträge aus der Tagung der Deutschen Sektion der Internationalen Vereinigung für Rechts- und Sozialphilosophie (IVR) in der Bundesrepublik Deutschland vom 11. und 12. Oktober 1982 in Berlin (West). Archiv für Rechts- und Sozialphilosophie, Beiheft Nr. 18,* Wiesbaden: Franz Steiner Verlag.

Krölls, Albert (1983): *Kriegsdienstverweigerung. Das unbequeme Grundrecht,* Frankfurt am Main: Europäische Verlagsanstalt.

Laird, John (1968): *Hobbes,* New York: Russell & Russell.

Löw, Konrad (1977): *Die Grundrechte. Verständnis und Wirklichkeit in beiden Teilen Deutschlands,* Munich: Verlag Dokumentation.

Lübbe, Hermann (1963): *Politische Philosophie in Deutschland. Studien zu Ihrer Geschichte,* Basle and Stuttgart: Beno Schwabe & Co. Verlag.

Melamed, Samuel Max (1909): *Theorie, Ursprung und Geschichte der Friedensidee. Kulturphilosophische Wanderungen,* Stuttgart: Verlag von Ferdinand Enke.

Möhle, Volker, and Christian Rabe (1972): *Kriegdienstverweigerer in der BRD. Eine empirisch-analytische Studie zur Motivation der Kriegsdienstverweigerer in den Jahren 1957–1971,* Opladen: Westdeutscher Verlag.

Mommsen, Wolfgang (1990): *Nation und Geschichte. Über die Deutschen und die deutsche Frage,* Munich and Zurich: R. Piper & Co.

Orwin, C. (1975): 'On Sovereign Authorisation', *Political Theory,* 3 (1): 26–44.

Platon (1976): *Država,* Belgrade: BIGZ (original: Plato: *Politeia*).

Popper-Lynkeus, Josef (1921): *Krieg, Wehrpflicht und Staatsverfassung,* Vienna: Rikola Verlag.

Runham Brown, H. (1930): *Der Durchbruch. Studie über Kriegsdienstverweigerung und die Internationale der Kriegsdienstgegner,* Enfield: War Resisters International (Internationale der Kriegsdienstgegner).

Schmitt, Carl (1937): 'Der Staat als Mechanismus bei Hobbes und Descartes', in: C. A. Emge (ed.): *Dem Gedächtnis an René Descartes (300 Jahre Discours de la Méthode),* Berlin: Verlag für Staatswissenschaften und Geschichte.

Schmitthenner, Paul (1937): *Politik und Kriegführung in der neueren Geschichte,* Hamburg: Hanseatische Verlagsanstalt.

Sombart, Werner (1915): *Händler und Helden. Patriotischen Besinnungen,* Munich and Leipzig: Duncker & Humblot.

Strauss, Leo (1971): *Prirodno pravo i istorija,* Sarajevo: Veselin Masleša (original: *Natural Right and History*).

Warrender, Howard (1961): *The Political Philosophy of Hobbes. His Theory of Obligation,* Oxford: Clarendon Press.

Whittome, Candy (1989): 'Prigovor savjesti vojnoj službi: Što je s ljudskim pravima?', *Pitanja* 20 (4–6): 5–33.

13

The Legal Status of National Minorities in the Federal Republic of Yugoslavia

Marijana Santrač

International Law and Legal Acts in the FRY

In international law there is no generally accepted and binding definition of national minorities; however, all relevant definitions of this term mostly contain the same basic elements. According to the lawyer Kapotorty, a national minority is a group which is smaller in numbers than the rest of the dominant population of a country, whose members, the country's subjects, have ethnic, religious or linguistic characteristics different from the rest of the population and implicitly show a feeling of solidarity in keeping their own culture, tradition, religion and language. A similar definition is given by the Sub-Commission (of the Human Rights Committee) on Prevention of Discrimination and Protection of Minorities: a minority is a group of citizens of a country, smaller in number and subordinate, with ethnic, religious or linguistic characteristics that mark it off from the majority of the population, whose members show solidarity and, even if it is only implicit, a collective will to survive, and who aim at real and legal equality with the majority.

The rights and status of minorities are defined, with regard to their importance, by the highest legal acts of the country as well as international legal documents.

International legislation

The formal importance of international legal regulations lies in the obligations that follow from the international conventions taken over by the FRY, as it claims to be the only successor of the SFRY, in terms of regulating and protecting the rights of national minorities. However, *ratio legis* of this normative field, in the situation when pure ethnic states are rare, is in the contribution to the social and political stability and security both on the country level and the level of the region and the international community. Besides, the question of national minorities is one of the questions that do not belong exclusively to the domain of the state any more.[1]

In international treaties, the protection of national minorities dates back to the Peace of Westphalia (1648), and there is a tendency in the twentieth century to supplement the abstract protection of minorities through the protection of their basic human rights for all people without any distinction[2] by formulating special rights of national minorities which derive from their specific status. In this respect, Article 27 of the International Covenant on Civil and Political Rights (1966) represents a turning point.

United Nations documents

THE CHARTER OF THE UNITED NATIONS (1945)
It states that the purposes of the United Nations are, among other things, to achieve international cooperation in promoting and encouraging respect for human rights and for fundamental freedoms for all without distinction as to race, sex, language, or religion.

THE UNIVERSAL DECLARATION OF HUMAN RIGHTS (1948)
Everyone is entitled to all the rights and freedoms set forth in this Declaration, without distinction of any kind, such as race, colour, sex, language, religion, political or other opinion, national or social origin, property, birth or other status.

THE INTERNATIONAL COVENANT ON ECONOMIC, SOCIAL AND CULTURAL RIGHTS (1966)
Pursuant to the Covenant, each signatory state undertakes immediate application of the prohibition of discrimination in the enjoyment of the rights enumerated on grounds of race, colour, sex, language, religion, or political or other opinion; national or social origin; property; and birth or other status.

THE INTERNATIONAL COVENANT ON CIVIL AND POLITICAL RIGHTS (1966)
Apart from Article 2, which requires each state party to respect and to ensure to all individuals the rights recognized in the Covenant without distinction of any kind, such as race, colour, sex, language, religion, political or other opinion, national or social origin, property, birth or other status, and Article 26, which claims that all are equal before the law and forbids any discrimination, Article 27 explicitly designates the right of ethnic, religious, or linguistic minorities to enjoy their own culture, to profess and practise their own religion, and to use their own language.

The General Commentary of the Human Rights Committee for this Article (1994) stresses that this right of national minorities should neither be understood as the right to self-determination, nor mixed with the obligation of a country to undertake to respect and to ensure to all individuals the rights recognized in the Covenant without distinction of any kind and to guarantee equality before the law. Article 27 has been explained to the effect that individuals who should be protected by it neither have to be subjects of the respective country nor have to have permanent residence within its territory. The term culture is too broadly defined and includes the specific way of life which can be connected with the way of exploiting land and other resources as well as with traditional activities. In addition, the right of minorities to use their own language, as a special right, should be distinguished from everyone's right to freedom of expression, as well as from the narrower right of the defendant to use his own language in a legal process. Generally speaking, the rights stipulated in Article 27 should not be mixed with other individual rights guaranteed to each human being.

THE UNITED NATIONS DECLARATION OF THE ELIMINATION OF ALL FORMS OF RACIAL DISCRIMINATION (1963)

It prohibits the realization, incitement or complicity in discrimination as to the enjoyment of human rights and freedoms on the grounds of race, colour or ethnic origin. The prevention of discrimination is especially designated in terms of civil rights: nationality, education, religion, employment, profession and residence, the right to use public facilities, and furthermore in terms of political rights, especially the right to take part in elections through the general and equal right to vote and taking part in governing bodies.

THE INTERNATIONAL CONVENTION ON THE ELIMINATION OF ALL FORMS OF RACIAL DISCRIMINATION (1965)

It defines racial discrimination as any distinction, barring, restricting or giving priority on the grounds of race, colour, descendants, national or ethnic origin. The adoption of measures in the areas of politics, legislation, social security of culture is necessary, and the demand for the elimination of discrimination includes a wider spectrum of civil and political rights in comparison with the previous Convention.

THE INTERNATIONAL CONVENTION ON THE SUPPRESSION AND PUNISHMENT OF THE CRIME OF APARTHEID (1973)

The participating states will take measures in order to prevent and censure the practice and policy of racial segregation in countries such as South Africa, where apartheid was widely practised.

THE CONVENTION ON THE PREVENTION AND PUNISHMENT OF THE CRIME OF GENOCIDE (1948)

Genocide means any of the following acts committed with intent to destroy, in whole or in part, a national, ethnic, racial, or religious group, such as: killing members of the group, causing serious bodily or mental harm to members of the group, deliberately inflicting on the group conditions of life calculated to bring about its physical destruction in whole or in part, imposing measures intended to prevent births within the group, forcibly transferring children of the group to another group. Conspiracy, incitement, attempt, and complicity in genocide are also made punishable. Perpetrators may be punished whether they are constitutionally responsible rulers, public officials, or private individuals. The states are obliged to extradite their own nationals for trial.

DECLARATION ON THE RIGHTS OF PERSONS BELONGING TO NATIONAL OR ETHNIC, RELIGIOUS OR LINGUISTIC MINORITIES (1992)

Apart from the provisions regarding the protection of national minorities and the provisions of Article 27 of the International Covenant on Civil and Political Rights concerning the rights of persons belonging to minorities, this Declaration affirms that persons belonging to minorities have the right to participate effectively in cultural, religious, social, economic and public life, the right to participate effectively in decisions on the national and, where appropriate, regional level concerning the minority to which they belong or the regions in which they live, in a manner not incompatible with national legislation, the right to establish and maintain their own associations, the right to establish and maintain contacts with other members of their group within their country or across frontiers. States shall take measures where required to ensure that persons belonging to minorities may exercise fully and effectively all their human rights and fundamental freedoms without any discrimination and in full equality before the law, except in cases when these practices represent a violation of national laws or when they are contrary to international standards. States should take appropriate measures so that, wherever possible, persons belonging to minorities may have adequate opportunities to learn their mother tongue or to have instruction in their mother tongue. States should, where appropriate, take measures in the field of education, in order to encourage knowledge of the history, traditions, language and culture of the minorities existing within their territory. Persons belonging to minorities should have adequate opportunities to gain knowledge of the society as a whole. National policies and programmes shall be planned and implemented with due regard for the legitimate interests of persons belonging to minorities. However, the exercise of the rights set forth in the present Declaration shall not prejudice the enjoyment by all persons of universally recognized human rights and fundamental freedoms, and may not permit any activity contrary to the purposes and principles of the United Nations, including sovereign equality, territorial integrity and political independence of States.

THE UNESCO CONVENTION AGAINST DISCRIMINATION IN EDUCATION

The term 'discrimination' includes any distinction, exclusion, limitation or preference which, being based on race, colour, sex, language, religion, political or other opinion, national or social origin, economic condition or birth, has the purpose or effect of nullifying or impairing equality of treatment in education and in particular of depriving any person or group of persons of access to education of any type or at any level, or of limiting any person or group of persons to education of an inferior standard. The state parties to this Convention recognize the right of members of national minorities to carry on their own educational activities, including the maintenance of schools and the use or the teaching of their own language, provided, however, that this right is not exercised in a manner which prevents the members of these minorities from understanding the culture and language of the community as a whole and from participating in its activities, or which prejudices national sovereignty. The standard of education may not be lower than the general standard laid down or approved by the competent authorities, and attendance at such schools is optional.

Documents of the Conference on Security and Co-operation in Europe (CSCE)[3]

THE HELSINKI FINAL ACT 1975
Apart from respect for human rights and fundamental freedoms, including the freedom of thought, conscience, religion or belief, for all without distinction as to race, sex, language or religion, the participating states will respect the right of national minorities to equality before the law, will afford them the full opportunity for the actual enjoyment of human rights and fundamental freedoms, and will, in this manner, protect their legitimate interests in this sphere.

THE MADRID CONCLUDING DOCUMENT (1983)
The participating states will promote constant progress in the realization, respect and actual enjoyment of human rights of national minorities, as well as the protection of their legitimate interests.

THE VIENNA CONCLUDING DOCUMENT (1989)
The participating states will take all the necessary legislative, administrative and other measures in order to protect human rights of persons belonging to national minorities, they will protect and create conditions for the promotion of the ethnic, cultural, linguistic and religious identity of national minorities and ensure their full equality with others. Persons belonging to national minorities can establish and maintain contacts with the citizens of other states with whom they share a common national origin or cultural heritage, and cherish and develop their own culture in all aspects, including language, literature, religion and the preservation of cultural and historical monuments and objects. The participating states will ensure that persons belonging to national minorities have access to, disseminate and exchange information in their native language, and facilitate education of minorities in terms of their own culture, including learning the language, religion and cultural identity by transferring it from parents to their children.

THE SECOND MEETING OF THE CONFERENCE ON THE HUMAN DIMENSION OF THE CSCE, COPENHAGEN (1990)
Apart from the Articles stating that persons belonging to national minorities have the right to exercise fully and effectively their human rights and

fundamental freedoms without any discrimination and in full equality before the law, to which purpose the participating states will adopt, where necessary, special measures, it is established that to belong to a national minority is a matter of a person's individual choice and no disadvantage may arise from the exercise of such choice. Besides the right to preserve their identity and to maintain and develop their culture, persons belonging to national minorities have the right to use freely their mother tongue in private as well as in public; to establish and maintain their own educational, cultural and religious institutions, organizations or associations in conformity with national legislation; to profess and practise their religion; to establish and maintain contacts among themselves within their country as well as contacts across frontiers; to disseminate, have access to and exchange information in their mother tongue; to establish and maintain organizations or associations within their country and to participate in international non-governmental organizations. The participating states will protect the ethnic, cultural, linguistic and religious identity of national minorities; they will endeavour to ensure that persons belonging to national minorities have adequate opportunities for instruction of their mother tongue or in their mother tongue, as well as, wherever possible and necessary, for its use before public authorities; in the context of the teaching of history and culture in educational establishments, they will also take account of the history and culture of national minorities; the participating states will respect the right of persons belonging to national minorities to effective participation in public affairs. On the other hand, national minorities have no right to engage in any activity or perform any action in contravention of the purposes and principles of the Charter of the United Nations, including the principle of territorial integrity of states.

CHARTER OF PARIS FOR A NEW EUROPE (1990)
It affirms that the ethnic, cultural, linguistic and religious identity of national minorities will be protected and that persons belonging to national minorities have the right freely to express, preserve and develop that identity without any discrimination and in full equality before the law. The participating countries further acknowledge that the status of national minorities should be promoted and the rights of persons belonging to these minorities must be fully respected as part of universal human rights.

REPORT OF THE CSCE MEETING OF EXPERTS ON NATIONAL MINORITIES, GENEVA (1991)
It is established that issues concerning national minorities, as well as compliance with international obligations and commitments concerning the rights of persons belonging to them, are matters of legitimate international concern and consequently do not constitute exclusively an internal affair of the respective state. However, all ethnic, cultural, linguistic or religious differences do not necessarily lead to the creation of national minorities. In areas inhabited mainly by persons belonging to a national minority, the

human rights and fundamental freedoms of persons belonging to that minority, of persons belonging to the majority population of the respective state, and of persons belonging to other national minorities residing in these areas will be equally protected. Respecting the right of persons belonging to national minorities to effective participation in public affairs, the participating states consider that when issues relating to the situation of national minorities are discussed within their countries, they themselves should have the effective opportunity to be involved, in accordance with the decision-making procedures of each state. The participating states will create conditions for persons belonging to national minorities to have equal opportunity to be effectively involved in public life and economic activities, they will take the necessary measures to prevent discrimination against individuals, particularly in respect of employment, housing and education, and they confirm the importance of refraining from hindering the production of cultural materials concerning national minorities. The participating states reaffirm, and will not hinder the exercise of, the right of persons belonging to national minorities to establish and maintain their own educational, cultural and religious institutions, organizations and associations, and to participate in international non-governmental organizations, as well as maintain contacts with the members of their group within their own country or across international frontiers. In access to the media, they will not discriminate against anyone based on ethnic, cultural, linguistic or religious grounds. The states will make efforts to collect, publish on a regular basis, and make available to the public, data about crimes on their respective territories that are based on prejudice as to race, ethnic identity or religion and they will, on a voluntary basis, distribute information to other participating states about the situation of national minorities in their respective territories. Moreover, the Report suggests measures, taken by some states, which proved to be efficient in this area.

THE THIRD MEETING OF THE CONFERENCE ON THE HUMAN DIMENSION OF THE CSCE, MOSCOW (1991)
The participating states confirm the decision and obligations of all the previous CSCE documents concerning national minorities issues.

CSCE HELSINKI DOCUMENT (1992)
The participating states decide to establish a High Commissioner on National Minorities. His mandate is to provide 'early warnings' and, as appropriate, 'early action' as an instrument of conflict prevention at the earliest possible stage. The states will intensify in this context their efforts to ensure the free exercise by persons belonging to national minorities the right to participate fully, in accordance with the democratic decision-making procedures of each state, in the political, economic, social and cultural life of their countries, including through democratic participation in decision-making and consultative bodies at the national, regional and local level, *inter alia*, through political parties and associations. National minority issues will be addressed

by peaceful means and through dialogue and the states will refrain from resettling and condemn all attempts, by the threat or use of force, to resettle persons with the aim of changing the ethnic composition of areas within their territories.

Domestic legislation

The legal status of national minorities is defined by the Constitution of the Federal Republic of Yugoslavia, the Constitution of the Republic of Serbia, the Constitution of the Republic of Montenegro, and federal as well as republic regulations in Serbia and Montenegro. As the Constitution of the Republic of Serbia was passed in 1990, and the majority of relevant federal and republic acts are from the period before the Federal Constitution was introduced, taking into consideration the fact that there has been no coordination between these acts and the Federal Constitution, which is the fundamental legal act, it can be concluded that there is inconsistency in domestic legal acts.

THE CONSTITUTION OF THE FEDERAL REPUBLIC OF YUGOSLAVIA (1992)
Five Articles in the Yugoslav Constitution are explicitly devoted to the rights of national minorities. Yugoslavia recognizes and guarantees all rights of national minorities in maintaining, developing and expressing their ethnic, cultural, linguistic and other identity, as well as the right to use of national symbols (Art. 11). The language and alphabet of national minorities are officially used in areas inhabited to a certain extent by a national minority (Art. 15.2). Persons belonging to a national minority have the right to education and access to public information in their own language (Art. 46), as well as the right to establish and maintain their own educational, cultural and religious institutions, organizations and associations (Art. 47). They also have the right to establish and maintain unimpeded contacts with the members of their group within their own country or across international frontiers, and the right to participate in international non-governmental organizations (Art. 48).

The constitution determines that the rights stated in Article 11 can be used in accordance with international law, the rights stated in Articles 15.2, 46 and 47 in accordance with the law, and the rights stated in Article 48 can be used, but not in contravention of the interests of Yugoslavia or its republics.

There are some important provisions which also protect the special rights of persons belonging to national minorities, such as: equality before the law without any distinction as to race, sex, language, religion, political or other belief, education, social origin, wealth and other personal characteristics (Art. 20.1; 2), the freedom of expressing their national origin, culture and the use of their language and alphabet (Art. 45), the censure of incitement or complicity in discrimination on the grounds of ethnic origin, race, religion or any other grounds, incitement of hatred and hostility (Art. 50), and the recognition and guarantee of human and civil rights and freedoms in conformity with international law (Art. 10), to name but a few.

Persons belonging to national minorities have the right to profess and practise their religion, in private or in public, and to perform religious rites (Art. 43.1).

According to the Yugoslav Constitution, distribution of newspapers and dissemination of other information, as well as the work of political, trade union or other organizations can be banned if they incite ethnic, racial or religious discrimination and hatred (Art. 28.2 and Art. 42.1).

The right to use their own language is guaranteed to all individuals in detention or incarceration (regarding the information on the reasons for their imprisonment) and to all individuals in procedures before state authorities and organizations which in exercising their responsibilities decide on the rights and duties of the individuals (Art. 23.3 and Art. 49).

THE CONSTITUTION OF THE REPUBLIC OF SERBIA (1990)

Taking into consideration special ethnic, historical, cultural and other characteristics (Art. 108), the constitution establishes the Autonomous Province of Vojvodina and the Autonomous Province of Kosovo and Metohija as forms of territorial autonomy (Art. 6).

Instead of the term 'national minorities', the term nationalities is used, and explicitly only in two Articles; the one proclaiming the right to use a minority language and alphabet officially in the areas where they live, the other proclaiming the right of nationalities to maintain education in their own language (Art 8.2 and Art. 34.2). Both rights are used in conformity with the law.

The constitution guarantees the right to all citizens to express their national identity and culture, as well as the freedom to use their language and alphabet (Art. 49).

Freedom of professing religion is guaranteed (Art. 41.1).

All citizens have equal rights and duties and enjoy equal protection before authorities, without any distinction as to race, sex, birth, language, ethnic identity, religion, political or other belief (Art. 13).

Political work or distribution of newspapers and dissemination of other information can be banned in the case of incitement or complicity in ethnic, racial and religious hostility and hatred (Art. 44.2 and Art. 46.6).

THE CONSTITUTION OF THE REPUBLIC OF MONTENEGRO (1992)

It uses the term 'persons belonging to national and ethnic groups' instead of the term 'persons belonging to national minorities' and devotes a special section to their rights.

Articles 67 to 76 guarantee: protection of national ethnic, cultural, linguistic and religious identity of persons belonging to national minorities in conformity with international protection of human and civil rights, the right to use freely their language and alphabet, the right to education and information in their mother tongue, the right to use and display their national symbols, the right to maintain educational, cultural and religious associations with financial assistance from the state. Curricula in schools also include the history and culture of national and ethnic groups. Persons belonging to national and ethnic groups have the right to use their language in procedures before state authorities, the right to proportional representation in the public sector, governing bodies and local autonomous bodies, the right to maintain contacts with citizens outside Montenegro with whom they share a common national origin, the right to participate in regional and international non-governmental organizations, as well as the right to appeal to international institutions in order to protect their constitutional rights.

The exercise of special rights of persons belonging to national and ethnic groups cannot be performed in contravention of the constitution, principles of international law and the principle of territorial integrity of Montenegro, and the right to maintain contacts can be exercised only if it does not result in any harm to Montenegro.

In order to protect the rights of national and ethnic groups, this constitution designates the establishment of a special body – the Republic Council for the Protection of the Rights of Persons Belonging to National and Ethnic Groups.

FEDERAL REGULATIONS

1. *The Yugoslav Criminal Code* (1976) prescribes punishment for criminal acts of incitement or complicity in national, racial or religious hatred, dissension, or hostility among peoples and nationalities by the use of propaganda or offending the citizens (Art. 134).

2. *The Law on Maintaining Citizens' Associations, Social Organizations and Political Organizations founded on the territory of the FRY* (1990) prohibits the foundation of organizations whose aims, and the realization of those aims, are set to incite national, racial or religious hatred and hostility and proclaims equality and equal legal protection of all organizations (Art. 2 and Art. 3.2).

3. *The Law on the Basis of Mass Media* (1990), in discussing the responsibilities of editor-in-chief, prohibits media orientation aimed at inciting national, racial or religious hatred and hostility (Art. 17.1).

4. *The Law on Criminal Procedure* (1977) establishes equality in the use of language and alphabet, the possibility of writing petitions in the language of a nationality which is not officially used in court and sending summons in the language of the nationality to persons belonging to that nationality who used that language in the procedure if the language is officially used in court (Art. 5, Art. 6.2 and Art. 8.2).

5. *The Law on Litigation* (1977) defines the use of language of nationalities in the same way as the Law on Criminal Procedure, apart from a provision that the expenses for translating into the language of peoples and nationalities will be charged to the court (Art. 103.2, Art. 104.1 and Art. 105).

6. *The Law on Disclosure of Federal Laws and Other Federal Legislative and General Acts* (1992) affirms that texts published in Albanian and Hungarian are also authentic (Art. 4).

REGULATIONS IN THE REPUBLIC OF SERBIA

1. *The Serbian Criminal Code* (1977) punishes acts of mockery of peoples or nationalities in Yugoslavia or ethnic groups (Art. 100).

2. *The Law on Mass Media* (1991) designates incitement of ethnic, racial or religious hostility as a reason for the ban on the distribution of newspapers and dissemination of information in the mass media (Art. 20).

3. *The Law on Radio and Television* (1991) states that preparation and production of radio and TV programmes should also be done in languages of nationalities.

4. *The Law on Elementary Schools* (1992) establishes that instruction for persons belonging to nationalities should be done in the language of the nationality or bilingually, the minimum requirement being fifteen pupils. If there are less than fifteen pupils, a special permit should be obtained from the Education Secretary. This curriculum includes a course in Serbian. If instruction is in Serbian, persons belonging to nationalities have the right to study their mother tongue with elements of their culture (Art. 5).

5. *The Law on Grammar Schools* (1992), in the same way as the Law on Elementary Schools, establishes the right of persons belonging to national minorities to have instruction in their mother tongue, i.e. the right to study their mother tongue.

6. *The Law on Community Colleges* (1992) stipulates that instruction can be performed in the language of national minorities, to which purpose, if the founder is not the Republic of Serbia, a special permit from the Republic government should be obtained (Art. 4.2 and 3).

7. *The Law on Universities* (1992) establishes that instruction can be performed in the language of other peoples and nationalities if there is a minimum of thirty students in the same year of study. If instruction is performed in the language of national minorities, registers, records and official identity documents will also be issued (transcribed) in that language at all levels of education.

8. *The Law on the Official Use of Language and Alphabet* (1991) stipulates that official use of the Roman script as well as the language and alphabet of nationalities is defined in the Statute of each municipality, i.e. autonomous province. The lower procedure in which the rights and duties of citizens are established can be performed in the language of a nationality which is not officially used in that institution and which can be determined by that institution only in cases of disagreement between the involved parties, while the Serbian language will be given priority if it has been suggested as one of the languages. Documents of the second-degree procedures will be translated by the lower institution into the language used in the first instance. In areas where languages of nationalities are not officially used persons belonging to nationalities have the right to use their language and alphabet in the procedure, lodge petitions, receive summons and give statements. They have the right to have the record translated (as it is written in Serbian), and all expenses for translation will be charged to that institution. Registers, official identity documents and their forms will also be kept and/or issued in the

language of the minority in official use, and geographical names, names of streets and squares, bodies and organizations, companies, information and traffic signs will also be written in languages of nationalities in official use in that area.

REGULATIONS IN THE REPUBLIC OF MONTENEGRO

1. *The Montenegrin Criminal Code* (1978) punishes discrimination in the enjoyment of all rights on grounds of national, ethnic identity etc., the prevention of peoples and nationalities using their language and alphabet (Art. 52) and mockery of peoples or nationalities in Yugoslavia (Art. 90).

2. *The Law on Mass Media* (1990) prohibits incitement of national, racial and religious hatred and hostility as the orientation of the mass media (Art. 20).

3. *The Law on Citizens' Associations* (1990) prohibits associations and political organizations formed with an aim of inciting national and other hatred and hostility, and stipulates that persons previously convicted of these criminal offences cannot be founders of such organizations (Art. 4 and 5).

4. *The Law on Violation of Public Order and Peace* (1987) punishes offences against national, religious or racial feelings in public places (Art. 34).

5. *The Law on the Seal of the Republic of Montenegro and Seals of State Institutions* (1984) stipulates that the name of an institution situated in areas where bilingual administration is performed should be written in Albanian as well (Art. 9).

6. *The Law on Elementary Schools* (1991) determines that schools or classes with instruction in Albanian should be founded in areas inhabited by a great number of persons belonging to Albanian nationality, and that in areas where persons of Yugoslavian and Albanian nationality live together bilingual schools and classes can be established. In all other cases education in Albanian will be introduced depending on its feasibility. When instruction is in Albanian, Serbian must be studied.

7. *The Law on Grammar Schools* (1991) stipulates that instruction, depending on its feasibility, can be in Albanian, i.e. bilingual, whereas Serbian is compulsory (Art. 14).

Certificates of enrolment and graduation certificates in schools where instruction is in Albanian will also be issued in Albanian, at all levels of education.

The principal characteristic of the legal status of national minorities in Yugoslavia is that this subject, due to the federal form of government, is regulated by three constitutions. They differ in this matter not only as to the term for defining the concept of national minorities, but also in terms of the place of these rights in general systematization, the number and contents of legal norms formulating these rights and their concordance with standards of international law.

The Yugoslav Constitution regulates the rights of national minorities in accordance with the standards of the CSCE (OSCE). However, the consequences of general inconsistency of domestic legal order are reflected in this field as well. The lack of coordination of the constitutions and regulations of the republics with those on the federal level reduces the effects of satisfactory formulation of the rights of national minorities set in the Federal Constitution.

The Constitution of the Republic of Montenegro devotes a special section to the rights of national and ethnic groups which not only emphasizes their importance but contributes to the establishment of a full system of legal protection as well. By constituting explicitly a special corpus of rights of national minorities, defined elaborately and completely, with solutions adequately following modern tendencies in the regulation of this issue, the Constitution of Montenegro is in accord with the international legal standards in this area. Additional quality in the institutionalization of the protection of the rights of national minorities lies in the establishment of a special body, as it is described in the very text of the constitution, for the protection of these rights, i.e. the Republic Council for the Protection of the Rights of Persons Belonging to National and Ethnic Groups. The head of the Council is the president of Montenegro.

The rights of national minorities are explicitly mentioned in the Serbian Constitution only in two articles (Art. 8.2 and Art. 32.4) and using the term 'nationalities'. In the modern constellation of social, political and legal relations, when the rights of national minorities are generally accepted as special rights within general human rights, it is unacceptable that the concept of national minorities (ethnic minority, national or ethnic group) does not even exist in the Serbian Constitution. With due respect to the fact that the Serbian Constitution was passed before the other two aforementioned constitutions (at a specific political moment, while the former SFRY still existed), its brief and sporadic treatment of the rights of national minorities cannot be excused. Despite the establishment of two autonomous provinces as a means of respecting the special interests of persons belonging to national minorities, in order to regulate the full legal status of national minorities their rights should be elaborated in the constitution, a country's principal legal act. A full structure of the rights of national minorities, complex in its contents and adjusted to modern international standards, would contribute to overcoming the present standard of the rights of national minorities as defined in the Serbian Constitution, which is in conformity with the year 1966 and Article 27 of the International Covenant on Civil and Political Rights.

In the Yugoslav legal system the rights of national minorities are regulated within three heterogeneous legal structures. The legal status of national minorities, as designated in the Federal Constitution, is in conformity with international legal standards, but the effects of the rights set in the constitution are hindered by the inconsistency of the domestic legal system. Legal systems of the republics show a totally different approach to this issue. While the Constitution of the Republic of Montenegro fully respects internationally accepted standards of the rights of national minorities, the Constitution of the Republic of Serbia respects only certain basic principles.

Translated by Vladimir Ignjatović

Notes

This paper is a comparative analysis of international standards and domestic legal regulations in the domain of the rights of national minorities and does not examine either the issues such as the compulsory disclosure of international documents or the implementation of domestic legal acts. The documents used in this paper have been selected from *Meatunarodni dokumenti o zaštiti nacionalnih manjina i njihov položaj u ustavnom poretku SRJ,* Belgrade, 1994.

1. V. Dimitrijević and M. Paunović (eds): *Prava i slobode – meatunarodni i jugoslovenski standardi,* Belgrade, 1995, p. 144.
2. The exceptions are certain peace accords after World War I and declarations of some countries on their joining the League of Nations which require respect for special rights of minorities.
3. Since 1994 this has been known as the Organization for Security and Co-operation in Europe.

14

Women's Rights as Human Rights: Toward a Re-Vision of Human Rights

Charlotte Bunch

Significant numbers of the world's population are routinely subject to torture, starvation, terrorism, humiliation, mutilation and even murder simply because they are female. Crimes such as these against any group other than women would be recognized as a civil and political emergency as well as a gross violation of the victims' humanity. Yet, despite a clear record of deaths and demonstrable abuse, women's rights are not commonly classified as human rights. This is problematic both theoretically and practically, because it has grave consequences for the way society views and treats the fundamental issues of women's lives. This paper questions why women's rights and human rights are viewed as distinct, looks at the policy implications of this schism, and discusses different approaches to changing it.

Women's human rights are violated in a variety of ways. Of course, women sometimes suffer abuses such as political repression that are similar to abuses suffered by men. In these situations, female victims are often invisible, because the dominant image of the political actor in our world is male. However, many violations of women's human rights are distinctly connected to being female – that is, women are discriminated against and abused on the basis of gender. Women also experience sexual abuse in situations where their other human rights are being violated, as political prisoners or members of persecuted ethnic groups, for example. In this essay I address those abuses in which gender is a primary or related factor because gender-related abuse has been most neglected and offers the greatest challenge to the field of human rights today.

The concept of human rights is one of the few moral visions ascribed to internationally. Although its scope is not universally agreed upon, it strikes deep chords of response among many. Promotion of human rights is a widely accepted goal and thus provides a useful framework for seeking redress of gender abuse. Further it is one of the few concepts that speak to the need for transnational activism and concern about the lives of people globally. The Universal Declaration of Human Rights,[1] adopted in 1948, symbolizes this world vision and defines human rights broadly. While not much is said about women, Article 2 entitles all to 'the rights and freedoms set forth in this Declaration, without distinction of any kind, such as race, colour, sex, language, religion, political or other opinion, national or social origin, property, birth or other status'. Eleanor Roosevelt and the Latin American women who fought for the inclusion of sex in the Declaration and for its passage clearly intended that it would address the problem of women's subordination.[2]

Since 1948 the world community has continuously debated varying interpretations of human rights in response to global developments. Little of this discussion, however, has addressed questions of gender, and only recently have significant challenges been made to a vision of human rights which excludes much of women's experiences. The concept of human rights, like all vibrant visions, is not static or the property of any one group; rather, its meaning expands as people reconceive of their needs and hopes in relation to it. In this spirit, feminists redefine human rights abuses to include the degradation and violation of women. The specific experiences of women must be added to traditional approaches to human rights in order to make women more visible and to transform the concept and practice of human rights in our culture so that it takes better account of women's lives.

In the next part of this essay, I will explore both the importance and the difficulty of connecting women's rights to human rights, and then I will outline four basic approaches that have been used in the effort to make this connection.

I Beyond Rhetoric: Political Implications

Few governments exhibit more than token commitment to women's equality as a basic human right in domestic or foreign policy. No government determines its policies towards other countries on the basis of their treatment of women, even when some aid and trade decisions are said to be based on a country's human rights record. Among non-governmental organizations, women are rarely a priority, and Human Rights Day programmes on 10 December seldom include discussion of issues like violence against women or reproductive rights. When it is suggested that governments and human rights organizations should respond to women's rights as concerns that deserve such attention, a number of excuses are offered for why this cannot be done. The responses tend to follow one or more of these lines: (1) sex discrimination is too trivial, or not as important, or will come after larger issues of survival that require more serious attention; (2) abuse of women, while regrettable, is a cultural, private, or individual issue and not a political matter requiring state action; (3) while appropriate for other action, women's rights are not human rights per se; or (4) when the abuse of women is recognized, it is considered inevitable or so pervasive that any consideration of it is futile or will overwhelm other human rights questions. It is important to challenge these responses.

The narrow definition of human rights, recognized by many in the West as solely a matter of state violation of civil and political liberties, impedes consideration of women's rights. In the United States the concept has been further limited by some who have used it as a weapon in the Cold War almost exclusively to challenge human rights abuses perpetrated in communist countries. Even then, many abuses that affected women, such as forced pregnancy in Romania, were ignored.

Some important aspects of women's rights do fit into a civil liberties framework, but much of the abuse against women is part of a larger socioeconomic web that entraps women, making them vulnerable to abuses which cannot be delineated as exclusively political or solely caused by states. The inclusion of 'second generation' or socioeconomic human rights to food, shelter and work – which are clearly delineated as part of the Universal Declaration of Human Rights – is vital to addressing women's concerns fully. Further, the assumption that states are not responsible for most violations of women's rights ignores the fact that such abuses, although committed perhaps by private citizens, are often condoned or even sanctioned by states. I will return to the question of state responsibility after responding to other instances of resistance to women's rights as human rights.

The most insidious myth about women's rights is that they are trivial or secondary to the concerns of life and death. Nothing could be further from the truth: sexism kills. There is increasing documentation of the many ways in which being female is life-threatening. The following are a few examples:

- Before birth. Amniocentesis is used for sex selection, leading to the abortion of more female foetuses at rates as high as 99 per cent in Bombay, India; in China and India, the two most populous nations, more males than females are born even though natural birth ratios would produce more females.[3]
- During childhood. The World Health Organization reports that in many countries, girls are fed less, breastfed for shorter periods of time, taken to doctors less frequently, and die or are physically and mentally maimed by malnutrition at higher rates than boys.[4]
- In adulthood. The denial of women's rights to control their bodies in reproduction threatens women's lives, especially where this is combined with poverty and poor health services. In Latin America, complications from illegal abortions are the leading cause of death for women between the ages of fifteen and thirty-nine.[5]

Sex discrimination kills women daily. When combined with race, class and other forms of oppression, it constitutes a deadly denial of women's right to life and liberty on a large scale throughout the world. The most pervasive violation of females is violence against women in all its manifestations, from wife battery, incest and rape, to dowry deaths,[6] genital mutilation[7] and female sexual slavery. These abuses occur in every country and are found in the home and in the workplace, on streets, on campuses, and in prisons and refugee camps. They cross class, race, age and national lines; and at the same time, the forms this violence takes often reinforce other oppressions such as racism, 'able-bodyism' and imperialism. Case in point: in order to feed their families, poor women in brothels around US military bases in places like the Philippines bear the burden of sexual, racial and national imperialism in repeated and often brutal violation of their bodies.

Even a short review of random statistics reveals that the extent of violence against women globally is staggering:

- In the United States, battery is the leading cause of injury to adult women, and a rape is committed every six minutes.[8]
- In Peru, 70 per cent of all crimes reported to police involve women who are beaten by their partners; and in Lima (a city of seven million people), 168,970 rapes were reported in 1987 alone.[9]
- In India, eight out of ten wives are victims of violence, either domestic battery, dowry-related abuse, or, among the least fortunate, murder.[10]
- In France, 95 per cent of the victims of violence are women; 51 per cent at the hands of a spouse or lover. Similar statistics from places as diverse as Bangladesh, Canada, Kenya and Thailand demonstrate that more than 50 per cent of female homicides were committed by family members.[11]

Where recorded, domestic battery figures range from 40 per cent to 80 per cent of women beaten, usually repeatedly, indicating that the home is the most dangerous place for women and frequently the site of cruelty and torture. As the Carol Stuart murder in Boston demonstrated, sexist and racist attitudes in the United States often cover up the real threat to women; a women is murdered in Massachusetts by a husband or lover every twenty-two days.[12]

Such numbers do not reflect the full extent of the problem of violence against women, much of which remains hidden. Yet rather than receiving recognition as a major world conflict, this violence is accepted as normal or even dismissed as an individual or cultural matter. Georgina Ashworth notes that:

> The greatest restriction of liberty, dignity and movement and at the same time, direct violation of the person is the threat and realization of violence . . . However violence against the female sex, on a scale which far exceeds the list of Amnesty International victims, is tolerated publicly; indeed some acts of violation are not crimes in law, others are legitimized by custom or court opinion, and most are blamed on the victims themselves.[13]

Violence against women is a touchstone that illustrates the limited concept of human rights and highlights the political nature of the abuse of women. As Lori Heisse states: 'This is not random violence . . . [T]he risk factor is being female.'[14] Victims are chosen because of their gender. The message is domination: stay in your place or be afraid. Contrary to the argument that such violence is only personal or cultural, it is profoundly political. It results from the structural relationship of power, domination and privilege between men and women in society. Violence against women is central to maintaining those political relations at home, at work and in all public spheres.

Failure to see the oppression of women as political also results in the exclusion of sex discrimination and violence against women from the human rights agenda. Female subordination runs so deep that it is still viewed as inevitable or natural, rather than seen as a politically constructed reality maintained by patriarchal interests, ideology and institutions. But I do not believe that male violation of women is inevitable or natural. Such a belief requires a narrow and pessimistic view of men. If violence and domination are understood as a politically constructed reality, it is possible to imagine deconstructing that system and building more just interactions between the sexes.

The physical territory of this political struggle over what constitutes women's human rights is women's bodies. The importance of control over women can be seen in the intensity of resistance to laws and social changes that put control of women's bodies in women's hands: reproductive rights, freedom of sexuality whether heterosexual or lesbian, laws that criminalize rape in marriage, etc. Denial of reproductive rights and homophobia are also political means of maintaining control over women and perpetuating sex roles and thus have human rights implications. The physical abuse of women is a reminder of this territorial domination and is sometimes accompanied by other forms of human rights abuse such as slavery (forced prostitution), sexual terrorism (rape), imprisonment (confinement to the home) and torture (systematic battery). Some cases are extreme, such as the women in Thailand who died in a brothel fire because they were chained to their beds. Most situations are more ordinary, like denying women decent education or jobs, which leaves them prey to abusive marriages, exploitative work and prostitution.

This raises once again the question of the state's responsibility for protecting women's human rights. Feminists have shown how the distinction between private and public abuse is a dichotomy often used to justify female subordination in the home. Governments regulate many matters in the family and individual spheres. For example, human rights activists pressure states to prevent slavery or racial discrimination and segregation even when these are conducted by non-governmental forces in private or proclaimed as cultural traditions as they have been in both the southern United States and in South Africa. The real questions are: (1) who decides what are legitimate human rights; and (2) when should the state become involved and for what purposes. Riane Eisler argues that:

> the issue is what types of private acts are and are not protected by the right to privacy and/or the principle of family autonomy. Even more specifically, the issue is whether violations of human rights within the family such as genital mutilation, wife beating, and other forms of violence designed to maintain patriarchal control should be within the purview of human rights theory and action . . . [T]he underlying problem for human rights theory, as for most other fields of theory, is that the yardstick that has been developed for defining and measuring human rights has been based on the male as the norm.[15]

The human rights community must move beyond its male-defined norms in order to respond to the brutal and systematic violation of women globally. This does not mean that every human rights group must alter the focus of its work. However it does require examining patriarchal biases and acknowledging the rights of women as human rights. Governments must seek to end the politically and culturally constructed war on women rather than continue to perpetuate it. Every state has the responsibility to intervene in the abuse of women's rights within its borders and to end its collusion with the forces that perpetuate such violations in other countries.

II Towards Action: Practical Approaches

The classification of human rights is more than just a semantic problem because it has practical policy consequences. Human rights are still considered to be more important than women's rights. The distinction perpetuates the idea that the rights of women are of lesser order than the 'rights of man', and, as Eisler describes it, 'serves to justify practices that do not accord women full and equal status'.[16] In the United Nations, the Human Rights Commission has more power to hear and investigate cases than the Commission on the Status of Women, more staff and budget, and better mechanisms for implementing its findings. Thus it makes a difference in what can be done if a case is deemed a violation of women's rights and not of human rights.[17]

The determination of refugee status illustrates how the definition of human rights affects people's lives. The Dutch Refugee Association, in its pioneering efforts to convince other nations to recognize sexual persecution and violence against women as justifications for granting refugee status, found that some European governments would take sexual persecution into account as an aspect of other forms of political repression; but none would make it the grounds for refugee status per se.[18] The implications of such a distinction are clear when examining a situation like that of the Bangladeshi women who, having been raped during the Pakistan–Bangladesh war, subsequently faced death at the hands of male relatives to preserve 'family honour'. Western powers professed outrage but did not offer asylum to these victims of human rights abuse.

I have observed four basic approaches to linking women's rights to human rights. These approaches are presented separately here in order to identify each more clearly. In practice, these approaches often overlap, and while each raises questions about the others, I see them as complementary. These approaches can be applied to many issues, but I will illustrate them primarily in terms of how they address violence against women in order to show the implications of their differences on a concrete issue.

1. *Women's Rights as Political and Civil Rights.* Taking women's specific needs into consideration as part of the already recognized 'first generation' political and civil liberties is the first approach. This involves both raising the visibility of women who suffer general human rights violations as well as calling

attention to particular abuses women encounter because they are female. Thus, issues of violence against women are raised when they connect to other forms of violation such as the sexual torture of women political prisoners in South America.[19] Groups like the Women's Task Force of Amnesty International have taken this approach in pushing for Amnesty to launch a campaign on behalf of women political prisoners which would address the sexual abuse and rape of women in custody, their lack of maternal care in detention, and the resulting human rights abuse of their children.

Documenting the problems of women refugees and developing responsive policies are other illustrations of this approach. Women and children make up more than 80 per cent of those in refugee camps, yet few refugee policies are specifically shaped to meet the needs of these vulnerable populations who face considerable sexual abuse. For example, in one camp where men were allocated the community's rations, some gave food to women and their children in exchange for sex. Revealing this abuse led to new policies that allocated food directly to the women.[20]

The political and civil rights approach is a useful starting point for many human rights groups; by considering women's experiences, these groups can expand their efforts in areas where they are already working. This approach also raises contradictions that reveal the limits of a narrow civil liberties view. One contradiction is to define rape as a human rights abuse only when it occurs in state custody but not on the streets or in the home. Another is to say that a violation of the right to free speech occurs when someone is jailed for defending gay rights, but not when someone is jailed or even tortured and killed for homosexuality. Thus while this approach of adding women and stirring them into existing first generation human rights categories is useful, it is not enough by itself.

2. *Women's Rights as Socioeconomic Rights.* The second approach includes the particular plight of women with regard to 'second generation' human rights such as the rights to food, shelter, health care and employment. This is an approach favoured by those who see the dominant Western human rights tradition and international law as too individualistic and identify women's oppression as primarily economic.

This tendency has its origins among socialists and labour activists who have long argued that political human rights are meaningless to many without economic rights as well. It focuses on the primacy of the need to end women's economic subordination as the key to other issues including women's vulnerability to violence. This particular focus has led to work on issues like women's right to organize as workers and opposition to violence in the workplace, especially in situations like the free trade zones which have targeted women as cheap, non-organized labour. Another focus of this approach has been highlighting the feminization of poverty or what might better be called the increasing impoverishment of females. Poverty has not become strictly female, but females now comprise a higher percentage of the poor.

Looking at women's rights in the context of socioeconomic development is another example of this approach. Third World peoples have called for an understanding of socioeconomic development as a human rights issue. Within this demand, some have sought to integrate women's rights into development and have examined women's specific needs in relation to areas like land ownership or access to credit. Among those working on women in development, there is growing interest in violence against women as both a health and development issue. If violence is seen as having negative consequences for social productivity, it may get more attention. This type of narrow economic measure, however, should not determine whether such violence is seen as a human rights concern. Violence as a development issue is linked to the need to understand development not just as an economic issue but also as a question of empowerment and human growth.

One of the limitations of this second approach has been its tendency to reduce women's needs to the economic sphere which implies that women's rights will follow automatically with Third World development, which may involve socialism. This has not proven to be the case. Many working from this approach are no longer trying to add women into either the Western capitalist or socialist development models, but rather seek a transformative development process that links women's political, economic and cultural empowerment.

3. *Women's Rights and the Law.* The creation of new legal mechanisms to counter sex discrimination characterizes the third approach to women's rights as human rights. These efforts seek to make existing legal and political institutions work for women and to expand the state's responsibility for the violation of women's human rights. National and local laws which address sex discrimination and violence against women are examples of this approach. These measures allow women to fight for their rights within the legal system. The primary international illustration is the Convention on the Elimination of All Forms of Discrimination Against Women.[21]

The Convention has been described as 'essentially an international bill of rights for women and a framework for women's participation in the development process . . . [which] spells out internationally accepted principles and standards for achieving equality between women and men'.[22] Adopted by the UN General Assembly in 1979, the Convention has been ratified or acceded to by 104 countries as of January 1990. In theory these countries are obligated to pursue policies in accordance with it and to report on their compliance to the Committee on the Elimination of Discrimination Against Women (CEDAW).

While the Convention addresses many issues of sex discrimination, one of its shortcomings is failure to directly address the question of violence against women. CEDAW passed a resolution at its eighth session in Vienna in 1989 expressing concern that this issue be on its agenda and instructing states to include in their periodic reports information about statistics, legislation and support services in this area. [23] The Commonwealth Secretariat in its manual on the reporting process for the Convention also interprets the issue of violence against women as 'clearly fundamental to the spirit of the

Convention', especially in Article 5 which calls for the modification of social and cultural patterns, sex roles and stereotyping that are based on the idea of the inferiority or the superiority of either sex.[24]

The Convention outlines a clear human rights agenda for women which, if accepted by governments, would mark an enormous step forward. It also carries the limitations of all such international documents in that there is little power to demand its implementation. Within the United Nations, it is not generally regarded as a convention with teeth, as illustrated by the difficulty that CEDAW has had in getting countries to report on compliance with its provisions. Further, it is still treated by governments and most non-governmental organizations as a document dealing with women's (read, 'secondary') rights, not human rights. Nevertheless, it is a useful statement of principles endorsed by the United Nations around which women can organize to achieve legal and political change in their regions.

4. *Feminist Transformation of Human Rights.* Transforming the human rights concept from a feminist perspective, so that it will take greater account of women's lives, is the fourth approach. This approach relates women's rights and human rights, looking first at the violations of women's lives and then asking how the human rights concept can change to be more responsive to women. For example, the GABRIELA women's coalition in the Philippines simply stated that 'Women's Rights are Human Rights' in launching a campaign in 1989. As Ninotchka Rosca explained, coalition members saw that 'human rights are not reducible to a question of legal and due process . . . In the case of women, human rights are affected by the entire society's traditional perception of what is proper or not proper for women.'[25] Similarly, a panel at the 1990 International Women's Rights Action Watch conference asserted that 'Violence Against Women is a Human Rights Issue'. While work in the three previous approaches is often done from a feminist perspective, this last view is the most distinctly feminist with its woman-centred stance and its refusal to wait for permission from some authority to determine what is or is not a human rights issue.

This transformative approach can be taken toward any issue, but those working from this approach have tended to focus most on abuses that arise specifically out of gender, such as reproductive rights, female sexual slavery, violence against women, and 'family crimes' like forced marriage, compulsory heterosexuality and female mutilation. These are also the issues most often dismissed as not really human rights questions. This is therefore the most hotly contested area and requires that barriers be broken down between public and private, state and non-governmental responsibilities.

Those working to transform the human rights vision from this perspective can drawn on the work of others who have expanded the understanding of human rights previously. For example, two decades ago there was no concept of 'disappearances' as a human rights abuse. However, the women of the Plaza de Mayo in Argentina did not wait for an official declaration but stood up to demand state accountability for these crimes. In so doing, they helped to create a context for expanding the concept of responsibility for deaths at the hands of paramilitary or right-wing death squads which, even if not carried out by the state, were allowed by it to happen. Another example is the developing concept that civil rights violations include 'hate crimes', violence that is racially motivated or directed against homosexuals, Jews, or other minority groups. Many accept that states have an obligation to work to prevent such human rights abuses, and getting violence against women seen as a hate crime is being pursued by some.

The practical applications of transforming the human rights concept from feminist perspectives need to be explored further. The danger in pursuing only this approach is the tendency to become isolated from and competitive with other human rights groups because they have been so reluctant to address gender violence and discrimination. Yet most women experience abuse on the grounds of sex, race, class, nation, age, sexual preference and politics as interrelated, and little benefit comes from separating them as competing claims. The human rights community need not abandon other issues but should incorporate gender perspectives into them and see how these expand the term of their work. By recognizing issues like violence against women as human rights concerns, human rights scholars and activists do not have to take these up as their primary tasks. However, they do have to stop gate-keeping and guarding their prerogative to determine what is considered a 'legitimate' human rights issue.

As mentioned before, these four approaches are overlapping and many strategies for change involve elements of more than one. All of these approaches contain aspects of what is necessary to achieve women's rights. At a time when dualist ways of thinking and views of competing economic systems are in question, the creative task is to look for ways to connect these approaches and to see how we can go beyond exclusive views of what people need in their lives. In the words of an early feminist group, we need bread and roses, too. Women want food and liberty and the possibility of living lives of dignity free from domination and violence. In this struggle, the recognition of women's rights as human rights can play an important role.

Notes

1. Universal Declaration of Human Rights, adopted 10 December 1948, G.A. Res. 217A(III), U.N. Doc. A/810 (1948).

2. Blanche Wiesen Cook, 'Eleanor Roosevelt and Human Rights: The Battle for Peace and Planetary Decency', in Edward P. Crapol, ed., *Women and American Foreign Policy: Lobbyists, Critics, and Insiders* (New York: Greenwood Press, 1987), 98–118; Georgina Ashworth, 'Of Violence and Violation: Women and Human Rights', *Change Thinkbook II* (London: Change, 1986).

3. Vibhuti Patel, *In Search of Our Bodies: A Feminist Look at Women, Health and Reproduction in India* (Bombay: Shakti, 1987); Lori Heise, 'International Dimensions of Violence Against Women', *Response*, vol. 12, no. 1 (1989), 3.

4. Sundari Ravindran, *Health Implications of Sex Discrimination in Childhood* (Geneva: World Health Organization, 1986). These problems and proposed social programmes to counter them in India are discussed in detail in 'Gender Violence: Gender Discrimination Between Boy and Girl in Parental Family', paper published by CHETNA (Child Health Education Training and Nutrition Awareness), Ahmedabad, 1989.

5. Debbie Taylor, ed., *Women: A World Report, A New Internationalist Book* (Oxford: Oxford University Press, 1985), 10. See Joni Seager and Ann Olson, eds., *Women in the World: An International Atlas* (London: Pluto Press, 1986) for more statistics on the effects of sex discrimination.

6. Frequently a husband will disguise the death of a bride as suicide or an accident in order to collect the marriage settlement paid him by the bride's parents. Although dowry is now illegal in many countries, official records for 1987 showed 1,786 dowry deaths in India alone. See Heise, note 3 above, 5.

7. For an in-depth examination of the practice of female circumcision see Alison T. Slack, 'Female Circumcision: A Critical Appraisal', *Human Rights Quarterly* 10 (1988), 439.

8. C. Everett Koop, M.D., 'Violence Against Women: A Global Problem', presentation by the Surgeon General of the US, Public Health Service, Washington D.C., 1989.

9. Ana Maria Portugal, 'Cronica de Una Violacion Provocada?', *Fempress* special, 'Contraviolencia', Santiago, 1988; Seager and Olson, note 5 above, 37.

10. Ashworth, note 2 above, 9.

11. 'Violence Against Women in the Family', Centre for Social Development and Humanitarian Affairs, United Nations Office at Vienna, 1989.

12. Bella English, 'Stereotypes Led Us Astray', *The Boston Globe*, 5 Jan. 1990, 17, col. 3. See also the statistics in Women's International Network News, 1989; United Nations Office, note 11 above; Ashworth, note 2 above; Heise, note 3 above; and *Fempress*, note 9 above.

13. Ashworth, note 2 above, 8.

14. Heise, note 3 above, 3.

15. Raine Eisler, 'Human Rights: Toward an Integrated Theory for Action', *Human Rights Quarterly* 9 (1987), 297. See also Alida Brill, *Nobody's Business: The Paradoxes of Privacy* (New York: Addison-Wesley, 1990).

16. Eisler, note 15 above, 291.

17. Sandra Coliver, 'United Nations Machineries on Women's Rights: How Might They Better Help Women Whose Rights Are Being Violated?', in Ellen L. Lutz, Hurst Hannum and Kathryn J. Burke, eds., *New Directions in Human Rights* (Philadelphia: Univ. of Penn. Press, 1989).

18. Marijke Meyer, 'Oppression of Women and Refugee Status', unpublished report to NGO Forum, Nairobi, Kenya, 1985 and 'Sexual Violence Against Women Refugees', Ministry of Social Affairs and Labour, The Netherlands, June 1984.

19. Ximena Bunster describes this in Chile and Argentina in 'The Torture of Women Political Prisoners: A Case Study in Female Sexual Slavery', in Kathleen Barry, Charlotte Bunch and Shirley Castley, eds., *International Feminism: Networking Against Female Sexual Slavery* (New York: IWTC, 1984).

20. Report given by Margaret Groarke at Women's Panel, Amnesty International New York Regional Conference, 24 Feb. 1990.

21. Convention on the Elimination of All Forms of Discrimination Against Women, G.A. Res. 34/180, U.N. Doc. A/Res/34/180 (1980).

22. International Women's Rights Action Watch, 'The Convention on the Elimination of All Forms of Discrimination Against Women' (Minneapolis: Humphrey Institute of Public Affairs, 1988), 1.

23. CEDAW Newsletter, 3rd Issue (13 Apr. 1989), 2 (summary of U.N. Report on the Eighth Session, U.N. Doc. A/44/38, 14 April 1989).

24. Commonwealth Secretariat, 'The Convention on the Elimination of All Forms of Discrimination Against Women in the Reporting Process – A Manual for Commonwealth Jurisdictions', London, 1989.

25. Speech given by Ninotchka Rosca at Amnesty International New York Regional Conference, 24 Feb. 1990, 2.

Reproduced with permission from Charlotte Bunch, 'Women's Rights as Human Rights: Toward a Re-vision of Human Rights', *Human Rights Quarterly*, 12 (1990), pp. 486–98.

PART II
SUBVERSIVE DISCOURSE

15

Political Theory and the
Problem of Violence

Anthony Giddens

The problem of managing or limiting violence ranks as one of the most difficult and demanding in human affairs, but left and liberal political theory has only rarely touched on it. A great deal has been written about the origins of war and the possibility of peace. Yet for the most part this literature has remained unconnected with theories of the internal constitution of societies and governments – it has been preoccupied with the behaviour of nation-states in the international arena.

Left political thought has often taken up the question of revolutionary violence, and has discussed this in tandem with the repressive violence of the state. Leftists, however, have mostly assumed that violence would not be a problem in a socialist society and hence have given little thought to how social relations might become free from it. Most varieties of liberal thinking are not in the end too different; for liberal political thought has been built around the idea of the contract, and a contract is essentially a pacific negotiation of exchange.

Conservatives of various persuasions have given more attention to the role of violence, particularly of war, in social life. Some versions of conservative thought, indeed, have glorified war and martial values. What conservative philosophers by and large have not done, however, is to consider how war and violence might be transcended. For conservatives have tended to assume that these are generic to the human condition.

There are of course numerous contexts in which violence figures in human social life, almost always in relation to structures of power. Violence, as Clausewitz says, is normally at the other end of persuasion; it is one among other means whereby individuals, groups or states seek to impose their will on others. I shall not try to discuss the origins or nature of violence in general, nor shall I consider the issue of violence and crimes as such. I shall limit myself to the following issues (large though each of them still is). From the point of view of utopian realism, is it feasible to suppose that the role of warfare might diminish and how might such a process be furthered? What can be done to

245

limit the spread of sexual violence? How can we counter violence which develops on the basis of ethnic or cultural differences? These may seem like
disconnected issues, but in the light of the social transformations discussed earlier [in *Beyond Left and Right*: ed.] some clear connections, as I shall try to show,
exist between them.

I take it that each of these questions raises problems of pacification and I
take pacification to be as important a part of an agenda of radical politics as
any of the issues I have discussed earlier. For even if the Cold War has been
relegated to the past, the threat of nuclear conflict and other sorts of military
violence will remain for the indefinite future; and violence and the threat of
violence in social life can destroy or cripple the lives of millions.

Several provisos are in order here. There are respects, and some very
important respects, in which the use of violence is necessary to achieve widely
desired social ends. Thus pacification itself presumes a control of the means
of violence on the part of legitimate authorities. I think one can take it for
granted, though, that *all* forms of violence are to be minimized as far as possible, whether legitimate or illegitimate. In other words, the tendency of
governing authorities to secure a monopoly over the means of violence
should not be equated with an increasing *resort* to violence.

'Violence' has sometimes been defined in a very broad way. Johan Galtung,
for example, argues for an 'extended concept of violence' which would refer
to a wide set of conditions that inhibit the development of individuals' life
chances. Violence is any barrier which impedes the realization of potential,
where such a barrier is social rather than natural: 'if people are starving when
this is objectively avoidable, then violence is committed . . .'[1] As with Pierre
Bourdieu's idea of 'symbolic violence', the point is to apply the concept of violence to a wide variety of forms of oppression which people might suffer, and
thereby to relate it to general criteria of social justice. The problem with such
notions is that they make an already very widespread phenomenon ever-present. What is specific to violence as ordinarily understood – the use of force to
cause physical harm to another – becomes lost from view. I shall therefore
understand violence in this straightforward and conventional sense.

The State and Pacification

The issue of pacification has to be understood in relation to the long-term
development of modern institutions and the modern state. Violence and
the state, as rightist thinkers have always tended to emphasize, are closely connected; the state is the prime vehicle of war. In respect of their deployment
of violence, however, pre-modern states differed in a basic way from nation-
states. In the pre-modern state, the political centre was never able to sustain
a full monopoly over the means of violence. Brigandage, banditry, piracy and
blood-feuds were always common, and in most states local warlords retained
a good deal of independent military power. Moreover, the power of the political centre depended in a fairly immediate way on the threat of violence.
Pre-modern states were segmental in character: the centre normally had no

way of enforcing obedience from subjects in more peripheral areas save by a show of force. In spite of the despotic and bloodthirsty character which many pre-modern political regimes displayed, their level of substantive power in day-to-day social relations was relatively low.

As a result of a number of factors, including particularly improved communications and an intensifying of surveillance mechanisms, nation-states became 'sovereign powers': the agency of government was able to achieve much greater administrative control over its subject populations than ever before. To cut a long story very short, and to use a good deal of oversimplification, the result was a pervasive process of internal pacification, achieved in most 'classical nation-states' – those developing from the eighteenth century onwards in Europe and the United States.[2]

Pacification doesn't mean, of course, the disappearance of violence from the interior of states; and it is quite consistent with the waging of wars in the international arena. It refers, in this context at any rate, to the more or less successful monopoly of the means of violence on the part of the political authorities within the state. Internal pacification went along with the formation of professionalized armed services, 'pointing outwards' towards other states in the state system, rather than being preoccupied with the maintenance of internal social order. The convergent development of capitalism and parliamentary democracy, together with systems of centralized law, played a major role in 'extruding' violence from the immediate mechanisms of government.

Although processes of internal pacification have proved much harder to achieve in 'state-nations' and ex-colonial societies than in the classical nation-state, they have almost everywhere proceeded far compared with the pre-modern state. Civil war is by now a specifically abnormal situation in most states throughout the world, particularly in the economically advanced regions. In earlier forms of state, by contrast, it was almost the norm; contestation of the power of the ruling authorities by rival military groups was frequent and often protracted.

The era of the internal pacification of states was also the time of the industrialization of war: war changed its character as weaponry became mechanized and mass-produced. The industrialization of war destroyed militarism in one guise, although it sustained it in another. The 'warrior values' long promoted by aristocratic strata went into prolonged decline. War could no longer be seen as an occasion for display and ritual. The highly coloured clothing that had so often been favoured by warrior groups and traditional armies gave way to sober uniforms of camouflage. In the shape of admiration for valour, esprit de corps and military discipline, militarism survived in an altered form. Indeed, if 'militarism' be defined as the widespread support for military principles and ideas in the larger society – and the preparedness of civilian populations to support war *en masse* if need be – militarism became more rather than less common.

It can be argued, however, that with the further development of industrialization of war, and above all with the invention of nuclear weaponry, these processes started to go dramatically into reverse. During the Cold War, the existence of large-scale nuclear arsenals formed part of the (remote) experience of everyone – the most threatening of all high-consequence risks. Yet at the same time, Clausewitz's theorem became turned around. Although smaller wars were fought out 'by proxy' in many places, a nuclear confrontation was 'unthinkable' because of its devastating consequences. War could no longer be turned to when diplomacy failed; diplomacy had to have as its goal the avoidance of large-scale war altogether. From this point onwards, one could say, militarism started to go into decline.

The emergence of what Martin Shaw calls a 'post-military society' would certainly be of interest to any programme of radical politics in the present day.[3] A post-military society responds to the changing global situation following the Cold War, but also builds on longer-term trends within the developed societies. Militarism, Shaw argues, has been diminishing in many countries across the world since the end of the Second World War. It was a consequence of a state system which mixed internal pacification with external preparation for war. Its institutional backdrop was the sovereign state, the nation-in-arms and mass (male) conscription. Militarism, in the terminology used in *Beyond Left and Right*, was a characteristic of simple modernization. Current social, economic and political transformations undermine it.

Militarism in this sense was characterized by large-scale, hierarchical systems of command which paralleled the industrial and state bureaucracies. There was in fact a direct connection, often remarked on, between militarism and the early development of both democracy and the welfare state; citizenship rights were forged in the context of mass mobilization for war. Militarism has declined as a result of several trends: the shifting, and in some ways diminishing, autonomy of classical nation-states; the disappearance of clear-cut external enemies; the reduced influence of classical nationalism and the rise of substate nationalisms; and the functional obsolescence of large-scale war.

Can we see these processes, in so far as they are sustained or accelerate, as leading to a reduction of the role of military violence in settling disputes? Is there now an extension of internal pacification into external areas?

We might give a cautious assent to both of these questions. A post-military society is not one where the threat of large-scale military violence is removed, especially given the massive economic differences within the global system. Geopolitical rivalries are likely to remain strong, and destructive war remains a possibility in many parts of the world. A post-military order is none the less likely to be more resistant to mass mobilization for military purposes than used to be the case. Smaller, more 'civilized' armed forces may still wield large destructive power. Yet it seems likely that the military will become functionally more separate from other groups than before. The expectation that has affected the lives of young men for generations – their possible, even probable, involvement in war – could end.

I don't want to pursue here the difficult question of how the world might police itself if the post-military society, in combination with other trends, helps reduce tendencies to large-scale war. Pacification on a global scale is unlikely to reproduce the processes involved in the internal pacification of states. I shall consider only the implications for features of cosmopolitanism discussed earlier. Consolidating a post-military society would mean generalizing the attitude that violence should play less and less part in settling international tensions and problems. The active side of citizenship responsibilities would imply recognition of an obligation to nourish pacific rather than warlike values, this to be as basic a part of a democratized polity as any other.

Peace movements played an important role in producing the shifts in social consciousness – West and East – which contributed to the ending of the Cold War. Like ecological movements, peace movements were driven in the first instance above all by awareness of high-consequence risk: consequently, they were largely single-issue movements. They were oriented to the Cold War, and with its collapse have either disappeared or changed their form. The mass mobilizations such movements were periodically able to generate have more or less ceased, and don't look likely to be revived in the near future. How does one mobilize for peace in a society with no enemies – but many real military dangers? Peace movements have become peace organizations and they still have plenty of concrete tasks. They can seek to raise the consciousness of citizenries and governments concerning the dangers of nuclear proliferation and they can keep alive the debate over nuclear power, especially its connection with the political production of weaponry.

The single most important factor here, however, is the altered relation between peace movements and the interests of governments in an emergent post-military order. States without enemies, and marked by a concomitant decline in militarism, are in quite a different situation from either the Cold War or pre-existing systems of military alliance and national antagonism. Although border disputes may remain, and invasions sometimes occur, most states no longer have any incentive to wage offensive war. 'Peace' takes on quite different connotations in such circumstances than it did when it meant absence of war in a nation-state system permanently geared up for it. Hence the interests of governments and peace organizations are much more convergent than they used to be; and there is no reason why they shouldn't often work in tandem rather than in opposition.

Masculinity and War

So far as civic values and responsibilities are concerned, what should we make of the fact that the propagation of military violence has always been a resolutely male affair? Feminist authors have quite often drawn direct connections between masculinity and war: warfare is a concrete expression of male aggressiveness. The civic virtues that would promote peace rather than war, it is said, are those characteristically associated with the activities and values of women. Expressed in such a way, however, this thesis is somewhat implausible. War is not an expansion of a generalized aggressiveness, but associated with the rise of the state. Although there might be some men who actively relish war, the large majority do not.[4]

One couldn't deny, of course, that there is a relation between war, military power and masculinity. Men may have to be indoctrinated in order to wage war, but war and the military have formed part of the ethos of masculinity – or masculinities – in a deep-rooted way. This was true most especially of warrior aristocracies: war-making was glorified as the highest of all values. With the decline of the warrior ethic, military violence was no longer widely seen as the chief testing ground for heroism, honour and adventure – although some strands of Old Conservative thought long continued to regard this situation as reversible. Valour remained a dominant value in military circles, particularly in officer corps, but the professionalizing of the armed forces separated military ideals from the concrete experience of the rest of the male population. To 'serve' in the military became instead part of a shifting male ethos of instrumentality and protection. Masculinity came to be associated with a commitment to work and with 'providing' for dependants; assuming the role of soldier when called on to do so was part of the intrinsic maleness of the public domain.

In the post-military society there is a push and pull between the decay of ideals of masculinity in these various senses and the entry of women into the public arena. Women have gone into the armed forces in increasing numbers. They have mostly accepted existing military norms and have agitated for complete inclusion: that is, they expect to achieve full combat rights alongside men. In the meantime, the masculine values which went along with militarism are corroding or becoming ambiguous as a result of the advance of gender equality and the growth of social reflexivity. It is in this context that we should examine the idea of a war against women, most boldly developed by Marilyn French. French interprets such a war as a long-term phenomenon, dating back even to the first origins of civilization. Up to some six thousand years ago, she says, humans lived in small, cooperative groups in which the status and power of women was either equivalent, or superior, to that of men. With the formation of the first states, women became enslaved and subject to male domination – a situation which the advent of modernity only served to worsen:

> In personal and public life, in kitchen, bedroom and halls of parliament, men wage unremitting war against women . . . Men start repressing females at birth: only the means vary by society. They direct female babies to be selectively aborted, little girls to be neglected, under-fed, genitally mutilated, raped, or molested . . . The climate of violence against women harms all women. To be female is to walk the world in fear . . . Women are afraid in a world in which almost half the population bears the guise of the predator, in which no factor – age, dress or colour – distinguishes a man who will harm a woman from one who will not.[5]

As French describes it, the war against women is widespread indeed. It embraces all systems of patriarchal discrimination against women and is an expression of them. Male violence, 'the physical war against women', follows on from broader structures of inequality. The battering of women, rape and sexual murder form a material expression of the larger system of domination. Even much male on male violence, she suggests, is a sublimated form of violence that would otherwise have women as its object. 'When women are not available, men turn other males into "women". So male prisoners regularly rape other male prisoners and many ministers and priests betray the trust of little boys or male teenagers by molesting them.'[6]

I think one can in fact agree that there is a war of men, or some men, against women today, but not in the manner in which French represents it. A war is an exceptional rather than a permanent state of affairs, and it doesn't make much sense, except in a metaphorical way, to speak of such a thing as enduring for thousands of years. Moreover, such an analysis misses what is new about the situation of the present day. Patriarchy has indeed existed for millennia; however, the circumstances in which it has become contested, and has to some extent broken down, are of much more recent provenance. Over most of the course of human history, patriarchy was accepted by both sexes; collective women's protests against the male rule may have been staged sometimes, but the historical record is not littered with them in the way in which it is with other forms of rebellions, such as peasant rebellions.

As with other systems of power, patriarchy has never been sustained mainly through the use of violence. The power of men over women has endured because it has been legitimated on the basis of differentiated gender roles, values associated with these, and a sexual separation between private and public spheres. In terms of legitimacy, particularly important has been the schismatic view of women which contrasts 'virtue' with the corrupt or fallen woman. The fallen woman in pre-modern systems of patriarchy referred not only to a category of persons – prostitutes, mistresses, courtesans – who stood outside the pale of normal family life. To become 'fallen' was a disgrace that could happen to anyone if she did not abide by codes of virtue and proper behaviour.

Patriarchy in pre-modern cultures was maintained by women as well as by men: women wielded their own sanctions against those who transgressed. So far as control of the means of violence was concerned, however, this lay in the hands of men. As a means of last resort, violence was as significant a sanctioning mechanism of power in patriarchy as elsewhere. Kate Millett has summed up all this very well: 'We are not accustomed to associate patriarchy with force. So perfect is its system of socialisation, so complete the general assent to its values, so long and so universally has it prevailed in human society, that it scarcely seems to require violent implementation.' Yet, she goes on to add, it still had 'the rule of force to rely on . . . in emergencies and as an ever-present instrument of intimidation'.[7]

At this point, however, a major qualification needs to be added to Millett's view. The violence by means of which men policed patriarchy was not mainly directed at women. In many societies, including those of pre-modern Europe, women have been chattels of men and have no doubt often been treated with the casual violence that the status of a mere possession might provoke. But respect, even love, can be much more powerful forms of domination than the sheer use of force. Probably more often than not, men have treated ('virtuous') women with moral approval and esteem. The violence by means of which patriarchy was sustained was mainly from men towards *other men*. This was particularly true in respect of organized or semi-organized violence.

Hostile images of women, and physical maltreatment – such as the punishments meted out to witches – were important sanctioning mechanisms against female misbehaviour. Male on male violence, however, integrated the defence of patriarchy with the upholding of other forms of order. In many pre-modern societies a man's honour was directly dependent on the honour of his family, which he had a duty to uphold no matter where the threat was coming from. The reputation of a family could be tainted in various ways, but certainly this always included the virtue of its female members. Feuds conducted between kin groups commonly sprang from the defence of honour, or from an attempt to compromise it; but even where women were directly involved it was usually other men who were the targets of hostile response.[8]

What has happened today is that this system of violence has collapsed, or is collapsing, on a worldwide basis. Processes of internal pacification in most developed countries long ago displaced the feud, but remnants of the moral foundations of patriarchy were reshaped in the eighteenth and nineteenth centuries. Briefly put, the legitimation of patriarchy came to depend on a reiteration of the schism between the virtuous woman and the harlot – the second of these subjected to the sanctions of the state, the first bolstered by specific legal and moral structurings of the 'normal family'. Male sexuality was retraditionalized and was something that could be 'taken for granted', while female sexuality was in large part controlled through being subjected to an interrogatory gaze: it became understood as the 'dark continent', problematized by the first stirrings of the assertion of independent women's rights.

The large-scale entry of women into the labour force, together with universal democratization and the continued transformation of family forms, has radically altered the 'tradition in modernity' compromise which characterized simple modernization. Patriarchy can no longer be defended by violence directed by some men against others. Men (or, as one must say, some men) turn directly to violence against women as a means of shoring up disintegrating systems of patriarchal power – and it is in this sense that one might speak of a war against women today. It is not an expression of traditional patriarchal systems but, instead, a reaction to their partial dissolution.

Much of such violence, then, results from a system which is decaying; it results from the fact that women's challenge to patriarchy has in some part been successful. Its successes have provoked violent reactions; but they have also brought a great deal into the open that was previously hidden, and enforced an interrogation of much that was carried in tradition.[9]

From the point of view of utopian realism, overcoming male violence against women is contingent on the structural changes now affecting work, the family and the state, and the possibilities these yield – combined with an expansion of dialogic democracy. Masculinity and femininity are today identities and complexes of behaviour in the process of reconstruction. Increasing gender equality is paradoxical for the overall social community unless it goes along with structural changes which promote democratization and new forms of social solidarity – and unless there is a mutual emotional realignment of the sexes. Men's movements that have developed thus far are of various types, some seeking to reassert patriarchal forms of masculinity. In so far, however, as such movements contemplate and act on the detraditionalizing of masculinity in its diverse forms, they can be an important influence in promoting an emotional realignment. Although their influence thus far is tiny compared with that of the feminist movement, it makes sense to see them as the functional equivalents of peace movements – trying to help put an end to the undeclared war of men against women.

The transformation of masculinity and femininity, or rather their multiple forms, as inherited from the past, will depend in a basic way on how far a post-military society comes into being, and what consequences flow from the changing character of work, the family and sexual relationships. Male identity has undoubtedly been bound up with the centrality of work – as full-time permanent employment – in modern societies. Or rather, it has been bound up with the intersections between work, the family and sexuality. For commitment to full-time work in the paid labour force was not just an economic phenomenon – it was an emotional one. The engagements of men in the public sphere enforced a schism in men's lives of a different nature from that characteristic of women's experiences. Men, or many men, across different class categories, became cut off from the emotional sources of their own lives – the origins of the by now celebrated phenomenon of 'male emotional inexpressiveness'. They left women for the most part to manage these areas in their role as 'specialists in love'.

The fact that the higher echelons in most occupational domains are still dominated by men, while men continue to play a much smaller part in child-care than women, is quite often regarded as cause for despair. Yet is it surprising that things have not yet changed to the degree that most feminist thinkers would hope? For those same thinkers have demonstrated that patriarchy has been deeply entrenched for thousands of years; it would be surprising if they could be overcome over a number of decades.

Women have won a variety of legal rights they did not hold before, and are more strongly represented in most occupational domains than they used to be, including the higher levels. Rates of unemployment of men have risen more than those of women, and the 'feminizing' of some male careers is placing in question the old models of work associated with prductivism. Equal parenting – with the socioeconomic arrangements which might permit it – may still be utopian, but now carries more than a dash of reality.[10]

Male violence against women could be lessened if these developments progress and at the same time new forms of sexual identity are pioneered. As Lynne Segal has observed,

> The conscious subversion of men's power . . . is partly the work of those who travel the slow and grinding route taken by mainstream reformist political parties and organisations committed to sexual equality. It is also the work of those engaged in the more erratic, more radical, spurts and retreats along the volatile route of interpersonal sexual politics, as feminists, lesbians, gay and anti-sexist men refashion and live out their new versions of what it is to be 'woman' or 'man'. It is finally, as feminists have always preached and often practised, also a matter of cultural subversion – the creative work of remoulding the lives and experiences of women and de-centring the androcentric positioning of men in all existing discourses. Though it might be difficult to perceive, these routes do intersect. Interpersonal struggles to change men, attempts by men themselves to refashion their conceptions of what it is to be a man, always encounter and frequently collide with other power relations . . . It is not so hard to imagine a world free from the fear of too little work for men, and all too much work for women . . . It is just as easy to envisage a world free from fears of the interpersonal violence, rape, and child sexual abuse which, in their most dangerous and prevalent forms, are the violent acts of men . . .[11]

Easy to envisage, a critic might say, hard actually to bring about: how might the combating of male violence against women relate to other forms of pacification? There is a clear connection, as has been mentioned, with the decline of militarism. Male violence is certainly not all of a piece with the waging of wars, but there are common elements that spill over from one to the other. Mass rapes are quite often perpetrated in times of war; conversely, attitudes of adventurism found among some who enlist in the armed forces seem empirically linked to a tendency to violent behaviour towards women.[12]

More important, probably, are potential connections the other way around. The creation of a democracy of the emotions, as I have sought to show earlier, has implications for social solidarity and citizenship. Men's violence against women, or a great deal of it, can be understood as a generalized refusal of dialogue. Couldn't one see this as a Clausewitzean theory of interpersonal relations? Where dialogue stops, violence begins. Yet such violence is (in principle) as archaic in the personal domain as Clausewitz's theorem is in the wider public arena.

Violence, Ethnic and Cultural Difference

As I write these lines, a tenuous dialogue has been established between warring parties in Israel and in Bosnia; the armed conflicts in Somalia, Angola, Afghanistan and elsewhere look set to continue. To move from violence against women back towards such military confrontations might appear as heterodox as the link developed with overall processes of pacification. Yet the connections are there. The war in Bosnia, for example, witnessed the systematic rape of Muslim women as a deliberate way of humiliating them – and, as statements from those involved made clear, of humiliating their menfolk also.

Confrontations such as those in the former Yugoslavia and other regions might perhaps be a residue of the past – a clearing-up of lines of division and hostility. Alternatively, and more disturbingly, they may be the shape of things to come. For the very changes that act to reduce the possibility of wars between states might increase the chances of regional military confrontations – the more so since fundamentalisms of various kinds can act to sharpen pre-existing ethnic or cultural differences.

Under what conditions are the members of different ethnic groups or cultural communities able to live alongside one another and in what circumstances are the relations between them likely to collapse into violence? The question is again a large one, and I shall discuss only a few aspects of it. There are virtually no societies in the world where different ethnic groups are wholly equal to one another. Ethnic division, and some other kinds of differences, such as religious ones, are normally also differences of stratification. The inequalities associated with ethnicity are often sources of tension or mutual hostility, and thus play their part in stimulating conflicts which may lead to a collapse of civil order.

Yet such inequalities are too commonplace to provide sufficient explanations of outbreaks of major violence. Without seeking to analyse how common or otherwise such conflicts are likely to be, or what their main origins are, I want to discuss three sets of circumstances relevant to how they might be inhibited or contained. The first is the potential influence of dialogic democracy; the second, the countering of fundamentalism; the third, controlling what I shall call degenerate spirals of emotional communication. All relate to, or draw on, ideas discussed in other parts of *Beyond Left and Right*.

There are only a limited number of ways, analytically speaking, in which different cultures or ethnicities can coexist. One is through segmentation – through geographical separation or cultural closure. Few groups or nations, however, can sustain a clear-cut separation from others today. Small communities which try to cut themselves off from the outside world, or limit contact with it, nearly all become reabsorbed to a greater or lesser degree – as has happened, for example, with the vast majority of the communes of the 1960s. States which seek isolation, such as in a sense the whole Soviet bloc did, or China or Iran, have not been able to preserve it in the longer term.

As a 'solution' to problems of living along with clashes of values, then, segmentation is much less significant than it used to be, with the emergence of a global cosmopolitan order. Although complete withdrawal from the wider social universe has become problematic, various kinds of group separation and national differentiation can of course be maintained. Groups can keep to themselves and physical segregation has not lost all its meaning. In cities, for example, different ethnic groups often occupy distinct neighbourhoods which have only limited contacts with one another. Geophysical separation is one means by which the stratification of ethnic groups and under-classes is organized. Those in the poorer areas may lack the capacity to travel, while the members of more affluent groups rarely if ever visit the deprived neighbourhoods.

Given the diasporic character of many ethnic and cultural differentiations, however, and the penetrative influence of mass media, segmental cultures now only function with some degree of harmony in a cosmopolitan climate. Where segmentation has become broken down, and exit difficult, only two options remain: communication, or coercion and violence.

There is a tension between communication and violence, then, of a more acute kind than existed in earlier phases of modern social development – and this is true not only in the industrialized societies but on a global scale. In such a situation, whether combined with more orthodox democratic institutions or not, dialogic democracy becomes a prime means for the containment or dissolution of violence. It isn't far-fetched to see a direct line of connection here between male violence against women in everyday life and violence between subnational groups.

Difference – whether difference between the sexes, difference in behaviour or personality, cultural or ethnic difference – can become a medium of hostility; but it can also be a medium of creating mutual understanding and sympathy. This is Gadamer's 'fusion of horizons', which can be expressed as a virtuous circle. Understanding the point of view of the other allows for greater self-understanding, which in turn enhances communication with the other. In the case of male violence against women it is well established that dialogue can dispel the 'Clausewitzean theorem'. That is to say, violent individuals become less so – in other spheres of their lives also – if they manage to develop a virtuous circle of communication with a significant other or others.

Dialogue has great substitutive power in respect of violence, even if the relation between the two in empirical contexts is plainly complex. Talk can in many circumstances lead to hostility, and to the possibility of violence, rather than serving to undermine them. In a diversity of situations, a refusal to engage with the other is tied to systems of coercive power, as is its opposite, the absence of voice. The advance of dialogic democracy almost always depends on correlate processes of socioeconomic transformation. These things having been said, dialogic democratization is likely to be central to civil cosmopolitanism in a world of routine cultural diversity. Difference can be a means of a fusion of horizons; what is a potentially virtuous circle, however, can in some circumstances become degenerate. I would define a degenerate spiral of communication as one where antipathy feeds on antipathy, hate upon hate.

And this observation brings us full circle. For how else could one explain the events in Bosnia, and parallel happenings elsewhere? Fundamentalisms, as I have said earlier, are edged with potential violence. Wherever fundamentalism takes hold, whether it be religious, ethnic, nationalist or gender fundamentalism, degenerate spirals of communication threaten. What is originally merely an isolationism, or perhaps only an insistence on the purity of a local tradition, can, if circumstances so conspire, turn into a vicious circle of animosity and venom. Bosnia sits on a historic fault-line dividing Christian Europe from Islamic civilization. Yet one cannot produce a sufficient explanation of the Yugoslavian conflict only by reference to old hostilities. Those hostilities, when refocused in the present, provide a context; once conflict begins, and hate starts to feed on hate, those who were good neighbours can end as the bitterest of enemies.

Notes

1. Johan Galtung, 'Violence and Peace', in Paul Smoker et al., *A Reader in Peace Studies* (Oxford: Pergamon, 1990), p. 11.

2. I have discussed these changes at some length in *The Nation-State and Violence* (Cambridge: Polity, 1987). For an important analysis, see Charles Tilly, *Coercion, Capital and European States AD 990–1990* (Oxford: Blackwell, 1990).

3. Martin Shaw, *Post-Military Society* (Cambridge: Polity, 1991).

4. Jean Bethke Elshtain, *Women and War* (New York: Basic Books, 1988).

5. Marilyn French, *The War Against Women* (New York: Ballantine Books, 1993), p. 200.

6. Ibid., p. 198.

7. Kate Millett, *Sexual Politics* (Garden City: Doubleday, 1970), pp. 44–5

8. Sylvana Tomaselli and Roy Porter, *Rape* (Oxford: Blackwell, 1986).

9. One of the best discussions of these issues is to be found in Lynne Segal, *Slow Motion* (London: Virago, 1990), ch. 5.

10. Jon Gershuny, 'Change in the Domestic Division of Labour in the UK', in Nick Abercrombie and Alan Warde, eds, *Social Change in Contemporary Britain* (Cambridge: Polity, 1992).

11. Segal, *Slow Motion*, pp. 308, 317.

12. Diana Scully, *Understanding Sexual Violence* (London: Unwin Hyman, 1990).

Reproduced with permission from Anthony Giddens, 'Political Theory and the Problem of Violence', in his *Beyond Left and Right: The Future of Radical Politics* (Calif.: Stanford University Press, 1995), pp. 229–45.

16

Local and Global

Terry Eagleton

Because human beings are made up of both a body and a language, we all live a tension between the local and the universal, and one, moreover, which, if psychoanalysis is to be credited, we can never completely resolve. For the body will never be entirely at home in language, but will instead be scarred and fissured by it, as the cranking up of our needs to the level of linguistic demand and desire opens up that way of being forever extrinsic to ourselves which we know as the unconscious. Our creatureliness is somewhat at odds with our conceptuality. Language is one of the ways in which our bodies transcend themselves, along with labour and sexuality, but therefore one of the ways in which we can overreach and undo ourselves, as amphibious animals trapped between angel and beast, inhabiting simultaneously the realm of the sensuously somatic and that kingdom of universality which language opens up for us. It's these twin domains which Hegel thought he had finally reconciled in the idea, and it was a nice try, but looking round at postmodern immediacy on the one hand and multinational capitalism on the other it seems somehow not to have come off. More to the point, perhaps, look at the conflict in Hegel's own epoch between the culturalist Burke and the rationalist Paine – at the illusion that we are no more than our local prejudices and the chimera that we can definitively transcend them. It's a battle now being refought on the terrain of contemporary theory between the pragmatists and the Habermasians.

The problem of interrelating culture and politics is that culture seems to be local whereas politics appears to be universal. The former is a matter of the way we live the world on our bodies, the latter a question of that abstract extension of our bodies which we call society. Of course there are local politics and cosmopolitan cultures, so the distinction is dodgy from the outset; and if power, as Foucault reminds us, is a question of bodies, then culture is just as much a matter of discourse. One might claim that the mediation between the two is called ideology, which ratifies an abstract power-structure but does so by bringing it home to lived experience, transmuting it into 'culture'. And it isn't at all clear where an institution like the family, or sexuality in general, fits into some clean division between cultural form and political institution. This wasn't, however, the way it seemed to the radical Enlightenment. For the Enlightenment, culture, in the sense of stubbornly local allegiances, particularist prejudices, provincial and partisan commitments, was really the enemy of politics, that which prevented us from becoming citizens of the world. It's hard in a rampantly culturalist age like our own to think ourselves back into this extraordinary moment when all our own buzz-terms – culture, history, bodiliness, particularity – were dark and demonized, the enemy of a civilized and progressive politics. The brave, doomed dream of the anti-culturalist Enlightenment is to reinvent the kind of solidarity we had once supposedly experienced in culture at the level of universal Reason, to persuade us to invest in the political with all the psychic intensity we had imagined was reserved for the local, the cultural, the sensuously specific. This was a noble, liberating, utterly unreal vision, unreal because virulently anti-somatic and anti-materialist, cavalierly bypassing all those vital aspects of our 'species being' as the early Marx has it, which we share in common with stoats and badgers. It seemed that we could cease to be subjects of power, in the pejorative sense, only by ceasing to be subjects in the psychical sense at all. We were invited to become citizens of the world, but the price we had to pay was to stop being ourselves. Regionality was crushed beneath rationality – or at least it would have been, had it not been for that wonderfully convenient nineteenth century invention, the nation-state.

The point of the hyphen in 'nation-state' is to fuse culture and politics, to create an identity between the life-forms of a specific people and the structures of political power. What distinguishes nationalism originally isn't a claim to sovereignty over a specific bit of territory – a claim familiar enough to Renaissance princes – but the sovereignty of a particular people, who happen to be territorially located; what distinguishes the territorial claims of nationalism, in other words, is a form of republicanism, the wedding of people and state, the insertion of the one into the other with all the tightly bonded unity of signifier and signified. This, of course, was only ever an approximate equation, as indeed is the case with the signifier: hardly any nation-states have actually clung to the contours of some distinct ethnicity, and one reason why postcolonial states have tended to preserve the national boundaries bequeathed to them by their colonizers is because ethnic mayhem might otherwise ensue, as indeed it is doing as I write. Another problem is class: the nation-state can't really represent a divided people, can't figure forth contradiction in its formal structures, so that as its bourgeois architects find themselves eventually confronted by the proletariat its consensuality will begin to crumble. But the nation-state was also a device for reconciling regionality with universal reason, since it was the place where a potentially international community of free, equal citizens could be locally instantiated. It was the *patria* which 'interpellated' you as a French revolutionary subject, but interpellated you as the locus of a more global freedom and reason. The problem lay in preserving the delicate equipoise between local and universal, or if you like between culture and politics. Political nationalism sometimes found it convenient to summon a cultural nationalism to its aid, but was also in danger of being ousted by it. For the more the universal-rational form of the nation-state underpins its power by drawing on local cultural resources, the more this cultural particularism threatens to undermine the forms of universal reason. Think, in Irish terms, of the conflict between the anti-culturalist O'Connell and the culturalist Young Irelanders, or between Parnell and Arthur Griffith. Culture is the medium of political authority but also its potential antithesis and undoing; indeed just as in the nineteenth century culture in its narrower sense – the arts, basically – becomes constituted as anti-political, the spiritual opposite of all that dreary institutional stuff, so culture in the broader anthropological sense relevant to cultural nationalism becomes a kind of alternative to institutional politics. The anti-political animus of Irish cultural nationalism is very striking, to the point where 'cultural nationalism' begins to sound more and more like an oxymoron. 'State' and 'nation' seem to move at ontologically different levels and to resist any easy hyphenation. The state presents itself as the political locus of the national culture, its organic outcropping, as it were, in the political realm; but though this way of putting it makes the national culture seem prior to the state, the reality is that the state, or the state-in-waiting, largely brings that national culture into being, organizing it for particular political ends. It is, in truth, politics which constitutes culture, but – in cultural nationalism – in a way which seems to invert the relationship between them. And it isn't of course hard to believe that the way we speak and sing and dress is somehow more immediate, and so more fundamental, than who we vote on to the transport committee. There is, then, a conflict from the outset between cultural and political nationalism – the former more particularist and introspective but, precisely because of this, sometimes more militantly separatist and anti-colonialist (in Ireland, Davis, O'Leary, Pearse); the latter more cosmopolitan and 'rational' but precisely because of that more akin to the institutional forms of the colonizing nation and so more politically compromised (in Ireland, O'Connell, Parnell). But it can work the other way round too, since cultural nationalism's displacement of the political may lead it to be less politically minded or politically militant (Yeats), whereas the internationalism of a more 'enlightened' political nationalism (Tone, Connolly) may side-step this culturalist displacement for a more direct political confrontation.

If modernity dreamt of fusing culture and politics, or more radically of the latter eradicating all vestiges of the former, what gave the lie to this vision was modernism. For modernism is among other things the site of an immense disturbance of the relations between particular and universal, a sort of seismic upheaval in which local and universal, supposedly wedded in the Romantic symbol, fly apart and force each other into grisly caricatures of themselves. A remorseless abstraction and rationalization of reality now sits cheek-by-jowl with a kind of vividly irrationalist immediacy, and one name for this (mis)coupling is Joyce's *Ulysses*. The universal forms of mythology, and a naturalist tale of myopic particularism, now intersect only in irony. Modernism is at once the age of deep archetypal structures which now seem to have taken on an autonomous life of their own, and the tumultuous return of the sensuously repressed, as the 'primitive' and concrete and sensuous and ineffable rise up to do battle with a reified reason. And none of this is really intelligible outside the context of imperialism and monopoly capitalism, of a world in which the truth of the particular, the regional, the national, now seems to lie in an increasingly cosmopolitan structure which is always else-where. It is not that these specificities have vanished, just that (like modernist time and place) they seem increasingly fortuitous and interchangeable, gov-erned as they are by a structure which transcends them and is no longer uniquely instantiated by them. As with Saussure, whose work belongs to this period, the general linguistic structure gives rise to specific utterances which are arbitrary and untheorizable, and cannot itself be palpably present in its particular instances. The world is still nation-centred, and with the rise of fas-cism will become pathologically so; but that gross inflation of the particular which is national socialism or the imperial nation-state is caught up, as in modernist art, with a network of increasingly global operations. The cult of the concrete, whether as national *Zeitgeist* or a style of painting, is among other things a protest against universal reification, but one which is in strange collusion with it. Modernism and monopoly capitalism are at once cos-mopolitan and particularist, transcending specific cultures yet raiding them for their own purposes, whether as economic or cultural capital. If the cos-mopolitanism of the modernists is a subversive strike against still-powerful, claustrophobic national identities, their fascination with the concrete, the fragment, the deviant, the inarticulable, is a protest against the levelling, homogenizing global system which is now increasingly emerging, in which anywhere can be everywhere and modern-day Dublin merges smoothly into ancient Greece. Modernism thus cuts above and below the nation-state at a stroke, spurning its parochialism for the great cosmopolitan centres while reaching deep into the dimensions of folklore, mythology, the popular and the regional. The Eliot who airily permutates London, Geneva and Vienna is the same Eliot who is fascinated by music hall, folk dancing and Derby day. It is as though the hyphen leashing 'nation' to 'state', or culture to politics, is now palpably slackening: modernism skilfully exploits the resources of national cultures, but if it can permutate so many so indifferently it is partly because of an increasingly international political and economic order, to which the modernists as rootless cosmopolitans belong, which is in the process of transcending the political state. National cultures are, so to speak, released from their political proprietors and circulated on the global market, or in the pages of *Finnegans Wake*. Like commodities, they exchange, so to speak, at the same value; they are deprivileged, which is as offensive to the custodians of the nation-state, and so politically radical, as it is acceptable to the imperialists, and so politically reactionary.

Postmodernism can be read, among other things, as a pressing of this stalled dialectic between concrete and universal to an almost unimaginable extreme. As far as the universal goes, something quite dramatic happens between monopoly and multinational capitalism, which is that the international becomes the transnational, a semantically trivial but politically momentous shift. Internationalism extends but doesn't revolutionize our concept of space: there are still autonomous nations, but now they are inter-linked. Transnationalism signifies a qualitatively different sort of space altogether, which one can best express by noting that of the world's 100 largest economies, 47 of them are multinational corporations. There's a shift within that sentence between two distinct conceptions of space, the one familiarly territorial ('economies'), the other ('multinational corporations') not. The multinational company is a kind of virtual or hyperspace, one whose borders and coordinates are constantly shifting, a well-nigh infinitely malleable dimension which bears the same kind of relation to physical territory as a cube does to a square, or as the Roman Catholic Church does to a Roman Catholic church. To continue the religious analogy, the multinational resembles the Almighty Herself in being at once everywhere and nowhere, always more than any of its specific incarnations but more than just the totality of those individual places as well, like God Herself absolutely real but utterly invisible, that in which we live and breathe and have our being but too close to the eyeball to be represented or objectified. (We might note, incidentally, that one difference between colonialism and postcolonialism is that in the latter the ruling powers are increasingly invisible, which is hardly an unqualified advance.) It is as though in the multinational the visions or nightmares of modernist art have finally taken on flesh, and we now actually live in some Escher-type landscape where space curves endlessly back upon itself, where all apparent exits from this windless enclosure turn out to be *trompe l'oeils*. Likewise, the time of multinational capitalism is pure synchronicity, not at all the linear unfolding of a national destiny but the stack of international clocks in the stock exchange, a world of perpetual consciousness where like Orwell's Room 101 there is no darkness, and where there is no distance either, and so properly speaking no space at all. If monopoly capitalism extends space, multinational capitalism offers to abolish it. Not so much the end of history, you might say, as the end of geography. But just because this system appears entirely centreless, as disarticulated as a jellyfish, anywhere can be a centre, and a 'bad' universalism thus generates a 'bad' particularism as the flipside of itself. Think of the current US cult of communitarianism, a flight from a 'bad' globalism which seems to mean among other things that if you smoke on the street or commit adultery in South Carolina your neighbours come round and beat you up. We have seen that this bad kind of particularism (there's a good one too) was already becoming true with modernism, but with modernism, you might argue, there's still the sense of some abstract system, however elusive, which is the secret absent cause of the concrete, whereas with multinational capitalism that system threatens to evaporate entirely into its specific instances, so that it's now no longer a question of a system which is there but inscrutable but of there being apparently no system at all. What this means, of course, is that the system, financially speaking, is now so pervasive, so extended, that it's no longer a centred one, and since poststructuralism believes in its charmingly old-fashioned way that all systems have to have a centre, it can only conclude that this one isn't a system at all. (Note the epistemological parallel to this: either we have a God's eye view or we have scepticism. Note also that the absence of a centre may have something to do with the decline of US hegemony and the failure so far to fill this political vacuum.) The stalled dialectic of modernism is thus pressed to the point where the system is now so universalized as to implode upon itself, flip over into its own opposite and become no more than a host of random particulars and perspectives; for if objects, as Hegel reminds us, exist only be negation, by differentiating themselves from what they are not, then an apparently boundless system can logically not exist (just as God does not, for the astute theologian, strictly speaking exist). It is now no longer, as with the nineteenth century nation-state or the Romantic symbol, that the universal can become incarnate in the particular, nor, with modernistic imperialist monopoly capitalism, that system and particular are strangely askew, but the nominalist condition in which there is nothing but the particular, except of course for another rather similar-looking particular, which means that there is nothing particular at all. (Anyway, how can one have an individuality if one does not also have a universal to contrast it with?) Think, as David Harvey has pointed out, of the way that what is in fact an increasingly homogeneous world system must actually manufacture and commodify difference by, for example, making each of its cities apparently unique; nothing in such a world is more similar than difference, just as nothing is more international a phenomenon than nationalism.

The modernist fetish of the local, deviant or immediate is, I've argued, in part a last-ditch resistance to reification, and here modernism and postmodernism are surely in continuity rather than at odds. For the most obvious political fact about our world is that we are growing both more international and more tribal simultaneously, and the more phoney the internationalism the more morbid the tribalism. (I'm deeply uneasy with the word 'tribalism' but hope, like St Augustine on time, that you know what I mean.) Each phenomenon twists the other into a 'bad' version of itself; and one material cause of this among many is the erosion of that traditional mediator, the nation-state. Marx thought capitalist society a kind of dire parody of an authentic work of art, in which the particular becomes grotesquely inflated as the laws of the whole become correspondingly abstract, and so-called 'late' capitalism has now projected this condition onto a global scale. As far as the relations between culture and politics go, what we have in postmodernism is a kind of reversal of the Enlightenment in which, far from cranking up local culture to a cosmopolitan politics, or burying it beneath it, politics have now in effect slithered to a halt with the end of the Cold War, the final triumph of liberal capitalism and the consequent end of history, and what we have instead to link us is a thoroughly cosmopolitan culture. (Though actually, in so far as this culture bears the political stamp of the West, the depoliticization is only of course apparent.) One thinks of Lyotard's (in)famous declaration: 'one listens to reggae, watches a Western, eats McDonald's food for lunch and local cuisine for dinner, wears Paris perfume in Tokyo and "retro" clothes in Hong Kong . . .' But this isn't of course meant to be culture as a substitute for political community, as with Kant or Arnold or Leavis, for there is deliberately no community here at all. This hybridized, cosmopolitan, commodity culture is just an assemblage of differences, as much a reminder of how we aren't linked, or of how all such links are fortuitous, as any kind of culturalist substitute for political solidarity. What we consume here is exactly the 'foreignness' of the cultural products, which is as far removed as possible from culture as the immediate, the densely affective, the local piety. Or rather we have a culture which doesn't spurn the ethnic and local but exports it as international commodity, fashions an indifferent global mishmash out of the stubbornly specific, thus presenting us with a blend of 'bad' particularity and 'bad' universality. There's a parallel here with the multinationals, which adapt to some extent to the local culture or refashion it for their purposes; multinational companies have, legally speaking, multiple identities, which should give pause to those who think multiple identity an unequivocal boon. Postmodernism, at least in its more conservative varieties, collapses the classical opposition between culture and politics by simply passing culture through the exchange-circuits of international capitalism, just as the Wake passes the signifier through a sort of dizzying exchange of mythemes, so 'decathecting' it, stripping it of affect, emptying it of all that which once allowed it, however nostalgically, to act as a critique of the political status quo.

But this is only one half of the postmodernist story. The other, more positive half is a much more radical retrieval of the local, the vernacular, the somatic, the communitarian, the unincorporable particular history, in the teeth of an apparently homogenized globe. And this, of course, has always been the upbeat side of the nationalist story too. One contradiction of the present world system is that the nation-state is still needed to stabilize and regulate what would otherwise be a politically uncontrollable economic system, and needed too to lend that system its particular, hegemonizing national myths. However much multinational space may spurn the local, it knows that there are no disciplines like local ones; and it must thus prop itself up with modalities of power which in some ways run counter to its own logic. The state is thus now more powerful internally than it has ever been, even if externally speaking the nation-state is being increasingly squeezed out between the supranational on the one hand, and on the other hand a localism or regionalism which now seems to some people the only defence left to them, given the dwindling sovereignty of the nation-state, against the depredations of the global economy. So as the state delegates powers above itself, it becomes increasingly vulnerable to powers from below. The transnational nature of the economic base is constantly at war with the national political superstructure, which is why the British Tories are in such disarray on Europe. Base and superstructure, unlike classical capitalism, now occupy different spaces and temporalities, as capital shifts from place to place in accordance with global profit rather than local need. But another contradiction of the nation-state is that, like the sensuous particular in modernism, it can offer resistance to the very system within which it is caught. The most virulently anti-nationalist force in the world today is a multinational capitalism which keeps most of the globe in poverty and hunger. When commentators excoriate pathological or fundamentalist forms of nationalism, as indeed they should, they seem unaware of how these are often enough the dark side of the brave new streamlined world they themselves so euphorically endorse. And nobody can doubt the proven power of the nation-state, throughout the Keynsian era, of significantly limiting and repairing the damage of market forces. Anyone who thinks such a state now irreparably outmoded might consider just how progressive a force it could still be in comparison with the international banditry we happen to have. Back to Keynes would be forward indeed. Those who oppose anti-colonial nationalism in the name of difference seem to forget that it can make quite a difference – that if it often enough erases internal differences it also presses the claims of external difference, the right to differ from one's colonizers, as well as pressing the claims of identity (the right to share their right to self-determination). Anyway, there can surely be no more ambiguous political ideology than one which in Britain today means both a desire for centralization (English nationalism) and one for devolution (Scots and Welsh), which was used first as a weapon in the revolutionary overthrow of the ancien régimes, then in the late nineteenth century to ratify the triumphalist expansion of capitalism, again in the inter-war years of this century to rally an ailing capitalism and pose an alternative to socialism, and used yet again in the postwar period as a remarkably successful anti-imperialist force through the so-called Third World. An ideology which was originally coopted by the bourgeois states in the cause of internal stability and external expansion ended up in some cases hoisting them with their own petard. Perhaps the American troops, as they scrambled out of Saigon in 1975, consoled themselves with the thought that nationalism was just an inverted mirror-image of imperialism.

What we have been witnessing is not just a transition from the nation-state to a global order – not only because the nation-state remains fairly strong, but because this shift actually intensifies the local, regional, tribalist, communitarian as a form of last-ditch defence. The system conjures up its own opposite, just as international capitalism has always enlisted as well as subverted the nation-state. In some ways, this remains true: national élites in the so-called Third World, for example, draw power and privilege from the very global system which marginalizes them. But the tribalism which the political order once coopted now threatens to blast it apart. Whereas, in the classical nation-state, local and universal are meant to be at one, they are now increasingly at odds. In the Third World, where the 'rising' from local bonds to the class and citizenship which come with urbanization has always been a problem, the undermining of orthodox political systems by international capitalism leads to a resurgence of sectarian tribalism. In Europe, one consequence of the global system is neo-fascism. And if 'culture' in the local sense is out of synchrony with the global economy, so is politics, which has yet to find some way of calling the multinationals to democratic accountability. With the old nation-states, capitalism and a limited degree of democracy were able to coexist; with the new multinational economy, this is less and less the case. Another way of putting the local-universal conflict is to say that whereas capital is global, labour is local; the unemployed can't always just leave the country.

One problem, then, is what kind of cultural and political identity we can achieve in this situation which is neither commodified cosmopolitanism or a myopic particularism. How is the subject of this world to be interpellated? How are cultural forms to catch up with the international political and economic order?

It seems implausible right now that men and women will throw themselves on the barricades crying 'Long live the European Union!'. But we should remember that in the pre-modern period the nation, for which so many have since lived and died, seemed pretty abstract too. Anyone who believes that one can't fervently identify with an abstract global organization has obviously not been talking to a Roman Catholic. And if the new citizen of the world these days is the corporate executive, he or she is also the ecological campaigner, whose slogan is 'Think global, act local' (though in one sense what else can we ever do?). And if the multinational is non-territorial, so are forms of identity and solidarity like class or gender. Cultural identities will continue to be forced into pathological particularism, as we have witnessed in former Yugoslavia, as long as the international system is alienated rather than (necessarily) abstract, unresponsive to popular political control, and as long as it is forced to erase cultural specificity. It is not a matter of some eternal quarrel between culture and politics, but of how this conflict shapes up in an alienated global system. Culture is only divisive or non-divisive within specific political conditions, which means we need neither abolish it with the radical Enlightenment nor reify it with postmodernism. How we 'live' our relation as subjects to the new supranational order is in the first place a political rather than cultural matter, a question of citizenship and democracy; but we can expect this to overlap with other more local, ethnic, cultural forms of subjectivity, once political change, which must assume priority over culture here, has allowed these to depathologize themselves. There can no longer, in other words, be that dream of identity between rational and affective, civic and cultural, which the hyphen in 'nation-state' sought to secure. Instead, we will no doubt live in a world of multiple 'interpellations', some more affective or abstract than others. The local and universal will be neither identical nor in mutual contradiction. As for nationalism, this may represent a 'bad' particularism, as in an increasingly racist Europe, or it may be part of the redrawing of relations between regional and global – a democratic devolution of power within a wider international community. In this sense, ironically, nationalism could help to erode the hyphen in 'nation-state' rather than help to forge it. If the nation-state is increasingly unviable, it is partly because of the diluted sovereignty of the state, but also because of the increasingly diverse character of the nation. In this situation, the meanings of culture and community need urgently to be redefined to take account of both realities. If the left does not do the job, then we may be sure that it will be abandoned to a fight between liberal capitalism and right-wing reaction.

Time of Consumption and the Consumption of Time: Consumer Society and the 'End' of History

Rajesh Sampath

> Consumable pseudo-cyclical time is spectacular time, both as the time of consumption of images in the narrow sense and as the image of consumption of time in the broad sense. The time of image-consumption, the medium of all commodities, is inseparably the field where the instruments of the spectacle exert themselves fully, and also their goal, the location and main form of all consumption: it is known that the time-saving constantly sought by modern society, whether in the speed of vehicles or in the use of dried soups, is concretely translated for the population of the United States in the fact that the mere contemplation of television occupies it for an average of three to six hours a day. The social image of the consumption of time, in turn, is exclusively dominated by moments of leisure and vacation, moments presented at a distance and desirable by definition, like every spectacular commodity.
>
> Guy Debord, *Society of the Spectacle*[1]

The great philosophical problem of time is now an effect of the continuous paroxysm of time consumed and the time of consumption, time exchanged and the time of exchange. Modern political-economy offers itself images of time while its own time retreats into the vanishing image of society's contradictions. It is not that the future of time itself, the being of time, the dream of philosophy, is vanquished in consumer society which proliferates the uncertainty of its own time, but rather the time of consumption, the market of time, where time is bought and sold, conceals the ever-increasing complexity by which the contradictions of time, production and consumption multiply. Hence is it possible to undertake a study by which the three dimensions of time live and die before and after they live and die in consumer society? What contradictions belie modern consumer society's relation to time, its accumulation, circulation and waste? How does time appear and disappear for the consumer, a phenomenological advertisement, which shrouds the laws by which time is made to appear consumable and non-consumable?

Likewise what is the time of consumer society when it purports to absorb time into the fractured cyclicality of reproduction and return: the reproduction of the end of history and the return of history of the 'end' both of which inflect themselves within the still time of eternal consumption? The end has arrived in so far as its image is postponed continually within the consumption of every image: consumer society as the highest realization of the Absolute Spirit of History in so far as the *presence* of the deferral of the end of society terminates itself, while deferring the end of the end – the end of time is infinite, the infinite reprise of the finite. The present is never itself present in consumer society, only the anticipated future which arrives before anticipation. Hence an imaginary future takes the place of the future imagined as the future of a present, a continual return of futures which is substituted for the eclipsed present lost among circulated futures that are consumed; consumer society is its future, which means that it is always already there even before it attempts to arrive at itself. That being the case, the strange creature that it is, what is the time of consumption and the consumption of time?

On the one hand, time is desired as a commodity that should not be consumed, a reserve, which, paradoxically, *will* be used as the most consumable commodity within the time of consumption. For with ideological time accumulated as a surplus interval in which the time of labour *appears* to shrink, fetishized time is deferred to an ever closer future where time can be consumed, thus concealing the simultaneous expansion of production time required for time to appear reserved in the present. Every present divides itself into the necessary time by which consumption is deferred only to promise the consumption of what appears to be empty, unnecessary time. However, the distinction between necessary and unnecessary time is already the effect of consumer time and the cause of consumer society which perpetrates the distinction with respect to production and consumption. But what happens when the distinction confuses itself precisely when consumer society crosses both necessary and unnecessary time in the image of consumption and the shadow of production (and vice-versa) to determine the necessary font by which its regulations can be normalized and its ends realized? If indeed time is desired as a non-consumable necessity within the present deferral of the desired time of unnecessary consumption which is anticipated, then the structure of desire in consumer society is a time between present and future, necessity and contingency, production and consumption. Desired time is an interval, a pocket, a void of time betwixt the future event of consuming unnecessary time and the present event of desiring non-consumable necessary time; the presupposition of 'desired time' before and after it is consumed.

Modern consumer society is the contradiction of time lost and time regained within the *image* of consumption by which the question of time's value is presupposed. But if consumption itself is the image of time's devaluation, then what is the time of the condition by which time is consumed in its necessary and unnecessary forms, which in turn occludes the necessary expenditure of time within the productive cycles that make consumer society possible? What is the distinction between the time of consumption – that is the image of time, circulated within consumption as such and such (work or leisure) – and the consumption of time by which consumption can furnish an image of itself, which when in circulation fails to differentiate itself from the other deficit images of time? Time's return appears impossible in consumer society in so far as its image is continually recycled in the eternal return of consumption. Likewise the imminent dissolution of any novel image is the concealed work of consumer time by which society measures its virtual diachronic progress, a fetishization of time in the imagined completion of a cycle of consumption. Time moves on in consumer society when consumption repeats the destruction of its origin. Consuming the origin of consumption itself guarantees the eternal presence of the consumption of time against the potential vicissitudes of a time of society without consumption. No time for time in consumer society and too much time for its gluttonous anticipation. If a non-consumable theory of historical time is both the hope and the impossibility for consumer society to measure a time before and after consumption, then it is a theory based on the contradiction not between past and present, but between consumptive and non-consumptive time in relation to the mutable laws of the contradictions of consumer society. Baudrillard states,

> The entire discourse on consumption aims to transform the consumer into the Universal Being, the general, ideal, and final incarnation of the human species. It attempts also to make of consumption the premise of 'human liberation', to be attained in lieu of, and despite the failures of, social and political liberation. The consumer is in no way a universal being, but rather a social and political being, and a productive force. As such, the consumer revives historical problems.[2]

The consumer is the beginning and end of historical time in the age of consumption; he reverses the order by which the 'history' of historical time itself is understood. For the origin of the consumer himself is embroiled in a dreamed up history, a concoction of an unformed beginning of capital inscribed forever in its final end within the history of 'endings', which 'coincidentally' corresponds to the dominant image of the 'end of history' at the so-called end of *History*: the consumer is the end of history, and the ends of history, the target of history, who consumes the image of history's end. Hence to speak of the history of consumption in some senses deletes the possibility of speaking about a theory of history in which consumption appears as a non-consumable 'historical being', a reserve of pure historicity, rather than a manufactured sense of anachronistic historical time. Is it possible that the consumer, if considered the end and ends of history, is the threshold of a theory of historical time whose image consists of the polymorphous intersection of the three dimensions of time in *its* very consumption and not the asymmetrical prioritization of one dimension in its imagined and dissolved presence: the present that inherits the past to deliver the future? How is historical time consumed in 'age' when historical time is no longer one of the succession of ages, the successive consumption of ages? Or is the notion 'end' an alienated concept, which only indicates the origin of a great return of time, a revitalized form of virtual history, of which the Consumer marks the first epoch in the grand market of consumable things? The consumer is the site of the question of history in so far as he 'revives' the historicity of how history is produced and consumed.

The time of consumption appears to be a time lost within the possibility of measuring finitude in terms of continuous, linear historical time; the consumptive time of finitude leaves behind the remains of the concepts of origin and death after the event of their consumption. What remains after the consumption of death is not oblivion; historical time for the consumer creates the void of a present (consumes the present) first and then fills it with a non-consumable past (previous deferral of wasted time which returns and remains as non-consumable) instead of consuming the past in creating an absence which is then represented in the present, i.e. the consumable commodity of historical knowledge. Hence historical time is reversed in consumer society in so far as the present is already past in being consumed, while the past was never present in being non-consumable. To speak of transformation in history is to speak of the conditions by which the transformative process of consumption reconstitutes differing intervals of historicity within what appears a synchronic domain of consumer society; here change is impossible precisely because its possibility is recycled endlessly.

The paradox of consumer society as synchronic is not based on the fact that the eternity of the universal gem of liberated, endless desire has been uncovered beneath the dross of Man's search for his essence of history. Rather, the contradiction of consumer time is the 'historical' coincidence of the concept of the end of history and the continuous possibility of the proliferation of the image of the end within a 'historically' finite structure: consumer society presents itself as its very history within every instant of its apparent synchrony. Hence to think the relation between history and consumer society is to think again the question of time and history when history is forced to account for the conditions of its appearance, which means the conditions of its productions, from an indeterminate origin that is never a consumable present within historical time. Consumer society liberates the possibility of thinking again how history happens as such precisely because the object by which history is localized – the past – can be mistaken for the referent from where it is received – the present. Concomitantly, pasts are invented thus liquidating the ground of a present within history. As a result, if the past happens in the present, and the present passes but not into the past, then history is the logic of transferable regimes of temporality whose dominion is consumer society. Likewise, consumer society is the origin of the image of history happening in the profusion of a non-contemporaneity of all three dimensions of time: no longer a present which attempts to find itself in the past, but the past itself happening in the present, which becomes History, paradoxically, in the future.

The historical time of consumption, time in consumer society, and the process of consuming time reveal deep problems within the theoretical question of time in general and historical time. If indeed more complex dimensions of the problem are revealed, then maybe it is consumer society, itself, which reveals itself 'temporally' and 'historically' as the great mutation by which time *has, is* and *will* be thought. Consumer society may be the 'historic' revelation of the mystery of time in so far as the secret irrelevancy of the 'revelation' of History is revealed. If not, then the structures by which consumer society defers the possibility of its end in so far as it thinks it has ended history summon the ends of thinking to approach the 'history' of consumer society prior to the consumption of history, which has been produced as such. Either way what remains is the future and what becomes is the past: consumer society's involuted theory of historical time.

Notes

1. Debord, Guy, *Society of the Spectacle*. Detroit: Black and Red 1983, p. 153.

2. Baudrillard, Jean, *Selected Writings*. Ed. Mark Poster. Stanford: Stanford University Press 1988, p. 53.

The Perfect Crime

Jean Baudrillard

Were it not for appearances, the world would be a perfect crime, that is, a crime without a criminal, without a victim and without a motive. And the truth would forever have withdrawn from it and its secret would never be revealed, for want of any clues [*traces*] being left behind.

But the fact is that the crime is never perfect, for the world betrays itself by appearances, which are the clues to its non-existence, the traces of the continuity of the nothing. For the nothing itself – the continuity of the nothing – leaves traces. And that is the way the world betrays its secret. That is the way it allows itself to be sensed, while at the same time hiding away behind appearances.

The artist, too, is always close to committing the perfect crime: saying nothing. But he turns away from it, and his work is the trace of that criminal imperfection. The artist is, in Michaux's words, the one who, with all his might, resists the fundamental drive not to leave traces.[1]

The perfection of the crime lies in the fact that it has always-already been accomplished – *perfectum*. A misappropriation of the world as it is, before it even shows itself. It will never, therefore, be discovered. There will be no Last Judgment to punish or pardon it. There will be no end, because things have always-already happened. Neither resolution nor absolution, but inevitable unfolding of the consequences. Precession of the original crime – which we might perhaps be said to find in derisory form in the current precession of simulacra. After that, our destiny is the accomplishment of this crime, its inexorable unfolding, the continuity of the evil, the continuation of the nothing. We shall never experience the primal scene, but at every moment we experience its prolongation and its expiation. There is no end to this and the consequences are incalculable.

Just as we cannot plumb the first few seconds of the Big Bang, so we cannot locate those few seconds in which the original crime took place either. It is a fossilized crime, then, like the 'fossilized' background noise scattered about the universe. And it is the energy of that crime, like that of the initial explosion, which will spread through the world until, perhaps, it exhausts itself.

This is the mythic vision of the original crime, the vision of the alter-ation[2] of the world in the play of seduction and appearances, and of its definitive illusoriness.

This is the form the mystery takes.

The great philosophical question used to be: 'Why is there something rather than nothing?' Today, the real question is: 'Why is there nothing rather than something?'

The absence of things from themselves, the fact that they do not take place though they appear to do so, the fact that everything withdraws behind its own appearance and is, therefore, never identical with itself, is the material illusion of the world. And, deep down, this remains the great riddle, the enigma which fills us with dread and from which we protect ourselves with the formal illusion of truth.

On pain of dread, we have to decipher the world and therefore wipe out the initial illusoriness of the world. We can bear neither the void, nor the secret, nor pure appearance. And why should we decipher it instead of letting its illusion shine out as such, in all its glory? Well, the fact that we cannot bear its enigmatic character is also an enigma, also part of the enigma. It is part of the world that we cannot bear either the illusion of the world or pure appearance. We would be no better at coping with radical truth and transparency, if these existed.

Truth wants to give herself naked. She is desperately seeking nudity, like Madonna in the film which brought her fame. That hopeless striptease is the very striptease of reality, which 'disrobes' in the literal sense,[3] offering up to the eyes of gullible voyeurs the appearance of nudity. But the fact is that this nudity wraps it in a second skin, which no longer has even the erotic charm of the dress. There is no longer any need even of bachelors to strip her bare, since she has herself given up *trompe-l'œil* for striptease.

And, indeed, the main objection to reality is its propensity to submit unconditionally to every hypothesis you can make about it. With this its most abject conformism, it discourages the liveliest minds. You can subject it – and its principle (what do they get up to together, by the way, apart from dully copulating and begetting reams of obviousness?) – to the most cruel torments, the most obscene provocations, the most paradoxical insinuations. It submits to everything with unrelenting servility. Reality is a bitch. And that is hardly surprising, since it is the product of stupidity's fornication with the spirit of calculation – the dregs of the sacred illusion offered up to the jackals of science.

To recover the trace of the nothing, of the incompleteness, the imperfection of the crime, we have, then, to take something away from the reality of the world. To recover the constellation of the mystery [*secret*],[4] we have to take something away from the accumulation of reality and language. We have to take words from language one by one, take things from reality one by one, wrest the same away from the same. Behind every fragment of reality, something has to have disappeared in order to ensure the continuity of the nothing – without, however, yielding to the temptation of annihilation, for disappearance has to remain a living disappearance, and the trace of the crime a living trace.

What we have forgotten in modernity, by dint of constantly accumulating, adding, going for more, is that force comes from subtraction, power from absence. Because we are no longer capable today of coping with the symbolic mastery of absence, we are immersed in the opposite illusion, the disenchanted illusion of the proliferation of screens and images.

Now, the image can no longer imagine the real, because it is the real. It can no longer dream it, since it is its virtual reality. It is as though things had swallowed their own mirrors and had become transparent to themselves, entirely present to themselves in a ruthless transcription, full in the light and in real time. Instead of being absent from themselves in illusion, they are forced to register on thousands of screens, off whose horizons not only the real has disappeared, but the image too. The reality has been driven out of reality. Only technology perhaps still binds together the scattered fragments of the real. But what has become of the constellation of meaning in all this?

The only suspense which remains is that of knowing how far the world can de-realize itself before succumbing to its reality deficit or, conversely, how far it can hyperrealize itself before succumbing to an excess of reality (the point when, having become perfectly real, truer than true, it will fall into the clutches of total simulation).

Yet it is not certain that the constellation of the mystery is wiped out by the transparency of the virtual universe, nor that the power of illusion is swept away by the technical operation of the world. Behind all technologies one can sense a kind of absolute affectation and double game, their very exorbitance turning them into a game by which the world shows through, from behind the illusion of its being transformed. Is technology the lethal alternative to the illusion of the world, or is it merely a gigantic avatar of the same basic illusion, its subtle final twist, the last hypostasis?

Perhaps, through technology, the world is toying with us, the object is seducing us by giving us the illusion of power over it. A dizzying hypothesis: rationality, culminating in technical virtuality, might be the last of the ruses of unreason, of that will to illusion of which, as Nietzsche says, the will to truth is merely a derivative and an avatar.

On the horizon of simulation, not only has the world disappeared but the very question of its existence can no longer be posed. But this is perhaps a ruse of the world itself. The iconolaters of Byzantium were subtle folk, who claimed to represent God to his greater glory but who, simulating God in images, thereby dissimulated the problem of his existence. Behind each of these images, in fact, God had disappeared. He was not dead; he had disappeared. That is to say, the problem no longer even arose. It was resolved by simulation. This is what we do with the problem of the truth or reality of this world: we have resolved it by technical simulation, and by creating a profusion of images in which there is nothing to see.

But is it not the strategy of God himself to use images in order to disappear, himself obeying the urge to leave no trace?

So the prophecy has been fulfilled: we live in a world where the highest function of the sign is to make reality disappear and, at the same time, to mask that disappearance. Art today does the same. The media today do the same. That is why they are doomed to the same fate.

Because nothing wants exactly to be looked at any longer, but merely to be visually absorbed and circulate without leaving a trace – thus outlining, as it were, the simplified aesthetic form of impossible exchange – it is difficult today to recover a grasp on appearances. With the result that the discourse which would account for them would be a discourse in which there was nothing to say – the equivalent of a world where there is nothing to see. The equivalent of a pure object, of an object which is not an object. The harmonious equivalence of nothing to nothing, of Evil to Evil. But the object which is not an object continues to obsess you by its empty, immaterial presence. The whole problem is: on the outer fringes of the nothing, to materialize that nothing; on the outer fringes of the void, to trace out the mark of the void; on the outer fringes of indifference, to play by the mysterious rules of indifference.

There is no point identifying the world. Things have to be grasped in their sleep, or in any other circumstance where they are absent from themselves. As in the *House of the Sleeping Beauties*,[5] where the old men spend the night beside the women and, though mad with desire, do not touch them, and slip away before they wake. They too are lying next to an object which is not an object, the total indifference of which heightens the erotic charge. But the most enigmatic thing is that it is not possible to know whether the women are really asleep or whether they are not maliciously taking pleasure, from the depths of their sleep, in their seductiveness and their own suspended desire.

Not to be sensitive to this degree of unreality and play, this degree of malice and ironic wit on the part of language and the world is, in effect, to be incapable of living. Intelligence is precisely this sensing of the universal illusion, even in amorous passion – though without the natural course of that passion being impaired. There is something stronger than passion: illusion. There is something stronger than sex or happiness: the passion for illusion.

There is no point identifying the world. We cannot even identify our own faces, since mirrors impair their symmetry. To see our own face as it is would be madness, since we would no longer have any mystery for ourselves and would, therefore, be annihilated by transparency. Might it not be said that man has evolved into a form such that his face remains invisible to him and he becomes definitively unidentifiable, not only in the mystery of his face, but in any of his desires? But it is the same with any object which reaches us only in a definitively alter-ed state, even when it does so on the screen of science, in the mirrors of information or on the screens of our brains. Thus, all things offer themselves up without a hope of being anything other than illusions of themselves. And it is right that this should be so.

Fortunately, the objects which appear to us have always-already disappeared. Fortunately, nothing appears to us in real time, any more than do the stars in the night sky. If the speed of light were infinite, all the stars would be there simultaneously and the celestial vault would be an unbearable incandescence. Fortunately, nothing takes place in real time. Otherwise, we would be subjected, where information is concerned, to the light of all events, and the present would be an unbearable incandescence. Fortunately, we live on the basis of a vital illusion, on the basis of an absence, an unreality, a non-immediacy of things. Fortunately, nothing is instantaneous, simultaneous or contemporary. Fortunately, nothing is present or identical to itself. Fortunately, reality does not take place. Fortunately, the crime is never perfect.

Translated by Chris Turner

Notes

1. Henri Michaux (1899–1984), Belgian-born French poet and painter. [Trans.]

2. The French verb *altérer* has the sense of making something other than its (perfect?) self and thus of distorting, impairing or even falsifying it. The word has, therefore, sometimes been translated by an equivalent English term, such as 'impair'. However, since Baudrillard's argument depends both on (French) meaning and (shared French and English) etymology, I have found it necessary to invent an English verbal form 'alter-ed' and a related noun 'alter-ation', which I must ask the reader to understand as involving a *negative* alteration, a change *for the worse*. I have tried to use this as sparingly as possible, and wherever *altérer* seems to me to be employed to describe a relatively 'neutral' change, I have used the ordinary English 'alter'. [Trans.]

3. There is a play here on the French verb '*se dérober*', which normally means 'to hide or conceal itself'. [Trans.]

4. Baudrillard's expression '*la constellation du secret*' refers to a passage in Martin Heidegger's 'The Question Concerning Technology', which William Lovitt renders as 'the constellation, the stellar course of the mystery' (*The Question Concerning Technology and Other Essays*, Harper Colophon Books, Harper & Row, New York 1977, p. 33). For this reason, the French word 'secret' has been treated here as equivalent to the German *Geheimnis*. [Trans.]

5. By Kawabata Yasunari. [Trans.]

PART III
INVENTORY OF TEXTS

'A Painful Peace'

Noam Chomsky

Sometimes it requires judgment to select the lead stories of the day, but in November 1995 it's easy enough: on the domestic front, balancing the budget; in the international arena, the Middle East peace process, framed by two dramatic events, the signing of the Oslo II agreement by Israel and the PLO under Washington's guiding hand, and the assassination a few weeks later of Israeli Prime Minister Yitzhak Rabin, another 'martyr for peace', in President Clinton's words.

I will return to a word on the domestic story, but would like to concentrate on the 'historic trade' in which the two long-time adversaries abandoned their traditional goals, at last coming to recognize that a 'painful peace' requires compromise and sacrifice. Let's begin with the bare facts of Oslo II, then turn to background developments, the commentary that all of this has elicited, and finally the significance of the events themselves and the reaction to them.

I The 'Historic Trade'

On September 28, Israel and the PLO initiated the second major step in the peace process (Oslo II), dividing the West Bank into three zones, with extensive further arrangements (not fully available at the time of writing). The Palestinian National Authority (PA) is to exercise total control in Zone A while Israel exercises total control in Zone C. Zone B is the region of 'autonomy': here the PA administers Palestinian villages under overall Israeli 'security control'. Zone A consists of the municipal areas of towns populated exclusively by Palestinians. Zone C includes all Jewish settlements. Zone B is a collection of scattered sectors, about 100 of them according to Israeli maps.

In addition to Zones A, B and C there is a fourth zone that incorporates part of the occupied territories: Jerusalem, which is assigned without comment to Israeli control, including formerly Arab East Jerusalem and an indefinite region beyond. The maps published in Israel and the *New York*

Times identify the Jerusalem area as part of Israel (with slightly different borders). Arafat's announcement of a 'Jihad' to seek Palestinian rights in Jerusalem (in accord with the terms of Oslo I) aroused much fury in the United States, demonstrating that the devious old terrorist had not changed his stripes. Rabin's announcement that Israel's Jihad had been completed and that Jerusalem will be the eternal and undivided capital of Israel elicited no reaction; not did the maps published after Oslo II, ratifying that announcement. Official rhetoric aside, Israel's decision accords with US intentions, and is therefore legitimate by definition.

The delimitation of the three zones is not precisely clear. According to the analysis accompanying Israeli maps, Zone C covers two-thirds of the West Bank and Zone B another 30 per cent, with 3 per cent in the Palestinian Zone A. Prime Minister Rabin, however, informed the Knesset (Parliament) on October 5 that Zone C includes 73 per cent of the West Bank, the Israeli press reported. The map and analysis in the *New York Times* assign 70 per cent of the West Bank to Zone C. The authoritative Washington *Report on Israeli Settlement* estimates Zone A at 1 per cent of the West Bank, Zone C at 72 per cent (relying on published Israeli sources). Of the Palestinian towns, one was disputed, Hebron, with 450 Jewish settlers among some 100,000 Palestinians; Israel therefore retains substantial control. Zone C includes 140,000 Jews, Zones A and B 1.1 million Arabs. 'About 300,000 Israelis are living in the areas conquered by Israel in 1967', veteran Israeli correspondent Danny Rubinstein observes, about 150,000 of them 'in the municipal area annexed to Jerusalem after 1967'.[1]

Oslo II reaffirms the provision of the Cairo accords of May 1994 that Palestinian legislation cannot 'deal with a security issue that falls under Israel's responsibility' and cannot 'seriously threaten other significant Israeli interests protected by this agreement'. The basic terms of the Cairo accords apparently remain in force for all three zones, including their provision that the Israeli Military Administration retains exclusive authority in 'legislation, adjudication, policy execution' and 'responsibility for the exercise of these powers in conformity with international law', which the US and Israel interpret as they please. The meaning, as the knowledgeable Israeli analyst Meron Benvenisti observed after Cairo, is that 'the entire intricate system of military ordinances . . . will retain its force, apart from "such legislative regulatory and other powers Israel may expressly grant"' to the Palestinians, while Israeli judges retain 'veto powers over any Palestinian legislation "that might jeopardize major Israeli interests"', which have 'overriding power' (his quotes are from the text of the Cairo agreement).

Oslo II stipulates further that the Palestinian Council that is to be elected must recognize the 'legal rights of Israelis related to Government and Absentee land located in areas under the territorial jurisdiction of the Council'. In effect, the PA therefore accepts the legality of already existing Jewish settlements and any further ones that Israel may choose to construct, and recognizes Israeli sovereignty over parts of the West Bank that Israel decides to designate as state and absentee lands (unilaterally, as in the past):

up to 90 per cent of Area B, according to 'well-informed Palestinian sources' cited by the *Report on Israeli Settlement*, an estimate only, because the ruling authorities do not release information.[2]

By incorporating these provisions, Oslo II rescinds the position of virtually the entire world that the settlements are illegal and that Israel has no claim to the territories acquired by force in 1967. Oslo II reaffirms the basic principle of Oslo I: UN Resolution 242 of November 1967, the basic framework of Middle East diplomacy, is dead and buried; UN 242, that is, as interpreted by those who formulated it, including – quite explicitly – the United States until Washington switched policy in 1971, departing from the international consensus it had helped shape. The 'peace process' keeps to the doctrines that the US has upheld in international isolation (apart from Israel) for twenty-five years, a matter of no slight significance.

To summarize, Israel runs Zone C (about 70 per cent of the West Bank) unilaterally, and Zone B (close to 30 per cent) effectively, while partially ceding Zone A (1 per cent–3 per cent). Israel retains unilateral control over the whole West Bank to the extent that it (and its foreign protector) so decide, and the legality of its essential claims is now placed beyond discussion. The principles extend to the Gaza Strip, where Israel retains full control of the 30 per cent that it considered of any value.

To illustrate with an analogy, it is somewhat as if New York state were to cede responsibility for slums of South Bronx and Buffalo to local authorities while keeping the financial, industrial and commercial sectors, wealthy residential areas, virtually all of the usable land and resources, indeed everything except for scattered areas it would be happy to hand over to someone else, just as Israel is delighted to free itself from the burden of controlling downtown Nablus and Gaza City directly. Here and in the isolated villages of Zone B Palestinian forces are to manage the population on the standard models: the British in India, whites in South Africa and Rhodesia, the US in Central America, and so on. Israel has at last recognized the absurdity of using its own forces to keep the natives quiet.

To take another standard of comparison, recall that in 1988, at the most extreme period of US–Israeli refusal to recognize any Palestinian rights or to have any dealings with the PLO, Rabin called for Israeli control of 40 per cent of the West Bank and Gaza Strip, speaking for the Labour Party and reiterating its basic stand from 1968 (with some variations). In 1995, Rabin recognized the need to sacrifice, and at Oslo II was willing to accept Israeli control of only about twice as much as he had demanded before – 70 per cent–99 per cent of the West Bank and 30 per cent of the Gaza Strip – along with recognition of the legality of whatever Israel and its sponsor have done and may choose to do.

There has been another change from 1988: at Oslo, Rabin and Shimon Peres were willing to negotiate with the PLO and recognize it as 'the representative of the Palestinian people', at least in a side letter though not in the official agreement. In 1988, they had flatly refused any dealings with the PLO. That transformation has evoked much acclaim from US commentators, who were particularly impressed by Rabin's ability to overcome the revulsion he felt for his old enemy – and who prefer not to listen to the explanation offered by the objects of their admiration: 'There has been a change in *them*, not *us*', Peres informed the Israeli public as the Oslo I accords were announced; 'We are not negotiating with the PLO, but only with a shadow of its former self.' The new approved shadow effectively accepts Israel's demands, abandoning its call for mutual recognition in a two-state settlement, the programme that branded the PLO a terrorist organization unfit for entry into negotiations, according to the conventions of US discourse.

Without consideration of the actual background, discussion of the issues can hardly be serious. The crucial facts of recent history, however, have been almost totally banned, even from scholarship for the most part; again, a matter of no slight significance.[3]

Commenting on the early stages of the historic trade, Palestinian human rights lawyer Raji Sourani sees 'the beginning of a trend towards the militarization of Palestinian society', consistent with the standard model of population control by client forces. That trend proceeds, Middle East correspondent Graham Usher adds, alongside 'the repressive Israeli regime of containment that since Oslo [I] has killed 255 Palestinians in the West Bank and Gaza, while attacks by Palestinians have claimed 137 Israelis' (to mid-1995), and has arrested 2400 Palestinians 'for alleged "Islamist tendencies" between October 1994 and January 1995' alone.[4]

The ratio of Palestinians to Israelis killed has declined since Oslo I, a tendency described in Israel and the West as an increase in Palestinian terror; not false, but not quite the whole story either, even more so if we bring in the suppressed topic of international terrorism in Lebanon.

US–Israeli intentions to maintain those terrorist operations were made explicit the day that Shimon Peres assumed his duties as prime minister. 'Peres Sets Tone of Post-Rabin Era', a front-page *New York Times* headline read, introducing a report that 'Israeli warplanes shrieked over Lebanon' and 'pounded the bases of radical Palestinian guerrillas south of Beirut'. This is well beyond the 'security zone' that Israel runs in south Lebanon with the aid of a terrorist mercenary force, in violation of the demand of the UN Security Council in March 1978 that it withdraw immediately and unconditionally. Peres won only praise for this demonstration of his intention 'to assume Mr Rabin's soldier's mantle as the scourge of Arabs who reject Israel's offer of peace'. The adjacent column condemned the 'desperate act, a horrible act, the work of cowards', when terrorists attacked a US-run military training centre in Riyadh, Saudi Arabia, the same day. Two weeks later, Hizbollah fired rockets into northern Israel, wounding several civilians, an act of terrorism that it described as a 'warning response' to 'Israel's continuing aggressions', including the demolition of homes by the Israeli Army in Lebanon and the Israeli Navy's continuing refusal to allow Lebanese fishermen to fish off the Lebanese coast. As the rockets fell, a senior security official of Hizbollah was blown up by a car bomb. Hizbollah's terror was condemned as a violation of the 1993 agreement that neither side would carry out actions outside of

Israel's 'security zone', an agreement that Israel violates at will: for example, two weeks earlier as Peres took office, or a month before that, on October 13, when 'Israeli artillery bombarded villages outside the security zone', a tiny item reported, with 'no immediate word on casualties', in retaliation for the wounding of Israeli soldiers in Israel's 'security zone'.

As Peres took office, the knowledgeable Middle East correspondent Mary Curtius explained that 'Peres is expected to follow Rabin's course of selectively hitting at guerrilla targets rather than pouring huge numbers of Israeli troops into Lebanon and risking more Israeli casualties' – 'Rabin's course' in July 1993, when he reacted to guerrilla attacks on Israeli troops in south Lebanon by pouring a huge number of troops into Lebanon in an assault that killed 125 Lebanese and drove half a million people from their homes, as Curtius among others reported. Curtius also gives some historical background: Israel invaded Lebanonf in 1982 when the PLO 'regularly fired Katyushas at northern communities and sent guerrillas on cross-border attacks'. That is the standard way of referring to the fact that the PLO scrupulously adhered to the US-brokered truce while Israel stepped up its terrorist attacks in Lebanon, killing many civilians by bombing and other actions in a desperate attempt to elicit some response that could serve as an excuse for the long-planned invasion. The facts are uncontroversial, but unacceptable, therefore turned into their opposite here [in the US: ed.] with amazing regularity (though discussed frankly in Israel).

Israeli atrocities in Lebanon regularly pass without mention or comment. More than 100 Lebanese were killed by the Israeli Army or its local mercenaries in the first half of 1995, the London *Economist* reports, along with six Israeli soldiers in Lebanon. Israeli forces use terror weapons, including antipersonnel shells that spray steel darts (sometimes delayed action shells to maximize terror), which killed two children in July 1995 and four others in the same town a few months earlier, and seven others in Nabatiye, where 'no foreign journalists turned up' to describe the atrocities, British Middle East correspondent Robert Fisk reported from the scene. So matters continue. The occasional mention is usually in the context of a denunciation of Hizbollah terror against Israelis in retaliation.[5]

The brutality of the new Palestinian forces and their cooperation with the Israeli security apparatus have been reported extensively by the Israeli press and human rights monitors, and should come as no surprise. That, after all, was the announced plan. Speaking to the political council of the Labour Party on October 2, 1993, immediately after Oslo I, Prime Minister Rabin explained that the Palestinian security forces would be able to 'deal with Gaza without problems caused by appeals to the High Court of Justice, without problems made by [the human rights organization] B'Tselem, and without problems from all sorts of bleeding hearts and mothers and fathers'. His plan was as rational as it is conventional.

Small wonder that Henry Kissinger sees Rabin as a 'visionary', though reaching his full heights as 'a visionary late in life', on the path to Oslo I: 'When you sit where I do and have, the number of world class thinkers among statesmen is very limited – and he was one of them', Kissinger explained.[6]

Minister of Interior Ehud Barak, now foreign minister in the Peres government, announced that Oslo II 'ensures Israel's absolute superiority in both the military and economic fields'. Benvenisti points out that the Oslo II map, establishing the 'peace of the victors', conforms to the most extreme Israeli proposal, that of the ultra-right General Sharon in 1981. Not surprisingly, Sharon does not appear too dissatisfied with the outcome. Correspondents report that after Oslo II, he was 'smiling broadly as he talked about the bright future for' a new West Bank settlement that he had 'planned and helped build . . . and others like it' while watching the 'construction going on' and showing the press his own proposed map from 1977, now implemented by Rabin, with whom Sharon said he 'felt close', thanks to the congruence of their programmes. Yisrael Harel, the founder of the Yesha Council of West Bank settlers and editor of its extremist newspaper *Nekudah*, agrees with Sharon and the governing Labour Party: 'If they keep to the current plan, I can live with it', he says. Prime Minister Peres's right-hand man, Labour dove Yossi Beilin, explains that the Oslo II agreement 'was delayed for months in order to guarantee that all the settlements would remain intact and that the settlers would have maximum security. This entailed an immense financial investment. The situation in the settlements was never better than that which was created following the Oslo II agreement.'

In his report on Oslo II to the Knesset, Rabin outlined 'the main changes, not all of them, which we envision and want in the permanent solution'. In accord with these primary demands, hardly likely to be subject to negotiation, Greater Israel is to incorporate 'united Jerusalem, which will include both Ma'ale Adumim [a town to its east] and Giv'at Ze'ev [a suburb to its north]'; the Jordan Valley; 'blocs of settlements in Judea and Samaria like the one in Gush Katif [the southern sector of Gaza that Israel retains surrounding its settlements]'. These blocs are to include 'Gush Etzion, Efrat, Beitar and other communities' in the West Bank. The press reported that Ma'ale Adumim will be annexed to the greatly expanded Jerusalem area after expanded settlement establishes contiguity between the two urban areas.[7]

The meaning of the 'peace of the victors' has been spelled out accurately in the Hebrew press in Israel. Tel Aviv University Professor Tanya Reinhart observed after the Cairo agreement that the arrangements being imposed should not be compared with the end of apartheid in South Africa; rather, with the *institution* of that system, with its 'home rule' provisions for new 'independent states', as they were viewed by South African whites and their friends. The analysis, since reiterated by Benvenisti and others, is quite reasonable. Political scientist Shlomo Avineri points out that 'In one sense [Oslo II] is a major victory for Israel and a minimalist settlement for Arafat', who 'has done a relatively good job giving the impossible circumstances under which he is working'. That is almost accurate. It is necessary, however, to recall other features of the Third World model: Arafat, his cronies and rich

Palestinians can expect to do quite well in the client relationship, whatever the effects on the population.[8]

In brief, there is considerable agreement about the bare facts across a spectrum ranging from Sharon and Harel to the sharpest critics.

There is disagreement, however, about what the facts portend, a matter of speculation of course. Some believe that the foundation has been laid for Palestinian independence beyond the Bantustan level, even full Israeli withdrawal. To others, the more likely prospect conforms to the hopes expressed by *New Republic* editor Martin Peretz as he advised Israel to invade Lebanon in 1982 and administer to the PLO a 'lasting military defeat' that will drive notions of independence out of the minds of Palestinians in the occupied territories: then 'the Palestinians will be turned into just another crushed nation, like the Kurds or the Afghans', and the Palestinian problem, which 'is beginning to be boring', will be resolved.[9] Speculation aside, at least this much seems clear: it would be pointless for Israel to retain anything like the territory it controls under Oslo II. Presumably, the government will sooner or later decide to restrict its administrative burden while continuing to integrate within Israel whatever land and resources it finds valuable, at which point another 'historic trade' will be celebrated.

The 'historic trade' just consummated establishes the most extreme position of US–Israeli rejectionism that has been seriously put forth within the mainstream political spectrum. But however extreme a position may be, some will remain unsatisfied. Ten years ago, central elements of the Likud coalition reiterated their claim to Jordan, while conceding that 'in the context of negotiations with Jordan we might agree to certain concessions in Eastern Transjordan' (the largely uninhabited desert areas). A similar position had long been held by the mainstream of the Kibbutz movement, Ahduth Avodah, which played a leading role in the Golda Meir government. To my knowledge, such claims have never been renounced. Today, some sectors, Americans and ultraorthodox prominent among them, claim the right to every stone west of the Jordan.[10]

The pattern is the same everywhere. Saudi Arabia is the most extreme Islamic fundamentalist state in the world, but is under attack by Islamic fundamentalists for selling out to the West. If the recent terrorist bombing in Riyadh turns out to have been done by such groups, that will hardly prove the government to be 'moderate', just as one cannot seriously argue that Rabin was a 'moderate' on the grounds that he was murdered by a religious extremist. The point is equally obvious in both cases – understood in the first and commonly denied in the second, consistent with doctrinal imperatives.

II The Facts on the Ground

Looking more closely, we find that the expanding area of Greater Jerusalem–Ma'ale Adumim extends virtually to Jericho and the Jordan Valley, so that the anticipated permanent settlement effectively bisects the West Bank. A huge array of 'bypass roads' is being constructed to fragment the region further into 'cantons', as they are called in the programmes of the ultra-right now being implemented. The new roads link the territories under Israeli control so that settlers can travel freely without having to see the Arab villages scattered in the hills, or the municipal areas run by the PA. Construction of Israeli settlements, housing and infrastructure has accelerated since Oslo I was signed in September 1993, using funds provided by the US taxpayer with the agreement of the Bush and particularly the Clinton administrations. The government of Israel continues to provide inducements to Jews to settle in the territories, where they enjoy a subsidized lifestyle well beyond the reach of the general population; most recently, new efforts to encourage settlement in lands confiscated from Bedouins in Ma'ale Adumim, where a new bypass road was opened on October 23, 1995 and 6000 new housing units are to be erected by the year 2005 along with 2400 new hotel rooms, its population projected to grow to 50,000. Building starts increased by over 40 per cent from 1993 to 1995 (not including East Jerusalem), according to a report by Peace Now issued on October 10, though they are still well below 1992 levels.[11]

The same conception, Israel Shahak observes, has been implemented in Gaza, 'sliced into enclaves controlled by the bypass roads [that] cut the Gaza Strip in two, in its strategically most sensitive spot: between Gaza town and the big refugee camps to the south of it'. The settlements 'serve as pivots of the road grid devised to ensure Israeli control' over the areas granted 'autonomy', which are separated from Egypt and from each other. In both Gaza and the West Bank, these arrangements allow Israel to continue to imprison the population in whole or in part by road and area closures, as it has often done, sometimes for long periods.

The motive for curfew-closure may be punishment, or to deter possible terrorist action (particularly, after some Israeli atrocity, or for several weeks during the signing of Oslo II). Or simply to liberate Jewish citizens from the annoying presence of the locals, as when the Arab population of Hebron was locked up under twenty-four-hour curfew for four days during the Passover holidays in 1995 so that settlers and 35,000 Jewish visitors brought there in chartered buses could have picnics and travel around the city freely, dancing in the streets with public prayers to bring down 'the government of the Left', laying the cornerstone for a new residential building, and indulging in other pleasures under the protective gaze of extra military forces, using the opportunity 'to insult the Palestinians imprisoned in their houses and to throw stones at them if they dared to peek out of the windows at the Jews celebrating in their city,' and finally bringing the celebration to a close 'by settlers rampaging through the Old City, destroying property, and smashing car windows . . . in a city magically cleansed . . . of Palestinians'. 'Children, parents and old people are effectively jailed for days in their homes, which in most cases, are seriously overcrowded', able to turn on their TV sets to 'watch a female settler saying happily, "There is a curfew, thank God"', and to hear the 'merry dances of settlers' and 'festive processions', some to 'the Patriarchs Cave open only to Jews'. Meanwhile 'commerce, careers, studies, the family, love – all are immediately disrupted', and 'the medical system was paralyzed' so that 'many sick persons in Hebron were unable to reach hospitals during the curfew and women giving birth could not arrive in time at the clinics' (Yifat Susskind, Israel Shahak, Gideon Levy).[12]

In annexed East Jerusalem, Israel is free to extend its programmes to reduce Arab citizens to second-class status. These were devised and implemented by former Mayor Teddy Kollek, much admired here as an outstanding democrat and humanitarian, and are now being extended under his successor, Ehud Olmert of Likud. Their purpose, Kollek's adviser on Arab affairs Amir Cheshin explained, was 'placing difficulties in the way of planning in the Arab sector'. 'I don't want to give [the Arabs] a feeling of equality', Kollek elaborated, though it would be worthwhile to do so 'here and there, where it doesn't cost us so much'; otherwise 'we will suffer.' Kollek's planning commission advised development for Arabs if it would have 'a "picture window" effect', which 'will be seen by a large number of people (residents, tourists, etc.)'. Kollek informed the Israeli media in 1990 that for the Arabs, he had 'nurtured nothing and built nothing', apart from a sewage system – which, he hastened to add, was not intended 'for their good, for their welfare', 'they' being the Arabs of Jerusalem. Rather, 'there were some cases of cholera [in Arab sectors], and the Jews were afraid that they would catch it, so we installed sewage and a water system against cholera.' Under Olmert, treatment of Arabs has become considerably harsher, according to reports from the scene.[13]

The Kollek programmes are analysed by Israeli community planner Sarah Kaminker (a city council member and city planner in Kollek's administration) in a June 1994 report submitted to the High Court on behalf of Arab plaintiffs by the Society of St Yves, the Catholic Legal Resources Center for Human Rights. In Jewish West Jerusalem, the report concludes, 'there is large-scale illegal construction' which the municipality does not prevent and retroactively approves. In Arab East Jerusalem, standards are different. There, 86 per cent of the land has been made 'unavailable for use by Arabs'. The remaining 14 per cent 'is not vacant land but land that has already been developed'; vacant lands are reserved for development for Jews, or kept as 'open landscape views' (often for eventual development for Jews, so it regularly turns out). 'The dearth of land zoned for Arab housing is a result of government planning and development policy in East Jerusalem', where the Kollek administration conducted 'a consistent effort since 1974 to limit the land area available to Arabs for licensed construction'. The goal is 'demographic balance', partially achieved in 1993 when Kollek's municipality 'was able to announce that the number of Jews residing in East Jerusalem had surpassed the number of Arabs'.

The government has provided housing in formerly Arab East Jerusalem: 60,000 units for Jews, 555 for Arabs. Arabs whose homes have been demolished for Jewish settlement often 'come from the lowest economic strata of their community' and now 'live in makeshift hovels, doubled and tripled up with other families, or even in tents and caves'. Those who are willing to build

their own homes on their own lands are barred by law and subject to demolition if they proceed. The threat is executed, unlike in Jewish West
Jerusalem, where 'the problem of illegal construction . . . is as serious, if not
more so, than that in East Jerusalem'. 'Demographic balance' is advanced
further by discriminatory regulations on building heights, far more limited in
Arab than Jewish neighbourhoods of East Jerusalem. An array of zoning provisions and other legal instruments has been designed to intensify the
discrimination between Jews and Arabs, as throughout Israel itself, always
using funds provided by the US taxpayer directly or through tax-free donations, always with the approval of admiring US commentators.[14]

With Israel's Jihad for Jerusalem now officially over, such programmes can
be extended there and beyond. The cantonization of Arab regions and the
new stamp of legitimacy for the right of closure should also make it possible
to refine the long-term programme of inducing the population to go somewhere else, except for those who may find a place in industrial parks handed
over to Israeli and Palestinian investors, linked to foreign capital.

During the occupation, the military administration barred independent
development. An official order declared that 'no permits will be given for
expanding agriculture and industry which may compete with the State of
Israel', a device familiar from US practice and Western imperialism generally,
which typically permitted 'complementary development' only. The facts are
well known in Israel. As Oslo II was announced, Ronny Shaked recalled that
in the territories Israeli governments 'were only interested in calm and cheap
manpower. Decisions to develop any infrastructures, to create any industrial
or agricultural development, were taken only to promote a specific Israeli
interest and were forced on the inhabitants. In Hebron, for example, the
Civil Administration refused a request to set up a factory for making nails,
fearing competition with a factory in Tel Aviv. The health system, on the
other hand, was taken care of, because diseases in the West Bank might also
endanger residents of Tel Aviv.' The Civil Administration was cheap to run,
he adds, because its 'minuscule' budget was covered by taxes from the local
inhabitants. It effectively continues with little change under Oslo II.

Under the Israeli regime, the local population was left with few options
beyond exile or employment in Israel under terrible conditions that have
been bitterly condemned for years in the Israeli press, largely concealed
from those who pay the bills. The only comparative scholarly study concludes
that 'the situation of noncitizen Arabs in Israel is worse relative to that of non-
nationals in other countries' – migrant workers in the United States,
'guestworkers' in Europe, etc.

Even these options have now been sharply reduced as Palestinians are
being replaced by workers brought in from Thailand, the Philippines,
Romania and other places where people live in misery. Israeli investigative
reporters have documented 'inhuman' working conditions and treatment,
including virtual slavery and 'severe sexual harassment', much as in the Gulf
principalities and other client states. The curfews and closures in the territories had 'devastated the Palestinian economy and destroyed 100,000

families in Gaza alone', journalist Nadav Ha'etzni reported in May 1995, a 'trauma' that can only be compared with the mass dispossession and expulsion of Palestinians in 1948, he added. The situation is likely to deteriorate as imported semi-slave labour displaces the Palestinian workforce from the only employment that had been allowed them. In such ways, 'the Oslo Accords have created a truly new Middle East', Ha'etzni writes.[15]

The rights of Palestinian workers in the 'new Middle East' were spelled out in a May 1995 ruling by Justice Y. Bazak of the Jerusalem District Court, rejecting a lawsuit brought by the workers' rights group Kav La'Oved ('Worker's Hotline', Tel Aviv). The plaintiffs had requested restitution of $1 billion withheld from salaries for social benefits that Palestinian workers had never received (pensions, unemployment payments and so on); the funds ended up in the state treasury. The court dismissed the case, accepting the government's argument that Knesset legislation to implement the Oslo I accords retroactively legalized the robbery, thus removing any legal basis for the suit. The court also accepted the government's argument that Israel's National Insurance Law grants rights only to residents of Israel. The deductions were never intended to ensure equal rights for the Palestinian workers, Justice Bazak ruled, but were designed to keep wages for Palestinians high on paper but low in reality, thus protecting Israeli workers from unfair competition by cheap Palestinian labour. This is 'a worthy and reasonable purpose which is recognized by the Court', Justice Bazak explained, 'just as the legality of imposing customs taxes is recognized for the purpose of protecting the country's products . . .'

One can see why the Israeli judicial system must retain veto power over any legislation that the Palestinian authorities might contemplate; and why American taxpayers must be kept in the dark about the use of the huge subsidies they provide to Israel.

These subsidies, incidentally, are opposed by the public even more than most foreign aid, and are the one component that is immune from the sharp reductions now being instituted in the miserly US programme, an international scandal and virtually invisible if Israel and other US Middle East interests are excluded. It includes, for example, twenty-five of 'the most sophisticated fighter-bombers in the world', the British press reports, a deal that 'slid through Congress with no objections by legislators and virtually no comment in the American media'. This is 'the first time such high-performance military equipment has been sold unrestricted and unamended abroad since the Second World War' ('sold' means funded by US military aid), a 'decisive enhancement of Israel's military capabilities, giving it the power to strike at potentially dangerous nations far beyond its borders: Iran, Iraq, Algeria, and Libya for example.' The US 'appears to be reappointing Israel as local deputy sheriff, a role which ended with the disappearance of the communist threat in the Middle East' – which, rhetoric aside, was never the real threat as the extended appointment once again reveals, and has indeed been official conceded.[16]

Though Israel's barring of development in the territories was well known, its extent came as a surprise even to the most knowledgeable observers when they had an opportunity to visit Jordan after the Israel–Jordan Peace Treaty of October 1994. The comparison is particularly apt, Danny Rubinstein observes, since the Palestinian populations are about as numerous on both sides of the Jordan, and the West Bank was somewhat more developed before the Israeli takeover in 1967. Having covered the territories with distinction for years, Rubinstein was well aware that the Israeli administration 'had purposely worsened the conditions under which Palestinians in the territories had to live'. Nonetheless, he was shocked and saddened to discover the startling truth.

'Despite Jordan's unstable economy and its being part of the Third World', he found, 'its rate of development is much higher than that of the West Bank, not to mention Gaza', administered by a very rich society which benefits from unparalleled foreign aid. While Israel has built roads only for the Jewish settlers, 'in Jordan people drive on new, multiple-lane highways, well-equipped with bridges and intersections.' Factories, commerce, hotels and universities have been developed in impoverished Jordan, at quite high levels. Virtually nothing similar has been allowed on the West Bank, apart from 'two small hotels in Bethlehem'. 'All universities in the territories were built solely with private funding and donations from foreign states, without a penny from Israel', apart from the Islamic University in Hebron, originally supported by Israel as part of its encouragement of Islamic fundamentalism to undermine the secular PLO, now a Hamas centre. Health services in the West Bank are 'extremely backward' in comparison with Jordan. 'Two large buildings in East Jerusalem, intended for hospitals and clinics to serve the residents of the West Bank, which the Jordanians were constructing in 1967, were turned into police buildings by the Israeli government', which also refused permits for factories in Nablus and Hebron under pressure from Israeli manufacturers who wanted a captive market without competition. 'The result is that the backward and poor Jordanian kingdom did much more for the Palestinians who lived in it than Israel', showing 'in an even more glaring form how badly the Israeli occupation had treated them'.

Electricity is available everywhere in Jordan, unlike the West Bank, where the great majority of Arab villages have only local generators that operate irregularly. 'The same goes for the water system. In arid Jordan, several large water projects . . . have turned the eastern bank of the Jordan valley into a dense and blooming agricultural area', while on the West Bank water supplies have been directed to the use of settlers and Israel itself – about five-sixths of West Bank water, according to Israeli specialists.[17]

As reported by the London *Financial Times* last summer [1994], 'Nothing symbolises the inequality of water consumption more than the fresh green lawns, irrigated flower beds, blooming gardens and swimming pools of Jewish settlements in the West Bank', while nearby Palestinian villages are denied the right to drill wells and have running water one day every few weeks, polluted by sewage, so that men have to drive to towns to fill up containers with water or to hire contractors to deliver it at fifteen times the cost. In summer

1995 the Israeli national water company Mekorot cut supplies to the southern and central parts of Gaza for twenty days because people had no money to pay their bills. While a handful of Israeli settlers run luxury hotels with swimming pools for guests and profit from water-intensive agriculture, Palestinians lack water to drink – or, increasingly, even food to eat, as the economy collapses, apart from wealthy Palestinians, who are doing fine, on the standard Third World model.

Individual cases clarify the general picture. For example, the village of Ubaydiya, where 8000 Palestinians were deprived of running water for eighteen months while the nearby Jewish settlements are 'flourishing in the desert' (though Mekorot did promise to restore service to deter a hearing at the High Court of Justice, with outcome unknown at the time of writing). Or Hebron, where thousands of people had no water from their pipes in August 1995. Journalist Amiram Cohen reports that in 'the hot days of summer', 1995, each Arab of Hebron received less than one-quarter of the water allotment of a resident of the nearly all-Jewish settlement of Kiryat Arba.

The radically discriminatory use of water resources should persist under Oslo II, which 'continues the old policy of keeping [Palestinians] from thirsting to death', one analyst in Israel observes, while 'not allowing the increases that would be necessary for economic growth'. Water is denied for Arab industry or agriculture, restrictions that do not hold for Jewish settlers. Meanwhile Israel itself will continue to use the waters of the West Bank under its claim of 'historic use' since the 1967 occupation. The Oslo II accords provide that 'both sides agree to coordinate the management of water and sewage resources and systems in the West Bank during the interim period', basically preserving the status quo. Only the waters of the occupied territories are subject to discussion, consistent with the general framework of capitulation.[18]

The Israel–Jordan Peace Treaty has provisions on 'achieving a comprehensive and lasting settlement of all the water problems between [Israel and Jordan]'. They are outlined by David Brooks of Canada's International Development Centre, a specialist on water resources of the region and a member of Canada's delegation to the Middle East Multilateral Peace Talks on water and the environment, who comments that the terms are not 'particularly remarkable as water agreements go', with one exception: 'what is omitted, or, more accurately, who is omitted. Not a word is said about water rights for the Palestinians, nor about giving them a role in managing the waters of the Jordan valley.' 'Palestinians are not even party to the negotiations', Brooke observes: 'Their omission is staggering given that most of the Lower Jordan River (from Kinneret to the Dead Sea) forms the border between Jordan and what is likely in the near future to be Palestinian, not Israeli, territory.'[19]

His basic point is correct, but the omission becomes less staggering when we depart from the rhetoric about what lies down the road and attend to its factual basis: specifically, to the fact that Israel has always made very clear its intention to retain the Jordan Valley within Greater Israel, so that Palestinian cantons that may some day be called 'a state' will be largely cut off from the outside. Effective control over Palestinian enclaves by Jordan and Israel, if that proves to be the outcome, will bring to a natural conclusion the co-operative efforts of Israel and Jordan's Hashemite monarchy that go back to the post-World War II origins of these states including the 1948 war.[20]

Neither Jordan nor Israel (nor the pre-state actors) has ever had any use for Palestinian nationalism, though there is a version that the US and Israel do advocate: Palestinian nationalism in the sense made explicit in the official US policy that provided the basis for the peace process initiated at Madrid in 1991. That conception had been spelled out in the Baker plan of December 1989, which identified the Shamir–Peres plan of Israel's coalition government as the sole 'initiative' to be considered in eventual negotiations. The basic principle of the Shamir–Peres–Baker plan was that there can be no 'additional Palestinian state in the Gaza district and in the area between Israel and Jordan' – the latter already a 'Palestinian state'. The terms of the Shamir–Peres–Baker plan, expressing the consensus of virtually the entire spectrum of US–Israeli politics, are scarcely to be found in the United States, and the occasional references involve substantial misrepresentation. The highly efficient suppression of official US policy makes good sense.[21]

The Jordan–Israel Treaty is a component of the 'truly new Middle East' that does receive attention in Western commentary, being far more significant than $1 billion stolen from Palestinians labouring under subhuman conditions or the assignment of crucial Palestinian resources to important partners in the peace process. Its major achievement is the integration of Israel within the US-dominated Middle East system. Long-standing tacit relations among participants are now becoming more overt and efficient, and Israel is taking on its intended role as a military-industrial-technological centre for the region (possibly financial centre as well). This goal was difficult to achieve as long as the Palestinian issue remained a festering sore, a source of unrest in the Arab world. But Arafat's acceptance of 'the peace of the victors', in the apparent hope of salvaging some shreds of his waning authority by becoming an agent of the powerful, has helped to suppress the Palestinian issue, at least for the present (there are other factors, including the disintegration of secular Arab nationalism and the disarray of the South generally). One notable consequence of this success is 'the real peace dividend for Israel', as the *Wall Street Journal* describes the fact that 'the barriers are now down in the fastest-growing markets in the world, which are in the Far East, not the Middle East'. The Middle East is already pretty much in Washington's pocket, but for a US outpost to position itself in the contested Asia–Pacific region is a useful further accomplishment.

These consequences of the Oslo peace process are reflected in the rapidly rising level of foreign investment in Israel, which is increasingly seen as 'the fulcrum of economic development in the region' (Lord Sterling, chairman of a major UK shipping company). 'Israel will look back on 1995 as the year when international finance and business discovered its thriving economy', the *Financial Times* observed – 'thriving' in the usual manner of 'economic miracles', mimicking its patron by achieving unusually high rates of inequality and dismantling social services.[22]

Another important component of the 'peace of the victors' is the end of even a gesture towards Palestinian refugees. The Oslo settlement effectively abolishes their 'right of return', endorsed unanimously by the UN General Assembly in 1948 as the most direct application of Article 13 of the Universal Declaration of Human Rights, adopted the previous day, and reiterated regularly since. Immediately after Oslo I, in another 'visionary' pronouncement, Rabin had dashed any hopes that refugees might return to the areas of Palestinian autonomy (let alone anywhere else). That is 'nonsense', he explained: 'if they expect tens of thousands, they live in a dream, an illusion.' Perhaps some 'increased family reunification', nothing more. While the Clinton administration offered $100 million to the PA, mostly for security forces (in contrast to $3 billion to Israel, perhaps twice that if we add other devices), it cut by $17 million the US contribution to UNRWA, the largest single employer in the Gaza Strip and responsible for 40 per cent of its health and education services as well as for Palestinian refugees elsewhere. Washington may be planning to terminate UNRWA, which 'Israel has historically loathed', Graham Usher observed. Breaking with earlier policies, the Clinton administration voted against all General Assembly resolutions pertaining to Palestinian refugees in 1993 and 1994, on the grounds that they 'prejudge the outcome of the ongoing peace process and should be solved by direct negotiations', now safely in the hands of the US and its clients. As a step towards dismantling UNRWA, its headquarters are to be moved to Gaza, which should effectively terminate international support for the 1.8 million Palestinian refugees in Jordan, Lebanon and Syria. The next step may be to defund it completely, UN sources report.[23]

III 'A Day of Awe'

The signing of Oslo II and the Rabin assassination received enormous attention and coverage. Typical headlines after the signing give the flavour. 'Israel agrees to quit West Bank'. 'Israel Ends Jews' Biblical Claim on the West Bank' in 'Rabin's historic trade with Arabs', a 'historic compromise'. 'Israelis, Palestinians find a painful peace', establishing an 'undeniable reality: The Palestinians are on their way to an independent state; the Jews are bidding farewell to portions of the Holy Land to which they have historically felt most linked'. 'Score One for Clinton'. 'At White House, symbols of a Day of Awe'.

Editorials added that 'the latest Israeli–Palestinian accord is a big one, making the historic move toward accommodation of the two peoples all but irreversible.' A Reuters chronology published here and abroad identified the Day of Awe, September 28, as the day on which 'Israel and the PLO sign agreement extending Palestinian rule to most of West Bank'. The *New York Times* lead story after the assassination reported that Rabin had 'conquered the ancient lands on the West Bank of the Jordan' and then 'negotiated the accord to eventually cede Israeli control of them to the Palestinians'. The major *Times* think piece on Rabin focused on the 'evolution' in his thinking that was 'taking place before your eyes', as 'his language underwent a remarkable transformation and so did his ideas about peace with the Palestinians'; 'it was astonishing how far he had roamed from where he stood in 1992'. The former Jerusalem bureau chief of the *Washington Post* reported that 'when Rabin offered the Israelis the possibility of "separation" – of walling off the Gaza Strip and West Bank and getting Palestinians out of sight and out of mind – the majority responded with enthusiasm.' 'Those who murdered Rabin, and those who incited them, didn't do so because they opposed plans to create a Palestinian Bantustan', the *New Statesman* correspondent reported from Jerusalem, chiding Edward Said for thinking otherwise. 'No: they knew that the course Rabin was charting would lead, unless stopped, to a Palestinian state.'[24]

That's a fair sample.

One intriguing feature is that the factual assertions are not even close to true. Israel did not 'agree to quit West Bank' or 'End Jews' Biblical Claim on the West Bank'. It signed no 'agreement extending Palestinian rule to most of the West Bank' or 'to eventually cede Israeli control of West Bank lands to the Palestinians'. Rabin never so much as hinted at an offer 'of walling off the Gaza Strip and West Bank'; quite the contrary, he was adamant, clear and consistent in stressing that nothing of the sort was even a remote possibility. And although Rabin's 'ideas about peace' had indeed 'roamed far' from 1992, it was not quite in the direction indicated: in 1992, as in 1988 and before, Rabin was advocating the traditional Labour Party stand that Israel should keep about 40 per cent of the occupied territories, not the far greater proportion he accepted on the Day of Awe.

As for what is 'undeniable' and 'irreversible', readers can make their own guesses, recognizing that these are speculations lacking any serious factual basis. Those who 'know' that Rabin's course would lead to an authentic Palestinian state, not 'a Palestinian Bantustan', might want to explain why they dismiss out of hand not all relevant facts, but also the explicit statements of the leadership, not only Rabin, but also Shimon Peres, even more of a 'visionary dove' than Rabin. Explaining the Oslo II accords to a gathering of ambassadors in Jerusalem, Peres responded to the question whether the permanent settlement could involve a Palestinian state by making it crystal clear that 'this solution about which everyone is thinking and which is what you want will never happen'. Two weeks before, journalist Amnon Barzilai reports further in *Ha'aretz*, Peres responded with a resounding 'No' when asked at a meeting with the editorial board of *Newsweek* whether a Palestinian state might be the eventual outcome. He proceeded with a 'learned explanation', which, however, was never completed, because the verdict in the O. J. Simpson trial was just then broadcast so that the meeting had to stop, and afterwards the *Newsweek* editors were 'too excited about the verdict' to return to his thoughts.[25]

Part of the standard story is indeed true. We should 'Score One for

Clinton' and observe what happened with Awe. The scale of the victory can only be appreciated by reviewing the history, almost totally suppressed in the US – and, quite interestingly, by now largely forgotten abroad, not only in Europe but in Latin America and elsewhere. The facts are not in dispute, and need not be reviewed here once again. In brief, from 1967 to 1971 the US led the international consensus in support of a diplomatic settlement based on UN 242, which it understood as implying full peace in return for full Israeli withdrawal from the territories occupied in 1967 (with perhaps minor and mutual modifications). When President Sadat of Egypt accepted these terms in February 1971 in what Rabin describes in his memoirs as a 'famous . . . milestone' on the road to peace, the US had to decide whether to keep to the policy it had crafted or join its Israeli ally in rejecting it. Kissinger insisted on 'stalemate' – no negotiations, only force – and won out in the internal conflict, setting the US on a lonely path as leader of the rejectionist camp, not only ignoring Palestinian rights (as did UN 242 and Sadat's offer as well) but also rejecting one of the two paired requirements of UN 242: Israeli withdrawal. US isolation deepened a few years later as the international consensus shifted to support for a two-state settlement incorporating the wording of UN 242, compelling Washington to veto Security Council resolutions, vote alone annually at the General Assembly (with Israel, and occasionally some other client state), and block all other diplomatic initiatives, a task that became increasingly complex from the early 1980s as the PLO more forcefully called for negotiations leading to mutual accommodation, but was handled with ease, thanks to the services of the intellectual community.[26]

It was not until the Gulf War established 'What We Say Goes', in George Bush's words, that the US was able to initiate the Madrid negotiations, an authentic 'peace process' because it was unilaterally run by Washington and restricted to its extremist agenda. The establishment of Washington's rejectionist stand in Oslo I, and its affirmation in Oslo II, is an impressive achievement.

The character of the triumph is revealed in a different way when we compare the reaction to the Rabin assassination with other cases, the most obvious one being the assassination of Abu Jihad (Khalil al-Wazir) by Israeli commandos in Tunis in April 1988. This act of international terrorism was probably intended mostly for morale-building in Israel at the height of the popular uprising (Intifada), which Israel was then unable to suppress, despite considerable brutality. On little credible evidence, Abu Jihad was charged with directing the Intifada, a claim reported as fact in the US media, which did, however, recognize that Abu Jihad was known 'as one of the more moderate and thoughtful officials in the PLO hierarchy' (*Washington Post*). The *Post* also reported that 'many Israelis celebrated his killing as evidence of Israel's willingness and ability to strike back at alleged terrorist leaders' and that the assassination evoked 'widespread applause from Israelis, ranging from the liberal left to the far right'. The State Department condemned 'this act of political assassination', but that was the end of the matter. There were no regrets, flags at half-mast, laments about the fate of the peace process, or other moving commentary. Abu Jihad was not a 'martyr for peace'.[27]

Why not? One possible reason is that he was a terrorist; true, but plainly irrelevant. His terrorist career, while bloody enough, did not even bring him close to those honoured as 'men of peace', including Rabin and Peres, or still more obviously, the statesmen who praise them. Another possible reason is that he opposed the 'peace process'. That too is true, at least in a technical sense. He did oppose US–Israeli rejectionism, joining most of the rest of the world in advocating a two-state settlement to be achieved by negotiations leading to mutual recognition. If we adopt the usage of doctrinal convention, he opposed 'the peace process', insisting on something other than a peace of the victors in which the Palestinians become 'just another crushed nation'.

Adopting the technical usage, we can make sense of the weird comments of Dennis Ross, chief Middle East negotiator for the Bush and Clinton administrations, reported by *Times* Middle East specialist Elaine Sciolino. Ross describes how in March 1993 Rabin presented Clinton with a 'brilliant, cogent, clear-cut argument' explaining 'exactly why the delegates then negotiating on behalf of the Palestinians would not be able to deliver' – to deliver a non-rejectionist settlement recognizing the rights of the indigenous population alongside of Israel, Sciolino refrains from adding. But the PLO refused to accept Rabin's brilliant argument: 'at that point they hadn't demonstrated they were prepared to make peace', Ross 'recalled'; Sciolino's term 'recalled' implies that the recollection is accurate (one doesn't 'recall' what didn't happen), as indeed it is, if 'making peace' means accepting US–Israeli terms, rejecting UN 242 and any thought of self-determination. When we adopt the conventions, Ross's statement is transformed from gibberish to simple truth, and Sciolino is not misleading her readers by reporting all of this as factually accurate. A little confusing perhaps, but with a proper education it all works out.[28]

We might ask what the authentic martyr for peace was up to when Abu Jihad was assassinated – at Rabin's 'enthusiastic' initiative. *Times* correspondent John Kifner reported from Jerusalem. Then defence minister, Rabin had ordered his troops to suppress the Intifada by brutality and terror, and shortly after, to attack villages using plastic bullets, because 'more casualties . . . is precisely our aim', 'our purpose is to increase the number of [wounded] among those who take part in violent activities'. Their 'violent activities' are to dare to assert that they are free, Rabin explained: 'We want to get rid of the illusion of some people in remote villages that they have liberated themselves', and by military attacks that produce 'more casualties', we 'make it clear to them where they live and within which framework', teaching familiar lessons in Western Civ. Shortly after, when the US was driven to a 'dialogue' with the PLO in a last-ditch effort to derail their increasingly irritating calls for negotiations leading to mutual recognition, Rabin assured a delegation of Peace Now leaders that the dialogue was of no significance, merely a delaying action intended to grant Israel at least a year to suppress the Intifada by 'harsh military and economic pressure' – exactly what happened, allowing the 'peace process' to resume on course.[29]

Plainly, Rabin is a martyr for peace and Abu Jihad a terrorist who deserved his fate.

We might also ask what Washington's men of peace were doing at that crucial moment in 1988 when the US and Israel were desperately trying to fend off the growing threat of diplomatic settlement. The leading figure among them was surely George Shultz, untainted by Reaganite scandal. Just before Abu Jihad was assassinated, Shultz was pursuing his 'peace mission' in Jordan, where he 'explained his understanding of the aspirations of Palestinians', Elaine Sciolino reported, offering the example of the United States, where Shultz is a Californian and George Bush a Texan, but they have no problem living in harmony. Palestinian aspirations can be handled in the same civilized way, under whatever arrangements US–Israeli power dictate; blandly reported, plainly uncontroversial.[30]

Shultz's understanding of the adversary's aspirations has echoes elsewhere, as recent news reminds us. A week before Rabin's assassination, Fathi Shiqaqi, head of Islamic Jihad, was shot in the back and killed in Malta, 'probably by Israeli agents', the *Times* reported. As in the case of Abu Jihad, Israel did not take responsibility, though the press did so with 'huge headlines', Israeli correspondent Haim Baram reports, extolling 'the long arm of Israel' and 'the night of revenge', while articles praised the murder and warned that 'Israel will punish whoever is responsible for the killing of Jews', and 'both Rabin and Peres hinted gleefully that Mossad was involved'. Peres commented that 'Islamic Jihad are killers, so it's one less killer' – true enough, though again one might observe that Peres's own achievements put them well in the shade, not to speak of George Shultz.[31]

Shiqaqi's position on peace was the mirror image of Shultz's. Shiqaqi probably understood the 'aspirations of Israelis' in the Shultz style, and would have accepted an outcome in which Jews lived submissively under Palestinian rule. On non-racist assumptions, then, either both Shultz and Shiqaqi are men of peace, or both are murderous terrorists who deserve the fate that only one has suffered. Fortunately, such assumptions are unthinkable, so we need not pursue the exercise.

While Abu Jihad and (obviously) Fathi Shiqaqi do not enter the Pantheon, some Arabs do. When Rabin was assassinated, alongside the front-page story in the *Boston Globe* reporting that 'peace has claimed another victim', the adjacent column recalled the assassination of Anwar Sadat – who qualifies as a peacemaker not because of his acceptance of a full peace treaty with Israel in terms of official US policy in 1971, a 'famous milestone' banned from history, but because of his visit to Jerusalem in 1977, opening the way to the Camp David settlement, admissible because it kept to Washington's rejectionist demands.[32]

IV Power and Propaganda

The phrase 'Day of Awe' is not out of place. The US has carried out a very impressive power play. The events are a remarkable testimony to the rule of force in international affairs and the power of doctrinal management in a sociocultural setting in which successful marketing is the highest value and the intellectual culture is obedient and unquestioning. The victory is not only apparent in the terms of Oslo I and II and the facts on the ground, but also in the demolition of unacceptable history, the easy acceptance of the most transparent falsehoods, and the state of international opinion, now so submissive on this issue that commentators and analysts have literally forgotten the position they and their governments advocated only a few years ago, and can even see that 'Israel agrees to quit West Bank' when they know perfectly well that nothing of the sort is true. That is really impressive, and instructive.

The most important aspect of any doctrinal system is the way issues are framed and presented, the presuppositions that are insinuated to bound discussion, remaining invisible, beyond reflection or analysis. In the old Soviet Union, the game was over if the question under debate was whether the Kremlin had made a mistake in its defence of Czechoslovakia and Afghanistan; or in Nazi Germany, if the issue was whether the threat of the Jews to civilization had been exaggerated. In the present case, what is important is the conquest of the notion 'peace process', which must be deprived of its meaning and restricted to a technical usage that ensures that the game is over before it begins. That has been done, very effectively, not by the exercise of any particular skill, but by sheer power. It is by now unimaginable that the term 'peace process' would refer to the effort to achieve peace.

To be sure, that concept of 'peace process' is too broad. Everyone wants peace, even Hitler and Genghis Khan. The question always is: on what terms? Under whose direction? In our highly disciplined intellectual culture, the answer to those questions is a virtual reflex: on Washington's terms, and under its direction.

The conventions have useful consequences. One is that the phrase 'the US government is trying to advance the peace process' is true by definition, whatever Washington happens to be doing – say, undermining diplomatic efforts to achieve peace. And the phrase 'the US government is trying to undermine the peace process' is meaningless, unthinkable, even if plainly true, as it often is, dramatically so in the present case for twenty-five years.

Though there is no space to review the matter here, the lead domestic story (the budget) reflects a similar achievement of the doctrinal institutions. The only issue is how long it should take to balance the budget, seven years or a bit longer. There are other possible questions. Is that what the population wants? Demonstrably not, by very large margins. Does the plan make sense? It surely does for some sectors, those that hope to maintain a powerful nanny state for the rich while the majority 'learn responsibility' under rigorous market discipline, enforced by the unaccountable private tyrannies that are to rule untroubled by unruly noises from below. But does it make sense for the health of the economy understood in terms that have to do with human interest and concerns, even economic growth? That is hardly obvious, to put it mildly. But no such questions arise once we have restricted debate to a spectrum bounded at one extreme by statist reactionaries of the Gingrich variety, and at the other by the president, who tells us: 'Let's be clear: of course – of course – we need to balance the budget', though not quite as fast as those a few millimetres to the right would like, while 'centrists' like Paul Tsongas and Bill Bradley seek a more 'moderate' course between the extremists of left and right. And if Americans think they oppose budget balancing under any realistic conditions, they can be reassured that they are wrong about their beliefs by tuning in to the ultraliberal media, for example, National Public Radio, where co-host Robert Siegel of 'All Things Considered' assures them that 'Americans voted for a balanced budget', detailing the cuts in social spending pursuant to the public will (and irrelevantly, over its overwhelming opposition, during the election and since, at least if opinion polls are anywhere near accurate).[33]

In case after case, that is just what we find. Open discussion is a fine thing, as great as democracy itself, if only it is kept within the bounds that support power and privilege. It's about as close to a true historical generalization as one can find that respectability is won by adhering to these fundamental principles, and that rending these chains is a first step towards freedom and justice.

Notes

1. *Yediot Ahronot*, Oct. 6; Serge Schmemann, *NYT*, Nov. 17; editorial, *Ha'aretz*, Oct. 6 (*Middle East International*), 1995. Rubinstein, *Palestine-Israel Journal*, Winter 1995. *Report on Israeli Settlement*, Foundation for Middle East Peace (Washington), 5.6, Nov. 1995.

2. Ibid. Benvenisti, *Ha'aretz*, May 12, 1994 (Israel Shahak, 'Translations from the Hebrew Press', June 1994).

3. For recent reviews and updates, see my *Necessary Illusions* (South End, 1989); *World Orders, Old and New* (Columbia, 1994); *Powers and Prospects* (South End, 1996). Norman Finkelstein, *Image and Reality of the Israel–Palestine Conflict* (Verso, 1995); *The End of Palestine* (Minnesota, 1996). Naseer Aruri, *The Obstruction of Peace* (Common Courage, 1995). On 1993–95, see Edward Said, *Peace and its Discontents* (Vintage, 1995) and Graham Usher, *Palestine in Crisis* (Pluto, 1995). One recent standard source is Mark Tessler, *A History of the Israeli–Palestinian Conflict* (Indiana, 1994), one of the better histories, though not without serious flaws, particularly with regard to the topics considered here; see *Powers and Prospects* on one crucial case.

4. Usher, op. cit.

5. Serge Schmemann, Elaine Sciolino, *NYT*, Nov. 14; Schmemann, *NYT*, Nov. 29; Curtius, Nov. 29, 1995. Reuters, Oct. 13, 1995. Curtius, *BG*, July 30, 1993. On Israel's 1993 invasion, which has largely been excised from history, see my article in *Z* magazine, Sept. 1993. *Economist*, July 15; Reuter, *Guardian*, July 10, 1995. Fisk, *Independent*, Oct. 22, 1994.

6. Rabin, *Yediot Ahronot*, Oct. 3, 1993. Kissinger, *Australian Financial Review*, Nov. 13, 1995.

7. Barak, Benvenisti, *Ha'aretz*, Oct. 12 (*The Other Front*, Jerusalem, October, 1995); 'The Taba Interim Agreement, Another Capitulation by Arafat', *Ha'aretz*, July 6 (Shahak translations, Sept. 1995). Sharon, Ethan Bronner, *Boston Globe*, Nov. 17; Harel, Schmemann, op. cit.; Beilin, *Ma'ariv*, Sept. 27 (Shahak translations); Rabin, *Report on Israeli Settlement*, Nov. 1995; Rabin and press reports, *Ha'aretz*, Oct. 6 and *Kol Ha'ir*, Oct. 13 (*Challenge* [Jerusalem], Dec. 1995).

8. Reinhart, *Ha'aretz*, May 27, 1994. Aineri, cited by John Battersby, *Christian Science Monitor*, Sept. 28, 1995.

9. Interview, *Ha'aretz*, June 4, 1982.

10. See *Necessary Illusions* and my 'Israel's Role in U.S. Foreign Policy', in Zachary Lockman & Joel Beinin, eds., *Intifida* (South End, 1989).

11. *The Other Front*, Oct. 1995; *News from Within*, Nov. 1995. For further details, see references in note 3.

12. Shahak, *MEI*, 17 Nov. 1995; *Ideology as a Central Factor in Israeli Policies* (Hebrew), May–June 1995. Susskind, *Challenge*, No. 32; Levy, *Ha'aretz*, April 23, 1995.

13. *B'Tselem Report*, May 1995, citing Sarah Kaminker; summary and excerpts in *Ha'aretz*, May 15; *News from Within*, June 1995. Also Aaron Back and Eitan Felner, senior staff members of B'Tselem, *Tikkun* 10.4, 1995. Graham Usher, *MEI*,, 12 May 1995. See also Clyde Haberman, *NYT*, May 14,15, 1995.

14. Sarah Kaminker and Associates, *Planning and Housing Issues in East Jerusalem*, June 1994.

15. Israeli Ministry of Defence, *Jerusalem Post*, Feb. 15, 1985; cited by Anthony Coon, *Town Planning Under Military Occupation* (Al Haq, Ramallah, 1992). Shaked, *Yediot Ahronot*, Oct. 13, 1995. Moshe Semyonov and Noah Lewin-Epstein, *Hewers of Wood and Drawers of Water* (Cornell, 1987). Shlomo Abramovitch, *Sheva Yamim*, March 3; editor Hanoch Marmari, *Ha'aretz*, March 9 (Shaha translations, April); Ha'etzni, *Ma'ariv*, May 5, 1995.

16. Kav La'Oved *Newsletter*, Oct. 1995. Aid, see *Powers and Prospects*. Said Aburish and Tim Llewellyn, *Independent*, 23 June, 1995.

17. Rubinstein, 'Two Banks of the Jordan', *Ha'aretz*, Feb. 13, 1995 (Shahak, 'Translations,' April). See *World Orders, Powers and Prospects*, for further details.

18. Julian Ozanne and David Gardner, *FT*, Aug. 8; Stephen Langfur, Allegra Pachecho (Society of St Yves), *Challenge*, Nov.–Dec. (also *MEI*, 3 Nov.); Cohen, *Ha'aretz*, Aug. 21, 1995.

19. *Outlook* (Vancouver), Oct./Nov. 1995.

20. See particularly Avi Shlaim, *Collusion across the Jordan* (Columbia, 1988).

21. See my 'Art of Evasion: Diplomacy in the Middle East', *Z*, Jan. 1990; *Deterring Democracy* (Hill & Wang, 1992), 'Afterword'; *World Orders*, chap. 3.

22. Amy Dockser Marcus, *WSJ*, Nov. 2; Julian Ozanne, *FT*, Oct. 24, 1995. On the tacit alliance, see my April 1977 article in *Le Monde diplomatique*, reprinted in *Towards a New Cold War* (Pantheon, 1982). It is most illuminating, but beyond the scope of this discussion, to see how these facts are finally entering mainstream scholarship.

23. Rabin, interview, *Jerusalem Post International Edition*, week ending Oct. 16, 1993. Usher, *MEI*, 6 Jan. 1995.

24. Derek Brown, *Manchester Guardian Weekly*, lead story, Oct. 1; John Battersby, *CSM*, Sept. 28; Ethan Bronner, *BG*, Sept. 28; R.W. Apple, *NYT*, Sept. 29; David Shribman, *BG*, Sept. 29; editorial, *WP* weekly, Oct. 2–8; Reuters, *BG*, Nov. 5, *FT*, Nov 6; Serge Schmemann, *NYT*, Nov. 5; Clyde Haberman, *NYT*, Nov. 6, 1995; Glenn Frankel, *WP* weekly, Nov. 27–Dec. 3; Stephen Howe, *NS*, 17 Nov. 1995.

25. Barzilai, *Ha'aretz*, Oct. 24, 1995.

26. For documentation, see references in note 3.

27. Loren Jenkins, *WP*, April 17; Glenn Frankel, *WP*, April 18, 20; Robert Pear, *NYT*, April 19, 1988.

28. Sciolino, *NYT*, Nov. 6. 1995.

29. Kifner, *NYT*, April 23, 1988. See *Necessary Illusions*.

30. Ibid., citing *NYT*, April 6, 8, 1988.

31. Serge Schmemann, *NYT*, Nov. 5; Baram, Graham Usher, *MEI*, 3 Nov. 1995.

32. David Shribman, Peter Canellos, *BG*, Nov. 5, 1995.

33. AP, *BG*, Oct. 1, 1995, reporting Clinton's radio address. NPR, May 12, 1995.

20

Critique and Analysis in Media Studies: Media Criticism as Practical Action

Paul Jalbert

Introduction

The concern over what counts as analysis in communication studies is general and mass media studies in particular has generated mixed commentary on the part of several reviewers of work which is informed by ethnomethodological insights and which simultaneously explicates the critical expressions intelligible therein. My analysis of the US network television coverage of the Lebanon War in 1982[1] can serve to demonstrate this concern. The treatment of that work by critics both positive and negative has been peculiar. The negative assessments almost uniformly complained that I had produced a 'polemic' regarding the coverage and not an 'analysis' of it. The positive comments indicated that I had been successful in 'exposing' media partisanship, while also arguing that, in so doing, I had transgressed the boundaries of the analytical project and crossed over into the 'critique' of ideological positions. While it is true that critical assessments along ideological lines could emerge as a by-product of the explication of the meaning-options made available to members[2] in the reports I analysed, such critical assessments (e.g. of 'bias') were ascribed to *me* as *my* assessments of the coverage rather than to *possible members with certain specifiable background commitments*. This was a curious situation and it encouraged me to become clearer about the methodological, conceptual and analytical enterprise in which I am engaged. The result is this essay.

What Should Analysis Look Like?

The task of analysis of media reportage is to attempt to explicate, to unveil the social constructions that allow people to make sense of the world: the access that I seek to do this, the medium through which I seek to make this available, is through the study of mass communication media representations of events and states of affairs. I am *not* trying to uncover *which*

'meanings' particular members actually discern, but to elucidate such meanings as *could* intelligibly be achieved. These meanings can logically be argued
to inhere in actual texts in virtue of their organization etc.; the issue is what
is available to be grasped from them. While we do not know how many possible understandings could be derived from a particular text or
communication, we can nonetheless make arguments of the *kinds* of understandings that can be achieved, and, in many instances, for *very specific*
understandings which can be derived. To make such arguments does *not*
mean that the analyst is 'instructing' people as to which meanings are actually achieved or *should* be achieved; although much of media 'analysis' does
exactly that (see Anderson and Sharrock, 1979).

If, in the logic of the explication, it so happens that certain renditions, certain versions of the world, become elucidated and, in doing so, the results
look like, have the appearance of being, a critical formulation, that *should not
be seen as a departure from the analysis. The 'critical edge' is itself an achieved phenomenon on the part of a possible recipient and the analyst.* What ends up looking
like a critique a *fortiori* emanating from the explicative analysis should not be
case aside as undercutting an *analytical* programme. Why should a critical
implication, inferential option, etc. undercut the analysis? Why should the
analyst be accused of engaging in a polemic because some of those critical
factors emerge in the analysis? Aside from the very real possibility that the
analyst may himself[3] be critical of a text he is analysing – one of the goals of
the analyst could be to be critical – the critical implications attendant upon
the analysis is not necessarily the product of a diatribe or a polemic. For
example, media analysts obviously will adopt any one of the range of existing
ethical positions concerning the abortion controversy. Consider the case of
one such analyst who characterizes the logic of categorization embodied in
the dispute in the following way: wherever a protagonist in the controversy
speaks of abortion as a matter of 'murdering babies', he obliterates the conceptual distinctions between 'babies', 'foetuses', 'embryos', 'gametes' and
'zygotes', along with their very different ethical and even theological implications. Moreover, the available categorization of anti-abortion activists as
'pro-life' can be argued to postulate an implicit contrast to a derogatory construction 'anti-life', i.e. what would it mean to be 'anti-life'? Surely, this would
be to beg the question. It may very well be argued that such an account of the
logic of the controversy already embodies elements of '*pro*-abortion' reasoning. However, there is absolutely nothing which precludes an analyst trading
upon his own *critical* resources for the production of an analysis of meaning-
options: after all, these are not idiosyncratic to him but rather elucidate
exactly the parameters of a critical interpretation, just as an ethnomethodologist has no choice but to draw upon his practical knowledge as
common-sense resources in an elucidation of the *logic* of any such resources.
As Turner argues:

> At every step of the way, inevitably, the sociologist will continue to employ his
> socialized competence, while continuing to make explicit *what* these resources

are and *how* he employs them. I see no alternative to these procedures, except to pay no explicit attention to one's socialized knowledge while continuing to use it as an indispensable aid. In short, sociological discoveries are ineluctably discoveries *from within* the society. (1974: 205)

This also applies to media analysts in terms of their deployment of 'socialized competence' or common sense resources, not excluding their *critical* faculties. The issues here are: to avoid explicit *advocacy* of a contending position within the analysis itself; to be able to identify succinctly the parameters of socially distributed points-of-view with which one may be in personal disagreement as well as those with which one may be in agreement; and to argue for an analysis without presupposing the validity (or otherwise) of the critical viewpoint being advanced. Often, those best able to elucidate the structure of a particular argument may well be among its most committed protagonists. However, rather than construe this as a defect, it should be appreciated as a potential advantage. Unless all we wish to read, study and analyse are treatments of matters sympathetic from the outset to our own commitments and presuppositions, in which case we will forever shield ourselves from an elucidation of our own taken-for-granted ways of reasoning, arguing and using language in general, the only way we can have analytical access to the cultural phenomena by which the concept of 'criticality' can be measured is to recognize its character as *an emergent feature* of the actual analysis. Moreover, the analyst engaged in such explications should not be accused of *distorting* analysis for the sake of a 'critique' or a 'polemic'. On the contrary, in so far as critical posture can itself *facilitate* analysis of some contested position, argument or text, why should we impoverish the domain of analysis? Max Weber made a similar claim in different historical circumstances in his essay 'The Meaning of "Ethical Neutrality" in Sociology and Economics':

> One of our foremost jurists once explained, in discussing his opposition to the exclusion of socialists from university posts, that he too would not be willing to accept an 'anarchist' as a teacher of law since anarchists deny the validity of law in general – and he regarded his argument as conclusive. My own opinion is exactly the opposite. An anarchist can surely be a good legal scholar. And if he is such, then indeed the Archimedean point of his convictions, which is outside the conventions and presuppositions which are so self-evident to us, can *equip him to perceive problems in the fundamental postulates of legal theory which escape those who take them for granted.* (1949: 7; emphasis added)

Weber was not endorsing anarchism as a political philosophy in this comment: he was taking stock of the kind of intellectual insight which can be won by adopting such a (critical) vantage-point as a methodological device whether or not the one who adopts it does so for more than a methodological purpose. I propose that our earlier example pertaining to the use of categories taken from a consideration of the abortion controversy is exactly analogous.

Within the context of ethnomethodological inquiries, a related issue has arisen which requires some comment. Ethnomethodologists are required to analyse practical actions, including (centrally) communicative actions, without any commitment to their adequacy, correctness or otherwise. This policy of 'ethnomethodological indifference' is then sometimes held to preclude the kind of methodological device under discussion whereby adopting a *critical* standpoint toward some phenomenon can enable us to obtain access to aspects of its organization, logic or structure otherwise not readily available. According to Garfinkel and Sacks:

> Ethnomethodological studies of formal structures are directed to the study of such phenomena, seeking to describe members' accounts of formal structures wherever and by whomever they are done, while abstaining from all judgements of their adequacy, value, importance, necessity, practicality, success, or consequentiality. We refer to this procedural policy as 'ethnomethodological indifference'. (1970: 345)

In the course of analytical practice, however, such a policy has its own logical limitations: in what sense could it be considered 'indifferent', for example, to conceptualize the practice of 'water divination' as a *reasoned* procedure as distinct from, say, mysticism or irrationality? Could ethnomethodologists 'indifferently' treat astrological or phrenological judgments as 'achievements' of reason in contrast to 'defects' of reason? Garfinkel and Sacks themselves actually include 'divinational reasoning' alongside legal and psychiatric reasoning as if they were unproblematically equivalent:

> Persons doing ethnomethodological studies can 'care' no more or less about professional sociological reasoning than they can 'care' about the practices of legal reasoning, conversational reasoning, divinational reasoning, psychiatric reasoning, and the rest. (1970: 346)

I do not deny the importance of striving to bracket off assumptively theoretical treatments of reasoning and activity as far as is possible. My only point here is to draw attention to the fact that some phenomena are *constituted* by 'judgements of their adequacy, value . . . success, or consequentiality', such as memory, the achievement of gender, making a scientific discovery, or arriving at a determination that someone has committed suicide, all of which phenomena have been investigated ethnomethodologically. After all, a recollection is not an *apparent* recollection, a scientific discovery is not a failed attempt at one, etc. Given these inherent limitations to the implementation of a strict policy of 'ethnomethodological indifference', and given Weber's argument in favour of adopting a critical standpoint as a methodological procedure for identifying and elucidating fundamental assumptions in a domain of human behaviour, I see no reason to limit ourselves as analysts to orientations exclusive of *critical* ones. The only caveat is not to transgress the boundaries between explication and advocacy under the auspices of analysis.

In dealing with media representations of controversies, political phenomena and similar areas of investigation, analysis is to be understood as
anti-intentionalist. It is rather *conventionalist*. There is neither the evidence
nor the argumentation provided to support ascribing to actual reporters
intentions to bias, to under-report, etc. The only issue is, *using the texts and
only the texts, the communicated reports and only the reports, as data,* how to provide
for whatever viewings such materials can be claimed to make available to
viewers. Naturally, to a critical recipient, bias or neutrality can be determined,
whereas, to a non-critical or counter-critical recipient, these dimensions of
assessment do not become relevant. Whatever dimensions of assessment can
be made are intelligible/invokable *only if these are logical options in the first
instance.* That is, some reports cannot logically be determined in any way, for
any recipient, to exhibit bias of a particular sort, just as other reports for any
recipient cannot possibly (i.e. logically) be found to exhibit neutrality in
respect of some position. In my work on the coverage of the Lebanon War, I
encountered frequently the objection from reviewers that I had tried to
demonstrate bias. This is not the case: what I had tried to demonstrate was
that a recipient *could have logical grounds for discerning bias within a communicative object.* Whether he does, or should, is not my concern. *Whether he
would* is the issue, and the only issue, I address analytically. Moreover, if we are
looking at what could be understood, and one such understanding has a critical character, then what does it look like? How is it achieved? Surely, this is
as worthy of analysis as any other comprehension option.

The methodological issue at stake here is this: a member may view 'bias'
etc. in a report only given his background knowledge/belief(s), moral orientations and like commitments. However, against any such background
(which can be described as a possible – even a conventional – background for
viewing a report), how could this inform an orientation to a text? Surely, we
can analyse the options for a characterization any text embodies, *along with
a description of various backgrounds (e.g. historical knowledge/belief, political perspective, etc.) for its reception*, and arrive at a conclusion such as: against
background *B*, text *T* can, in virtue of its analysable intelligibility struc-
tures/devices, be heard as, inter alia, biased (for or against position *P*) or
neutral. Other dimensions of assessment available to members include:
balanced/unbalanced; accurate/inaccurate; partisan/non-partisan; complete/
incomplete; objective/subjective, etc. It takes logical, ethnomethodological
and linguistic analysis to show 'the *how*' of any such achieved understanding
that members may arrive at.

This approach proposes that the 'text' (the embodiment of categorization
practices and conceptual arrangements through them) be the object of
inquiry. While this is not a new approach in principle, there have been some
orientations to texts which have created problems. For example, due to a
Kantian prejudice, a traditional conception has been to think of texts as *passive*, inert phenomena, requiring the activity of the mind of a viewer to
impose structure, intelligibility or otherwise upon them.[4] Against this, a more
recent argument has proposed that the text is itself *active* (Smith, 1982) in

organizing whatever orientations a member *can* logically find *in* it. However, we should not take this position to mean that we are substituting a model of an active text and passive mind for the Kantian one of an active mind and a passive text: rather, *both are active*! In this sense, we have outlined a method-ological procedure to elucidate conjointly the structures of textual organization and design with respect to the analysis of available backgrounds for orienting them. (By 'mind' here, of course, we are not involving any Cartesian category of a *res cogitans* – we could just as well say 'member', 'viewer', 'hearer', 'reader', 'listener', etc.)

The Matrix of Criticality and its Permutations

There are many interrelated levels at which the concept of 'criticality' can operate in our domain of interest. Consider, as a first approximation, the fol-lowing distinctions (often conflated or overlooked): the *non-theoretical* recipient of a text can be critical of (a) the text, (b) the producer of the text, (c) the organization for which the producer of the text works, etc. The *theo-retical* critic can be critical of (a) the text, (b), a given non-theoretical characterization of it, (c) a given background commitment on the part of a non-theoretical recipient of it, (d) the background commitment of a rival theoretical recipient of it, (e) the producer of it, (f) the organization for which the producer works, etc. The analyst, *by contrast*, who restricts himself to that form of analysis which begins and ends with the *text*, which locates the *text* at the centre of his analytical attention, is *never* interested in criticizing producers or recipients, their background commitments or organizational affiliations: he is interested only in portraying as faithfully as possible the intelligibility structures and devices inhering in the text as well as the back-ground commitments which interact with any such structures or devices so as to generate a given possible understanding and assessment of it. In so far as some such assessments can be demonstrably critical of a text (and, by transi-tivity, of its producer, his affiliation, etc.) they also need to be grounded in the possibilities made available by the analysis of the text. To provide for the log-ical option of criticality of a text is not *eo ipso* to concur in that assessment as one that *should* be adduced. Should we discover, for example, that a given text makes available for someone of a given background commitment the determination that *X* is the case whereas *X* is not the case *in fact*, must we, as a matter of *analytical strategy*, state that *X* is not the case in fact lest we be taken to concur in its facticity? Surely not. (The converse can also be proposed: namely that when a text makes available that *X* is not the case, whereas in fact *it is*, the analyst must say so as a part of his analysis – again surely not.) To claim that this is essential *for analysis* is to commit the fundamental error of arguing that an analyst must be *complicit* with one specific account of text and viewer as a *condition of analysis*. The fallacy involved in this, however, should not be confused with the perfectly reasonable proposal that, given a text *T*, its analysis and a description of background commitment(s) *B*, position *P* can be found as generatable by *T* in its interaction with *B*, where *B* may very well

be defensible, conventional knowledge (or indefensible, conventional ignorance) of a particular sort, or where P may well be indefensible (or
defensible) from other points of view.

Just because an elucidation of some P given some T and B may make some
fellow analyst *uncomfortable* (politically, ethically), this is insufficient reason
(a) for their refusing to grant, on *technical* grounds, the claim that P was
indeed a generated option from the interaction of T and B and (b) for their
discrediting and/or rejecting an analyst's work. For example, it can be shown
that, given a specific background:

B^1: Acceptance of an historical account of the West Bank and Gaza Strip
which depicts it as an unjustified occupation of other people's territory.

a specific text:

T: 'The new arrivals from the Soviet Union were taken to their homes in
Judea and Samaria to enjoy their new-found freedom from anti-semitism.'

can generate position:

P^1: 'T is biased in favour of the Israeli official position.'

Now, consider the *gestalt* opposite. Holding T constant, but varying B, T
can generate a different P. Thus, with background:

B^2: The West Bank and Gaza Strip were historically and rightfully Jewish
under the biblical names of Judea and Samaria.

text:

T: 'The new arrivals from the Soviet Union were taken to their new homes
in Judea and Samaria to enjoy their new-found freedom from anti-semitism.'

can generate:

P^2: 'T is simply a factual account of the situation being described.'

Both positions[5] can intelligibly be generated from the same text given the
difference in background commitments. How is this possible? That is a
matter for analysis to reveal. It can proceed to do so by explicating the internal structure of the text. For example, given that any location can be
described with more than one set of categories, what procedural basis can be
found to animate any given selection? Correctness is not enough, since many
alternative depictions can have a claim to correctness (e.g. 'West Bank and
Gaza Strip', 'the [Israeli-] Occupied Territories', 'Judea and Samaria', etc.).
Thus, any given selection can be found, *varying B*, to have been *differentially*
grounded. The analyst does not have to be *complicit* with one or another of
these positions or their associated background commitments to explicate it
and to connect it to the broader theme of categorial logic in account production.

From the above argument, the following corollary may be drawn: it is not
permissible to ascribe the deliberate production of any P from T by an author
(A) or reporter (R). Although common sense would tell us that there are
some reporters who can determine the possible range of background
assumptions on the part of their constituency in order to manipulate or
manufacture their consent to some particular position in virtue of the way in
which they design their account, nothing in the above argument could warrant any such determinate attribution.

'Criticality' is as much a part of common sense reasoning as 'conformity', exercised or not. Members routinely engage in common sense *critical* appraisals of wide varieties of ongoing perceptual phenomena. Their criticality can be achieved at both the *tacit* and *witting* levels. One legitimate objective of analysis is to demonstrate how critical viewings are achievable. In order to clarify the distinction between what I shall call partisan common sense critics, on the one hand, and the explication of 'options for criticality', on the other, I have elected to contrast the treatment by Joshua Muravchik of US network coverage of the Lebanon War with my own analysis of that coverage.

Some Contrasting Conceptions of Media 'Criticism': A Case Study

In 1983, Muravchik and I, independently and for very different purposes, had occasion to use the resources of the Vanderbilt University Television News Archive in order to study US television network coverage of the Israeli invasion of Lebanon which occurred in 1982. Muravchik published his report in the journal *Policy Review* (23, Winter 1983), and I presented my (more extensive) analysis to Boston University in partial satisfaction of the requirements for the PhD degree (Spring, 1984c). Among the many points of contrast between our respective treatments of the same corpus of media materials were the following: my analysis was based upon my reproduced transcriptions of substantial segments of the actually appearing coverage; my analytic effort employed techniques drawn from logic, linguistics and ethnomethodology; and my objective was the elucidation of the meaning structures of the media depictions of the war.

Muravchik's study, on the other hand, was an exercise in ideological criticism whose aim was to argue that US network coverage could be generally characterized as having been anti-Israeli in tone and substance.[6] His direct quotations from network media coverage were selected to enable him to make this argument.[7] Among his conclusions was the remark that: 'None of the networks achieved . . . [a] rigorous standard in reporting on the events in Lebanon. CBS, however, seemed to be trying the hardest, and it succeeded a good part of the time. ABC's coverage was erratic; NBC's gave the impression that the network was on a crusade' (Muravchik, 1983: 41).

I read Muravchik's discussion with great interest: it was the only serious and relatively thorough assessment of the materials upon which I had been working that I could find in print. My own ideological conclusion, however, was diametrically opposite to Muravchik's. This discrepancy posed for me the following intellectual issue: was there a methodological procedure that could be used to decide between our competing conclusions? After all, both of us could hardly expect to represent more than a fraction of the materials we had examined: what criteria of 'representativeness' could be proposed for our respective 'samples'?[8] Was a logic of 'sampling' relevant to this issue at all? Were our divergent assessments primarily a function of our different political/ethical starting points, or, as I continue to believe, were they more a function of our different sensitivities to the logic of the *detail* of our common corpus of empirical data?

Let us consider the issue of 'sampling' from a technical point of view. A parallel consideration has been addressed in connection with conversation-analytic methodology. How are we to treat the transcribed data extracts which analysts reproduce for explication – are they to be construed as samples or in some other way? Coulter has proposed that:

> The options that are actually adopted in any given conversational interaction cannot be assigned probability frequencies for the simple reason that the universe of possible instantiations of any given sequence class is unknown [and unknowable: it is indefinitely large]. Consequently, the study of any particular instantiation of a sequence class [e.g. arguments] must be motivated not by an interest in empirical generalization to the class but by an interest in the *a priori* relations between illocutionary actions. (1990: 182–3)[9]

If our interest is not statistical, but 'logical', then our reproduced data sets are not samples but perspicuous instances.

> . . . I do not have to see *n* games of chess in order to grasp the *a priori* relationship between the two pawns of the same colour in the same column and the act of having used one of them in an earlier move to take a piece. Given a knowledge of the concepts in question, or of the game in question, and the datum that speakers and players are abiding by the rules of proper use, then one can see that two or more contingent states of affairs are conceptually connected. (Coulter, 1983: 371)

Both conceptual and conversation analysis, then, must invoke a model of 'grammatical' rather than statistical inquiry as their epistemological rubrics. Their interests are logical and conceptual, although founded upon instances of actual usage, and not purely empirical in the sense of an inquiry into mere 'contingent regularities'. Media analysis involving the elucidation of meaning structures is also, necessarily, a model of conceptual inquiry in an extended sense. The rules governing category selections, presuppositions and implications, practical inferences, sequential organization, utterance design and other phenomena of technical interest are derived from, and are answerable to, empirical data in the form of actual cases of, among other phenomena, media reportage. However, the adequacy of such elucidations is, with few exceptions, not decidable with reference to the sheer frequency of empirical instances.

For Muravchik, however, there is no methodological scruple involved in his selection of instances, no sense of the problematics of either sampling or conceptual analysis, and no constraint adhered to (or even recognized) in the derivation of critical inferences. Observations such as the following naturally lend themselves to such scrutiny:

Except for the reporting of Alan Pizey and Bob Simon from Beirut, CBS tended to avoid the tendentious or loaded wording that was used often by Peter Jennings, Barrie Dunsmore, and Mike McCourt on ABC, and by almost everybody on NBC. (Muravchik, 1983: 43)

How does Muravchik *know* (or even claim to know) that CBS 'tended to avoid' loaded wording? How often did they 'load words' as contrasted to using 'neutral language'? What could constitute 'neutral language' by reference to which a characterization of 'loaded wording' might be justified? According to what evidence are we to hold the entire network accountable for the instances of 'loaded wording' putatively detected by Muravchik in *some* of its reporters' coverage? Did these reporters intentionally, deliberately, set out to load their words, as it were, or is there something else at work which could account for their categorial selections?

Muravchik is perfectly entitled to his 'opinions' about US network coverage of the Lebanon War. The question that faces us is to develop methods whereby we can maintain a principled distinction between an 'opinion' (or a set of opinions comprising a 'polemic') and a critical inference grounded in a logical analysis of the same corpus of empirical materials. In order to give this distinction some flesh and blood, I have selected for discussion a fragment of news reportage from NBC television news on Saturday, 12 June 1982. Remember that, for Muravchik, 'NBC's [coverage] gave the impression that the network was on a crusade [against Israel] . . . CBS tended to avoid the tendentious or loaded wording that was used often . . . by almost everybody on NBC.' Here is the fragment:[10]

> NBC News, Saturday, 12 June 1982 (18:35:30)
> (Paul Miller in Nabatiyeh)
> While Israelis patrolled the streets *looking for terrorists*, they also looked for ways of winning over the Lebanese people. In small villages like this, the Israelis and their *Christian* allies are being welcomed. (18:35:40)

It will not suffice to complain against Muravchik that Palestinian guerrilla forces were frequently categorized as 'terrorists', a designation *not once* employed to categorize the Israeli Defence Forces. What has to be shown is *how* such a categorial selection was actually used and in what discursive environment. Editorializing commentaries, manifestly direct quotations of Israeli politicians, officials or spokesmen and similar partisan contexts are domains within which such a derogatory characterization of the Palestinian forces as 'terrorists' may be encountered routinely without generating an impression of biased news reportage. (It should, of course, be noted that the sustained and cumulative usage of this category in reference to only one party to the conflict may well have generated prejudicial attitudes on the part of some viewers.)[11] In the extract reproduced above, however, the category is embedded within a live news report by a reporter (not by an editor or network administrator). He is not engaged in direct quotation of an Israeli or anti-Palestinian spokesman. Nonetheless, I claim that his use of this category, according to a logic which I will specify, constitutes grounds for the attribution of bias against the persons so categorized (the Palestinian forces). What is this logic?

Without having to enter into any debate about the correctness or incorrectness of the category selection according to criteria of a moral or political nature, it can be argued that the design of Miller's report affiliates him to the official Israeli (or pro-Israeli) political position.[12] Whether or not the category 'terrorist' is, by some standards, a reasonable one to invoke, is not the issue here. The issue is, rather, that the category is a 'disjunctive' one in the technical sense that while it may be ascribable, it is not self-avowable.[13] Of course, this is not to argue that there is a universal rule preferring self-avowable categories to ascribable ones in cases of conflict. If such a rule were in force, we should all be constrained to characterize Joan of Arc as a visionary and not as an hallucinator and the Stalinist Gulag as a People's Democracy and not as a totalitarian abomination. It is clear that many categories from disjunctive sets are specifically *not* self-avowable by those being categorized. However, a selection from a disjunctive categorial pair (or set) which privileges an extrinsically ascribable category over a self-avowable one (e.g. which selects 'hallucinator' over 'visionary', 'terrorist' over 'freedom fighter', etc.) *where the ascribable category is specifically not self-avowable* (irony apart) observably commits the categorizer to a contrastively unsympathetic perspective on those being categorized.[14]

Consider, further, the availability of an option in this instance for marking the categorization as *de dicto* – i.e. 'While Israelis patrolled the streets looking for *those they call* terrorists . . .' contrasts with the *de re* characterization actually produced by Paul Miller, i.e. 'While Israelis patrolled the streets looking for terrorists . . .' Juxtaposing *de dicto* with *de re* categorizations can be consequential for certain contexts and purposes. In this context, neglecting to mark the selection of the non-self-avowable category as *de dicto* presumptively establishes it as *de re*.[15] Such a presumption links the reporter's perspective on these events to that of one side of the conflict at the expense of the perspective of the other. This holds whether or not the reporter intended to display, was conscious of displaying, or would have admitted to, such an affiliation. As I remarked earlier, my analysis is non-intentionalist in character. Muravchik, on the other hand, employs intentionalist and motive-ascribing formulations at every turn.

Although I do not want to belabour my treatment of this argument, an additional point about it is worthy of mention. Mr Miller spoke of 'the Israelis and their Christian allies . . .' The category 'Christian' was indeed the self-avowed one for those whom Palestinian and their *allied* Lebanese combatants referred to with a variety of non-religious categories, among which were 'Phalangist' (the English translation of their political affiliation deriving from their historical relationship to Franco's Fascist party), 'Isolationist', etc. It could be argued that the category 'Christian' was simply the recognitional preference for an American audience, given the embeddedness of the alternatively correct categories within a relatively less perspicious political frame of reference. The problem which this selection engenders, however, is that it tacitly projects a religious rather than political-military explanation for the minority Lebanese alliance with the Israelis, and one with which many otherwise disinterested Christian Americans could be expected to identify.

Muravchik singles out John Chancellor of NBC News for special opprobrium, referring to his 'crusade' against Israel's invasion of Lebanon (1983: 54).[16] However, it was clear that Chancellor accepted consistently fundamental (pro)-Israeli assumptions in his editorial commentaries. Likening the Palestine Liberation Organization to 'Al Capone's mob', he remarked that 'It is inconceivable that Israel would deliberately get itself into a situation like that [the siege of West Beirut] . . . What is much more likely is that Israel blundered into it and now is stuck with it' (NBC News, Friday, 6 August 1982, 17:51:00 to 17:52:20). Three days later, Chancellor is explaining to his audience how so many Palestinians came to live in Lebanon. Ignoring the civil war in Jordan in 1970–71 between Palestinian and Jordanian forces which resulted in a massive influx of Palestinian refugees from Jordan to Lebanon, Chancellor focuses upon the first wave of Palestinian immigration to Lebanon in 1948. Characteristically for this conflict, as for most others, the events of 1948 have already been conventionally articulated in a disjunctive category-pair, 'War of Independence'/'War of Conquest'. The former is the official Israeli category preference, the latter is that of Palestinians.[17]

> NBC News, Monday, 9 August 1982 (17:50:40)
> (John Chancellor commentary in Lebanon)
> Some of these people [Palestinians] came here to Lebanon in the Israeli *War of Independence*. That's how the Palestinians became refugees. (17:50:50)

Chancellor's usage affiliates him to the official Israeli position, hardly the perspective of an anti-Israel 'crusader'.

D'Arcy (1963: Ch. 1) analysed a mode of elision in the construction of factual accounts which is pertinent here. For example, I may truthfully say of someone that he entertained his friends at the party, but I will be found morally culpable of misleading my interlocutor if it turns out that the entertainment consisted in torturing someone. I cannot be found to have *lied*: my 'sin' is rather one of omission. Similarly, were I to describe the Nazi physician Mengele simply as having 'conducted medical experiments', it is not that I have lied but rather that I have elided morally significant information. We do not need to ramify such examples in order to establish the validity of D'Arcy's 'Non-elidability Principle' for morally consequential accounts. Did Paul Miller, and those other commentators who selected the category 'Christian' to describe Israel's allies in Lebanon, violate this principle? Muravchik does not even raise this question. The issues that Muravchik does raise might have otherwise been analytically interesting had he deployed a methodological framework within which to explicate them. I contend that what is unfolding in these methodological discussions and explicative analyses of actual texts in such a methodological apparatus, one which is capable of transforming an otherwise polemical orientation into a critical analytical attitude.

Background, Text, Position

Among the reasons I have for objecting to Muravchik's style of media critique are his choice of instances of reportage as a matter of his argumentative convenience alone, his failure to motivate his own readings of his materials by anything beyond his own initial preconceptions about the Lebanon War, and his neglect of the problem of ruling out alternative readings of his preferred instances. I cannot claim that anyone in media studies has yet been able to produce a theoretically definitive account of the structures and devices whereby messages are conveyed, impressions created and inferences facilitated. However, earlier in this essay I outlined a framework for beginning to work out some of these issues, and now I shall try to indicate to what extent it may succeed.

In order to proceed cautiously, I shall consider Muravchik's treatment of a brief fragment from the ABC News coverage supplied by its State Department correspondent, Barrie Dunsmore. Muravchik had earlier characterized Dunsmore as someone 'who repeatedly went out of his way to work little digs at Israel in his stories' (1983: 49). Whether or not this assertion can be justified is not relevant here: I include it only as data to illustrate a manifest component of the Background Knowledge/Belief Commitments attributable to Muravchik as a viewer/listener. Here is his treatment of Dunsmore's report:

On 14 June, Mr Dunsmore reported:
Lebanese police said today that as many as ten thousand people may have been killed in the fighting. To deal with such casualty figures Israel seems to be gearing up a campaign to justify its actions. Israel sources told ABC news today they had captured hundreds of tons of weapons and documents and have dealt international terrorism an extreme blow.

There were two pieces of news here. One was the Lebanese police casualty figure which deserved to be reported and to be treated with a degree of skepticism. The other was the Israeli announcement of some of the documents and equipment they had captured. Mr Dunsmore combined the two in a way that negated the second story by implying that it was nothing more than a part of an Israeli effort at self-justification. As the same time he implicitly confirmed the fallacious Lebanese police statistic by saying this was the cause of Israel's need for self-justification. (1983: 49)

Using our analytical scheme – Background, Text and Position – to organize our discussion, we can treat the direct quotation of Dunsmore's report as constituting T and Muravchik's commentary upon it as constituting P. The main elements of P are:

1. The Lebanese police casualty figure cannot be trusted – indeed it was fallacious.
2. Israel's announcement of its capture of weapons and documents was independent of the announcement of the casualty figure by the Lebanese
   police.
3. Given the dubious or fallacious nature of the casualty figure Israel's
   announcement could not have been an effort at self-justification.
4. Israel's claim to 'have dealt international terrorism an extreme blow' was
   correct and not merely a function of some 'need for self-justification'.

The issue for analysis now is to specify how *T* and *P* relate within a structure
of reasoning. And the question to be posed is: is that structure coherent
independently of *B*?

Consider first Muravchik's inattention to Dunsmore's use of modal qualifiers: 'Lebanese police said . . . people *may have been* killed in the fighting' and
'Israel *seems to be* gearing up to a campaign . . .' Because modal qualifiers *can*
be strategically used to protect, by preserving deniability, an account-pro-
ducer from the fuller implications of a *knowledge*-claim, they can sometimes
be challenged by an account-recipient, but not *disattended*. Muravchik must
have made up his mind on the basis of other, undisclosed evidence of
Dunsmore's anti-Israeli partisanship that he 'implicitly confirmed the fallacious Lebanese police statistic': the logic of the text itself provides no
confirmation whatsoever of this attribution to Dunsmore. Indeed one could
argue that Dunsmore's use of modal qualifiers itself built into his account
Muravchik's desired 'degree of skepticism'.

Muravchik claims that Dunsmore's combination of the Lebanese police
report and the Israeli announcement 'negated' the Israeli claim. His basis for
this way of hearing the report is simply to assert that because Dunsmore had
characterized the Israeli claim as a 'justification', its status as correct or true
had thereby been undermined. This is singularly strange, since presumably
things which count as justification *can* without contradiction be correct or
true in their factual status. To say something counted as a justification is not
thereby to diminish its truth. Of course, people can (and often may well) produce accounts in justification of their actions which are false, but this does
not mean that justifications have that property as a universal feature. Quite
the contrary: the more truthful the account, the more effective the justification it accomplishes.

On what basis does Muravchik deny the possibility that the Lebanese police
statistic (reported by Dunsmore as tentatively given) was accurate? Why does
it '[deserve] to be . . . treated with a degree of skepticism'? For some answer
to this, we must consult Muravchik's already manifested Background
Knowledge/Belief Commitments. Muravchik is openly pro-Israeli and
defended Israel's actions in Lebanon. He has expressed serious misgivings
about Dunsmore's attitude to Israel earlier in his article, quoted above. From
this vantage-point, we can begin to develop an answer to our question. If we
partition the antagonists in the Lebanon War simply as 'Israelis' and 'Arabs',

then, since the Lebanese are Arabs, and Arabs are in conflict with Israel, any Arab – including any Lebanese Arab police officer – who produces a war-related account is immediately open to the charge of exaggeration, lying, self-serving bias, etc. However, Muravchik does not give any basis for his inclusion of the Lebanese police force within the set of actual opponents of Israel. No evidence is given to implicate this police force in fighting Israel's armed forces, in expressing anti-Israel sentiments as a matter of official policy, nor in anything other than a neutral posture. (In fact, from other sources one can develop a view of the Lebanese police force which may tend to align them against PLO and their Lebanese militia allies.) Thus, Muravchik's critique of Dunsmore's text is based, in this respect, exclusively upon incorrigible commitments already held: after all, if one did not hold such views, the Lebanese police report, however tentatively articulated, might have led one seriously to question Israel's use of such deadly force in Lebanon.

I do not want to be understood here as holding that Muravchik had no right to hear/read *T* in the way he did. From a purely *political* point of view, I am unsympathetic to virtually every aspect of his Background commitments. From an *analytical* point of view, the validity of our respective political positions is entirely irrelevant. The issues involved in the critical analysis of media materials are conceptual and methodological: otherwise, the field degenerates into an extension of the very political conflicts whose representations it is trying to understand. In their article 'Biasing the News: Technical Issues in "Media Studies"', a well-known critique of mainstream media studies, Anderson and Sharrock comment:

> We are not trying to argue that one *cannot* arrive at the kinds of conclusions that media scholars reach. We argue only that these conclusions are not *necessarily* to be drawn from those [textual] materials, *and* that those conclusions are not the only ones which can legitimately be drawn from those same materials. (1979: 367)

In developing the kind of analysis exemplified here, the constraints which Anderson and Sharrock recommend are accepted. Only *logical grammars* can have a necessitarian status. The analyst is precluded from stipulating a *definitive* content to any given hearing/reading/viewing for any given text. The purpose of analysis, including especially *critical* analysis, is to elucidate the structure of possibilities derivable from the interaction of any given *B*, *T* and *P* and *thereby to indicate whatever arbitrary contrivances and logical limitations are to be uncovered within the exhibited reasoning which links B, T and P.*

Concluding Comments

I have been arguing for wider recognition on the part of professional analysts of media materials of the existence of criticality as a *practical activity* and not just as a theorist's privilege. Ethnomethodology has taught us to recognize the constitutive presence within the social world of pre-theoretical hermeneutics: it has so far had little to say of the presence of pre-theoretical *critical* orientations.[18] This may well be explained, at least in part, by a general adherence to a restrictive interpretation of the policy of 'ethnomethodological indifference'.

In the preceding discussion, I have tried to show how an interest in the *workings* of criticality may be investigated in the domain of media studies. This required the formulation of an analytical methodology and a detailed case study involving its application. In order to demonstrate its relative cogency, I sought to specify the results of its application to a corpus of materials and to contrast them to a substantive media critique (that of Muravchik). Further, I tried to show how Muravchik's critique embodied the elements of a proto-methodology which was too weak to sustain his own critical observations. Among these elements were his reliance upon a primitive mode of sampling selection, his preference for stipulated determinate meanings instead of explicating a logic of meaning-options and his penchant for basing critical inferences almost exclusively on what, from an analytical point of view, are arbitrary preconceptions of a political kind. This is *not* to say that preconceptions are avoidable, only that they must themselves be treated as phenomena, as part of the domain of data.

Just as no ethnomethodologist, linguist or logician can work with materials in a state of amnesia regarding his common sense resources and institutions, neither can effective explicatory work be accomplished on political, ethical or other contentious human constructions if the analyst is required to put aside in their entirety his ordinary critical faculties, including his *own* ideological and/or moral commitments. A recurring problem has been to circumvent the criticism which awaits him at every turn, namely that he has transgressed the boundary between explication and ideological evaluation, or between a critical analysis and a political polemic. I wish to claim that, while there are no guarantees against being systematically misunderstood, the approach being recommended here goes further than others of which I am aware in addressing itself to a resolution of this difficulty.

Notes

1. This ethnomethodological analysis examined the ABC, NBC and CBS reportage of the Israeli invasion of Lebanon. The data were drawn from the Vanderbilt Television News Archive and a detailed explication of the texts elucidated the ideological phenomena embodied in them.

2. By 'members', I intend to include all perceptually relevant categories, such as 'readers', 'hearers', 'listeners', 'viewers', etc.

3. By employing the masculine gender in third-person references, I am only trying to help establish a convention which would stipulate that male members employ masculine pronouns and female members feminine ones in their discourse.

4. The Kantian-inspired classical tradition of literary criticism and hermeneutic approaches to texts more generally have exhibited this assumption. (For an illuminating discussion of the hermeneutic schools, see Palmer, 1969.) A more contemporary preoccupation with the mind's 'assignment of meaning' to cultural objects, including texts,

is to be found in the *verstehende* methodology of Weber and the interpretive sociology of the symbolic interactionist perspective in the social sciences. A good reference for these and some contrasting views is Truzzi (1974).

5. I am ignoring here a consideration of the other major inferential option recoverable from the text concerning anti-semitism in the Soviet Union.

6. For a political discussion which argues the opposite, i.e. that the US coverage was pro-Israeli, see my '"News Speak" About the Lebanon War' (Jalbert, 1984b).

7. Note that Muravchik also drew upon print media coverage to construct his argument. For the purposes of the present discussion, I shall restrict myself to an assessment of that part of print media coverage. See my unpublished paper, 'Media Analysis: On Distinguishing a Polemic from a Critique' (Jalbert, 1984a), which can be obtained from the author.

8. Muravchik complains that '. . . a number of commentaries by Bill Moyers . . . though tempered by an effort to understand Israel's point of view, were clearly critical of Israel's actions, sometimes hyperbolically so. On 15 June, Mr Moyers said that Israel had waged "total war" and added that "war unbounded follows the logic of hornets – everything in their path is their enemy"' (1983: 43).

The contrary can be argued: in a number of commentaries, Bill Moyers can be found articulating opinions hostile to the Palestinian cause. On Friday, 11 June 1982, broadcasting on CBS News at 17:52:30, Moyers characterized the Palestinian people as 'a people displaced and abused, bloodless abstractions and born losers', after having remarked twenty seconds earlier that 'the war has improved Israel's security to the north'. Two months later, on Monday, 23 August 1982, broadcasting on CBS News at 17:51:40, Moyers castigated 'Arafat and his allies' for not having accepted 'the reality of Israel', and adds that they had 'established within Lebanon a terrorist state sworn to Israel's destruction'. This is surely hyperbolic commentary in the reverse direction to that lamented by Muravchik. My purpose here is not simply to score points against Muravchik's untenable assessment of US network coverage as biased against Israel. Rather, I am drawing attention to the dangers involved in playing the sampling game. Perhaps Muravchik could dredge up further examples to suit his purpose and I could reply with a similar volley of counter-examples until both of us ran out of patience. (My own data set consists of hours of video recordings of network coverage spanning all four months of the war; only by subjecting these materials to the most distorting operationalization could it be rendered amenable to sampling of any kind. Muravchik does not even raise this issue, let alone supply a solution.)

9. For a more extensive methodological discussion of this issue, see Coulter (1983).

10. In reproducing a transcript from actual excerpts from US television network news broadcasts, I adopt the convention of italicizing words, phrases or larger linguistic units solely for the purpose of highlighting those fragments to be analysed or discussed. In no case should this practice be taken to signify anything about the original broadcast, e.g. emphasis, intonation, affect or any other endogenous property of the report. In addition, I have included references to the exact time of the broadcast fragments reproduced as data by using EST as the metric. Thus, after giving the date, the reader will encounter a series of numerals such as (17:30:40) marking the beginning of the fragment and another at its conclusion.

11. Two years prior to the Israeli invasion of Lebanon, a clear linkage had already become widely established in the US between the categories 'Palestinian' and 'terrorist', largely due to media depictions of the Israel-Palestine conflict. A 1980 *Time* poll reported that '30 per cent of the US public think Palestinians are best described as "terrorists", 17 per cent regard them as "displaced persons who will eventually settle in another country", and 19 per cent think of them as "refugees seeking a homeland"' (*Time*, 14 April 1980: 42, col. 3). One is left wondering, however what sentiments the remaining 34 per cent of the US public might have expressed on the issue, as this was not reported.

12. As I argued in '"News Speak" About the Lebanon War': Miller's use of the category 'terrorist' in this way instances a point made by the logician W. B. Gallie (1955–6). He argued that, to the degree that descriptions and categorizations of social phenomena are (uncritically and contentiously) taken to be what those who have an interest in them and who have already described and categorized them assert they are, to that degree one is

involved in the use of contestable concepts. To the extent that Miller uncritically takes the categorization of the PLO by the Israelis (i.e., 'terrorist') and imports it into the apparatus of his own report, to that extent he is involved in an *ideological enterprise* (1984: 27).

For further discussion of the notion of 'contestable concepts', see Shapiro (1981: ch. 7).

13. Building upon Sacks's notion of 'standardized relational pairs' (1972: 28–9) Coulter develops the notion of 'disjunctive category-pairs': 'At the level of the social organization of their use, we can speak of the categories "belief and knowledge" as forming disjunctive *category-pair*. We shall mark this by the use of an oblique as follows: knowledge/belief. Other such pairs would include: vision/hallucination, telepathy/trickery, ghost/illusion, flying-saucer/UFO, and ideology/science. Where one part of these pairs is involved to characterize some phenomenon seriously, *the speaker's belief-commitment may be inferred, and the structure of subsequent discourse may be managed in terms provided for by the programmatic relevance of the disjunctive category-pair relationship.* Thus, to the nonbeliever, Joan of Arc suffered hallucinations; to the believer, divine visions. To the nonbeliever, Uri Geller is a sophisticated conjurer; to the believer, telepath and telecinethicist, and so on' (Coulter, 1979: 181).

In every conflict, disjunctive categorization operates and very often through the use of disjunctive category-pairs such as government/junta, mob/crowd, extremist/moderate, etc. Israeli General Ariel Sharon became highly sensitive to the operation of one such pair in the description of the departure of Palestinian forces from Beirut: during a CBS News report from Jerusalem on Friday, 19 August (17:38:40), he protested: '[This is] about the *expulsion* not about *withdrawal.* It is not a *withdrawal.* It is an *expulsion.* It is not a *withdrawal*' (17:38:50).

14. On the logic of disjunctive categorization practices, see Coulter (1979), Jayyusi (1984: ch. 5) and Jalbert (1989).

15. *De dicto/de re* conflations were occasionally avoided, as in the following extract from NBC News, Wednesday, 30 June, 1982 (17:36:20), presented by Tom Brokaw: 'In south Lebanon, meanwhile, the Israelis presented what they called evidence against the PLO and Rick Davis has that story . . .' (17:36:30). The use of the explicit *de dicto* marker 'what they called' disaffiliated the reporter from the truth value of the object-complement 'evidence against the PLO'. After all, evidence is to be distinguished from putative evidence: had Brokaw simply asserted that the Israelis presented evidence against the PLO, its status as evidence would have been presupposed *de re.* For further discussion of the properties of *de re/de dicto* modalities, see Jalbert (1983).

16. Muravchik even invokes FCC's 'fairness doctrine' against Chancellor on the grounds that his many commentaries on the Lebanon War 'were consistently critical of Israeli policy' (1983: 53).

17. For details regarding elision and the categorial phrase 'War of Independence', see Jalbert (1994: 143).

18. David Bogen (1989) alerts us to several problems which arise in attempts to reconcile Habermas's 'universal pragmatics' with ethnomethodological studies of practical action and practical reasoning. My own perspective differs from that of Habermas while preserving his interest in grounding critical reflections on communication and other social phenomena within the domain of the 'lifeworld'.

Bibliography

Anderson, D.C. and Sharrock, W.W (1979), 'Biasing the News: Technical Issues in "Media Studies"', *Sociology* 13(3), September: 367–85.

Bogen, D.E. (1989), 'A Reappraisal of Habermas's *Theory of Communicative Action* in Light of Detailed Investigations of Social Praxis', *Journal for the Theory of Social Behaviour* 19(1): 47–77.

Coulter, J. (1979), 'Beliefs and Practical Understanding', in G. Psathas (ed.), *Everyday Language: Studies in Ethnomethodology,* pp. 163–86, New York: Irvington.

Coulter, J. (1983), 'Contingent and *A Priori* Structures in Sequential Analysis', *Human Studies* 6: 361–76.

Coulter, J. (1990), 'Elementary Properties of Argument Sequences', in G. Psathas (ed.), *Interaction Competence*, pp. 181–204, Washington, DC: University Press of America.

D'Arcy, E. (1963), *Human Acts: An Essay in Their Moral Evaluation*, Oxford: Clarendon Press.

Gallie, W.B. (1955–6), 'Essentially Contested Concepts', *Proceedings of the Aristotelian Society* 56: 167–98.

Garfinkel, H. and Sacks, H. (1970), 'On Formal Structures of Practical Actions', in J.C. McKinney and E.A. Tiryakian (eds.), *Theoretical Sociology*, pp. 337–66, New York: Appleton-Century-Crofts.

Jalbert, P.L. (1983), 'Some Constructs for Analysing News', in H. Davis and P. Walton (eds.), *Language, Image, Media*, pp. 282–99, Oxford: Basil Blackwell.

Jalbert, P.L. (1984a), 'Media Analysis: On Distinguishing a Polemic from a Critique', unpublished paper.

Jalbert, P.L. (1984b), '"News Speak" About the Lebanon War', *Journal of Palestine Studies* XIV(1) (53), Fall: 16–35.

Jalbert, P.L. (1984c), 'Structures of "News Speak": US Network Television Coverage of the Lebanon War', Summer 1982, doctoral dissertation, Boston University.

Jalbert, P.L. (1989), 'Categorization and Beliefs: News Accounts of Haitian and Cuban Refugees', in D.T. Helm, W.T. Anderson, A.J. Meehan and A. Rawls (eds.), *The Interactional Order: New Directions in the Study of Social Order*, pp. 231–48, New York: Irvington.

Jalbert, P.L. (1994), 'Structures of the "Unsaid"', *Theory, Culture & Society* 11(4): 127–60.

Jayyusi, L. (1984), *Categorization and the Moral Order*, Boston, MA: Routledge & Kegan Paul.

Muravchik, J. (1983), 'Misreporting Lebanon', *Policy Review* 23, Winter: 11–66.

Palmer, R. (1969), *Hermeneutics*, Evanston, IL: Northwestern University Press.

Sacks, H. (1972), 'An Initial Investigation of the Usability of Conversational Data for Doing Sociology', in D. Sudnow (ed.), *Studies in Social Interaction*, pp. 31–74, New York: Free Press.

Shapiro, M. J. (1981), *Language and Political Understanding: The Politics of Discursive Practices*, New Haven, CT: Yale University Press.

Smith, D.E. (1982), 'The Active Text: An Approach to Analyzing Texts as Constituents of Social Relations', paper presented to the Annual Convention of the International Sociological Association, Mexico City, August.

Truzzi, K., ed. (1974), *Verstehen: Subjective Understanding in the Social Sciences*, Reading, MA: Addison-Wesley.

Turner, R. (1974), 'Words, Utterances and Activities', in R. Turner (ed.), *Ethnomethodology*, pp. 197–215, Harmondsworth: Penguin.

Weber, M. (1949), *The Methodology of the Social Sciences* (trans. and ed. E.A. Shils and H.A. Finch), New York: Free Press.

Reproduced with permission from Paul L. Jalbert, 'Critique and analysis in media studies: media criticism as practical action', *Discourse and Society*, 1995, vol. 6 (1), pp. 7–26.

21

Metaphor, Ontology and Scientific Truth: Against Some Dogmas of the New Anti-Realism

Christopher Norris

Introduction

Anti-realism is currently the prevailing trend across many schools of thought in epistemology and philosophy of science. There are, to be sure, some strong countervailing voices and some well-developed arguments in support of an alternative (ontological-realist or causal-explanatory) approach.[1] But these latter have enjoyed nothing like the same degree of acceptance among workers in other disciplines – history of science, sociology of knowledge, cultural studies, etc. – where anti-realism is nowadays the orthodox line. Nor is it hard to understand why this should be the case. For those disciplines clearly have a large investment in the idea of scientific 'truth' or 'reality' as relative to – or constructed within – some culture-specific discourse, framework of enquiry, historical paradigm, conceptual scheme, or whatever.[2] Hence the rapid diffusion of arguments from recent (post-Kuhnian) philosophy of science which are taken as lending powerful support to the anti-realist case. Other sources include W. V. Quine (on ontological relativity, meaning-variance, and the underdetermination of theories by evidence); late Wittgenstein (on language-games and cultural 'forms of life'); Heidegger, Gadamer, and other proponents of a depth-hermeneutical approach; Foucault's relentlessly sceptical 'genealogies' of power/knowledge; postmodernists such as Lyotard with their talk of paralogism, narrative pragmatics, and 'performativity' as the sole criterion of scientific truth; and the 'strong programme' in sociology of knowledge with its declared principle of according equal treatment to all scientific theories, whether true or false as judged by our present-day cultural lights.[3] What they all have in common is the turn toward language – or some version of the socio-discursive constructivist argument – deployed as a counter to realist claims of whatever variety.

In so far as these arguments have found support from within the Anglo-American philosophical community it has come mostly from 'post-analytical' thinkers – Richard Rorty prominent among them – who seek to demote science (and philosophy of science) from its erstwhile position of high prestige.[4] Of course there are others like Michael Dummett who continue the analytic project (broadly defined) but who none the less espouse an anti-realist position according to which we can have no grasp of verification-transcendent truth values.[5] On this view – in short – it is strictly unintelligible that our present best notions of truth, method, observational warrant, theoretical adequacy and so forth might *not* correspond to the way things stand 'in reality'. That is to say, we could have no possible grounds for suspecting this to be the case given the fact that any reasons adduced would always be reliant on criteria derived from those same (for us truth-constitutive) standards of evidential reasoning. It is mainly under pressure from arguments of this sort that philosophers like Hilary Putnam have retreated from a strong realist position – such as Putnam took during the early 1970s – to a stance of (so-called) 'internal realism' which concedes most of the adversary case while hoping to avoid its more extreme relativist implications.[6]

Still it is clear that the 'linguistic turn' in its various forms has done more to promote anti-realist than realist approaches to philosophy of science. That is to say, it has most often been enlisted in support of conventionalist, instrumentalist, or cultural-relativist doctrines, all of which manifest an elective affinity with the idea of truth as a discursive construct devoid of any real-world ontological grounding.[7] In what follows I shall take a rather oblique route by way of addressing these issues. My main concern is with Derrida's essay 'White Mythology: Metaphor in the Text of Philosophy', a work that is often read – mistakenly I think – as adopting an extreme anti-realist (or 'textualist') position with regard to philosophical truth-claims.[8] Of particular interest in the present context are Derrida's lengthy and detailed discussions of the role of metaphor in scientific concept-formation and its bearing on matters of ontology and epistemology as raised by philosophers of science from Aristotle to Bachelard and Canguilhem.

Derrida and Benveniste on Aristotle

Let me give more substance to this generalized claim by quoting a passage from 'White Mythology', this time at a length adequate to convey the complexity of Derrida's argument. The passage has to do with Aristotle's account of metaphor and its place within what Derrida calls 'the great immobile chain of Aristotelian ontology, with its theory of the analogy of Being, its logic, its epistemology, and more precisely its poetics and its rhetoric' (p. 236). It is also concerned with Aristotle's attempt to distinguish human from non-human (animal) modes of being on the basis of a theory of language – a philosophical grammar – that would define man as a speaking-and-reasoning creature as opposed to a mere producer of pre-articulate, meaningless, unintelligible sounds. Hence the importance of the letter (*stoikheion*), the minimal distinctive element that possesses no meaning – no semantic content – in and of itself but whose role it is, within Aristotle's system, to create the possibility of

articulate utterance by accomplishing the passage from 'sound without signification' (*phone asemos*) to meaningful speech-production (*phone semantike*).
From this point, so Aristotle argues, one can go on to derive the entire inven-
tory of human linguistic resources – from syllables, *via* nouns and verbs, to
the highest, most complex levels of logico-grammatical structure – which set
human beings decisively apart from the rest of the animal creation.[9] Yet
there is also another distinctive human attribute, one that enables us to
acquire knowledge, to 'perceive resemblances', to apply words to objects in
habitual or unaccustomed ways, or to reason analogically from one context of
knowledge, usage or experience to another. *Mimesis* and *metaphor* are the
two chief terms that Aristotle uses in connection with this range of capacities.
And since they occupy such a crucial place in his system – since without
them that system would fall apart – therefore it is wrong (a misreading of
Aristotle) to assign them a subordinate or derivative role.

Here is the relevant passage from 'White Mythology', omitting those
extended citations in the original Greek which Derrida is careful to provide
but which are not (I think) necessary here.

> This is the difference between animals and man: according to Aristotle both
> can emit indivisible sounds, but only man can make of them a letter . . .
> Aristotle does not analyze this difference; he interprets it by teleological ret-
> rospection. No internal characteristic distinguishes the atom of animal sound
> and the letter. Thus, it is only on the basis of the signifying phonic composition,
> on the basis of meaning and reference, that the human voice should be dis-
> tinguished from the call of an animal. Meaning and reference: that is, the
> possibility of signifying by means of a noun. What is proper to nouns is to sig-
> nify something, an independent being identical to itself, conceived as such. It
> is at this point that the theory of the name, such as it is implied by the concept
> of metaphor, is articulated with ontology. Aside from the classical and dog-
> matically affirmed limit between the animal without *logos* and man as *zoon
> logon ekhon*, what appears here is a certain systematic indissociability of the
> value of metaphor and the metaphysical chain holding together the values of
> discourse, voice, noun, signification, meaning, imitative representation, resem-
> blance; or, in order to reduce what these translations import or deport, the
> values of *logos, phone semantike, semainein, onoma, mimesis, homoiosis* . . . *Mimesis* is
> never without the *theoretical* perception of resemblance or similarity, that is, of
> that which will always be posited as the condition for metaphor. *Homoiosis* is not
> only constitutive of the value of truth (*aletheia*) which governs the entire chain;
> it is that without which the metaphorical operation is impossible; 'To produce
> a good metaphor is to see a likeness'. The condition for metaphor (for good
> and true metaphor) is the condition for truth. ('White Mythology', pp. 236–7)

Again this is couched in Derrida's mixed-mode style of direct or oblique
citation from the source-text (Aristotle) combined with analytic commentary
and critical exegesis. Moreover, as the context makes clear, it is offered by way
of an illustrative statement of precisely those 'classical' presuppositions which

have governed the philosophic discourse on metaphor and – beyond that – the predominant (post-Aristotelian) way of thinking about issues in ontology, epistemology, philosophical semantics and kindred disciplines. So there can be no question of reading the passage as an affirmation of Aristotle's views or even as signalling partial assent to any link in the 'great chain' of Aristotelian argument.

Yet it is equally unjustified – here as elsewhere in Derrida's work – to suppose that a deconstructive reading is a *priori* committed to the disarticulation of all truth-claims and the undoing of any theory (such as Aristotle's) predicted on values of truth, reason, logical form, conceptual adequacy, empirical warrant and so forth. For this is once again to mistake the whole purpose and argumentative tenor of an essay like 'White Mythology': namely, its critical questioning of such values in a manner that itself maintains the highest standards of analytical consistency and rigour while not taking anything for granted in the way that those standards have hitherto or traditionally been applied. In other words deconstruction carries on the critique of established (common sense, naturalized, or consensus-based) modes of perception or conceptualization which has characterized philosophy in the tradition from Aristotle to Descartes, Kant and Husserl.[10] No doubt it does so through a method of analysis – the rhetorical close-reading of various cardinal texts in that tradition – which departs very markedly from other, more conventional ideas of what constitutes a proper philosophical critique. No doubt it raises issues – about truth, representation, the extent to which metaphors can be 'adequately' conceptualized or intuitions brought under 'adequate' concepts – that have provoked consternation (or outright dismissal) among many philosophers. Yet the above passage should at least give pause to anyone who is tempted to regard 'White Mythology' as a mere exercise in 'textualist' mystification or an argument devoted to such simplified (pseudo-deconstructive) slogans as that 'all concepts are metaphors', 'reality just a fictive or rhetorical construct', or 'truth just a product of the will-to-power vested in figural language'.

Thus Derrida is not for one moment suggesting that *just because* Aristotle has recourse to metaphor – or to metaphor-related notions like resemblance, *mimesis*, the 'perception of similarity', etc. – at crucial points in his argument, *therefore* his entire ontology and epistemology (along with his logic, metaphysics, and conception of enquiry in the natural of physical sciences) comes down to nothing more than a series of figural tropes and substitutions, indifferent with regard to their truth-content or capacity for conceptual elucidation and critique. Nor is he committed to the absurd view that truth and reality *just are* what we make of them according to this or that favoured rhetoric, language-game, discourse, vocabulary, or whatever. Such a doctrine could be extracted from 'White Mythology' only by ignoring those many passages – among them the sections on Aristotle, Canguilhem and Bachelard – that offer a precise and detailed account of the critical epistemology of metaphor and its role in the process of scientific knowledge-production. In short: '[m]etaphor, as an effect of *mimesis* and *homoiosis*, the manifestation of analogy, will be a means of knowledge, a means that is subordinate, but certain' (p. 238).

This is not to deny – what is in any case quite evident – that Derrida is here paraphrasing Aristotle and drawing attention to the way in which metaphor has traditionally been treated as 'subordinate' to other (more directly reliable) means of acquiring knowledge. Thus: 'metaphor . . . is determined by philosophy as a provisional loss of meaning, an economy of the proper without irreparable damage, a certainly inevitable detour, but also a history with its sights set on, and within the horizon of, the circular reappropriation of literal, proper meaning' (p. 270). To this extent Derrida is describing – and calling into question – an entire set of axioms (along with an implicit teleology) aimed towards the 'proper' understanding of metaphor as a detour on the path to adequate conceptual knowledge. This is why, as he writes,

> the philosophical evaluation of metaphor has always been ambiguous: metaphor is dangerous and foreign as concerns *intuition* (vision and contact), *concept* (the grasping or proper presence of the signified), and *consciousness* (proximity or self-presence); but it is in complicity with what it endangers, is necessary to it in the extent to which the de-tour is a re-turn guided by the function of resemblance (*mimesis* or *homoiosis*), under the law of the same. (p. 270)

But again we shall mistake Derrida's purpose – or (not to beg the intentionalist question) the logic of his argument in 'White Mythology' – if we read such passages as opening the way to a wholesale metaphorization of philosophy, or a levelling of the metaphor/concept distinction that would view it as merely a symptomatic instance of this drive for the 'reappropriation' of metaphor by the philosophic will-to-truth. For there could then be no accounting for that other (often strongly counter-intuitive) process of conceptual 'rectification' that enables scientific metaphors, models and analogies to bring about genuine advances in our knowledge of physical objects, processes and events. Empson makes the point more succinctly when he remarks – in a review of E. A. Burtt's book *The Metaphysical Foundations of Modern Science* – that 'it is unsafe to explain discovery in terms of man's intellectual preconceptions, because the act of discovery is precisely that of stepping outside preconceptions.'[11]

One could go into a lot more detail with respect to Derrida's position on these issues of ontology, epistemology and the logic of scientific enquiry. A crucial text here would be his essay 'The Supplement of Copula' where he argues – as against the linguist Emile Benveniste – that Aristotle's table of the categories (the various forms and modalities of predicative judgment) cannot be treated as mere products of a particular language, namely the ancient Greek, whose lexical and grammatical resources they erect into an absolute (quasi-transcendental) set of laws for the conduct of rational thought.[12] Of course there is a very real question – much debated by philosophers, Kant among them – as to whether Aristotle's really was, as he thought, a complete and exhaustive (*a priori* deducible) listing of the categories concerned.[13] Also there are problems, as scarcely needs remarking, with Aristotle's essentialist definition of 'substance' as that to which the categories apply but which cannot itself be qualified or modified in its essence by any such categorical predicates. However Derrida's argument has to do with Benveniste's more sweeping (and strictly unintelligible) claim that the very idea of 'categoriality' is one that could only arise within the context of a given natural language that provided the lexico-grammatical means for its expression. For this involves Benveniste in a confusion of terms, a failure to observe the crucial distinction between particular categories (which may indeed be language-dependent) and *categoriality* as the precondition for making any judgments whatsoever, including judgments with regard to the priority of 'language' over 'thought' or – as the issue presents itself here – linguistics over philosophy. The latter is a *transcendental* question, taking the term 'transcendental' (as Derrida specifies) 'in its most rigorous accepted sense, in its most avowed "technicalness", precisely as it was fixed in the course of the development of the Aristotelian problematic of the categories'.[14] In this sense of the term, quite simply, 'transcendental means transcategorial', i.e. pertaining to the condition of possibility for thought and judgment in general. It literally signifies 'that which transcends every *genre*', every particular (as it might be linguistically instantiated) mode of categorical predication.

Thus 'none of the concepts utilized by Benveniste could have seen day, including that of linguistics as a science and the very notion of language, without a certain "small document" on the categories [i.e. Aristotle's table]' ('Supplement of Copula', p. 188). And again, more pointedly:

> Philosophy is not only *before* linguistics as one might find oneself facing a new science, a new way of seeing or a new object; it is also *before* linguistics, preceding linguistics by virtue of all the concepts philosophy still provides it, for better or worse; and it sometimes intervenes in the most critical, and occasionally in the most dogmatic, least scientific, operations of the linguist. (p. 188)

I must refer the reader to Derrida's essay if he or she wishes to follow this argument in all its intricate and rewarding detail. Sufficient to say that it operates both through the mode of transcendental-deductive reasoning – as defined above – and through a critical exegesis of Benveniste's text alert to those items of empirical (i.e. natural-language) evidence that contradict his avowed thesis. Thus, as Derrida remarks, '[w]hat is not examined at any time is the common category of the category, the *categoriality in general* on the basis of which the categories of language and the categories of thought may be dissociated' (p. 182). And as a matter of empirical evidence there is the case of Ewe – a language spoken in Togo – which according to Benveniste possesses no equivalent (no *lexical* equivalent) of the verb 'to be' in its jointly existential and copulative function, but which turns out, *on Benveniste's own submission*, to require that those resources be ascribed to it (in whatever lexico-grammatically distributed form) if Ewe is to make any sense in its various social and communicative contexts. Thus the transcendental argument receives confirmation at the level of empirical research, that is, through Benveniste's reflection on the evidence of how Ewe speakers actually communicate as distinct from his preconceived ideas about linguistic or ontological relativity.

There is another passage from Benveniste – cited at length by Derrida – which brings out the close relationship between these issues in the fields of linguistics, anthropology, philosophical semantics, epistemology and philosophy of science. 'Surely it is not by chance', Benveniste suggests,

> that modern epistemology does not try to set up a table of categories. It is more productive to conceive of the mind as a virtuality than as a framework, as a dynamism than as a structure. It is a fact that, to satisfy the requirements of scientific methods, thought everywhere adopts the same procedures in whatever language it chooses to describe experience. In this sense it becomes independent, not of language, but of particular linguistic structures. Chinese thought may well have invented categories as specific as *tao*, the *yin* and the *yang*; it is nonetheless able to assimilate the concepts of dialectical materialism or quantum mechanics without the structure of the Chinese language proving a hindrance. No type of language can by itself alone foster or hamper the activity of the mind. The advance of thought is linked much more closely to the capacities of man, to general conditions of culture, and to the organization of society than to the particular nature of a language.[15]

It is a remarkable passage for several reasons, not least its espousal of an extreme dualism between 'language' and 'thought', its casual (as if unnoticed) throwing away of the linguistic-relativist thesis, and its distinction – equally fatal to Benveniste's arguments elsewhere – between language in general and 'particular languages'. What emerges through all these manifest contradictions is the acknowledgment that there must be some order of reality that thought can apprehend or that language (language-in-general) can articulate quite aside from all mere relativities of time and place. Thus the 'advance of thought' seems a process that can indeed occur – whether in quantum physics or Chinese philosophy – through a process of conceptual development that cannot be attributed to the formative influence of this or that 'particular language'. Rather it belongs to the 'capacities of man' as a knowledge-acquisitive agent, with perhaps some allowance – and here Benveniste slides back toward a relativist stance – for 'general conditions of culture' or the 'organization of society'. But these latter conditions are apparently conceived as belonging to an order more permanent – or at any rate of far longer duration – than anything else on the scale (historic or geographical) that Benveniste associates with 'particular' localized languages or cultures. In short, the whole passage tends towards a transcategorial conception of thought, language, reason and truth which Benveniste cannot bring himself to endorse explicitly – given his linguistic-relativist credentials – but which comes through in his argument *despite and against* its overt professions of belief.

Quantum mechanics has become a standard *topos* in current debates about ontological relativity and the issue of linguistic representation.[16] It has spawned a great range of philosophical positions – realist and anti-realist – with regard to the status of quantum phenomena and their implications for philosophy of science, epistemology and interpretation-theory. Benveniste makes only passing reference to this debate in the above-cited passage. However it does lend support to the view that some degree of ontological realism is presupposed in any discussion of quantum mechanics that seeks an 'advance of thought' through the elaboration and testing of specific conjectures. This applies even to highly speculative thought-experiments – such as the famous series conducted by Einstein and Bohr – for which, as yet, there existed no means of observational or experimental proof.[17] For those experiments would quite simply have lacked all probative force had they not presupposed certain realist postulates concerning – for instance – the space-time trajectory of photons or electrons, the effects of particle charge, the well-defined limits placed upon simultaneous measurement of location and momentum, the behaviour of waves and/or particles under certain specified conditions, etc.[18] Nor is this argument in any way refuted by their having given rise to heterodox ideas (complementarity, undecidability, Heisenberg's uncertainty-principle) that on the face of it would appear incompatible with a realist interpretation. For here again it is the case that these theories were arrived at only in response to certain deep-laid conceptual problems, problems that would not have arisen – or required such strongly counter-intuitive 'solutions' – except on the premise (the ontological-realist premise) that they captured something that was deeply and genuinely puzzling in the quantum-physical domain.[19]

I should not wish to place too large a philosophical burden on Benveniste's brief reference to quantum mechanics or on Derrida's citation of it in support of his case – as against Benveniste – for the impossibility of relativizing truth to language. Still it is a passage of some significance in the present context of argument. This emerges more clearly if one considers Benveniste's suggestion that 'modern epistemology' has no need of anything like Aristotle's table of the categories since 'it is more productive to conceive of the mind as a virtuality than as a framework, as a dynamism than as a structure'.[20] There is an echo here of Whorfian ethnolinguistics, more specifically of Whorf's much-debated claim that the ideas of relativity-theory or quantum mechanics could be better expressed in Hopi Indian than in any of the modern European (Greek-influenced) languages since Hopi manifested a different metaphysics, a world-view unencumbered by the subject/object dualism or the rigid categorical framework of predicative grammar and logic.[21] What is curious about this claim, as many commentators have noted, is the fact that these theories were expounded and developed not – as it happens – in Hopi but in a range of other (mainly European) languages that on Whorf's account should have put up maximal resistance to their adequate expression.

All of which suggests that Davidson is right: that there is no making sense of the argument for ontological relativity if that argument is pushed to the point of denying the very possibility of adequate translation from one language to another.[22] What is involved here (once again) is a kind of thought-experiment, in this case an experiment with the idea of 'radical translation' conducted – as by Whorf or by Quine – with a view to establishing the incommensurability of diverse languages, conceptual schemes, ontological frameworks, etc.[23] But the result is rather to prove just the opposite: that any evidence adduced in support of such claims (whether ethnolinguistic evidence like Whorf's or hypothetico-deductive 'evidence' like Quine's) will always presuppose the possibility of comparing languages and hence, *a fortiori*, of translating between them. Thus, as Davidson remarks, Whorf is here attempting to have it both ways, on the one hand declaring that Hope cannot be 'calibrated' with English, while on the other presuming to describe *in English* those various lexical and grammatical features of Hopi that supposedly render such description impossible.

My point in all this is that thought-experiments may have various (positive and negative) kinds of results. In some cases – like the Einstein/Bohr debates and subsequent quantum-physical conjectures – they serve as a means of formulating and testing theories which cannot at present be physically verified but which none the less require that their terms be taken as referring to certain entities, processes or events whose behaviour under given conditions is (to put it simply) what the experiment is all about. In other cases – as with Quine, Whorf and Benveniste – what begins as an argument *against* ontological realism (and in support of the linguistic-relativist case) ends up by undermining its own thesis and thus showing such ideas to be strictly unintelligible. Nor should we be over-impressed by the fact that quantum mechanics has so frequently figured as a paradigm instance of ontological relativity in the thinking of Quine and others.[24] For this is to ignore what emerges very clearly in detailed accounts of those original thought-experiments; that is, the extent to which they all *necessarily* relied on a realist understanding of quantum phenomena even if the results turned out to require some drastic modification to accepted ideas about the ontology of the microphysical domain, the limits of precise measurement, the wave/particle duality, or the distinction between observing 'subject' and observed 'object'. In this respect the Einstein/Bohr conjectures were on a par, ontologically speaking, with such previous classic thought-experiments as that by which Galileo proved the uniform (mass-independent) rate of gravity-induced acceleration for bodies in a state of free fall. He imagined the case of two such bodies, a cannonball and a musket ball, securely fastened together. 'Go figure!', as they say; the experiment is enough to demonstrate conclusively, as a matter of conceptual necessity, what Galileo would later put to the proof by his better-known series of empirical tests at the leaning tower of Pisa.[25]

Notes

1. See especially Roy Bhaskar, *Scientific Realism and Human Emancipation* (London: Verso, 1986); Bhaskar, *Reclaiming Reality: A Critical Introduction to Contemporary Philosophy* (London: Verso, 1989); Rom Harré, *The Principles of Scientific Thinking* (Chicago: University of Chicago Press, 1970); Rom Harré and E. H. Madden, *Causal Powers* (Oxford: Blackwell, 1975); Wesley Salmon, *Scientific Explanation and the Causal Structure of the World* (Princeton, N.J.: Princeton University Press, 1984); J. J. C. Smart, *Philosophy and Scientific Realism* (London: Routledge & Kegan Paul, 1963); also – from a range of philosophical standpoints – Michael Devitt, *Realism and Truth* (2nd edn., Oxford: Blackwell, 1986); Jarrett Leplin (ed.), *Scientific Realism* (Berkeley & Los Angeles: University of California Press, 1984); W. H. Newton-Smith, *The Rationality of Science* (London: Routledge & Kegan Paul, 1981); Edward Pois, *Radical Realism: Direct Knowing in Science and Philosophy* (Ithaca, N.Y.: Cornell University Press, 1992); Nicholas Rescher, *Scientific Realism: A Critical Reappraisal* (Dordrecht: D. Reidel, 1987); Peter J. Smith, *Realism and the Progress of Science* (Cambridge: Cambridge University Press, 1981); Roger Trigg, *Reality at Risk: A Defence of Realism in Philosophy and the Sciences* (Brighton: Harvester, 1980); Gerald Vision, *Modern Anti-Realism and Manufactured Truth* (London: Routledge, 1988).

2. See for instance Barry Barnes, *About Science* (Oxford: Blackwell, 1985); Augustine Brannigan, *The Social Basis of Scientific Discoveries* (Cambridge: Cambridge University Press, 1981); Steve Fuller, *Philosophy of Science and its Discontents* (Boulder, Colo.: Westview Press, 1989); Alan G. Gross, *The Rhetoric of Science* (Cambridge, Mass.: Harvard University Press, 1990); Sandra Harding, *The Science Question in Feminism* (Ithaca, N.Y.: Cornell University Press, 1986); K. Knorr-Cetina and M. Mulkay (eds.), *Science Observed* (London: Sage, 1983); Bruno Latour, *Science in Action* (Milton Keynes: Open University Press, 1987); Bruno Latour and Steve Woolgar, *Laboratory Life: The Social Construction of Scientific Facts* (London: Sage, 1979); Andrew Ross, *Strange Weather: Culture, Science and Technology in the Age of Limits* (London: Verso, 1991); Joseph Rouse, *Knowledge and Power: Toward a Political Philosophy of Science* (Ithaca, N.Y.: Cornell University Press, 1987); Steve Woolgar, *Science: The Very Idea* (London: Tavistock, 1988); Woolgar (ed.), *Knowledge and Reflexivity: New Frontiers in the Sociology of Knowledge* (London: Sage, 1988).

3. See Rouse, *Knowledge and Power* (op. cit.) for a synthesis of these various cultural-relativist, 'strong' sociological, language-based, depth-hermeneutic, and kindred anti-realist trends.

4. See especially Richard Rorty, 'Science as Solidarity', 'Is Natural Science a Natural Kind?', and 'Texts and Lumps', in *Objectivity, Relativism, and Truth* (Cambridge: Cambridge University Press, 1991), pp. 35–45, 46–62, 78–92.

5. See for instance Michael Dummett, *Truth and Other Enigmas* (London: Duckworth, 1978); also Crispin Wright, *Realism, Meaning and Truth* (Oxford: Blackwell, 1986) and *Truth and Objectivity* (Cambridge, Mass.: Harvard University Press, 1992).

6. Hilary Putnam, *The Many Faces of Realism* (La Salle: Open Court, 1987); *Realism with a Human Face* (Cambridge, Mass.: Harvard University Press, 1990); *Renewing Philosophy* (Harvard, 1992).

7. See entries in note 2, above.

8. Jacques Derrida, 'White Mythology: Metaphor in the Text of Philosophy', in *Margins of Philosophy*, trans. Alan Bass (Chicago: University of Chicago Press, 1982), pp. 207–71.

9. Derrida refers to various of Aristotle's texts in this connection, chiefly the *Topics*, the *Rhetoric* and the *Poetics*.

10. See in particular the essays collected in Derrida, *Margins of Philosophy; 'Speech and Phenomena' and Other Essays on Husserl's Theory of Signs*, trans. David B. Allison (Evanston, Ill.: NorthWestern University Press, 1973); *Writing and Difference*, trans. Alan Bass (London: Routledge & Kegan Paul, 1978); *Dissemination*, trans. Barbara Johnson (London: Athlone Press, 1981); also Rodolphe Gasché, *The Tain of the Mirror: Derrida and the Philosophy of Reflection* (Cambridge, Mass.: Harvard University Press, 1986) and Christopher Norris, *Derrida* (London: Fontana, 1987).

11. William Empson, review of E. A. Burtt, 'The Metaphysical Foundations of Modern

Science', reprinted in Empson, *Argufying: Essays on Literature and Culture*, ed. John Haffender (London: Chatto & Windus, 1987), pp. 530–33; p. 531.

12. Derrida, 'The Supplement of Copula: Philosophy before Linguistics', in *Margins of Philosophy* (op. cit.), pp. 175–205; Emile Benveniste, *Problems in General Linguistics*, trans. Mary E. Meek (Coral Gables: University of Miami Press, 1971). For the main texts of Aristotle in question here, see *Categories*, Chapter 4 and *Metaphysics*, Chapter 6.

13. See Immanuel Kant, *Critique of Pure Reason*, trans. Norman Kemp Smith (London: Macmillan, 1965), pp. 113–14.

14. Derrida, 'The Supplement of Copula' (op. cit.), p. 195. Further references given by title and page number in the text.

15. Benveniste, *Problems in General Linguistics* (op. cit.), pp. 63–4.

16. In this connection see especially Quine, 'Two Dogmas of Empiricism' (op. cit.); also Harvey R. Brown and Rom Harré (eds.), *Philosophical Foundations of Quantum Field Theory* (Oxford: Clarendon Press, 1988); Arthur Fine, *The Shaky Game: Einstein, Realism, and Quantum Theory* (Chicago: University of Chicago Press, 1986); Peter Forrest, *Quantum Metaphysics* (Oxford: Blackwell, 1988); Hans Reichenbach, *Philosophical Foundations of Quantum Mechanics* (Berkeley & Los Angeles: University of California Press, 1944); Paul Teller, 'Relational Holism and Quantum Mechanics', *British Journal for the Philosophy of Science*, Vol. 37 (March 1986), pp. 71–81.

17. A. Einstein, B. Podolsky and N. Rosen, 'Can the Quantum-Mechanical Description of Reality be Considered Complete?', *Physical Review*, series 2, Vol. 47 (1935), pp. 777–80. Niels Bohr, article of same title, *Physical Review*, Vol. 48 (1935), pp. 696–702. See also J. S. Bell, *Speakable and Unspeakable in Quantum Mechanics: Collected Papers on Quantum Philosophy* (Cambridge: Cambridge University Press, 1987); Fine, *The Shaky Game* (op. cit.); John Honnez, *The Description of Nature: Niels Bohr and the Philosophy of Quantum Physics* (Oxford: Clarendon Press, 1987); Tim Maudlin, *Quantum Non-Locality and Relativity: Metaphysical Intimations of Modern Science* (Oxford: Blackwell, 1993); Michael Redhead, *Incompleteness, Nonlocality and Realism: a Prolegomenon to the Philosophy of Quantum Mechanics* (Oxford: Clarendon Press, 1987).

18. See James Robert Brown, *The Laboratory of the Mind: Thought Experiments in the Natural Sciences* (London: Routledge, 1991) and *Smoke and Mirrors: How Science Reflects Reality* (London: Routledge, 1994); also Paul Davies, 'The Thought that Counts: Thought-Experiments in Physics', *New Scientist*, May 6th 1995, pp. 26–31.

19. For a strong defence of this ontological-realist view, see Karl R. Popper, *Quantum Theory and the Schism in Physics* (London: Hutchinson, 1982).

20. Benveniste, *Problems in General Linguistics* (op. cit.), p. 63.

21. Benjamin Lee Whorf, *Language, Thought and Reality: Selected Writings*, ed. J. B. Carroll (Cambridge, Mass.: M.I.T. Press, 1956).

22. Davidson, 'On the Very Idea of a Conceptual Scheme', in *Inquiries into Truth and Interpretation* (Oxford: Clarendon Press, 1984), pp. 183–98.

23. See Quine, *Ontological Relativity and Other Essays* (op. cit.); Also *Word and Object* (Cambridge, Mass.: M.I.T. Press, 1960); *The Roots of Reference* (La Salle: Open Court, 1974); Donald Davidson, 'Radical Interpretation', in *Inquiries into Truth and Interpretation* (op. cit.), pp. 125–39.

24. See Quine, 'Two Dogmas of Empiricism' (op. cit.).

25. Galileo, *Discourse on Two New Sciences*, trans. S. Drake (Madison, Wisc.: University of Wisconsin Press, 1974); see also Brown, *Smoke and Mirrors* (op. cit.), pp. 113–16.

PART IV

WAR IN THE TRIBAL ZONE: YUGOSLAVIA

Parallel Worlds: NGOs and the Civic Society

Obrad Savić

> However, the difference between worlds can be found in that
> all that belongs to the one, does not belong to the other.
> (Nelson Goodman, *Ways of Worldmaking*)

In this text I would like to suggest one of the possible interpretations of the history of the inception and activities of the NGO (non-governmental organizations) scene in Belgrade.[1] *Parallel Worlds*, the title I chose for this article, may perhaps seem confusing. Nevertheless, with it I wish to preempt any eventual misunderstanding in regard to the intentions of the text. *Parallel Worlds* carries with it the aspiration of announcing the central theme and the main direction in which the sociopolitical analysis of the alternative civic option in Serbia – founded during the disintegration of the former Yugoslavia – is heading. I begin with the assumption that the Belgrade NGO network is moving toward a new parainstitutionalized type of activity inside the civic scene of the Federal Republic of Yugoslavia.

Three ideal types of strategy on that civic scene – *critical, nomadic* and *parallel* – can be (re)constructed. That is, there is no 'natural' place which this work seeks to bring to light, no 'substantial' space which needs to be revealed. On the contrary, it is with this text that I wish to 'construct' and in some way promote this nearly invisible scene. The civic scene is outlined as a decentralized, diffused social model in which there is no privileged place, no centre from which all the activities of the Belgrade NGO scene emanate.

Here I attempt to reconsider the social, political and legal consequences of the activities of that civic, at the same time real and virtual, scene, which announces the possibility of being the constant *corrective of the political society*. This new scene did arise out of the context of undeveloped forms of civic society, which, just like any ecosystem, had to constantly cleanse itself of political pollution. On the other hand, a political decontamination of civic society presupposes constant correction of the administrative complex, which in turn must ensure political and legal systems that will protect the citizens

335

from possible state oppression. According to its regulatory principles, a democratic state must function as the operational service of civic society. Only the states which respect the general will of the people are able to depend on the stable legality, and more or less consensual legitimacy.

To get right to the point, as a new social, political and cultural fact, the Belgrade NGO network (the one that is in question here) arose out of direct opposition to the *binary logic of political differentiation*. This logic has (seemingly) split the whole society into two antagonistic camps. Even though the place for self-exposure, which I will call here the third option, was becoming narrower, the protagonists of the so-called 'Other Serbia'[2] bravely tried to show that they have a different project of a civic society. They were unwilling to give in to the general practice of political differentiation, as they were led by the correct attitude that civic society cannot be imposed from *above*, because it simply (self)expresses from *within*.[3] The NGO network did not permit itself to be drawn into the binary political option that was imposed on Serbia by the 'Socialist' government, as well as its mostly nationalist-oriented opposition. In contrast to the nationalist opposition in Belgrade, the NGO scene did not indicate any desire to become the officially simulated, manufactured opposition of the regime in Serbia. Faced with the problem of political legitimization, the government authority almost 'legalized', in other words, institutionalized the opposition, and, in the process, the multi-party system. On the one hand, the opposition took upon itself the coerced and thankless task of feigning political pluralism in the parliament, while on the other it acted out an open society at mass rallies. Perhaps this, hopefully temporary simulation will some day produce some real effect. In contrast to the nationalist-oriented opposition, the civic alternative stood cautiously on the sidelines, refusing to participate in the seductive announcement of redistribution of political power and distribution of administrative authority.

The NGO scene managed to maintain control over the displacing technique, which permitted it to avoid the parasitic symbiosis between the authorities and its nationalistic opposition. The public sphere in Serbia was colonized by those political formations which sought a privileged role in the redistribution of current power, as well as an exclusive primacy in the general circulation of authority. Society has been reduced to a specific political zone, which is based on the exploitation of simple party polarity. Crossed-over, self-serving interests are reciprocally legitimized by a populist conception of democracy, totally steeped in nationalistic jargon. This pre-political concept of democracy in Serbia draws its energy from 'the soul of the Serbian people', 'the greatness of a nation awakened', and 'the spirit of national community'. The profound banality of such rhetorical figures inhabited the entire symbolic space in Serbia. Of course, such slogans of the day were intended to preserve the nationalistic fervour in Serbia. Public space for civic initiatives had been entirely endangered. In order to survive within the global political surroundings, the NGOs had to form *local counter-alliances*. The NGO network could only (self)constitute in a new, nearly invisible space, not controlled by the 'Socialist' regime and its nationalist opposition. The energetic self-defence of the civic perspective could only be nurtured at a great distance from state 'Socialism', and, of course, from socialized nationalism. Only under the conditions of a *global withdrawal strategy* could the NGO scene develop its own *transpolitical position*, together with its profound moral sovereignty. Only those who did not expose themselves to the coercion of structural assimilation shall have the opportunity to construct an *other*, *different*, *parallel* world.

The concept of the parallel world did not arise from theoretical curiosity, nor from discursive inquisitiveness. On the contrary, it came out of the burning questions of the moment, and it uses the language of necessity. The concept originated in the context of the frightening explosion of *negative signs and events* which 'madly' multiplied all over the former Yugoslavia. It followed many years of confrontation with the new, until then unknown, waves of hatred that appeared all around us. It focused a new experience, an experience of one's personal political and, above all, cultural milieu as an *unfriendly territory*! The Project of the Parallel Serbia originated in a brave attempt of the protagonists of the Belgrade NGO scene to protect and systematically differentiate themselves from the crude, primitive order, in which the worst forms of aggression, crime, xenophobia, racism were intermixed. These are national and religious spectres and fanaticism with which we are all too well acquainted, although we did not recognize them in time, and did not think them through thoroughly. The frightening signs of brutal nationalism violently infiltrated the entire government machine, as well as all the mechanisms of authority and modes of power. That militant populism suddenly forced itself onto this anachronistic society, which, under the attack of official nationalism, completely imploded. Despite an unavoidable implosion, this worn-out system attempted in vain to revive itself through militaristic fascination, and sought rebirth through the 'discourse of war'. The 'Socialist' government and the nationalistic opposition were immersed in this yearning for battle ('la nostalgie du front').

In both camps, war patriotism revived homeopathically the myth of the Greater Serbia, on whose behalf, literally, the most senseless words were uttered, and the most horrible crimes committed. War was imposed as a pathological form of transition, as a demonic appearance of transformation. The NGO scene in Serbia, including the representatives of the Belgrade Circle, refused to participate in 'the conformist correction' of the old, perishing world which had to be hastily abandoned.[4] The attitude of firm denial of any arrangement with that 'exotic' world in Serbia – a world which had not as yet succeeded in 'defeating the plague or overcoming metaphysics' – was announced in the first issue of the official publication of the Belgrade Circle.

In the Introduction to the first issue of the international journal *Belgrade Circle*, a complete abandonment of the old, pre-modern world in Serbia was announced – an abandonment of a world in which the difference between the striving for heights and the plunging into the abyss is hardly noticeable. How could one understand an environment in which the most hideous crimes were committed in the name of the noblest ideals of the 'Heavenly

Serbia'? For every lucid citizen who had no difficulty in assigning a name to an awful Reality, the monsters of collective glee and traditional euphoria belonged to the *system of radical evil*. It was clearly evident to the members of the NGO scene in Belgrade that pragmatic rationalization of civic society belongs to a project of a future social system. A displaced, indirect strategy of public activity of the NGO scene in Serbia was announced in the aforementioned Introduction: 'The critical energy mobilized by *The Other Serbia* has no intention of being parasitically linked to the "*one reality*" which should be saved at any price". On the contrary, the Belgrade Circle articulates that alternative scene which readily *constructs a different reality, which builds new, parallel worlds*. As the public voice of the Belgrade Circle, the editors of this journal will attempt to draw clear distinctions and borders between themselves and the anachronistic and immature Serbia, which is tired of its years, of its past, of its heritage. Our starting point will not be the old and spent Yugoslavia, even if it commands respect, it will be the *idea of a new Europe* which does not yet exist, but which we could all build together. We have no intention of assuming the role of nostalgic guardians of the Old Continent, of nurturing a sentimental memory of the European past. On the contrary, we wish to cooperatively participate in the symbolic process of the creation of a *new European spirit*, one which will not apply only in the too narrow geopolitical field, from within that administrative entity known as the European Union. We are aware that it is only through the spirit of a new, different and distinct Europe that we *can become part* of the international community, and participate in the "planetary conversation of peoples". Should it turn out that the spirit of this new Europe eludes us, that we cannot succeed in interiorizing it, we shall not hesitate to herald it persistently.'[5]

Why had the Belgrade Circle and the greater part of the NGO network in Belgrade chosen such an indirect and certainly long-range strategy of parallel action? Why had not a choice been made for other, more direct, certain and efficient ways of local exposure and self-establishing? Why this need for persistent distancing from the dangerous proximity of the government authorities and the opposition, this constant withdrawal from solidarity between militant socialism and nationalism?

Perhaps it might be in order to offer here a warning with regard to this seemingly rhetorical question. Namely, this question could equally well be answered by those who, for whatever reason, decided to stay in Serbia, as well as by those who decided, either temporarily or permanently, to leave the country. The latter could cast a glance backward at their destroyed homeland, at that place of painful memories, the terrifying toponym of memory. However, those who decided to remain at the crime scene could testify to what transpired during the general incrimination of the society, especially in the period of nationalist mummification of 'really existing Socialism'.

In spite of the pressures of state nationalism, which for a while functioned as the official ideology in Serbia, the intellectuals in the Belgrade NGO scene did not fall for the political trick of nationalist self-interpretation by the Serbian regime. The arrogant abrogation of the second Yugoslavia was interpreted in this scene as an expression of perverted particularization of small nations which dreamed of becoming great. The short-lived course of nationalism had to ensure a legitimizing alibi to those political regimes on the territory of former Yugoslavia who, together with their nationalistic oppositions, emerged out of the old, communist nomenclature. The emphasized shift of the ideological centre (the totalitarian communist system was replaced by nationalist fundamentalism) did not yield a *structural liberalization of the society*. What was lacking was a total democratization of the administrative and political complex. The programmed attack on Western culture and civilization ('The New World Order') had as its goal the protection of an autocratic society and its governmentalized economy from the infiltration of polytheistic tendencies (popularly known as 'privatization'). Instead of the economic dissemination of the capital-process, it was precisely through war – i.e. through bloodshed – that in Serbia a centralized monotheistic model of the economy, which appears as a poor parody of industrial accumulation, was imposed. What emerged instead was the singular monopolization of power in whose midst operated the competing egoisms of the government and the opposition. The entire political space had been petrified by their joint egotism and attempts to trick each other. From such a molten midst emerged a gigantic operation of irreversible monopolization at all levels of social power. The virus of twofold political coercion, occasionally neutralized within the struggle of principled egoisms, penetrated through all the zones of the social system and colonized the entire lifeworld. The 'Socialist' regime and its nationalist opposition did not hide that their one-off competition in anti-Western propaganda had a place in the civilizational surrounding which they rhetorically denied. Given that the naive abolition of Modernity forcibly unfolded on the ground of modernism itself, it was only a matter of time when the local chain of violence would settle scores with the international community. The series of 'peacekeeping interventions' had placed the onus on the expansionist goals of a regime which did not know how to protect itself from the international trauma of submission. Not even the monotonous rhetoric of the official pacifism ('Peace has no alternative'), which appeared in the post-Dayton phase, could remove the traces of such deadly politics. Those who willingly created this war, and who irresponsibly reduced tactical competition between the republics to strategic antagonism between the states, could not expect to be showered with international respect. In spite of the real defeat of the project of the 'Greater Serbia', symbolic insistence on a national identity did not lose significance. Such a nearly consensual identity became the dominant form of social reflection. For this reason, it is not surprising that the imagined superiority of the nationalists draws its strength from the resources of this provincial, local, populist culture. The collectivist euphoria undoubtedly revealed that the citizens of Serbia were still unprepared to accept the principles of a rational, personal responsibility. The self-conscious actions of the civic forms of living – their particular contribution to a society which requires structural innovation – will for a long time be a question of systematic undermining. In nationalist circles, civic forms of solidarity are really condemned to a life of diaspora, whose centre is else-where.

Deprived of the understandings and sympathy of their political surround-ings, the representatives of the NGO scene reverted again to their original summons with their initial plea for caution. With that strength of new repul-sion, they laid ground for a permanent (self)identification of civic forms of society. They definitely lost every illusion in connection with the productive rationalization of the old system. There was no readiness for the application of critical energy to a destroyed model. In any case, the activists in the NGO scene in Belgrade took on an Enlightened theoretical and, of course, politi-cal culture within which it became evident that the global project of the *critical tradition* had suffered a collapse. Nobody believed any longer in the productive effects of persistent engagement in a *critical strategy*. It became widely believed that every critical challenge to the existing system in Serbia is immediately integrated and transformed into its opposite. It also appeared that every negation upon its recurrence is changed into an affirmation. Paradoxically, critical gestures almost parasitically revived the subject which they wished to abolish. It is precisely this unproductive critical urge that appears as the central motive of political action of the Serbian opposition. Right from its dissident beginnings, the opposition was obsessed with its proximity to power. In the flaring conflicts on many political fronts (party coalitions) where exhaustive battles were waged for the increase of power and government, the civic option cautiously stood on the sidelines. It quietly took a *depoliticized position* from which it did not wish to offer attractive pro-grammes or engaging solutions. Such a practice of the normative project of society can function only within the (post)traditional social complex. Who may be ready to expose oneself in an incurable vulgarity, in order to publicly express what is the allegedly unspoken truth for everyone? It is only those aggressive appropriators of the (political) convictions of others who permit themselves such an outrage, to represent the conscience of the people, nation, class and party. Inside this 'spider's web of power and authority', a fierce battle for prestige was waged for the empty place of the leader, or the father of a nation. In this, even good intentions were articulated in a manner of false superiority. The structural rationality of an acephalous society, freed from charismatic personalities, still has no place here! The sceptical dis-tance – that amplified caution of the NGO scene – thus appears exceptionally significant, especially if we take into account the latent possibility of a general amalgamation of heterogeneous social formations into a unified national front. Because of this front, the bullying rhetoric and aggressive propaganda of the government and the opposition could equally well adapt to every political option and to every political programme. It is because of this that one finds the painless shifts in the voting patterns in Serbia. In truth, Serbia is ruled by a hybrid virus whose trademark is 'muddling'. The political history of this 'muddling' has yet to be written, a history in which the intellectuals close to the government and the opposition are particularly caught up. The transversals of power and the overlapping of authority are equally adopted by both sides. The marginalized NGO scene had understandably suggested to party-affiliated intellectuals that the question does not only concern the ascent to power, but also the undermining of one's own authority. In the Serbian political space, as with any other place of public activity, nobody is 'innocent'; everyone can at the same time be both the object and the instrument of power. By contrast with perverted political manners which systematically reproduce the chains of power, the civic initiatives are actively struggling against those forms of authority in which they could participate. The NGO scene withdrew from the political space, from the dense appearances of power which systematically influence other, peripheral techniques of social discipline. Whoever wishes to escape from the risk of totalizing political unification must radically step out of this enchanted, global and local circulation of power. Such a proposition, even when led by profound political passions, cannot be fulfilled by the critical mind. Its germinal formulas, its all too quickly spent undermining resources, are irreparably reintegrated in the overpopulated space of a political sense.[6]

It appears that this figure of spent and concluded critical meaning is destined to remain in this space. Under the force of further transmission, the critical tradition warns us that 'politics must be like Fate – to have history as a career, sovereignty as an emblem, and sacrifice as an approach'. Is there a need to expose ourselves to this, in our case, impressive history of the political nationalist sacrifice? Do civic forms of society have a reason to associate with and critically fix themselves to a particular model of political authority which is getting too isolated and justly renounced?

In spite of the daily compulsion of dramatic events on the territory of the former Yugoslavia, representatives of the Belgrade NGO scene did not wish to allow for any sort of premature or inadequately thought-out concession to the Serbian authorities. Furthermore, it never succumbed to immediate effects of the criticisms of the regime by the opposition, criticisms which daily dithered between naiveté and cynicism. The NGO scene did not wish to assume a parasitic role over the political effects which the opposition occasionally, or permanently, seized from the authorities. On the contrary, it reasonably pointed out the paradox of irresponsible and undifferentiated criticism of the ruling system. Let us remember the infantile populist slogan 'All, all, all!' (so dear to the Serbian nationalist opposition), which always evoked fear. By contrast with this populist call with which the collectivist movement was staged, the NGO scene patiently announced the spirit of a new hope, a rational wish that the *future be obtained by the culture of small steps*. In that culture there is no room for a perverted, hyperdimentionalized political banality. Today, only those who lack style on the Serbian political scene can be assimilated and absorbed by the nationalist orgies.

The representatives of the NGO scene reacted with a gesture of *sovereign indifference* to the violent, almost euphoric stress on national politics. They refused to participate in the significant process of ethnic and national legitimization of a regime which once again is assuming the primacy of politics over all other spheres of public life.

The general nationalist exultation caused the representatives of the NGO network to withdraw from the public scene in Serbia. Evil was radicalized to such an extent that no rational motivation existed for refined corrections of authority and unintrusive social reform. This withdrawal and this marginalization were unavoidable.

Invisible positioning through the fragmented NGO network became a question of basic moral and political conviction. The obtaining of a new, marginal, or, if you like, *nomadic style of activity* – that subtle art of sudden disappearance and surprising reappearance – imposed itself as the primary civic task. Caught in the middle of an expanding social 'desert', the representatives of the NGO scene strove to conquer the *nomadic strategy*, which will not transform itself into a static space that can be easily appropriated. In the worst case scenario, there could have been a void, a gap in which others could break in undisturbed. In other words, such a nomadic strategy requires constant mobility and persistent manoeuvring. Of course, this exterritorial game of hide-and-seek, this trembling of the nomadic form, could not harm the ruling regime in Serbia. To put it simply, this changing form permitted the citizens not to fall into the shifting stands of nationalistic euphoria.

In this regard, the project of 'The Flying Classroom/Workshop'[7] (FCW) represents an exemplary model of the efficient use of nomadic practice. Caught in the middle of the 'nationalist desert', the members of this project, the so-called FCWs (intellectuals from the territory of the former Yugoslavia), bravely practised the spirit of nomadic solidarity. They acted with their influence across strange shores and hidden coves of the then already war-torn Yugoslavia. Of course, FCWs did not wander the boastful highways of local politics and media. Quite the contrary, these adventurers of the marginal always hovered around the edges of periphery. Such a situationalistic crossing of dangerous grounds, such a contingent fleeting across unfriendly territory, was almost unbearable. It appears that the nomadic strategy, like an endlessly moving spiral, necessarily appropriates from its actors any firm foundation. The nomadic strategy is a particularly wasteful and exhausting form of action, since at the very moment of its realization, it demands movement and disappearance. Loyalty to such an ecstatic form of action threatens self-entrapment of the protagonists of the NGO scene, especially when it denies them any, even the smallest degree of certainty. It is practically impossible to extend out to the limits of such an invisible motion, such rhythms of sudden appearance and disappearance, in which things could really happen. The absence of momentary effects and the lack of short-term consequences are included in the logic of the nomadic gesture! Such a gesture relies on the postponed and invisible results of its action. Despite an impressive persistence, the NGO scene still could not be effectively realized through the practice of nomadic influence. This strategy became its delayed fascination and perhaps its complete anti-destiny.

The unusual rivalry of the *critical* and the *nomadic* models could not ensure a stable consensus on the question of (non)political practice of non-government organizations in Belgrade. Under the pressure of a specifically

Serbian situation, this new form of civic engagement sloppily involved itself in daily political events. Numerous motifs, which effected the transformation of the non-governmental institutions into the anti-governmental ones, could be listed: the social, the legal, the political and cultural motifs. In the forced conditions of war, nationalism, the shortage of legal procedures and constant postponement of democracy, non-government organizations were exposed to the danger of becoming a party workshop for the politically affiliated marketplace. Despite the occasional stepping out into 'global politics', the activists of the Belgrade NGO scene did not betray their principal criterion, the basic demand for a civic society. They disassociated themselves from the primary and secondary effects of the national homogenization in Serbia. Moreover, the NGO scene took upon itself a big risk in suggesting, with great foresight, the new *culture of singularization.*

A culture which insists on operating in the first person singular is forced into staging a strong crisis of collectivist representation. The undermining of representative culture (the global practice of speaking and acting for someone else!) became the minimal guarantee for the correct exposure of a civic option. In the programmatized concern for the individual, such molecular structures of civic society had to be intertwined, so as to achieve the traffic density which is beyond the scope of any administrative control. The protagonists of the Second Serbia did not wish to overcome, or, on a higher level, to keep the conflicting elements of the old, populist Serbia. The particular interest of the authorities and the narrow-minded ambitions of the opposition both still depended on the 'mass loyalty' of the privileged ones. The structural coercion which is connected with the machines of daily obedience – the traditional mechanism of a political monopoly – could not (re)integrate itself into these, as I would call them, *imaginary institutions.* In this network of 'independent instances' the principle of state loyalty did not dominate; the one that did, was the principle of *civic solidarity.* The Belgrade NGO scene persistently insisted on the creation of a new theoretical and practical outline, inside which it could build a different sort of civic complexity.

A great wave of delegitimization of power tended in this direction here, in Serbia, where the authorities could no longer possibly count on an 'intimate agreement with the laws' that were otherwise voted for behind the back of the public. The representatives of some opposition coalitions and blocs occasionally took part in the parliamentary conspiracies against the citizens. The energetic invoking of human rights paradigmatically showed that the NGO scene did not accept the rule of power, but the rule of law; it refused to accept political games, and accepted legal norms.

In any case, the problem of the rule of law became the central theme of the entire NGO network in Serbia. The constant effort to remove the concept of human rights from the academic frame, and raise it to the basic level of the legal and social system, marks the key moment in the development of the civic consciousness on the Belgrade NGO scene. The legal obligation of sparing the citizen from a dependence, a dependence whose sole objective could not be the citizen, became the primary legal, political and social oblig-ation. In truth, the unavoidable turnover in the order of business of solving civic problems occurred in favour of human rights. The sole responsibility for this, without question, goes to the NGO scene, which did everything to edu-cate, on the basis of the logic of Peace and Reason, the new, different, Parallel Serbia. The objective acknowledgment of formal universality can pacify uncontrolled spontaneity, and it can bridle the cheap expression of passions and feelings, that in Serbia, as a rule, had always resulted in hatred, aggression and war. Of course, a diffused nationalism stubbornly tries to sur-vive outside the sphere of influence of the universal idea of human rights. Under the old regime, the international concept of law and justice will never become the *political law of the peoples.*

The delicate work on the legal reform of a society, the lawful arrangement of the lifeworld, presents the most significant intention of the Belgrade NGO scene. The conviction that the legal sector and its infrastructure need to create a formal outline for further rationalization of the remaining segments of an as yet incompletely differentiated society is taking root. Legal proce-dures temporarily took over the risk of evolving the political subsystem, the legal system, public administration, market economy, free media, culture, etc. Of course, legal rationality cannot efficiently establish norms for all the other (competing) subsystems inside a society. Molecular forms of this scene con-sensually congregate and network with solidarity, so as to permit the potential basis of civic self-regulation. In the absence of *permanent* social, political union and professional movements in Serbia, the NGO scene took upon itself the responsibility of generating new, socially integrated forms of civic life. Here we find the political, moral, legal and cultural resources of the NGO scene in Belgrade. The NGO scene is not ready to give them away easily to the government-party complex, or to voluntarily permit them to be tampered with by the political formations of the opposition. The NGO scene never participated in the opposition's fight for joint acceptance, in their fight for a new redistribution, in their struggle for social respect. Moreover, its practice and production were forced by the establishment into the dark-ness of a nearly private preserve. Expelled from public life and obscured, today the NGO scene does not wish to fit into their world-view, to fill in their voids, to be their ideal absence. However the repertoire of civic culture may differ from the stereotypical nationalist narrations,[8] it will always be repre-sented as the latest, most *representative icon of the national culture.* In this charming fraud – the one that suggests that a great harmony will not come from the negation and loss of all traditions, each one heading towards the same (national) aim – one ought not to participate! This staunch refusal is the elementary ethos of emancipated citizens, who should not fall for anachronistic courting by the nationalist opposition, nor accept the seductive offers made by the 'Socialist' government.

Translated by Aleksander Bošković

Notes

In this text I wished mainly to initiate a theoretical debate about the NGO scene. Legal, political and moral obligations which have been adopted in this scene should not hinder the constant effort to responsibly consider this new form of civic engagement. In any case, theoretical culture is the integral part of a sophisticated civic consciousness.

1. The Belgrade network of non-governmental organizations originated at the beginning of the war on the territory of former Yugoslavia. The period from 1990 to 1995 saw the founding of nearly all significant non-government organizations in Belgrade, Serbia: The Belgrade Circle, CAA, The Helsinki Committee for Himan Rights in Serbia, The Foundation for Humanitarian Rights, Women in Black, The Republic, The Belgrade Centre for Human Rights, Center for Women's Studies, SOS Telephone, European Movement in Serbia, Bridge, Eco Centre, Group 484, etc. See the useful book: Petrović Branka, Paunović Žarco, *Non-Government Organizations in Yugoslavia*, Otvoreni Univerzitet, Subotica, 1994.

2. The term 'Other Serbia' was used for the first time in public sessions of the Belgrade Circle held in 1992. When the book (*Druga Srbija*, eds., Ivan Čolović, Aljoša Mimica, Beogradski Krug, Borba, Beograd, 1992) came out, this term took on a much broader meaning, becoming a synonym for supporters of the New, Different, Alternate, Parallel Serbia, and, of course, SR Yugoslavia. The term is frequently used in the service of precise differentiation of nationalist, populist and above all militarist options, as well as the government option itself. See the international editions of that book: *Une Autre Serbie*, Les Temps Modernes, Paris, No. 570–571/1994; *L'altra Serbia*, Selene Edizione, Milan, 1995.

3. For an instructive view of the crisis of civic society in the FRY see: Vukašin Pavlović, ed., *Potisnuto Civilno Društvo*, Eko Centar, Belgrade, 1993.

4. By late 1992 there appeared the public petition (over a hundred signatures of the most distinguished members of the Belgrade Circle) in which an announcement was made regarding the cessation of all cooperation with government media in Serbia. The greater part of signators followed this public announcement, this public call for caution. With this gesture of withdrawal, public discourse remained at the mercy of the West. Ultimately, the nationalist intelligentsia could manufacture, undisturbed, the media 'exultation in national roots'.

5. *Belgrade Circle Journal*, no. 1, 1994, p. 6.

6. 'That which is called totalitarianism is the complete representation of (critical) sense in truth . . . In the fascist version, truth is the life of a community; in the nation(alist) version it is the inflammation of people, and in the communist version, it is humanity which is created as humanity.' (Jean-Luc Nancy, *The Sense of the World*, trans. Jeffrey S. Librett, University of Minnesota Press, 1998.)

7. The distinguished Belgrade author Biljana Jovanović (1953–1976) is the conceptual creator of the project 'The Flying Classroom/Workshop' – FCW. With the cooperation, solidarity and support of many friends from all parts of former Yugoslavia, that project was realized in the years 1992–1994. Under nearly impossible conditions FCWs fleetingly functioned in all the territories of former Yugoslavia (Ljubljana, Maribor, Skopje, Belgrade, etc.). Some traces of these first, pioneering attempts at the conquest of nomadic culture in this geographic area are documented in: Iveković Rada, Jovanović Biljana, Krese Maruša, Lazić Radmila (Hrsg), *Briefe von Frauen über Krieg und Nationalismus*, Suhrkamp Verlag, Frankfurt am Main, 1993. See the Serbo-Croatian translation of this book, *Vjetar ide na jug i obrće se na sjever*, Radio B-92, Belgrade, 1994.

8. An especially impressive analysis of symbolic (narrative and iconographic) production of nationalism can be found in: Homi K. Bhabha, ed., *Nation and Narration*, Routledge, London and New York, 1994.

A German version of this article was published under the title 'Parallele Welt – Die Belgrader NGO-Szene' in Irina Šlosar (Hrsg), *Verschwiegenes Serbien*, Wieser Verlag, Klagenfurt-Salzburg, 1997.

Speed Memories (III)

Obrad Savić

The Banality of Evil

Morality in Serbia has acquired a bad reputation, and now only children and madmen indulge in it. What else can one expect from a state in which the authorities are both legally and illegally – thus, doubly – corrupt? What else can one expect from the inhabitants of a country who maintain that smuggling is in the national interest? Such a country can be ruled only by those who are completely mired in the self-will of generalized evil. In *Fragments from a Damaged Life*, Adorno wrote that in a gangster society, only criminals could succeed! The unfortunate founder of the modern Serbian language, Vuk Karadžić, benignly noted that the national morality of the Serbs had become mired in the customariness of pure will: peasants simply liked to lie, and, the truth be told, also to steal!!! Collective consciousness in such cases operates on instinct, passion, opinion and witticisms. The power of custom rules individuals' lives by its 'natural authority'. Its trademark is precisely that dumb naiveté, that 'pure desire' which has infiltrated all pores of society. Collective flourishing of evil, tabooization of customs, credulous use of lies, theft, cheating, corruption, etc., are all spreading. The hyperinflation of evil has taken over the whole state, all the institutions of power and authority. Crime has become the principle of state, the delirious signifier of our economy, politics and, of course, international diplomacy. This can no longer be termed a crisis of morality, law, economy or politics. It is precisely the opposite, it is a fatal etatisation of customariness, an accelerated catastrophe of state evil.

Apocalypse Postponed

According to the Belgrade daily *Blic* (22 April 1997, p. 3), a paper specialized in the petit-bourgeois joy of information, a 'Declaration against genocide on the Serb people' is to be made public soon, with the inevitable blessing of His

Holiness the Serbian Patriarch Pavle. Of course, this initiative has been formulated by the wise heads, over sixty of them, respected personalities from
the Church, the Serbian Academy of Sciences and Arts, the Writers'
Association and Serbian public and political life in general. This apocalyptic
declaration should finally reveal and unmask the great secret of the world
dimension of Serbian suffering. As Europe is forgetful, and the New World
Order uninterested, the Declaration first reminds the reader of the horrible
suffering and injustice to which Serbs were subjected during the two World
Wars. It goes on to say that 'the exodus of the Serb people continues even
now, at the end of the 20th century'. This probably refers to the *completely
unprovoked* (!) expulsion of Serbs, to that great (self)expulsion which took
place after the Lost War for so-called Greater Serbia. Truly, how can the
Western World calmly watch the expulsion of Serbs from their holy places,
their historical settlements in Croatia and Bosnia-Herzegovina?

The signatories of the Declaration appeal to the international community
to condemn all past, present and future genocides against Serbs. Serbs are
morally clean, politically correct, so that this appeal is intended to wake up
the dormant conscience of mankind. Our concerned signatories (Milorad
Ekmečić, Kosta Mihailović, Nikša Stipčević, Dejan Medaković, Mihailo
Marković, Ljubomir Tadić, Zoran Đinđić, et al.) are no longer satisfied with
eternal justice, the absolute Judgment of History. Very soberly, our pragmatic patriots demand the establishing of a new international tribunal of
honour, which, in place of the Russell Court or the Hague Tribunal, could be
called, for example, the Tribunal of St. Sava. This tribunal would have the
task of introducing into international legal, diplomatic and political discourse a lordly, sublime and apocalyptic tone. It would have no space or
time for boring legal procedure. If the world is ready, the Serb mystagogues –
those who initiate into the secret – can immediately make public the exalted
vision of Serb suffering. Our prophetic voices, that aristocratic wisdom which
bears the apocalyptic hope, will no longer tolerate the infectious haughtiness
of Europe, the garrulous arrogance of the West.

The Extraordinary Fast

Any call to fasting, especially to an extraordinary fast, appeals to believers to
find in themselves 'deeper reserves of health'. It is, therefore, not unusual
that the Patriarchate has recommended to sick Serbia, tired of war, misery
and poverty, a further abstention from the elementary necessities of livelihood, and maybe even from pleasure. To those uninitiated in the ways of the
Serbian Orthodox Church, it may seem strange, cynical even, that on the
occasion of St. Sava Day the impoverished and miserable faithful are called
to redoubled hunger. Once they hunger as citizens of devastated Serbia,
once as the faithful of its official church. This appeal to total asceticism by
the people, to a liminal temptation of existence, has been sent out by His
Holiness the Serbian Patriarch Pavle. His appeal has come at the right time,
as it will best be understood by those who rummage in dumpsters, hoping to

find their salvation in the garbage. According to the official interpretation of the secretary of the Serbian Patriarch's Cabinet, Archdeacon Momir Lečić, only an extraordinary fast can save us from the evil which has befallen us! Blessed are the starving around the dumpsters, for theirs is the Kingdom of Heaven! After all, in front of God one should be simple, obsequious, sad and hungry. Merriment is the politeness of the rich.

Eucalyptus*

The eucalyptus is the favourite plant of the loudest propagator of Serbian nationalism, academician Ljubomir Tadić. Our oral Dionysus knows what the real thing is: one should only cultivate that tree whose flower remains closed even after blooming! This secret of nature has been revealed by the sociologist Tadić. It is small wonder, then, that our zoological visionary likes the limelight, the frightening noise of the media. The public sphere is where one can most effectively hide, painlessly conceal oneself. This subject of eschatological discourse, this garrulous visionary, has been obsessed by the Belgrade Circle for years. His euphoric attacks have no end. (By the way, I have recently been accused of being the founder of anti-Serb mondialism: 'Their ideological paradigm has been formulated by Obrad Savić'; *Vreme*, 1 February 1997, p. 32.) What is the basis of the libidinal economy of this nationalist juggler? Why does he renounce with such largesse all other aims and purposes for the sake of Serbhood? The trick is that this political euca-lyptus wishes to say everything precisely in order to say nothing. Tadić's public discourse is nothing but expression of gooseflesh, spasms and screams of a soul which must announce its cold lunacy. There are no semantics there, only mere gestures. No ideas, only frigid writhing. No meaning, only earthly excitement. No spirit, only mere breath and spasmodic mouthing.

Translated by Srđan Vujica

---

eucalyptus, n. Any of a genus of (*Eucalyptus*) of large, chiefly Australian evergreen trees of the myrtle family; widely used as timber, for ornamental purposes, and in the preparation of drugs, especially the volatile, pungent, essential oil of eucalyptus. (Gk. *eu-* well – *kalyptos-* covered <*kalyptein* cover: from the covering of the buds.)

Bibliography:
International Publications relating to
Human Rights

compiled by Obrad Savić

Aiderson, J., *Ljudska Prava I Policija*, Hrvatski kulturni dom, Rijeka, 1995.
Airaksinen, Timo, *Practical Philosophy and Action Theory: Human Rights*, Transaction Books, New Brunswick, 1993.
Alderman, Ellen, *The Right to Privacy*, Vintage Books, New York, 1997.
Aleksic, Zivojin and Paunovic, Milan, ur, *Ljudska Prava I Nacija*, Pravni Fakultet, Belgrade, 1992.
Amnesty International, *Report on Torture*, Duckworth, London, 1973.
Amnesty International, *Torture in the Eighties*, Amnesty International Publications, London, 1984.
Andrews, J. A. and Hines, W. D., *Key Guide to Information Sources on the International Protection of Human Rights*, Mansell Publishing, London, 1987.
An-Na'im, Abdullahi and others, eds., *Human Rights and Religious Values*, Eerdmans, Grand Rapids, 1995.
Arendt, H., *Eichmann in Jerusalem – A Report on the Banality of Evil*, Penguin Books, Harmondsworth, 1976.
Askin, Richard, *Defending Rights*, Harvard University Press, Cambridge, Mass., 1996.
Barry, Brian, *Theories of Justice*, University of California Press, Berkeley, 1989.
Bereis, P., *Pour de Nouveaux Droits L'Homme*, Editions J. C. Lattes, Paris, 1985.
Biserko, Sonja, ed., *In the Name of Humanity*, Helsinski odbor za ljudska prava u Srbiji, Belgrade, 1996.
Biserko, Sonja, *Izvestaj o Stanju Ljudskih Prava u Srbiji za 1996 Godinu*, Helsinski odbor za ljudska prava u Srbiji, Belgrade, 1997.
Bloed, A. and P. van Dijk, eds., *The Human Dimension of the Helsinki Process*, The Vienna Follow-up Meeting and its Aftermath, 1991.
Bosnia–Herzegovina: Gross Abuses of Basic Human Rights, International Secretariat, London, 1992.
Boward, James, *Lost Rights*, St. Martin's Griffin, New York, 1995.
Brown, P. and MacLean, D., eds., *Human Rights and US Foreign Policy*, Lexington Books, Lexington, Mass., 1979.
Brownlie, Ian, ed., *Basic Documents on Human Rights*, Clarendon Press, Oxford, 1977.
Brownlie, Ian, ed., *Documents on Human Rights*, Oxford University Press, Oxford, 1983.
Brownlie, Ian, ed., *Basic Documents in International Law*, Clarendon Press, Oxford, 1995.
Brownlie, Ian, *Principles of Public International Law*, Oxford University Press, Oxford, 1997.
Buergenthal, T., ed., *Human Rights, International Law and the Helsinki Accord*, Allanheld, Osmun and Universe Books, Monclair and New York, 1977.
Buergenthal, T. and others, eds., *Protecting Human Rights in the Americas: Selected Problems*, N. P. Engel Publishers, Strasbourg, 1982.

Cameron, Iain and Eriksson, Kirilova Maja, eds., *An Introduction to the European Convention on Human Rights*, Justus Forlag, Uppsala, 1995.

Campbell, Tom, ed., *De We Need a Bill of Rights?*, Temple Smith, London, 1980.

Campbell, Tom and others, eds., *Human Rights: From Rhetoric to Reality*, Basil Blackwell, Oxford, 1986.

Capotorti, Francesco, *Study of the Rights of Persons Belonging to Ethnic, Religious and Linguistic Minorities*, United Nations, New York, 1979.

Carey, John, *UN Protection of Civil and Political Rights*, Syracuse University Press, New York, 1970.

Cassese, A., *International Law in a Divided World*, Clarendon Press, Oxford, 1986.

Cassese, A., *Violence and Law in the Modern Age*, Polity Press, Cambridge, 1988.

Cassese, A., *Human Rights in a Changing World*, Temple University Press, Philadelphia, 1990.

Caudill, David S. and Gold, Steven J., eds., *Radical Philosophy of Law*, Prometheus Books, New Jersey, 1995.

Champan, John, *Human Rights – Nomos XXIII*, New York University Press, New York, 1981.

Chomsky, Noam and Hermann, Edward, *The Political Economy of Human Rights*, South End Press, Boston, 1979.

Cicak, Zvonimir Ivan, ur, *Kriza Hrvatskog Sudstva: Nijekanje Vladavine Prava*, Hrvatski helsinski odbor za ljudsak prava, Zagreb, 1995.

Claude, Pierre Richard and Weston, H. Burns, eds., *Human Rights in the World Community*, University of Pennsylvania Press, Philadelphia, 1992.

Coleman, Jules and Paul, Ellen, eds., *Philosophy and Law*, Blackwell, Oxford, 1989.

Cornell, Drucilla et al., eds., *Deconstruction and the Possibility of Justice*, Routledge, London and New York, 1992.

Cranston, Maurice, *What Are Human Rights?*, Basic Books, New York and London, 1973.

Crawford, James, ed., *The Rights of Peoples*, Clarendon Press, Oxford, 1988.

Daniels, Norman, ed., *Reading Rawls: Critical Studies on Rawls's 'A Theory of Justice'*, Stanford Series in Philosophy, Stanford, Calif., 1989.

Davies, P., ed., *Human Rights*, Routledge and Kegan Paul, London and New York, 1988.

Delmas-Marty, Mireille, *The European Convention for the Protection of Human Rights: International Protection Versus National Restrictions*, Martinus Nijhoff Publishers, Dordrecht, 1992.

Derrida, Jacques, *Sila Zakona: Misticni Temelj Autoriteta*, Svetovi, Novi Sad, 1995.

Devetak, Silvo, *Manjine, Ljudska Prava, Demokratija*, Oslobodjenje, Sarajevo, 1989.

Dimitrijevic, Vojin, *Neizvesnost Ljudskih Prava: Na Puto Od Samovlasca Ka Demokratiji*, Sremski Karlovci, Novi Sad, 1993.

Dimitrijevic, Vojin, *Strahovlada: Ogledi O Ljudskim Pravima I Drzavnom Teroru*, Dosije, Belgrade, 1997.

Dimitrijevic, V. and Paunovic, M., eds., *Prava I Slobode: Medjunarodni I Jugoslovenski Standardi*, Beogradski centar za ljudska prava, Belgrade, 1995.

Dimitrijevic, Vojin and Paunovic, Milan, *Ljudska Prava*, Beogradski centar za ljudska prava, Belgrade, 1997.

Dinstein, Yoram-Tabory, Mala, *The Protection of Minorities and Human Rights*, Kluwer Academic Publishers, Dordrecht, 1992.

Donnelly, Jack, *Universal Human Rights in Theory and Practice*, Cornell University Press, Ithaca, NY, 1989.

Donnelly, Jack, *International Human Rights*, Westview Press, Boulder, Colo. and San Francisco, 1993.

Droits de l'Homme et Droits des Peuples, Fondation Lelio Basso pour le Droit et la Libération des peuples, San Marino, Ministero de la Cultura, 1983.

Dworkin, Ronald, *Taking Rights Seriously*, Harvard University Press, Cambridge, Mass., 1977.

Dworkin, Ronald, ed., *The Philosophy of Law*, Oxford University Press, Oxford, 1977.

Dworkin, Ronald, *A Matter of Principle*, Harvard University Press, Cambridge, Mass., 1985.

Dworkin, Ronald, *Life's Domination: An Argument about Abortion, Euthanasia and Individual Freedom*, Vintage Books, New York, 1993.

Dworkin, Ronald, *Morality, Harm and the Law*, Westview Press, Boulder, 1994.

Dworkin, Ronald, *Law's Empire*, Harvard University Press, Cambridge, Mass., 1994.

Dworkin, Ronald, *Freedom's Law*, Harvard University Press, Cambridge, Mass., 1996.

Easton, Susan, *The Problem of Pornography Regulation and the Right to Free Speech*, Blackwell, Oxford, 1994.

Egeland, J., *Humanitarian Initiatives Against Political 'Disappearances'*, Henry Dunant Institute, Geneva, 1982.

Eide, Asbjorn and Hagtvet, Bernt, eds., *Human Rights in Perspective: A Global Assessment*, Basil Blackwell, Oxford, 1992.

Eide, A., Eide, B. and Goonatilake, S., eds., *Food as a Human Right*, United Nations University Library, Tokyo, 1984.

Eide, A. and Hegelsen, J., *The Future of Human Rights Protection in a Changing World*, Oslo, 1991.

European Workshop on the Universal Declaration of Human Rights: Past, Present and Future, United Nations, New York, 1989.

Eze, O., *Human Rights in Africa*, Nigerian Institute of International Affairs, Lagos, 1984.

Falk, Richard A., *Human Rights and State Sovereignty*, Holmes & Meier Publishing, New York, 1984.

Farelly, Colin, *Discourse of Ethics and Human Rights*, McMaster University, Department of Philosophy, 1988.

Fawcett, Sir James, *The Application of the European Convention on Human Rights*, Clarendon Press, Oxford, 1987.

Feinberg, Joel, *Rights, Justice and the Bounds of Liberty*, Princeton University Press, Princeton, NJ, 1980.

Feministicke Sveske, Belgrade, br.1/1994.

Fish, Stanley, *There's No Such Thing as Free Speech*, Oxford University Press, Oxford, 1994.

Fiss, Owen, *The Irony of Free Speech*, Harvard University Press, Cambridge, Mass., 1996.

Flajner, Tomas, *Ljudska Prava I Ljudsko Dostojanstvo*, Gutenbergova Galaksija, Belgrade, 1996.

Flathman, Richard, *The Practice of Rights*, Cambridge University Press, Cambridge, 1976.

Forsythe, P. David, *Human Rights and International Relations*, Cambridge University Press, Cambridge, 1986.

Forsythe, P. David, *Human Rights and World Politics*, Lincoln, Neb. and London, 1989.

Forsythe, P. David, *The Internalization of Human Rights*, Lexington Press, Lexington, Mass., 1991.

Forsythe, P. David, *Human Rights and Peace*, University of Nebraska Press, Lincoln, Neb. and London, 1993.

Friedelbaum, Stanley H., ed., *Human Rights in the States: New Directions in Constitutional Policy Making*, Greenwood Publishing Group, New York, 1988.

Gaskins, Richard, *Burdens of Proof in Modern Law Discourse*, Yale University Press, New Haven, Conn. 1992.

Gewirth, Alan, *Human Rights: Essays on Justification and Applications*, The University of Chicago Press, Chicago, Illinois, 1982.

Gilbert, Alan, *Democratic Individuality and Law*, Cambridge University Press, New York, 1990.

Glintic, Tatjana, *Pravda, Sloboda, Jednakost: Rols I Vulser*, FDS, Belgrade, 1995.

Gomien, Dona, *Kratak Vodic Kroz Evropsku Konvenciju O Ljudskim Pravima*, Beogradski centar za ljudska prava, Belgrade, 1996.

Gorecki, Jan, *Justifying Ethics: Human Rights and Human Nature*, Transaction Publishers, New Brunswick, 1996.

Graefrath, B., *Die Vereinten Nationen und die Menschrechte*, VEB Deutscher Zentralverlag, Berlin, 1956.

Graefrath, B., *Menschenrechte und Internationale Kooperation*, Akademic-Verlag, Berlin, 1988.

Green, Herbold Reginald, *Human Rights, Human Conditions and Law: Some Explorations Towards Interaction*, IDS, Brighton, 1989.

Griffin, Stephen and Moffat, Robert, eds., *Radical Critique of the Law*, University Press of Kansas, Lawrence, Kans., 1997.

Guinier, Lani, *The Tyranny of the Majority*, Marton Kessler Books, The Free Press, New York, 1994.

Habermas, Jürgen, *Between Facts and Norms: Contributions to a Discourse of Law and Democracy*, The MIT Press, Cambridge, Mass., 1996.

Hannum, H., ed., *Guide to International Human Rights Practice*, University of Pennsylvania Press, Philadelphia, Penn., 1984.

Hart, H. L. A., *The Concept of Law*, Clarendon, Oxford, 1961.

Hartley, T.C., *Osnovi Prava Evropske Zajednice*, COLPI-Beogradski centar za ljudska prava, Belgrade, 1998.

Hayek, F. A. von, *Law, Legislation and Liberty*, Vols. I–III, Routledge and Kegan Paul, London, 1979.

Henkin, Louis, *The Rights of Man Today*, Westview Press, Boulder, Colo., 1978.

Henkin, Louis, *The International Bill of Rights – The Covenant on Civil and Political Rights*, Columbia University Press, New York, 1981.

Henkin, Louis, *The Age of Rights*, Columbia University Press, New York, 1990.

Henkin, Louis and Hargrove, H. John, eds., *Human Rights: An Agenda for the Next Century*, Washington DC, 1994.

Horowitz, I. L., *Genocide: State Power and Mass Murder*, Transaction Publishers, New Brunswick, New York and London, 1976.

Horowitz, I. L., *Taking Lives: Genocide and State Power*, Transaction Publishers, New Brunswick, New York and London, 1980.

Hufton, Olwen, ed., *Historical Change and Human Rights*, The Oxford Amnesty Lectures, Basic Books, Oxford, 1995.

Human Rights: A Compilation of International Instruments, United Nations, New York, 1983.

Human Rights in International Law: Basic Texts, Strasbourg, Council of Europe, 1985.

Imamovic, Goran, *Uvod U Ljudska Prava*, Forum gradjana Tuzle, Tuzla, 1994.

Ishay, Micheline, *The Human Rights Reader*, Routledge, London and New York, 1997.

Ivanovic, Vane and Djilas, Aleksa, ur, *Zbornik O Ljudskim Pravima*, Demokratske reforme, London, 1983.

Jacobs, Francis, *The European Convention on Human Rights*, Clarendon Press, Oxford, 1975.

Janis, Mark W., Kay, Richard S. and Bradley, Anthony W., *European Human Rights Law*, Clarendon Press, Oxford, 1995.

Jaspers, T. and Betten, L., eds., *25 Years European Social Chapter*, Kluwer, Dewenter, 1988.

Kandic, Natasa, ed., *Praksa Krsenja Ljudskih Prava U Vreme Oruzanih Sukoba*, Fond za humanitarno pravo, Belgrade, 1995.

Kandic, Natasa, ed., *Ljudska Prava U Srbiji I Crnoj Gori*, Fond za humanitarno pravo, Belgrade, 1996.

Kandic, Natasa, ed., *Postupanje Organa – Protivpravno Postupanje Organa Unutrasnjih Poslova U Srbiji I Crnoj Gori*, Fond za humanitarno pravo, Belgrade, 1997.

Kandic, Natasa, ed., *Haski Tribunal*, Fond za humanitarno pravo, Belgrade, 1997.

Kandic, Natasa, ed., *Politicka Upotreba Policije Protiv Gradjanskog Protesta U Beogradu 1996–97 Godine*, Fond za humanitarno pravo, Belgrade, 1997.

Kandic, Natasa, ed., *Izbor Presuda Evropskog Suda Za Ljudska Prava*, Fond za humanitarno pravo, Belgrade, 1997.

Khushalani, Yougindra, *Dignity and Honour of Women as Basic and Fundamental Human Rights*, Nijhoff, The Hague, 1982.

King, Richard, *Civil Rights and the Idea of Freedom*, The University of Georgia Press, Athens, Geogia and London, 1996 (1st edition 1992).

Kingdom, Elisabeth, *What's Wrong with Human Rights? Problems for Feminist Politics of Law*, Edinburgh University Press, Edinburgh, 1991.

Kolm, Serge-Christopher, *Modern Theories of Justice*, The MIT Press, Cambridge, Mass., 1996.

Konvitz, S., ed., *Judaism and Human Rights*, W. W. Norton & Co., New York, 1972.

Kosutic, Budimir, *Medjunarodnoprana Zastita Ljudskih Prava I Pravni Sistem Savezne Republike Jugoslavije*, Belgrade, 1995.

Kriegel, Blandine, *The State and the Rule of Law*, Princeton University Press, Princeton, NJ, 1995.

Kukathas, Chandran, *Law*, Stanford University Press, Stanford, Calif., 1990.

Kuper, L., *Genocide: Its Political Use in the Twentieth Century*, Penguin Books, London, 1981.

Kuper, L., *International Action Against Genocide*, Minority Rights Group, Report no. 53, London, 1984.

Kuper, L., *The Prevention of Genocide*, Yale University Press, New Haven, Conn. and London, 1985.

Laqueur, W. and Rubin, B., eds., *The Human Rights Reader*, New American Library, New York, 1987.

Lauterpacht, Hersch, *An International Bill of the Rights of Man*, Columbia University Press, New York, 1945.

Lauterpacht, Hersch, *International Law and Human Rights*, Shoe String, Hamden, 1968.

Lawson, Edward, ed., *Encyclopedia of Human Rights*, Taylor & Francis, New York, 1991.

The Legal Protection of Human Rights in the Western Hemisphere, Interamerican Bar Foundation, Washington, DC, 1978.

Lillich, R. B. and Newman, C. F., eds., *International Human Rights*, Little, Brown and Co., Boston, 1979.

Litowitz, Douglas, *Postmodern Philosophy and Law*, University Press of Kansas, Kansas, 1998.

Ljudska Prava I Multikulturalnost, Dijalog, Sarajevo, br. 5/1996.

Lorimer, *The Institutes of the Law of Nations*, William Blackwood, Edinburgh and London, 1883.

Luban, David, *Legal Modernism*, The University of Michigan Press, Ann Arbor, 1994.

Macdonald, M. and others, eds., *The European System for the Protection of Human Rights*, European Union Publishers, The Hague, 1993.

Macdonald, R. St. and Johnson, D. M., eds., *The Structure and Process of International Law: Essays in Legal Philosophy*, Martinus Nijhoff, Leyden, 1983.

Mandela, Nelson, *The Struggle is My Life*, International Defense and Aid Fund for Southern Africa, London, 1986.

Maritain, J., *The Rights of Man and Natural Law*, Charles Scribner & Sons, New York, 1943.

Martin, D., ed., *The New Asylum Seekers: Refugee Law in the 1980s*, The Ninth Sokol Colloquium on International Law, 1988.

Matcher, F. and Petzold, H., eds., *Protecting Human Rights: The European Dimension – Studies in Honour of Gerald J. Wiarda*, C. Heymans Verlag KC, Cologne, 1988.

Matulovic, Miomir, ed., *Ljudska Prava: Zbornik Tekstova Iz Savremenih Teorija Ljudskih Prava*, ICR, Rijeka, 1992.

Matulovic, Miomir, *Ljudska Prava: Uvod U Teoriju Ljudskih Prava*, Hrvatsko filozofsko drustvo, Zagreb, 1996.

McDougal, M., Lasswell, H., Chen, L., *Human Rights and World Public Order*, Yale University Press, New Haven, Conn., 1980.

Medina Quiroga, Cecilia, *The Battle of Human Rights: Gross, Systematic Violations and the Inter-American System*, Martinus Nijhoff, Dordrecht, 1988.

Melden, I., *Rights and Rights Conduct*, Oxford University Press, Oxford, 1959.

Melden, I., ed., *Human Rights*, Wadsworth Publ. Co., Belmont, 1970.

Meron, Theodor, *Human Rights, Law-Making in the United Nations*, Clarendon Press, Oxford, 1986.

Meron, Theodor, *Human Rights and Humanitarian Norms as Customary Law*, Clarendon Press, Oxford, 1989.

Meron, Theodor, ed., *Human Rights in International Law: Legal and Policy Issues*, Oxford University Press, Oxford, 1984.

Mertus, Julije and others, eds., *Zenska Ljudska Prava*, Devedesetcetvrta, Belgrade, 1995.

Michele, Carter, ed., *Philosophy of Law*, Westview Press, Boulder, Colo., 1990.

Mikaelson, L., *European Protection of Human Rights*, Sijthoff and Noordhoff, Germantown, 1980.

Milenkovic, Branislav, ed., *Medjunarodni Dokumenti O Zastiti Nacionalnih Manjina I Njihov Polozaj U Ustavnom Poretku Sr Jugoslavije*, Belgrade, 1994.

Milenkovic, Branislav, ed., *Dokumenti KEBS-a 1975–1995*, Beogradski centar za ljudska prava, Belgrade, 1995.

Milenkovic, Branislav, *Medijske Slobode: Prava I Ogranicenja*, Beogradski centar za ljudska prava, Belgrade, 1996.

354 BIBLIOGRAPHY

Milenkovic, Branko, ed., *Govor Mrznje*, Centar za antiratnu akciju, Belgrade, 1994.
Milenkovic, Slobodan, *Unutrasnja Nadleznost Drzava I Medjunarodna Zastita Ljudskih Prava*, Belgrade, 1974.
Milne, M., *Human Rights and Human Diversity: An Essay in the Philosophy of Human Rights*, State University of New York Press, Albany, NY, 1986.
Milne, M., *Freedom and Rights*, London, 1968.
Milojevic, Momir, *Polozaj Pojedinca I Njegov Aktivni Subjektivitet U Medjunarodnom Pravu*, Belgrade, 1987.
Molnar, Aleksandar, *Osnovna Prava Coveka I Raspad Jugoslavije*, Visio Mundi, Novi Sad, 1994.
Molnar, Aleksandar, *Drustvo I Pravo, Tom – II*, Visio Mundi, Academic Press, Novi Sad, 1994.
Morrisson, Clovis, *The Developing European Law of Human Rights*, Sijthoff, Leyden, 1967.
Mrdjenovic, Dusan, *Temelji Moderne Demokratije: Izbor Deklaracija I Povelja O Ludskim Pravima*, Nova Knjiga, Belgrade, 1989.
Mrsevic, Zorica, *Zenska Prava Su Ljudska Prava*, SOS telefon za zene, Belgrade, 1994.
Murphy, Jeffrie G., *Philosophy of Law*, Westview Press, Boulder, Colo. and San Francisco, 1990.
Muzaffar, Chandra, *Human Rights and the New World Order*, South End Press, Boston, 1994.
Nanda, P. Ved and others, eds., *Global Human Rights and NGO Strategies*, Westview Press, Boulder, Colo., 1980.
Nickel, W. James, *Making Sense of Human Rights: Philosophical Reflection on the Universal Declaration of Human Rights*, University of California Press, Berkeley, 1987.
Nizich, Ivana, *War Crimes in Bosnia–Herzegovina*, Helsinki Watch, New York, 1992.
Obradovic, Konstantin, *Pocetnica Za Ljudska Prava*, Centar za antiratnu akciju, Belgrade, 1994.
Obradovic, Konstantin, *Pravo I Ljudsko Pravo*, Beogradski centar za ljudska prava, Belgrade, 1996.
Obradovic, Konstantin, ed., *Humanitarno Pravo: Savremena Teorija I Praksa*, Beogradski centar za ljudska prava, Belgrade, 1997.
Paine, Thomas, *The Rights of Man*, Collins, London, 1969.
Paul, Ellen and others, eds., *Human Rights*, Basil Blackwell, Oxford, 1986.
Paunovic, Milan, *Jurisprudencija Evropskog Suda Za Ljudska Prava*, Pravni fakultet, Belgrade, 1993.
Paunovic, Milan, ur, *Zbirka Medjunarodnih Dokumenata O Ljudskim Pravima*, Beogradski centar za ljudska prava, Belgrade, 1996.
Pavlovic, Zoran, *Medjunarodne Nevladine Organizacije I UNESCO*, Sremski Karlovci, 1993.
Pennock, J. R. and Champan, J. W., eds., *Human Rights*, New York University Press, New York, London, 1981.
Perry, M., *The Constitution, the Courts and Human Rights*, Yale University Press, New Haven, Conn., 1982.
Pollis, Adamantia and Schwab, Peter, eds., *Human Rights: Cultural and Ideological Perspectives*, Praeger, New York, 1979.
Porter, J. N., ed., *Genocide and Human Rights: A Global Anthology*, University Press of America, Washington, DC, 1982.
Posner, Richard, *Overcoming Law*, Harvard University Press, Cambridge, Mass., 1996.
Posner, Richard, *The Economics of Justice*, Harvard University Press, Cambridge, Mass., 1996.
Prokopijevic, Miroslav, ur, *Ljudska Prava*, Instiut za evropske studije, Belgrade, 1996.
Prvulovic, Vladimir, *U Ime Coveka – Ljudska Prava I Slobode U Odnosima Istok–Zapad*, Gornji Milanovac, 1988.
Pusic, Eugen, ur, *Francuska Revolucija – Ljudska Prava I Politicka Demokracija Nakon Dvjesto Godina*, Globus, Zagreb, 1991.
Radulovic, Radoje, ed., *Ljudska Prava I Demokratija*, Novi Sad, 1993.
Ramcharan, B. G., ed., *International Law and Fact-Finding in the Field of Human Rights*, Martinus Nijhoff, The Hague, 1982.
Ramcharan, B. G., *The Concept and Present Status of International Protection of Human Rights: Forty Years After the Universal Declaration*, Martinus Nijhoff, The Hague, 1989.
Ramcharan, B. G., *Humanitarian Good Offices in International Law: The Good Offices of the*

United Nations Secretary-General in the Field of Human Rights, Martinus Nijhoff, The Hague, 1983.

Ramcharan, B. G., *The Right to Life in International Law*, Martinus Nijhoff, The Hague, 1985.

Raoul, M., *Déclaration Universelle des Droits de l'Homme et Réalités Sud-Africaines*, Unesco, Paris, 1983.

Raphael, D. David, ed., *Political Theory and The Rights of Man*, Indiana University Press, Bloomington, 1967.

Rawls, John, *A Theory of Justice*, Harvard University Press, Cambridge, Mass., 1989.

Rembe, N., *Africa and Regional Protection of Human Rights*, Romai Leoni, 1985.

Ren, Elisabet, *Izvestaj Specijalnog Izvestioca Komisije Za Ljudska Prava*, Beogradski centar za ljudska prava, Belgrade, 1997.

Rhode, Deborah, *Justice and Gender*, Harvard University Press, Cambridge, Mass., 1989.

Robertson, A., *Human Rights in Europe*, Manchester University Press, Manchester, 1976.

Robertson, A., *Human Rights in the World*, Manchester University Press, Manchester, 1982.

Robinson, A., *The Universal Declaration on Human Rights*, 1958.

Robinson, N., *The Genocide Convention – A Commentary*, Basic Books, New York, 1960.

Rodley, N., *The Treatment of Prisoners under International Law*, Clarendon Press, Oxford, 1987.

Rols, Dzon, *O Liberalizmu i Pravednosti*, ICR, Rijeka, 1993.

Rosenbaum, Alan, ed., *The Philosophy of Human Rights*, Greenwood Press, Westport, 1980.

Rossilahti, Hannu, *How to think about Human Rights: Some Methodological Considerations in Practical Philosophy and Action Theory*, Transaction Books, New Brunswick, 1993.

Russo, Alessandra del Luini, *International Protection of Human Rights*, Lerner Law Book Co., Washington, DC, 1971.

Sabrina, Ramet, *Whose Democracy? Nationalism and the Doctrine of Collective Rights in Post-1989 Eastern Europe*, Rowman & L. Publishers, Lanham, 1997.

Sali, Sevima, Terzic, Zlatan, eds., *Medjunarodni Dokumenti o Ljudskim Pravima. Instrumenti Ustava Federacije Bosne i Hercegovine*, Pravni centar, Sarajevo, 1996.

Salt, Henry Stephens, *Animals' Rights*, International Society for Animals, 1980.

Sarat, Austin, ed., *The Rhetoric of Law*, The University of Michigan Press, Ann Arbor, 1996.

Sattler, M. J., ed., *Staat und Recht, die Deutsche Staatslehre im 19. und 20. Jarhundert*, List Verlag, Munich, 1972.

Scelle, G., *Manuel de Droit International Public*, Editions Domat – Montchrestien, Paris, 1948.

Schnur, R., *Zur Geschichte der Erklaerung der Menschrechte*, Darmstadt, 1964.

Schwab, Peter, ed., *Human Rights: Cultural and Ideological Perspectives*, Praeger, New York, 1979.

Schwab, Peter and Pollis, Adamantia, eds., *Toward a Human Rights Framework*, Praeger, New York, 1982.

Shapiro, Ian, *The Evolution of Rights in Liberal Theory*, Cambridge University Press, Mass., 1986.

Shue, Henry, *Basic Rights: Subsistence, Affluence, and U.S. Foreign Policy*, Princeton University Press, Princeton, NJ, 1980.

Shute, Stephen and Hurley, Susan, eds., *On Human Rights*, Basic Books, New York, 1993.

Sieghart, P., *The International Law of Human Rights*, Oxford University Press, Oxford, 1983.

Sieghart, P., *The Lawful Rights of Mankind*, Oxford University Press, Oxford, 1986.

Skok, Dobrisa, ed., *Ljudska Prava. Osnovni Medjunarodni Dokumenti*, Skolske novine, Zagreb, 1991.

Sohn, Louis B., *International Protection of Human Rights*, Bobbs-Merrill, Co., Indianapolis, Ind., 1973.

Solomon, Robert, ed., *What is Justice?*, Oxford University Press, Oxford, New York, 1990.

Spragens, Thomas, *Reason and Democracy*, Duke University Press, Durham, NC, 1990.

Stackhouse, Max, *Creeds, Society and Human Rights: A Study in Three Cultures*, Eerdmans, Grand Rapids, New York, 1984.

Status of International Instruments on Human Rights, Centre for Human Rights, Geneva, United Nations, New York, 1987.

Steiner, Hiller, *An Essay on Rights*, Blackwell, London and New York, 1994.

Strier, Franklin, *Reconstructing Justice*, The University of Chicago Press, Chicago, 1994.

Sudre, R., *Droit International et Européen des Droits de l'Homme*, Presses Universitaires de

France, Paris, 1989.

Sunga, S., *Individual Responsibilities in International Law for Serious Human Rights Violations*, Basic Books, New York, 1991.

Thompson, Janka, *Justice and Order*, Routledge, London and New York, 1992.

Thompson, Kenneth, ed., *Imperatives of Human Rights*, Washington DC University, Washington, 1980.

Thoolen, H. and Verstappen, B., *Human Rights Missions: A Study of the Fact-finding Practice of Non-governmental Organizations*, Martinus Nijhoff, Washington, DC, 1986.

Thornberry, Patrick, *Minorities and Human Rights Law*, The Minority Rights Group Report, London, 1987.

Uviller, Richard, *Virtual Justice*, Yale University Press, New Haven, Conn. and London, 1996.

Vallat, F., ed., *An Introduction to Human Rights*, Europa, London, 1972.

van Boven, Theo, *La Charte Africaine des Droits de l'Homme et des Peuples*, Cologne, 1988.

van Dijk, P. and von Hoof, M, *Theory and Practice of the European Convention on Human Rights*, Kluwer, Deventer, 1998 (3rd edn).

Van Dyke, Vernon, *Human Rights, Ethnicity and Discrimination*, Greenwood Press, Westport, 1985.

van Egmond, Aad, ed., *Human Rights and Religious Values*, Eerdmans, Grand Rapids, 1995.

Vandenberg, Donald, *Education as a Human Right: A Theory of Curriculum and Pedagogy*, New York Teachers College Program, New York, 1990.

Vasak, Karel, ed., *The International Dimension of Human Rights*, Vol. II, Greenwood Press and Unesco, Westport and Paris, 1982.

Vasilijevic, Vladan, ed., *Prava Coveka i Savremena Ketanja u Kriminalnoj Politici*, Institut za kriminoloska i socioloska istrazivanja, Borba, Belgrade, 1989.

Vasilijevic, Vladan, ed., *Prava Coveka: Zbornik Dokumenata o Pravima Coveka*, Institut za kriminoloske studije, Belgrade, 1991.

Vasilijevic, Vladan, *Zlocin i Odgovornost*, Institut za kriminolske studije, Belgrade, 1995.

Vincent, R. J., *Human Rights and International Relations*, Oxford University Press, Oxford, 1988.

Vodinelic, Vladimir and others, eds., *Pravo Medija s Modelom Zakona o Javnom Informisanju*, Beogradski centar za ljudska prava, Belgrade, 1998.

Vucinic, Nebojsa, *Medjunarodno-Pravni Status I Zastita Osnovnih Ljudskih Prava I Sloboda*, Pravni fakultet, Podgorica, 1994.

Vukas, Budislav, *Medjunarodnopravna Zastita Prava Voceka U Poretku Ujedinjenih Naroda*, Belgrade, 1978.

Vulkovic-Sahovic, Nevena, *Prava Deteta U Svetu I Jogoslaviji*, Beogradski centar za ljudska prava, Belgrade, 1997.

Waldron, Jeremy, *Theories of Human Rights*, Oxford Readings in Philosophy, Oxford University Press, Oxford, 1988.

Wallington, Peter and McBride, Jeremy, eds., *Civil Liberties and a Bill of Rights*, Cobden Trust, London, 1976.

Walzer, M., *The Spheres of Justice: A Defence of Pluralism and Equality*, M. Robertson, Oxford, 1983.

Warnike, Georgia, *Justice and Interpretation*, The MIT Press, New York, 1994.

Weeston, H., Lukes, A. and Hnatt, M., *Regional Human Rights Regimes: A Comparison and Appraisal*, Vanderbilt Journal of Transnational Law, 1987.

White, Alan, *Rights*, Clarendon Press, Oxford, 1984.

Winfield, Richard, *Reason and Justice*, State University Press of New York, New York, 1988.

Wringe, Colin A., *Children's Rights: A Philosophical Study*, London, 1981.

Zbornik Medjunarodnih Dokumenata O Ljudskim Pravima I, Osnovni Instrumenti, Beogradski centar za ljudska prava, Belgrade, 1996.

Zbornik Medjunarodnih Dokumenata O Ljudskim Pravima II: Krivicni Postupak I Izvrsenje Kanze, Beogradski centar za ljudska prava, Belgrade, 1996.

Zbornik Medjunarodnih Dokumenata O Ljudskim Pravima III: Evropski Dokumenti, Beogradski centar za ljudska prava, Belgrade, 1996.

Zilic, Ahmed, *Bosnia I Hercegovina – Kodeks Ljudskih Prava*, Amadeus, Slavonski Brod, 1996.

Ziolkowski, Theodore, *The Mirror of Justice*, Princeton University Press, Princeton, NJ, 1997.

Notes on Contributors

(in order of appearance)

Terry Eagleton is the Warton Professor of English Literature at St. Catherine's College, Oxford University. His previous books include *Criticism and Ideology*, 1978; *Walter Benjamin*, 1981; *Literary Theory: An Introduction*, 1985; *The Ideology of the Aesthetic*, 1990; *Ideology: An Introduction*, 1991; *The Illusions of Postmodernism*, 1996.

Obrad Savić teaches History of Social Sciences at the University of Belgrade. He is editor-in-chief of the *Belgrade Circle Journal*, and author and editor of the following collections: *Philosophical Readings of Freud*, 1988; *Musil and Philosophy*, 1988; *Freud and Modernity*, 1990; *The European Discourse of War*, 1995; *Serbia – Wake Up!* (Open Society Fund Bosnia and Herzegovina, Sarajevo, forthcoming); *Balkan as a Metaphor* (MIT Press, Cambridge, in preparation).

John Rawls is Emeritus Professor of Philosophy at Harvard University. His widely discussed work *A Theory of Justice* was published in 1971. He is also the author of *Liberty, Equality and the Law*, 1987; *Justice as Fairness*, 1991; *Two Concepts of Rules*, 1991; *Political Liberalism*, 1993.

Emmanuel Lévinas was the Directeur de l'Ecole Normale Israélite Orientale. He is the author of *De l'existence à l'existant*, 1947; *Totalité et infini: essai sur l'extériorité*, 1971; *Autrement qu'être ou au-delà de l'essence*, 1974; *Ethique et infini*, 1982; *Hors sujet*, 1987; *A l'heure des nations*, 1988.

Jürgen Habermas is Emeritus Professor of Philosophy at the University of Frankfurt. He is the author of *Technik und Wissenschaft als Ideologie*, 1968; *Theorie und Praxis*, 1971; *Erkenntnis und Interesse*, 1973; *Philosophisch-politische Profile*, 1981; *Theorie des kommunikativen Handelns*, vols. I–II, 1981; *Der philosophische Diskurs der Moderne*, 1985; *Nachmetaphysisches Denken*, 1988;

Erläuterungen zur Diskursethik, 1991; *Faktizität und Geltung*, 1992.

Richard Rorty is Professor of Humanities at the University of Virginia, Charlottesville. He is the author of the books *Philosophy and the Mirror of Nature*, 1979; *The Consequences of Pragmatism*, 1982; *Contingency, Irony and Solidarity*, 1989; *Philosophical Papers*, vols. I–II, 1991; *Rorty and Pragmatism: The Philosopher Responds to His Critics*, 1995; *Debating the State of Philosophy: Habermas, Rorty and Kolakowski*, 1996.

Peter Dews is Head of the Philosophy Department at the University of Essex. He is the author of the books *Logics of Disintegration: Post-Structuralist Thought and the Claims of Critical Theory*, 1988; *Autonomy and Solidarity: Interviews with Jürgen Habermas*, 1992; *Deconstructive Subjectivities*, 1996; *The Limits of Disenchantment: Essays on Contemporary European Philosophy*, 1996.

Charles Taylor is Professor of Philosophy and Political Science at McGill University, Montreal. He is the author of the books *Hegel*, 1975; *Sources of Self: The Making of the Modern Identity*, 1989; *The Ethics of Authenticity*, 1991; *Multiculturalism: Examining the Politics of Recognition*, 1992.

Jon Elster is Professor of Political Science and Philosophy at the University of Chicago. He has been one of the major figures in a movement known as 'analytic Marxism', and is the author of *Logic and Society: Contradictions and Possible Worlds*, 1978; *Ulysses and the Sirens*, 1984; *Sour Grapes: Studies in the Subversion of Rationality*, 1985; *The Multiple Self: Studies in Rationality and Social Change*, 1988; *Local Justice: How Institutions Allocate Scarce Goods and Necessary Burdens*, 1992; *Deliberative Democracy*, 1998.

Antonio Cassese is Professor of International Law at the University of Florence. He is the author of the books *International Law in a Divided World*, 1986; *Human Rights in a Changing World*, 1990; *Self-Determination of Peoples: A Legal Reappraisal*, 1995; *Inhuman States: Imprisonment, Detention and Torture in Europe Today*, 1996.

Robert Dahl is the Sterling Professor of Political Science Emeritus at Yale University. He is a winner of the 1991 Elaine and David Spitz Book Prize, given by the Conference for the Study of Political Thought for the best book published on liberal and/or democratic theory. He is the author of *Who Governs?*, 1961; *Preface to Democratic Theory*, 1963; *After the Revolution?*, 1970; *Polyarchy*, 1971; *Dilemmas of Pluralist Democracy*, 1982; *Democracy, Liberty and Equality*, 1986; *Democracy and Its Critics*, 1989; *Political Oppositions in Western Democracies*, 1996.

Jean-François Lyotard has taught at the Sorbonne and at the universities of Nanterre and Vincennes, as well as at the University of California, Irvine. He is the author of the books *Discours, figure*, 1971; *Economie libidinale*, 1974; *La* *condition postmoderne*, 1979; *Le différend*, 1984. His most recent publications include *Heidegger and 'the jews'*, 1990, and *Leçons sur l'analytique du sublime*, 1991.

Aaron Rhodes has been the Executive Director of the International Helsinki Federation for Human Rights (Vienna) since 1993. He was formerly associated with the Institute for Human Sciences (Vienna) and Boston University. He has taught at four institutions, most recently as Visiting Professor at Charles University (Prague). Born in New York, he was educated at Reed College (Oregon) in anthropology, and at the University of Chicago where he received his PhD in the Committee on Social Thought. He has published many articles on human rights.

Aleksandar Molnar teaches History of Social Theory at the Faculty of Philosophy, University of Belgrade. He is the author of the books *Society and Law*, 2 vols, 1994; *Basic Human Rights and the Dissolution of Yugoslavia*, 1994; *People, Nation, Race*, 1997.

Marijana Santrač is a student of the Faculty of Law, University of Belgrade. She has published articles in *The Annals of the Faculty of Law*.

Charlotte Bunch heads the Center for Women's Global Leadership at Rutgers University. She is the author of *Class and Feminism*, 1983; *Passionate Politics: Feminist Theory in Action*, 1988; *Gender Violence: A Development and Human Rights Issue*, 1992; *Voices from the Japanese Women's Movement*, 1996.

Anthony Giddens is Head of the London School of Economics, and was a Professor of Sociology, Faculty of Social and Political Science, and a Fellow of King's College, Cambridge. His previous books include *Capitalism and Modern Social Theory*, 1971; *Studies in Social and Political Theory*, 1976; *Central Problems in Social Theory*, 1979; *Constitution of Society*, 1984; *The Consequences of Modernity*, 1990; *Beyond Left and Right: The Future of Radical Politics*, 1995.

Rajesh Sampath teaches History at the University of California, Irvine, and is the author of numerous essays on contemporary French philosophy.

Jean Baudrillard was Associate Professor of Sociology at the University of Paris Nanterre. He is the author of *Le système des objets*, 1968; *La société de consommation*, 1970; *Pour une critique de l'économie politique du signe*, 1972; *Le miroir de la production*, 1973; *L'échange symbolique et la mort*, 1976; *Oublier Foucault*, 1977; *Simulacres et simulation*, 1978; *De la séduction*, 1979; *Les stratégies fatales*, 1983; *Amérique*, 1986; *Cool Memories*, 1987; *La transparence du mal*, 1990; *L'illusion de la fin*, 1992; *Le crime parfait*, 1994; *Fragments: Cool Memories III*, 1995.

Noam Chomsky is Professor of Linguistics at the Massachusetts Institute of

Technology, Cambridge. He is the author of the books *Aspects of the Theory of Syntax*, 1965; *The Logical Structure of Linguistic Theory*, 1975; *Knowledge of Language*, 1985; *What Uncle Sam Really Wants*, 1992; *World Order: Old and New*, 1994; *Class Warfare*, 1996; *Language and Problems of Knowledge*, 1996; *The Cold War and the University*, 1997; *Global Contradictions: Answers to Key Political Questions of Our Time*, 1997.

Paul Jalbert is Associate Professor of Communication Sciences at the University of Connecticut, Stamford. His research has focused on the explication of ideological phenomena in US television coverage of international conflicts, for which he draws upon analytical insights from pragmatics, speech art theory, ethnomethodology and ordinary-language philosophy. He is the author of numerous articles on communication sciences, and in 1999 published *Media Studies: Ethnomethodological Approaches*.

Christopher Norris is Professor of Philosophy at the University of Wales, Cardiff. He is the author of *Inside the Myth: Orwell – Views from the Left*, 1984; *Paul De Man: Deconstruction and the Critique of Aesthetic Ideology*, 1988; *Derrida*, 1988; *What's Wrong with Postmodernism: Critical Theory and the End of Philosophy*, 1991; *Uncritical Theory: Postmodernism, Intellectuals and the Gulf War*, 1992; *Reclaiming Truth: Contribution to a Critique of Cultural Relativism*, 1996; *Against Relativism: Philosophy of Science, Deconstruction and Critical Theory*, 1997.